A Comparative Study of Representative Systems

Yezhong Zhou

A Comparative Study of Representative Systems

商務印書館
SINCE 1897
The Commercial Press

Springer

Yezhong Zhou
School of Law
Wuhan University
Wuhan, Hubei, China

Translated by
Xiao Ma
School of Foreign Languages and Literature
Wuhan University
Wuhan, China

ISBN 978-981-15-4185-8 ISBN 978-981-15-4186-5 (eBook)
https://doi.org/10.1007/978-981-15-4186-5

Jointly published with The Commercial Press, Ltd.
The print edition is not for sale in China (Mainland). Customers from China (Mainland) please order the print book from: The Commercial Press, Ltd.
ISBN of the Co-Publisher's edition: 978-7-100-10261-2

This book is published with financial support from the Chinese Fund for Humanities and Social Sciences

This Springer imprint is published by the registered company Springer Nature Singapore Pte Ltd.
The registered company address is: 152 Beach Road, #21-01/04 Gateway East, Singapore 189721, Singapore

Preface

In the political life of modern countries, nothing is more worthy of people's obsessive aspiration and pursuit than "democracy". Withstanding the test of knife and sword and the trials of blood and fire from its early germination during the Classical period, the commodity economy sparked a war against the old relations of production, and finally swept them away with its tenacious vitality and mighty force. The exhilarating words like "democracy, freedom, and equality" immediately spread everywhere.

With the victory of the bourgeois revolution and establishment of the bourgeois state power, "democracy" has also evolved from a slogan, a declaration, or a guiding principle into the political practice of the people. Despite the fact that the bourgeoisie has been forced to guarantee "democracy" for the people in a legal sense, the nature of the private ownership of the means of production and the class attribute of the bourgeoisie determined that the democratic systems and forms in capitalist countries could only serve the interests of capital for various subjective and objective reasons.

The victory of the proletarian revolution and establishment of the proletariat state power has prompted a qualitative leap for "democracy", with the working class, originally at the bottom of the society, becoming the master of the country. As a result, the vast majority of the working people truly became their own masters. However, the construction of the democratic systems and democratic forms in socialist countries has been far from satisfactory due to people's misconceptions of democracy and the heavy burden of tradition, which in turn poses obstacles to the working people's exercise of the right of being the master of the country.

The practices of political life in modern countries have constantly revealed that the democratic form plays an indispensable role in the development of democracy: the completeness of the bourgeois democratic form has often sugarcoated its limitations, whereas the incompleteness of the socialist democratic form has usually blanketed its authenticity. Therefore, neither can we ignore the content and essence of democracy nor can we neglect the issue of democratic form in both theoretical research and political practice. Through a general overview of the history of democratic thought and development of democratic system, the forms of democracy, though multifarious, can be classified into two types: direct and indirect, as for whether people are personally involved in exercising the power of being the master. The vast territory and large

in elaborating on the specific activities of the representative organs; on the other hand, some scholars from socialist countries are enthusiastic about giving a boring introduction to the organizational structure and working system of the representative organs. The former fails to generalize the actual operational laws of the representative system by summarizing the diverse social relations arising in its operational process, especially through the examination of its specific functional effects; the latter, by avoiding the living realities of the political practice, is only content with knowledge introduction of the static structures of the representative system and specifications of why and how the representative system is organized, without a specific discussion of how it functions, which naturally leads to an inadequate account of the operational laws of the system. As the Japanese scholar Tomoaki Iwai pointed out, "Previously, most research was nothing more than an explanation of a system and some individual case studies".[3] However, the life and vitality of any political system lies in its ability to solve practical problems and regulate specific social relations because it is only its operational efficiency that promotes the social development, so we can only judge its merits and demerits in terms of its practical operation and its social effect. In fact, this is a specific manifestation and application of "practice being the sole criterion for testing truth". Therefore, in the study of the representative system, we must focus on the relevant systems that have an important influence upon the actual operation of the representative system. Only an adequate study of the relationship between the representative system and the sub-systems of the macro social system and their interaction, can we present a vivid picture of the representative system in the political life of the country. As some scholars have pointed out, the study of a political life cannot simply focus on systems or behavior, but on "interactive behavior".[4] Therefore, this book will devote several lengthy sections to the study of the relationships between the representative system and the electoral system, the representative system and the state structure, the representative system and the party system, and the representative system and the interest groups, so as to clarify the social and historical conditions for the existence and development of the representative system and summarize the laws of the emergence, development and operation of the system.

Any scientific research will get nowhere without an effective method, so it is with the study of the representative system. This research mainly adopts the method of comparative analysis, in addition to the methods of qualitative and historical analysis with a combination of theories and practice. But here, several issues need to be further clarified.

Firstly, the research perspective. The study of any issue has a point of departure, and different points of departure will lead to divergent conclusions. In the study of the representative system, the research perspectives are varied, ranging from practical and empirical to empty and hymnal. Although some have done work aimed at exploring the laws of the representative system, few have explicitly raised the issue of their research perspective, but the purpose of this research determines that this question

[3] Iwai, T. (1990) *Lifa guocheng* [Legal Process], trans. Li, W., The Economic Daily Press, p. 14.

[4] Zou, Y. X. et al. (1993) *Xiandai xifang guojia xueshuo* [Modern Theories of State in the West], Fuzhou: Fujian People's Press, p. 499.

must be addressed first. In my view, since the representative system has its own process of emergence and development in history, and exists in several social forms, the study of it must be carried out from the height of the historical development of human society. Only in this way, can we clearly see the stages and inheritances in the development of democratic forms.

From this perspective, the significance of the representative system is twofold: one is its significance as the operational mode of the state power. In this sense, the representative system has a specific purpose and task in different political, economic and cultural contexts, so it is closely related to the nature of the state power and state type. The other is its significance as a part of the human culture, i.e., the achievements of social civilization. In this sense, the representative system reflects the accumulation of human experience in searching for ways of state governance, and is the fruit of human progress and development. This determines that, in the process of our research, we should, on the one hand, clarify the nature of the representative system in different countries, or in different periods of a country; on the other hand, under the premise of affirming its nature, we can conduct a comparative analysis from the perspective of human culture, so as to find out its development trajectory.

Secondly, the comparability and reference system. This book mainly adopts the method of comparative analysis, so comparability is the primary issue to be addressed in the first place. Since the representative system has experienced several social forms in its historical development, it is inevitable to make a comparative analysis of the representative system in different types of countries in a comparative study, which involves the central issue of comparability. Although theorists came to agree that political systems of different types of countries in history are comparable, why do few of them touch upon the topic of comparability? In my view, the laws and political systems of any country are designed to solve certain social problems and deal with corresponding social relations. In the process of governing the state and the society, different countries may run into similar or identical social problems, and the comparison of the approaches to these problems in order to explore their similarities and differences and the reasons behind constitutes the initial reason for the comparison of political systems of different types of countries. Moreover, since the representative systems of different countries share some common characteristics in form, for example, they are all indirect democracy as opposed to direct democracy, these similar or even identical forms of the representative systems constitute the objective bases for the comparison of the representative systems of different countries.

Similarly, a comparative study must address the reference system for comparison. In my view, there are two issues we should take into consideration in the study of the representative system. First, the object of study. Since the emergence and operation of the representative system, it has mainly experienced two historical stages: the capitalist and the socialist. Therefore, the objects of the comparative study are primarily the capitalist representative system and the socialist representative system. Moreover, different capitalist and socialist countries naturally differ in the operation of the representative system due to their respective subjective and objective conditions, so it is necessary to conduct a comparative study of their respective situations. Hence, as far as the object of comparison is concerned, there are three major aspects: the comparison between the representative systems of capitalist countries, the comparison between the representative systems of socialist countries, and the comparison between the capitalist representative system and the socialist representative system. Second, the issue of historical environment. Karl Marx once pointed out: "Thus events strikingly analogous but taking place in different historic surroundings led to totally different results. By studying each of these forms of evolution separately and then comparing them one can easily find the clue to this phenomenon, but one will never arrive there by the universal passport of a general historico-philosophical theory, the supreme virtue of which consists in being super-historical".[5] Therefore, the object of comparison must be analyzed in a specific historical environment.

Thirdly, the relationship between "what is" and "what should be". In the study of political practice and political system, we often come across these two questions: "what is" and "what should be". According to Allen C. Isaac, an American political scientist, the former involves political science while the latter political philosophy.[6] To be sure, there is some truth in this distinction. "What is" aims at the realistic elaboration and summary of the objective existence of actual political life, while "what should be" is the ideal assumption of the political practice based on political ideals. However, Isaac does not clarify the relationship between the two. As a matter of fact, these two are independent yet interrelated, and the combination of the two will produce new understanding. In a sense, "what should be" is the sublimation of "what is". Just as the scientific research has revealed: When "what should be" to be transited to "what is", new concepts will arise related to "what should be".

This research mainly proceeds from the perspective of "what is" in studying the representative system to the height of "what should be", so as to improve the System of People's Congress in China and promote the construction of the Chinese representative democracy.

Fourthly, either similarities or differences. The confusion that exists in comparative studies comes from whether we focus on similarities or on differences in the process of comparison. In my view, research objectives and perspectives dictate research focus. If the study is carried out from the perspective of the development of human cultures, it should focus on the similarities, and its purpose is to explore the common norms of human cultures or the universal laws of the development of human society, which is a far-reaching and of great significance. However, if the study aims at finding something suitable for a country based on the history and present situation of the country, the focus should be placed on differences. As such, comparisons are often confined to a certain geographical area or a certain historical period, rather than arriving at a general conclusion through the coherent events relevant to the specific regions and time periods, and the emphasis should be put on differences. Such a conclusion drawn in this way may shed some light, but in reality, it may not have a

---

[5] *Makesi Engesi quanji* [Marx and Engels Collected Works] (1963/1965), Beijing: People's Publishing House, vol.19, p.131. cf. Marx, K. (1877) Letter to the Editorial Board of the *Otechestvenniye Zapiski.*

[6] Issac, A. (1987) *Zhengzhixue: fanwei yu fangfa* [Political Science: Scope and Methods], trans. Zhen, Y. N., Hu, C. and Tang, L., Hangzhou: Zhejiang People's Press, pp. 3–6.

profound historical significance because this kind of research is prone to the influence of pragmatism, and thus it possesses obvious limitations. Therefore, the research goal of this book determines that these two aspects must be taken into account, and at the same time coordinate the relationship between them. Therefore, in this research, the emphasis is usually given to differences in the specific discussions, while similarities are often highlighted in the generalization of rules and laws.

Wuhan, China Yezhong Zhou

References

Issac, A. (1987) *Zhengzhixue: fanwei yu fangfa* [Political Science: Scope and Methods], trans. Zhen, Y. N., Hu, C. and Tang, L., Hangzhou: Zhejiang People's Press.

Iwai, T. (1990) *Lifa guocheng* [Legal Process], trans. Li, W., The Economic Daily Press.

Makesi Engesi quanji [Marx and Engels Collected Works] (1963/1965), Beijing: People's Publishing House. cf. Marx, K. (1877) Letter to the Editorial Board of the *Otechestvenniye Zapiski.*

Naisbitt, J. (1984) *Da qushi: Gaibian women shenghuo de shige xin fangxiang* [Megatrends: Ten New Directions Transforming Our Lives], trans. Sun, D. Z., China Social Sciences Press.

Toffler, A. (1984) *Di sanci langchao* [The Third Wave], trans. Zhu Z. Y, Pan Q. and Zhang Y., Beijing: SDX Joint Publishing Company.

Zou, Y. X. et al. (1993) *Xiandai xifang guojia xueshuo* [Modern Theories of State in the West], Fuzhou: Fujian People's Press.

Contents

Chapter 1
Basic Theories of Representative System

In constitutional studies and political science, the "Representative System" is an old topic for discussion. Although the term "Representative System" in the modern sense has been in use only for centuries, its theoretical origin and political practice can be traced back to the distant classical era. Unfortunately, the reflections upon the "Representative System" within disparate theoretical frameworks are still far from thorough and sufficient. Therefore, in the systematic study of problems related to the representative system, the first step is to clarify the concept of the "Representative System" itself because the so-called basic theories of the "Representative System" are actually elaborations on this concept. Specifically, discussions on features, functions, and principles in the process of its organization and activities elaborate on the concept of "Representative System".

1.1 Some Concepts of Representative System

Fundamentally, the representative system is no more than a basic form of democracy, so democracy is the logical starting point for the study of the representative system.

1.1.1 Democracy and Democratic Forms

Karl Marx once pondered, "What is democracy? It must have a meaning, or it would not exist. It is all a matter, then, of finding the true meaning of democracy."[1] The word

[1] *Makesi Engesi Quanji* [Marx and Engels Collected Works] (1959), Beijing: People's Publishing House, vol. 7, p. 304. cf. Marx, K and F. Engels (1850) Review of *Latter-Day Pamphlets*, edited by Thomas Carlyle.

Y. Zhou, *A Comparative Study of Representative Systems*,
https://doi.org/10.1007/978-981-15-4186-5_1

"democracy" has its origin in the Greek vocabulary *demokratia*,[2] which means "the power of the people" or "people as the masters of the country", to be more exact, "the rule of the majority", or, as Lenin put it, a state where the minority is subordinate to the majority. Herodotus pointed out in *The Histories* that the characteristic of democratic politics is that political affairs should be "determined by the public"[3]; Thucydides expressed the same idea in the *History of the Peloponnesian War* and he argued, "[Our constitution's] administration favours the many instead of the few; this is way it is called a democracy."[4] In *Politics*, Aristotle divided the main types of polities according to the number of people in power, and pointed out that democracy refers to the rule of the majority. People in the modern age have varied understandings and interpretations of democracy, but they all affirm the traditional view that democracy refers to the rule of majority.[5] Therefore, the fundamental purpose of democracy is to guarantee the interests and political rights of the majority, and to recognize the will of the majority as the supreme will. Of course, for various reasons, democracy as the rule of the majority does not mean that the majority of members of the society directly become the rulers. The rule of the majority only means that the governance of the minority is carried out with the consent and authority of the majority, and is effectively constrained and supervised by the majority. Accordingly, the major problem to be solved by democracy is how to deal with the relationship between the governance of the minority and the interests and rights of the majority.

Democracy's historical origins reveal that the interrelation between governance of the minority and the interests of the majority is determined by the power distribution generated by the economic base and property rights relations. As a form of governance, democracy originated in clans. Of course, such so-called democratic forms of governance here are not the democratic system in the sense of a nation, but merely refer to a way of equally managing public affairs on the basis of the primitive public ownership, naturally established with people enjoying the equal labor right, that is, what Engels called, the "naturally developed democracy".[6] With the emergence of social division of labor and private ownership, the inequality of people's labor and property ownership arise, which leads to the antagonism between governors and laborers, and thus the primitive equal social relations are replaced. Similarly, the social management power held by governors is substituted by the state political power controlled by the ruling class (i.e. the so-called separation of the state from the society). As a result, the fundamental opposition of the ruling and ruled classes

---

[2] Some scholars hold that the word "Democracy" originated in the west, but the easterners first used it. cf. Huang, D. Q. et al. (1993) *Shehui zhuyi minzhu: kuashiji de chensi* [Socialist Democracy: Millennium reflection], Beijing: China Renmin University Press, p. 13.

[3] Herodotus (1959) *Lishi (II)* [Histories (II)], trans. Wang Y. Z., Beijing: The Commercial Press, pp. 80–82.

[4] Thucydides (2005) *Boluobennisa zhanzhengshi* (II) [The Peloponnesian War (II)], trans. Xie D. F., Beijing: The Commercial Press, p. 371. cf. https://www.globalgreyebooks.com/history-of-peloponnesian-war-ebook.html. p. 59.

[5] Cf. *Britannica Concise Encyclopedia,* entry "Democracy".

[6] *Makesi Engesi Xuanji* [Marx and Engels Selected Works] (1995), Beijing: People's Publishing House, vol. 4, p. 103. cf. Engels, F. (1884) *The Origin of the Family, Private Property and the State.*

in terms of political and economic interests determines that the power of state governance can only belong to the class and stratum in possession of social property, and cannot be equally distributed among all social classes. More specifically, the distribution of state power is exclusive to the ruling class. Therefore, "Democracy is the unity of opposites between equality and inequality in terms of power."[7] This unity of opposites implies that the ruling class in possession of the means of production will realize and consolidate its rule in the form of possession of power, while the ruled class will accept or resist being ruled in the form of possession of its corresponding power. In reality, the opposition between "consolidation" and "resistance" in democracy is the conflict between power and right. Therefore, what democracy concerns is, to some extent, the relationship between the governance of the minority and the interests of the majority, and as a matter of fact, it is also the relationship between power and rights. As Lenin pointed out, "Democracy is a form of the state, it represents, on the one hand, the organized, systematic use of force against persons; but, on the other hand, it signifies the formal recognition of equality of citizens, the equal right of all to determine the structure of, and to administer, the state."[8] In other words, democracy is the main approach for the majority to exercise the state power to determine, control and supervise the minority. It deals with three aspects of state power, namely: its source, constraints and attribution.

The existence of the class differences and unequal power distribution have determined that the practice of democracy in nature is the tool of class rule, be it bourgeois or socialist democracy. However, the realization of this nature is guaranteed by various effective forms of democracy. That's to say, the governance of a state by the ruling class is bound to be manifested through certain democratic forms, in other words, the class content of democracy must be realized through certain a democratic form, and democracy is thus an organic unity of both content and form. Therefore, in spite of divergent views on the issue of democracy, there is the consensus that the realization of the democratic content relies on the democratic form, in addition to the common view on the nature of democracy, i.e. "majority rule" or "people being the masters of their country". According to Dialectical Materialism, everything is the unity of the opposites between content and form. Content without form, or form without content, does not exist in the real world. The same is true of democracy, which also includes both content and form. The democratic content refers to the class attribute of the democracy and the degree of democratic realization; the democratic form refers to the systems, organizations, structures, institutions, measures and methods fit for the democratic content, generally including direct and indirect forms of democracy. While it is generally believed that the democratic content only refers to the class attribute of democracy, I'd like to clarify here why the degree of democratic realization must be attributed to the democratic content as an integral part. The class attribute is an important component of the democratic content, which

---

[7] Qiu, D. H. (1993) *Zhongguo minzhu zhengzhi lun* [On Chinese and Western Democratic Politics], Beijing: China Worker Press, p. 4.

[8] *Liening Xuanji* [Lenin Selected Works] (1995), Beijing: People's Publishing House, vol. 3, p. 201. cf. Lenin, V. (1917) *The State and Revolution.*

emphasizes to whom this democracy belongs mainly from a qualitative perspective. However, the connotation of democracy is far more than the ownership of the political power, but concerns all aspects of the national and social life. What's more, the existence and development of democracy are determined by such social and historical conditions as the politics, economy and culture. In other words, these objective conditions fundamentally confine various performances of democracy. Therefore, if the democratic content excludes the realization degree of democracy, it will not only be reduced to an abstract generalization, but also affect the accurate examination of democracy and the exploration of the approaches and methods for the development of democracy.

Looking into the theories and practices of democracy both in China and other countries, one will find some flaws in dealing with the issue of the relationship between the democratic content and form: the bourgeois democratic theories lay particular stress on the role of the democratic form, believing that the internal and economic content of democracy will be naturally realized so long as the formal and political form of democracy is achieved. This view not only reverses the relationship between the content and form of democracy, but also covers up the nature of the bourgeois democracy. Nevertheless, the socialist democratic theories often overemphasize the content of democracy while ignoring the form of democracy. Xu C. D. and He H. H. noted, "it seems that the study of state issues can only involve the nature and class dictatorship instead of the form and organization of the political power".[9] There is a misconception that the proletariat "does not haggle over the form". If anyone studies the democratic form and focuses on the democratic procedures, he will be criticized as "beating around the bush on the issue of form" and even labeled as a "bourgeois formalist". Xu and He further noted that the idea that the proletariat "does not bother about the trifling things of form... is both biased and extremely harmful".[10] Likewise, we could not do better in the construction of democracy if we could only recognize the decisive role of the content but fail to see the role of form in promoting or hindering the content or even the decisive significance of form under certain circumstances. The correct approach is to take the two aspects into account with equal emphasis and make timely adjustments according to various objective historical conditions.

In my opinion, at the present stage in China, the improvement of the democratic form is the key to the development of the socialist democracy. For one thing, the construction of the democratic form in China has long been neglected, which in turn has hindered the superior performance of socialist democracy. For another, it is also the requirement inherent in the development of the socialist democracy. The proletariat, in the process of seizing and building the state power, has undergone two phases in terms of democracy: the proletarian and the socialist democracy. In the former phase, the proletariat should aim at achieving the goal of people being the

[9] Xu, C. D. & He H. H. (1982) *Xianfa yu minzhu zhidu* [Constitution and Democratic System], Wuhan: Hubei People's Press, p. 45.

[10] Ibid, pp. 45–46.

masters of their own country and full acquisition of the political and economic dominance, etc., i.e. realizing the content of socialist democracy. Although the content and form are often inseparable, the fulfillment of the content will lead to the accomplishment of the form at the same time. It is during this phase that the development of democratic content should be the main focus. However, once the content is determined, the quality of democratic nature, which may develop with the changing of the objective situations, will maintain a considerable stability. Therefore, the development of the democratic content can only involve the enrichment, improvement and perfection of its nature. What's more, the transitional attribute of the socialist society determines that the development of socialist democratic content can only be extended from the state-form of democracy to the non-state form of democracy. Therefore, the development of the socialist democratic content appears to be more definite and stable, while the diversity and imperfection of the socialist democratic form definitively result in complexity that requires urgent understanding and exploration of the form most suitable for the content of socialist democracy.

1.1.2 Indirect Democratic Form and Representative System

There are two forms of democracy: direct and indirect. The form of direct democracy refers to the ways and methods in which people participate in the decision-making of the important state affairs in person. Generally speaking, the practice of direct democracy in a jurisdiction must meet the following requirements: First, it should be a small jurisdiction with a small population. As the direct democracy emphasizes the direct management of state affairs by the people, it is necessary to convene an assembly attended by all citizens to jointly handle the state affairs. Given a large territory and a large population, it is extremely difficult to practice direct democracy. Second, transportation should be well developed. A developed system of transportation is the basic requirement to guarantee that citizens can gather rapidly, attend the assembly of citizens and participate in the decision-making of the state affairs. Third, the state affairs should be simple. The complexity of state affairs is bound to exceed the bearing capacity of the assembly of citizens. Therefore, the practice of direct democracy is to be also restricted by the political factors in addition to the aforementioned geographical ones. Fourth, the citizens should be well-educated because the major task for the citizens in the direct democracy is to directly participate in law making. However, if citizens are poorly-educated, the assembly will be rendered incompetent for its function. That is why the direct democratic form is mainly adopted at the stage of the primitive democracy. As the forces of history push social progress,[11] the limitations of the direct democracy show up gradually, and the indirect democratic form thus comes into being. The form of indirect democracy refers to the ways and methods in which people participate in, decide and manage the major state affairs through their representatives. The indirect democratic form, which

---

[11] Cf. Chapter 2 of this book.

is created for remedying the defects of the direct democratic form, holds a dominant position relative to direct democracy in both capitalist and socialist societies later in the process of democratic development. Moreover, although direct democracy tends to increase the development of democratic form, the two forms of democracy are sure to coexist for a relatively long period of time. Additionally, as the direct democracy focuses more on the ideal aspect and neglects the practical level, on the contrary, the indirect democracy works the other way around,[12] the combination of the two can maximize their strengths and minimize their weaknesses. In this sense, the expansion of the direct democracy will not offset the existence of the indirect democracy, but only the focus will change with the political, economic and cultural conditions.

Besides, one thing must be clarified. Academics and the general public believe direct democracy means that the state power is exercised by citizens in person, while indirect democracy means that the representatives elected by the citizens exercise the state power instead. This view is not absolutely correct. Ancient Athens, for example, was generally believed to have practiced direct democracy. Although the ecclesia (assembly of citizens) held the supreme power in the executive, legislative and judicial areas, its duty in practice was only limited to deliberation, such as reviewing and approving the decision of declaring a war, while the executive power was entrusted to the consuls (executive officers), and judicial power was delegated to courts. Modern Switzerland is another example. It is generally considered that direct democracy is practiced in the country. However, its executive power belongs to the executive committee and the judicial power is entrusted to courts at all levels. Only the legislative power is directly exercised by the citizens. Obviously, neither the executive power nor the judicial power is exercised directly by citizens whether in the ancient or the modern ages. Therefore, the criterion to distinguish the difference between the direct and indirect democracy is only based on the form of exercise of the legislative power.

Although the indirect democratic form and the indirect democratic system have many connections, for instance, both of them belong to the indirect democracy and are counterparts of the direct democracy, but they are not the same things. Their differences mainly exist in their connotations and in the process of their production. In my opinion, the indirect democratic form appears prior to the indirect democratic system, in other words, the indirect democratic system is the outcome of the development of the indirect democratic form to a certain historical stage. In terms of connotation, the indirect democratic form mainly focuses on the indirect ways and methods, and its denotation may be one way and one method or two ways and two methods, that is to say, its denotation is wider; the indirect democratic system is a unified system comprised of a series of indirect democratic forms, thus its denotation is narrower. It is inappropriate but not completely wrong that the representative system under study in this book is often considered as a form of indirect democracy. In fact, the representative system belongs to the category of the indirect democratic system, and it is the main content and form of the indirect democratic system. In a

[12] Gu, B. X. (1988) *Minquan zhuyi minzhu zhengzhi lun* [On Principle of Civil Rights in Democratic Politics], Taipei: San Min Book Co., Ltd., pp. 393–396.

certain sense, the representative system has obviously become synonymous with the indirect democratic system in the modern democratic practices.

1.1.3 Comparison of Several Conceptions of Representative System

(1) **Conceptions of Representative System by Bourgeois Scholars**

The bourgeois scholars have many conceptions of the representative system. As far as I know, they are mainly as follows:

The first conception is that the representative system is equal to the establishment of the representative organ. In *Principles of Constitutional Law*, the renowned Japanese Constitutional scholar Minobe Tatsukichi noted that the representative system involves "the election and re-election of the parliament of citizens periodically by the people being represented as an institution speaking for the will of the people".[13] Some others hold that the representative system is just establishing a parliament as an institution representing the public will. The parliament is superior to the government, and all the important state affairs are to be first reviewed and approved by the parliament before they are executed by the government.

The second is that the representative system is the fundamental way for people to control the government. John Stuart Mill argued in his book *Considerations on Representative Government*, "The meaning of representative government is, that the whole people, or some numerous portion of them, exercise through deputies periodically elected by themselves, the ultimate controlling power, which, in every constitution, must reside somewhere. This ultimate power they must possess in all its completeness. They must be masters, whenever they please, of all the operations of government."[14]

The third is that the representative system is the indirect representation system. S. Reed Brett, the British constitutional expert said, "...for the idea of representation had not yet emerged—the idea, that is, that one man could represent another, or a number of others."[15] Others believe that the representative system can be defined as a system or a process where certain representatives, with evident consent of part or all of the citizens, impose their influence upon the government or the legislative power, and the effects are taken by the ones being represented.

---

[13] Tatsukichi, M. (1927) *Xianfaxue yuanli* [Principles of Constitutional Law], trans. Ou Z. Y. and He Z. L., Beijing: The Commercial Press, p. 227.

[14] Mill, J. (1982) *Daiyizhi zhengfu* [Representative Government], trans, Wang X., Beijing: The Commercial Press, p. 68. cf. Mill, J. (1861/2008) *Considerations on Representative Government*, London: The Electric Book Company, p. 87.

[15] Brett, S. (1936) *Yingguo xianzhengshi tan* [On the History of the British Constitution], trans. Chen S. D., Taipei: The Commercial Press, p. 81. cf. Brett, S. (1929) *The Story of the British Constitution*, London and Glasgow: Blackie & Son Limited, p. 81.

The fourth is that the representative system is regarded as a kind of polity. *Encyclopedia Britannica* defines the representative democracy, with which representative system has become synonymous as "a form of government where the citizens exercise the same right not in person but through representatives chosen by and responsible to them".[16] According to *Encyclopedia Americana*, "Representative government is the form of political rule in which the major laws and executive decisions in a state or community are made by a small number of persons who are believed to represent in some way the population or important parts of it."[17]

Although the conceptions mentioned above have all stressed the basic feature of indirectness of the representative system, their common defects are obvious: First, they fail to reveal the nature of the representative system except the mere descriptions of the phenomena and activities of the representative system in political practice. Second, they fail to comprehensively and completely generalize the content of the representative system other than defining it from one aspect or angle or another.

Still other points require classification. First, there are connections as well as differences between the representative system and the representative organ. Neither can be equated. Actually, the representative system is the abstraction and generalization of the representative organ system with the representative organ as the core, while the representative organ is a specified and structured representation of the principles and contents of the representative system. Second, the representative system is merely an approach to the realization of the interests and desires of the ruling class and its allies, but not a fundamental means for people to control the government in general,[18] because the government itself is the prime indication of the representative system. Third, the representative system connotes both "representing" and "deliberating", so it cannot be understood as the general meaning of "representing", as in "an individual representing the others or the majority". Fourth, the polity differs from the political system. The representative system is only the important content of the national political system, rather than the polity of the country. Fifth, theoretically, the representative system as a concept centers on the "indirect form", that is, a proportion of people representing the rest or the few representing the majority in the decision making of the important state affairs. As for its class attribute, it is given by its people. To put it another way, the class attribute of the representative system is determined by the purpose of the class or stratum who employs the system, its political and economic status. However, any study of political theory, if divorced from the real political life, will not only fail to reach any scientific conclusions, but also will not contribute to the development of the political practice. Therefore, revealing the nature of the representative system should be the core concept of its study.

---

[16] Benton, W. (ed.) (1929/1964) *Encyclopedia Britannica*, Chicago, London, Toronto, Geneva and Sydney: Encyclopedia Britannica, Inc., vol. 7, p. 215.

[17] *Meiguo baike quanshu* [The Encyclopedia Americana], vol. 2, p. 387. cf. The Encyclopedia Americana (1829/1985), Danbury: Grolier Incorporated, vol. 23, p. 410.

[18] The "government" here does not refer to "administrative organs", but a unity of legislation, jurisdiction and administration.

(2) **Conceptions of Chinese Scholars Concerning Representative System**

There are generally four common conceptions of the representative system held by Chinese scholars:

The first conception is that the representative system, also called "parliamentary system" or "congressional system", is a political system implemented in the capitalist countries, where the parliament is the center of the national political activities and the government is responsible to the parliament.[19]

The second one is that the representative system is the parliamentary system in a broad sense, where the parliament is formed by the elected members, exercises the legislative functions and supervises the government to a certain degree according to the principle of the separation of powers.[20]

The third is that the representative system refers to the system in which the capitalist countries divide constituencies across the country and elect members to form the parliament so as to carry out the power of legislation and supervision in the name of the voters.[21]

The fourth is that the representative system is "a form of indirect democracy. It has two characteristics: the first is that the members and representatives of the representative organ are elected by universal suffrage and have a certain term of office. The second is that the representative organ possesses the legislative power and occupies an important position in the system of state organs".[22]

It should be mentioned that the above conceptions basically avoid some defects of those proposed by the bourgeois scholars. However, I think there are still some points to be noted. Firstly, the counterpart of the representative democracy can only be the direct democracy instead of the socialist people's representative system, so it is biased to think that "the representative system is virtually the bourgeois parliamentary system".[23] Secondly, the discontinuity in the content and nature of democracy exists to some extent, but there is a certain inheritance in the form of democracy. Thirdly, the denotation of a concept is determined by its connotation, so we cannot demarcate the denotation before defining the connotation, otherwise, the preconception is bound to affect the scientific nature of the concept.

---

[19] Cf. *Jianming zhengzhixue cidian* [Concise Dictionary of Politics] (1985), Jilin People's Press; *Jianming zhengzhixue cidian* [Concise Dictionary of Political Science] (1986), Henan People's Press; *Zhengzhixue changjian mingci qianshi* [A Brief Explanation of Common Terms in Political Science] (1984), People's Publishing House; *Shijie yihui cidian* [Dictionary of World Parliaments] (1987), China Radio & Television Publishing House; Wang, Z. H. (1989) *Minzhu yu zhongguoren* [Democracy and Chinese People], China Radio & Television Publishing House, p. 52.

[20] Zhongguo da baikequanshu: Faxue [Encyclopedia of China: Law] (1984), Beijing: Encyclopedia of China Publishing House, entry "parliamentary system".

[21] Zhao, C. F. (1986) *Zhengzhixue xinlun* [New Theory of Politics], Changchun: Northeast Normal University Press, p. 154.

[22] He, H. H. (1992) *Renmin daibiao dahui zhidu de lilun yu shijian* [Theory and Practice of People's Congress System], Wuhan: Wuhan University Press, p. 1.

[23] Zhang, G. B. (1984) *Xianfa lun* [On Constitution], Changchun: Jilin People's Press, p. 95.

1.1.4 The Concept of Representative System

Lenin pointed out, "...the conditional and relative value of all definitions in general, ...can never embrace all the concatenations of a phenomenon in its full development."[24] Although the aforementioned conceptions of the representative system have certain drawbacks, we should be clear that they are all brought about by the different standpoints, methods, and perspectives of the researchers that propose them. Therefore, the representative system, on the basis of the above analysis, can be defined as a system in which the ruling class of a state elects a certain number of members who can reflect its interest and wills from different classes, strata and groups to form a representative organ for deciding and managing the major state affairs in terms of political, economic, cultural, and social life according to the principle of subordinating the minority to the majority. In this sense, this definition has not only refrained itself from the formalism of other definitions, but has also avoided the parochialism and the subjectivity on the issue of the representative system. Moreover, it has not only clearly revealed the nature and purpose of the representative system, but also comprehensively and systematically summarized its content. From this definition, we can understand that both the capitalist parliamentary system and the socialist people's representative system are only manifestations of different forms of the representative system.

Based on the definition above, the representative system can be divided into three main components in terms of its internal structure: the system of representation, the organizational system and the dispute resolution system of the representative organs. The integration of the three forms an organic whole. Here I'd like to elaborate on these points.

First, the system of representation. The system of representation is the core of the representative system, and the latter does not exist without the former. Since the concept of "representative" is used on different occasions in the social and political life, it is of great importance to clarify the connotation of the term "representative" as it is used in this book.[25] Here, the so-called "representative" is limited to the members of the representative organs elected according to law, such as members of parliament (MPs) or people's deputies. The system of representation refers to the system concerning the representatives' election, identity, status, obligation, supervision, recall, authority protection, operation and functions.

Second, the organizational system of the representative organ. The representative organ is the materialized framework of the representative system, and is the organizer and leader for the actual operation of the representative system. Therefore, the internal structure of the representative organ, the organization of its institutions, the obligations and authority of the institutions, and their mutual relations, etc. are closely related to the operation of the representative system.

---

[24] *Liening xuanji* [Lenin Selected Works] (1995), Beijing: People's Publishing House, vol. 2, p. 651. cf. Lenin, V. (1916) *Imperialism, the Highest Stage of Captitalism.*

[25] Professor Birch thinks that there are three applications of the term "representation". cf. Birch, A. H. (1971) *Representation*, London: Pall Mall Press Ltd., p. 19.

Third, the resolution system of the representative organ. The representative system not only needs the representatives and the representative organ, but also calls for the representative organ to perform its functions and powers and carry out various work according to law. Thus, the representative organ is required to establish a comprehensive and effective dispute resolution system by making 'rules and regulations' so as to guarantee the representative organ fully exercises its functions and powers.

1.2 Basic Features of Representative System

The basic features of the representative system refer to the most important features of the representative system, as the basic system of state governance, manifested in its organizational structure and in the status and role of the whole state system. Generally speaking, the representative system is characterized by "representing the deliberation", including both "representing" and "deliberating". The basic features are as follows.

1.2.1 Representation

The core feature of the representative system lies in the concept of "representation" in modern sense, which is different from the virtual concept that the king is the representative or delegate of the people in the Middle Ages. That is to say, in order for representatives to hold the state power, there must be a system of guarantees that actually ensures the nature of representation. In modern and contemporary bourgeois parliaments, at least the members of one house are elected, which is an institutional guarantee for "representation". Even in systems where the monarch possesses some representative quality, members of the lower houses of parliaments possess the quality to a much greater extent. In the socialist representative organs, all the representatives are elected. Therefore, election of representatives is the primary feature of the representative system.

1.2.2 Indirect

Closely associated with the feature of representation mentioned above, the indirectness indicates that the people do not manage the major state affairs directly. Since representation is the core feature of the representative system, which is a necessary intermediate link for the activation of the representative organ in order to give full play to the functions of the representative system, under the representative system, the people can only participate in the management of the country indirectly. Therefore, the indirectness is also one of the basic features of the representative system and an extension of representation as well.

1.2.3 Organizational

The representative system is a generalization and abstraction of a series of organizations and institutions with the representative organs as the core. In other words, the representative system is of significance only when the representative system is materialized into various organs and organizations. As stated above, the representative system is different from the representative organ, however, the former loses its intrinsic value without the latter. Because the representative system has its organizational feature, in order to give full play to the representative system and apply it scientifically and effectively, the key is to grasp its entities, namely, its various institutions and organizations. Only when all kinds of representative organs and organizations operate healthily and properly can the representative system function effectively.

1.2.4 Hierarchical

The representative system, in a sense, refers to the system of the representative organs at all levels of both central and local governments, that is to say, the representative system is not only an abstraction of the central representative organ system, but also the local ones. Therefore, it is the multilevel nature of the representative organ system that lead to the hierarchy of the internal composition of the representative system.

1.2.5 Accountability

Although the representative theories have failed to settle whether representative organs serve the function of "delegate" or "trustee",[26] none denies that both the representatives and the representative organs must be accountable for their own behavior, but their only differences lie in for what and to whom they should be accountable. The "trustee" conception of representative organs holds that the representatives must be accountable for the overall interests of the country, while the "delegate" conception

[26] Miller, D. and V. Bogdanor (eds) (1992) *The Blackwell Encyclopedia of Political Science*, New York: Wiley-Blackwell, p. 647.

holds that the representatives must be accountable to the voters of their constituencies. Therefore, the representative politics is in a sense a politics of accountability, and in turn accountability constitutes the feature of the representative system.

1.3 Basic Functions of Representative System

The basic functions of the representative system, i.e. the basic roles of the representative system in the social and political life, result from its establishment, improvement and practical operation by people. Classical theories posit that parliaments can do everything except make men women or women men, and that the functions of the representative system can be summarized as those of representation, unification and government-supervision, but theoretically, the representative system is created to provide the abstract power holders with specific ways to realize their power with the changing social and historical situation. Therefore, the most fundamental and core function of the representative system is to allocate the state power in the form of representative system. Specifically, the functions are: resolution, reconciliation, oversight and education.

1.3.1 Resolution Function

In terms of purpose, the organization of the representative organs and establishment of the representative system legitimize the status and powers of their subordinate institutions and organizations and properly solve various problems in the national and social life through their effective operation. As Tomoaki Iwai puts it, "'to endow legal status and legitimate qualification' is the most important function of the parliament in the democratic countries under the rule of law today."[27] Thus, "resolution" is one of the most basic functions in the operation of the representative system, which Birch defines as the function to endow the government with a particular kind of legitimacy.[28] In both its literal meaning and political practice, "resolution" entails "deliberation" and "decision", the two closely related but distinct parts. The so-called "deliberation", i.e., discussion or negotiation, is a process of drawing on collective wisdom and absorbing all useful ideas. It is also the basis for and prerequisite to a "decision", while a "decision" without "deliberation" entails loss of democracy, which easily leads to dictatorship. What's more, John Stuart Mill takes "deliberation", which fully reflects various opinions of the people, as a basic function of the parliament. He believes that politicians can find sound evidence for their policy making by observing the balance of power relations between those opinions displayed in the parliament.

---

[27] Iwai, T. (1990) *Lifa guocheng* [Legal Process], trans. Li W., Beijing: The Economic Daily Press, p. 3.

[28] Birch, A. (1971) *Representation*, London: Pall Mall Press Ltd., pp. 122–123.

Consequently, when someone accused the parliament of being "a place for mere talk and bavardage", Mill argued:

> There has seldom been more displaced derision. I know not how a representative assembly can more usefully employ itself than in talk, when the subject of talk is the great public interests of the country, and every sentence of it represents the opinion either of some important body of persons in the nation, or of an individual in whom some such body have reposed their confidence. A place where every interest and shade of opinion in the country can have its cause even passionately pleaded, in the face of the government and of all other interests and opinions, can compel them to listen, and either comply, or state clearly why they do not, is in itself, if it answered no other purpose, one of the most important political institutions that can exist anywhere, and one of the most foremost benefits of free government. Such 'talking' would never be looked upon with disparagement if it were not allowed to stop 'doing'.[29]

And such extensive deliberation provides the conditions for the formation of a correct decision. In this regard, Aristotle pointed out, "Now any member of the assembly, taken separately, is certainly inferior to the wise man. But the state is made up of many individuals. And as a feast to which all the guests contribute is better than a banquet furnished by a single man, so a multitude is a better judge of many things than any one individual."[30]

Here the term "decision" refers to decision-making or policy-making, which is the logical result of "deliberation". 'Deliberation' without "decision" is truly nothing but "mere talk", as meaningless as a vibration of the air. Thus, Rawls pointed out that "the authority to determine basic social policies resides in a representative body selected for limited terms by and ultimately accountable to the electorate. This representative body has more than a purely advisory capacity. It is a legislature with lawmaking powers and not simply a forum of delegates from various sectors of society to which the executive explains its actions and discerns the movements of public sentiment."[31]

1.3.2 Reconciliation Function

Unequal economic status and power allocation inevitably result in the contradictory movement between power and rights. Where interest differences are very popular and interest conflicts are extraordinarily complicated, the contradictions between power and rights are mainly manifested in three ways: (1) the contradiction between power and rights of different groups within the ruling class; (2) the contradiction

---

[29] Mill, J. (1982) *Daiyizhi zhengfu* [Representative Government], trans. Wang X., Beijing: The Commercial Press, p. 81. cf. Mill, J. (1861/2008) *Considerations on Representative Government*, London: The Electric Book Company, pp. 104–105.

[30] Cited in Lipset, S. (1993) *Zhengzhiren* [Political Man], trans. Liu G. M. & Nie R, Beijing: The Commercial Press, p1. cf. Lipset, S. (1960) *Political Man: The social bases of politics*, New York: Doubleday & Company, Inc., p. 1.

[31] Rawls, J. (1988) *Zhengyi lun* [A Theory of Justice], trans. He H. H., He B. G. and Liao S. B., Beijing: China Social Sciences Press, p. 212. cf. Raws, J. (1971/1999) *A Theory of Justice*, Massachusetts: The Belknap Press of Harvard University Press, p. 195.

between the power of ruling class and the rights of the ruled class; (3) the contradiction of rights among different strata and groups within the ruled class. From a philosophical point of view, there are a variety of solutions to these contradictions. However, reconciliation is the best way to resolve contradictions that need to be handled without undermining the existing social order, because managing contradiction entails a progression from basic solution to thorough solution, and reconciliation only involves the basic solution of contradictions; secondly, since contradictory factors can co-exist in unison in certain conditions, it is advisable to find common ground of mutual constraints so as to create such conditions to bring all those factors into a harmonious state through negotiation; thirdly, all aspects of contradictions can be transformed into one another under certain conditions, thus there must be an intersection that promotes mutual transformation, and reconciliation moves the "intersection" under given conditions in order that the nature of contradictions can be transformed without breaking the original unity of contradictions. Therefore, I believe that reconciliation is an important means to deal with the contradictory movement between power and rights under the premise of maintaining the basic stability of political and legal order in modern countries. In view of its organizational structure and actual operation, the representative system also has a significant function of reconciling various social contradictions.

First, in terms of the member composition of representative bodies, the existence of interest differences and interest contradictions prompts different classes, strata and groups to participate in and exert influence on the political life of the country to satisfy their own desires and realize their own interests. Since the representative body plays an important role in the political life of the country, being elected as a "member" or a "representative" is the best way to achieve the aforementioned purposes. In spite of the differences between countries with different class natures in the process of representing the different interests of the country and society—members of the representative bodies in capitalist countries mainly come from different interest groups and strata of the propertied class that only represent a small portion of the population, while members of the representative bodies in socialist countries come from various social classes and strata of the society that account for 98% of the population—they share something in common in terms of reflecting their respective interest differences, reconciling and solving their respective interest contradictions, and the only difference lies in that the members in the capitalist countries tend to only represent a part of the society and those in the socialist countries can represent the whole society. Lipset pondered the principal problem for a theory of democratic system, "Under what conditions can a society have 'sufficient' participation to maintain the democratic system without introducing sources of cleavage which will undermine the cohesion?"[32] Judging from the member composition of representative bodies, the representative system is the basic form to solve such a problem. Just as Easton

[32] Lipset, S. (1993) *Zhengzhi ren* [Political Man], trans. Liu G. M. & Nie R., Beijing: The Commercial Press, p. 18. cf. Lipset, S. (1960) *Political Man: The social bases of politics,* New York: Doubleday & Company, Inc., p. 32.

pointed out, "The differences among diverse groups may be shielded from aggravation by building into the system additional expressive structural means that give the groups an opportunity to attempt to resolve their differences, if at all possible, under acceptable ground rules. A major device for this purpose is to be found in all kinds of representative structures…".[33]

Regarding the operation of the representative system, since representative bodies are composed of interested representatives from different classes, strata and groups, their main task throughout the process of their activities is to reconcile conflicts of interest, solve various contradictions and properly handle the relationship between the overall interests of the country and the partial interests of the members or representatives. Whether it is a joint government of several classes as in the United Kingdom, or that of several parties as in France, or even that of only one ruling class in a country, reconciliation of contradictions between interests is one of the basic functions of the representative system. As Easton points out, "It may well be, as the constant success of representative democracy in reasserting itself in France testifies, that without the integrative character of representative institutions, the divisive forces in France might have won out"[34]; "Nevertheless, effective political expression for a demand, through the processes of representation, at least provides the satisfaction that an opportunity has been presented for trying to bridge the gap among differences."[35] In real political practice, the function of reconciliation is mainly manifested in two aspects. First, it reconciles the contradictions among different representatives and different state organs. Generally, the contradictions among different representatives and different state organs are usually internal contradictions within the ruling class, which are actually the contradictions between power and rights. Although there are no fundamental disputes within the ruling class, the differentiation of interests and the imbalance of power distribution among different strata and groups will inevitably lead to internal contradictions and conflicts. In order to maintain the stability of political and legal order, the representative system has to bring its reconciliation function into full play. Second, it reconciles the contradictions between the government and the people, which are also the manifestation of the contradictions between power and rights. Specifically, the contradictions between the rule of the minority and the interests of the majority. Therefore, such contradictions in capitalist countries are antagonistic but non-antagonistic in socialist countries. Regardless of the nature of the contradictions, the reconciliation function of the representative system remains the same. On the one hand, through communication channels provided by the representative system, the government is able to adequately understand the public will and

---

[33] Easton, D. (1989) *Zhengzhi shenghuo de xitong fenxi* [A Systematic Analysis of Political Life], trans. Wang P. Q., Beijing: Hua Xia Publishing House, p. 280. cf. Easton, D. (1965) *A Systems Analysis of Political Life*, New York, London and Sydney: John, Wiley & Sons, Inc., p. 251.

[34] Easton, D. (1989) *Zhengzhi shenghuo de xitong fenxi* [A Systematic Analysis of Political Life], trans. Wang P. Q., Beijing: Hua Xia Publishing House, p. 280. cf. Easton, D. (1965) *A Systems Analysis of Political Life*, New York, London and Sydney: John, Wiley & Sons, Inc., p. 252.

[35] Birch, A. H. (1971) *Representation*, London: Pall Mall Press Ltd., p. 123. cf. Easton, D. (1965) *A Systems Analysis of Political Life*, New York, London and Sydney: John, Wiley & Sons, Inc., p. 253.

interest to draft policies accordingly, and thereby win citizens' support and approval for the specific policies. On the other hand, these channels, which function like safety valves, enable entrusted citizens to vent their grudges.[36] As what Ralph Miliband pointed out, "The essence of parliamentarism is that it provides a buffer between government and people. It accords to the people the right to elect their representatives to engage in many forms of political activity; but it also binds the people to let their representatives bear the burden of sustaining or opposing the government of the day."[37] However, in the political practice of the capitalist countries, the reconciliation function contains profound class motives in that the bourgeoisie are clearly aware that they can effectively restrict citizens from participating in the political life of the country on the one hand and manipulate the state power via representatives on the other hand by means of the reconciliation function of the representative system. Montesquieu noted, "The great advantage of representatives is, their capacity of discussing public affairs. For this, the people collectively are extremely unfit, which is one of the chief inconveniences of a democracy." Montesquieu also criticized the direct democracy in ancient Greece, "One great fault there was in most of the ancient republics, that the people had a right to active resolutions, such as require some execution, a thing of which they are absolutely incapable. They ought to have no share in the government but for the choosing of representatives, which is within their reach."[38] When expounding the tradition of the Swedish representative system, Stan Lucan noted, "Now peasants have their own representative institution, which obviously relieves the pressure of demanding further expansion of power."[39] Therefore, fundamentally speaking, the bourgeois representative system aims to consolidate the dominant position of the bourgeoisie, while in contrast, the practice of the representative system in a socialist country aims to properly manage the relationship between the government and the people in order to truly ensure that the people as the masters of the country.

1.3.3 Oversight Function

John Stuart Mill maintained that the parliament cannot directly intervene in the legislative, executive and judicial activities, and that it should focus on the function of oversight and control rather than that of governance. He argued:

---

[36] Easton, D. (1989) *Zhengzhi shenghuo de xitong fenxi* [A Systematic Analysis of Political Life], trans. Wang P. Q., Beijing: Hua Xia Publishing House, pp. 280–281.

[37] Miliband, R. (1988) *Yingguo ziben zhuyi minzhuzhi* [Capitalist Democracy in Britain], trans. Bo Q. & Xiang D., Beijing: The Commercial Press, p. 47. cf. Miliband, R. (1982) *Capitalist Democracy in Britain*, New York: Oxford University Press, p. 38.

[38] Montesquieu (1982) *Lun fa de jingshen* [The Spirit of Laws], trans. Zhang Y. S., Beijing: The Commercial Press, pp. 158–159. cf. Montesquieu (1777) *The Spirit of Laws*, The Online Library of Liberty © 2004 Liberty Fund, Inc., p. 190.

[39] Wisti, F. (1990) *Beioushi minzhu* [Nordic Democracy], trans. Zhao Z. Q., Beijing: China Social Sciences Press, p. 51.

> Instead of the function of governing, for which it is radically unfit, the proper office of a representative assembly is to watch and control the government; to throw the light of publicity on its acts; to compel a full exposition and justification of all of them which any one considers questionable; to censure them if found condemnable, and, if the men who compose the government abuse their trust, or fulfil it in a manner which conflicts with the deliberate sense of the nation, to expel them from office, and either expressly or virtually appoint their successors.[40]

Mill's father, James Mill also pointed out that representative democracy is the only guarantee against oppression and the only means of supervising the rulers.[41] In theory, the representative system, with its representative bodies as the core, is the fundamental system for expressing and facilitating the popular will. In the political life of modern countries, the concept of "the popular sovereignty" has been deeply rooted in the minds of the people, so the will and interests of the people are bound to become the center of the political life of the country. Since the representative body is also an institution of public opinion, it has the power and responsibility to supervise the state organs to ensure the realization of the popular will, both in countries typical of "parliamentary supremacy" as in the United Kingdom and in the socialist countries in which the representative institutions are the highest organs of state power. Even in countries with a typical system of "separation of powers", since legislation is the main activities of the representative institutions and the laws are the essential codes of conduct for all institutions, organizations and individuals, their work of expressing the public opinions and safeguarding the popular will is largely performed through legislation and oversight of law enforcement. In this regard, the former U.S. President Woodrow Wilson pointed out:

> It is the proper duty of a representative body to look diligently into every affair of government and to talk much about what it sees. It is meant to be the eyes and the voice, and to embody the wisdom and will of its constituents. Unless Congress have and use every means of acquainting itself with the acts and the disposition of the administrative agents of the government, the country must be helpless to learn how it is being served; and unless Congress both scrutinize these things and sift them by every form of discussion, the country must remain in embarrassing, crippling ignorance of the very affairs which it is most important that it should understand and direct.[42]

In essence, the representative institution's supervision and control over the government guarantees supervision and control of the government by the people, so as to provide a way to keep political leaders openly accountable for their actions on the one hand, and to offer a mechanism for non-violent replacement of leaders on the other.[43]

---

[40] Mill, J. (1982) *Daiyizhi zhengfu* [Representative Government], trans. Wang X., Beijing: The Commercial Press, p. 80. cf. Mill, J. (1861/2008) *Considerations on Representative Government*, London: The Electric Book Company, p. 103.

[41] Cited in Miller, D. and Bogdanor, V. (eds) (1992). *The Blackwell Encyclopedia of Political Science*, New York: Wiley-Blackwell, p. 475.

[42] Wilson, W. (1990) *Guohui zhengti* [Congressional Government], trans. Xiong X. L. & Lv D. B., Beijing: The Commercial Press, p. 167. cf. Wison, W. (1885/2011) *Congressional Government*, Boston and New York: Houghton Mifflin Company, p. 150.

[43] Birch, A. H. (1971) *Representation*, London: Pall Mall Press Ltd., pp. 107–108.

In addition to the function of supervising the government, the representative system also implies the supervision over the representative institutions by the people since a representative institution is an agency of popular will as mentioned earlier. Are the public's opinions truly reflected by the representative institutions? To what extent has the popular will been achieved? The answers to these questions can only be obtained through the supervision and examination of the representative institutions by the people. Given that the "members" and "representatives" are elected by the people, the people directly supervise the representative institutions, and then indirectly supervise the government through the representative institutions, which constitutes the supervision system of the representative system. Theoretically, the effective operation of the supervision system can guarantee the status and role of the people as masters of the country. In this regard, Henry B. Mayo believes that the representative system, as a political system, is democratic to the extent that decision-makers are under effective popular control.[44] However, in the political practice of capitalist countries, such a supervision function is far from what has been theorized.

1.3.4 Education Function

Were one to discuss the function of education only in a general sense, I think there would be no need to elaborate on its function in study of the representative system. However, the representative system is the core of modern democratic politics, whose effective operation requires the participants to have certain qualifications, therefore, a brief discussion of education is necessary. When Montesquieu criticized the direct democracy of ancient Greece and advocated for the representative system, his basic rationale was that the average people were neither well trained and nor equipped with qualifications to manage state affairs. For the same reason, politicians and theorists in modern capitalist countries have also used lack of education as an excuse to prevent the people from participating in the political life of the country. Nevertheless, both Montesquieu and some later bourgeois spokesmen only saw what democracy asks from the people while ignoring the fact that democratic politics itself provides an ideal opportunity to improve the people's political competence and to develop their political character, a fact noticed by some other sensible thinkers. John Stuart Mill asserted that the representative government should be made to have both educational and utilitarian functions.[45] He argued that one of the important reasons why the representative government is called an ideal political system is that, through the process of political activities, it can educate the people, develop their own potential, improve their knowledge and moral standards, build up their good character, promote their personality and thus enhance their sense of commitment towards the country. The

---

[44] Mayo, H. B. (1960) *An Introduction to Democratic Theory*, New York: Oxford University Press, p. 60.

[45] Miller, D. and Bogdanor, V. (eds) (1992) *The Blackwell Encyclopedia of Political Science*, New York: Wiley-Blackwell, p. 475.

people's concern for and participation in the public affairs not only nutures positive attitudes, encourages autonomy and creates a better tomorrow, but also allows the people to realize political participation through the representative system, which will both promote them to go beyond the small circle of their personal lives to become members of a community and transcend their selfish mentality to become concerned with the public's interests. Compared with the autocratic political system that only requires the people to obey, the representative system that allows participation better promotes the social progress and improve the individual character of the people. Ideally, the best way to achieve these ends would be for everyone to participate in government affairs in person, though it is extremely difficult to achieve this in real life due to the constraints of social and historical conditions. Therefore, the representative system remains the best form of political system.[46]

On the other hand, Max Weber regarded the parliament as a training base for political leaders. He classified parliaments into two basic types. One is the so-called "symbolic" parliamentary system, which is weak in power and neither produces talent nor trains political leaders; the other is a strong one, under which the government is created by the parliament and is directly responsible to the parliament. And the main function of the parliament is to serve as a base for attracting and training future political leaders.[47] Undoubtedly, what Weber describes is also an important part of the educational function of the representative system.

In addition to the four functions mentioned above, the representative system also has the derivative function, which is actually an extension of the resolution function. The representative organ, composed of elected members or representatives, is entitled to make decisions on major political affairs including economic, cultural and social issues of the country. That is to say, by resorting to legislative activities, the representative organ expresses the will and interests of the ruling class in terms of politics, economy, culture, social life and other aspects in the form of law. Therefore, as a basic system of managing the country, the representative system can organize and build up a series of other systems to govern the state affairs in all fields by means of legislative activities. In this sense, the representative system has a derivative function since a series of other systems can be derived from it.

---

[46] Mill, J. (1861/2008) *Considerations on Representative Government,* London: The Electric Book Company, p. 92.

[47] Beetham, D. (1989) *Makesi Weibo yu xiandai zhengzhi lilun* [Max Weber and the Theory of Modern Politics], trans. Xu H. B., Xu J. H. & Kang L. W., Hangzhou: Zhejiang People's Publishing House, p. 99, p. 101.

1.4 Basic Principles of Representative System

1.4.1 General Principles

The general principles of the representative system refer to the principles that must be followed in the process of establishing, improving and operating the system, and are universally applicable to both the capitalist parliamentary system and the socialist people's representative system. Although these principles are applied by different classes in different countries so as to reflect different nature, they are affirmed in political theories and legal provisions by all the countries that carry out the representative system without exception. Specifically, the general principles of the representative system are as follows: popular sovereignty, universal suffrage, the rule of law, majority resolution, procedure and publicity.

(1) **The Principle of Popular Sovereignty**[48]

Popular sovereignty means that the vast majority of people in a country have the supreme power to rule the country, that is, the principle of sovereignty. It is a democratic principle put forward and confirmed by the bourgeoisie in the process of bourgeois revolution against the feudal autocracy. From the perspective of historical development, the principle of popular sovereignty is the fundamental guiding ideology of the representative system. Although this principle was not directly proposed as the representative system came into being in Britain, the principle of "parliamentary sovereignty", guiding the establishment and operation of the British parliamentary system, is actually designed to protect the interest of the emerging bourgeoisie, i.e. the so-called people's interest, therefore, its basic thrust does not differ from the principle of popular sovereignty. With the establishment of the capitalist relations of production and consolidation of the bourgeois regime, popular sovereignty and the representative system have competed to become significant parts of the bourgeois democracy, where the two are integrated perfectly in form. However, it is the privilege of capital that essentially determines this integration mainly serves the interests of the propertied class.

(2) **The Principle of Universal Suffrage**

As previously mentioned, the fundamental feature of the representative system is that representatives must be elected. Therefore, without elections, there can be no representative system. In this sense, we can say that the election is the foundation of the representative system. The so-called principle of universal suffrage here refers to the principle of universal right to vote. In general, the universal right to vote means that there are no extra qualifications for obtaining the right to vote other than age,

[48] This topic will be further discussed in Chap. 3.

citizenship, mental illness and legal deprivation of the political rights, and hence the principle of universal suffrage is practiced.

Universal suffrage was a key focus of the struggle for human rights and the slogan of the bourgeoisie against the feudal privileges in modern history. Under the feudal autocracy, officials were appointed by the feudal lords. In the first draft of *The Civil War in France*, Karl Marx used the term 'hierarchical investiture' to describe the system in which the feudal lords in the Middle Ages conferred vassals land, priesthood and official positions. The distinctive feature of this system was that people from the lower classes were completely at the mercy of the ecclesial and hereditary feudal lords from the higher classes. Under the monarchy in some western countries in the Middle Ages, there existed some sort of feudal hierarchical system of representation, yet in the "Estates General", the nobility and clergy enjoyed privileges while "the third estate" including peasants, artisans and bourgeois were completely deprived of rights or had them strictly restricted. For this reason, the representative assembly in the feudal society is fundamentally distinct from the bourgeois parliamentary system based on universal suffrage. In Chinese feudal society, there were also systems of so-called "selection of talents" and "recommendation of officials", which were designed to discover talents to serve the feudal lords, but they have nothing in common with the universal suffrage in a democracy. At the end of the feudal period, with the development of the capitalist commodity economy, the bourgeois revolution broke out under the slogan of equal rights. The slogan reflected exactly the needs of the capitalist commodity economy.

In the 1640s, British bourgeoisie brought up the issue of universal suffrage, but it did not come to fruition at that time. In 1832, Britain reformed its electoral system and lowered its high property qualifications. In July 1837, the London Working Men's Association launched the Chartist Movement, which Lenin called as the world's "first broad, truly mass and politically organized proletarian revolutionary movement."[49] Later, according to the Representation of the People Acts of 1918 and 1928, men and women alike enjoyed the equal right to vote in Britain. By 1948, equal suffrage based on the principle of "one man one vote" was implemented. In 1969, some amendments were made to the Representation of the People Act, stipulating that all British citizens over the age of 18 had the right to vote according to law.

According to the political practices in capitalist countries, whatever features it has, the bourgeois revolution has gone through a long and tortuous process of development in terms of the establishment of the universal suffrage and the implementation of the principle of universal suffrage. And the moment the bourgeoisie initially took control of state power, they turned their spearhead to the principle of universal suffrage and denied working people the right to vote. Afterwards, owing to the repeated struggles of the laborers, the bourgeoisie on the one hand had to abolish some overt restrictions and allowed the citizens to enjoy the suffrage in form, while, on the other hand, they actually undermined the principle of universal suffrage through more covert and circuitous means such as qualification restrictions, constituency division, and ballot

---

[49] *Liening quanji* [Lenin Collected Works] (1956), Beijing: People's Publishing House, vol. 29, p. 276.

calculation. In this way, the principle of universal suffrage, though created by the bourgeoisie, could only guarantee the suffrage of the rich as matter of fact under bourgeois parliamentary system. Just as Engels put it, "the propertied class rules directly by means of the universal suffrage."[50] And only in the socialist countries, where the people have truly become masters of their own countries and privileges are effectively eliminated, can the genuine democratic universal suffrage be possible.

(3) The Principle of Rule of Law

The rule of law, in contrast to the rule of man, refers to a way in which the ruling class institutionalizes and legalizes the state affairs according to the democratic principles, and manages them strictly in accordance with the law. It is an important principle advocated by the bourgeois enlightenment thinkers in the seventeenth and eighteenth centuries. For instance, John Locke, the British political philosopher, proposed that the governments "are to govern by the promulgated established laws, not to be varied in particular cases, but to have one rule for rich and poor, for the favourite at court, and the country man at plough".[51] Thomas Paine, the American political theorist, also expressed the similar view that in absolute governments the king is law and in free countries the law ought to be king. His core concepts are the rule of law, equal justice under the law, and opposition against any organization or individual enjoying privileges beyond the law. These views played a crucial role in the battle against feudal autocratic privileges, as well as in the establishment and maintenance of bourgeois democracy including the universal suffrage system and the representative system. After the victory of the bourgeois revolution, the capitalist countries generally implemented the spirit of the rule of law in political practice, and in their view, constitutions themselves demonstrate the implementation of the rule of law because they generally stipulate that all are equal before the law.

There are two questions to be clarified here. First, is the rule of law one of the fundamental principles of the representative system? The answer is affirmative. If the principle of universal suffrage is the foundation of the representative system and the principle of popular sovereignty is its fundamental guideline, then the rule of law is its fundamental guarantee. Only when the representative system is confirmed in the form of law and protected by legal means from interference and sabotage of any organization or individual, can the representative system operate smoothly. This is true for the capitalist parliamentary system, as is it for the socialist people's representative system. Cao P. L. et al. theorized that the principle of the rule of law in Britain is a bridge between the "parliamentary sovereignty" in law and "popular sovereignty" in politics, and a shield between the rulers and the ruled.[52] Second, can socialist countries follow and apply the principle of the rule of law? The answer is also affirmative. In the past 70 years of the socialist revolution and construction in China, the

---

[50] *Makesi Engesi xuanji* [Marx and Engels Selected Works] (1995), Beijing: People's Publishing House, vol. 4, p. 173. cf. Engels, F. (1884) *The Origin of the Family, Private Property and the State.*

[51] Locke, J. (1690/1988) *Two Treatises of Government*, London: Cambridge University Press, p. 363.

[52] Cao, P. L. et al. (1993) *Bijiao zhengfu tizhi* [A Comparison of Government System], Shanghai: Fudan University Press, p. 137.

building of democracy and the rule of law has not yet been established. An important reason is that the principle of the rule of law has not been strictly observed and effectively applied. Ironically, there are still some people in theoretical circles who regard the principle of the rule of law as something bourgeois, and they believe that the emphasis on the principle of the rule of law will lead to the bourgeois conception of the supremacy and omnipotence of law, and thus will negate the guidance of Marxism-Leninism and the guidelines, principles and policies of the Party. In this regard, I'd like to make the following points clear. First, the rule of law has proven to be the best means of governance in the history of mankind thus far. Although one must deny and criticize the essence of the bourgeois principle of the rule of law that mainly serves the privilege of capital, one can certainly build the socialist principle of the rule of law of our own. Secondly, we can affirm the "supremacy of law" while discarding the "omnipotence of law" advocated by the bourgeoisie, in that the "supremacy of law" is actually the inner core of the principle of the rule of law. Furthermore, the "supremacy of law" is different from the "omnipotence of law". The latter stresses the absolute function and role of law, exclusive of other factors, while the former refers to the high status of law and does not exclude others. Thirdly, observing the principle of the rule of law and adhering to the supremacy of law are not in conflict with the guidance of Marxism-Leninism and the leadership of the Party. Because it is under the guidance of Marxism-Leninism and the leadership of the Party that the Constitution and laws in China are formulated, and their contents are the standardization of the guidelines, principles and policies of the Party, to follow the principle of the rule of law and to adhere to the supremacy of law are consistent with the leadership of the Party and the guidance of Marxism-Leninism. Fourthly, the social ethics, conventions, etc. are also codes of conduct that people follow, but their status is under the law, and thus only the law enjoys supremacy.

In a word, the rule of law is the fundamental principle of the socialist people's representative system and also an important principle in building the socialist democracy and legal system. Moreover, the socialist rule of law should be more comprehensive and thorough than the current capitalist one.

(4) **The Principle of Majority Decision**

The essence of democracy is to draw on collective wisdom and make decisions based on the opinions of the vast majority. Therefore, in the process of deliberating and deciding on the state affairs, the representative bodies should first go through an extensive discussion and negotiation among deputies and then reach a resolution according to the opinions of the majority via voting. This is the principle of majority decision of the representative system.

In primitive societies, people had no notion of majority decision making, so they often resorted to force or even duel whenever they couldn't reach a consensus through negotiation. Therefore, achieving unanimity by force was the ultimate solution to conflicts in primitive societies. Later on, people came to realize that violence was harmful to both the winner and the loser. Consequently, alternatives to violence were suggested: one way was shouting, whereby the opposing sides shouted and whoever shouted louder than the other would win; and the other was lining up, whereby the parties stood in lines and whichever line longer than the other would prevail. This kind of decision by the number of people rather than duel is the origin of the majority rule. The principle of majority decision was adopted early in ancient Greece. In Sparta, for example, the five ephors were elected by majority vote. Similarly, there are also sayings in ancient Roman Law, "What the majority decides must apply to all." and "What is done by the majority of the popular assembly is regarded as what is done by all." So, the Senate voted on bills according to the majority. In this way, the principle of majority decision become a legal system.

The Germanic people adopted this principle mainly under the influence of the Roman law. Villages in northern Italy selected their chief by way of majority decisions, and many European countries followed suit thereafter. The Magna Carta, issued by the British King in 1215, stipulated that the 25 barons present at the meeting at Runnymede should be subject to the decision of the majority regardless of any disputes.[53] In 1356, the Roman Emperor Karl IV (or Charles the Fourth) issued an edict declaring that in the election of the prince electors and the emperor, the one who got the most votes would be elected. Since then, the principle of majority decision has been widely adopted in all countries around the world and still remains an important democratic principle.

Then why should the principle of majority decision be adopted? Due to differences in viewpoints, interests, knowledge, environments, morals, etc., people are unlikely to reach a consensus in times of disputes, which would give rise to majority opinions and minority opinions in most cases. Normally, there are two solutions in deliberating and deciding on an issue among people: one is to decide according to the opinion of the majority and the other is to reach a unanimous consensus by all. If the principle of unanimity were followed in decision making, the minority is very likely to control the majority, because one single objection would overthrow the whole resolution. In this way, it is neither reasonable nor fair that the decision-making on the state affairs according to the opinions of the people would result in the minority controlling and dominating the majority. And this is probably the reason why the principle of majority decision is accepted and taken as a crucial principle of democracy by all countries in modern times. So, what can be called a majority and what is the standard for establishing a majority? Usually, that which is approved by 1/2 or 2/3 of the attendance is the standard of majority.

Nevertheless, one should be clear that implementing the principle of majority decision does not reject the respect for the opinions of minorities. John Stuart Mill had his say early on, "Man for man, they would be as fully represented as the majority. Unless they are, there is not equal government, but a government of inequality and privilege: one part of the people rule over the rest: there is a part whose fair and equal

[53] Magna Carta, Article 61.

share of influence in the representation is withheld from them."[54] The leader of the British Labor Party, Clement Attlee once argued that democratic politics is not only the rule of majority, but also the majority rule plus due respect for the rights of the minority.[55] This is also valued by Proletarian theorists and Marxist classical writers. As Rosa Luxemburg once wrote, freedom only for the supporters of the government, only for the members of one party—however numerous they may be—is no freedom at all… all that is instructive, wholesome and purifying in political freedom depends on this essential characteristic, and its effectiveness vanishes when freedom becomes a special privilege.[56] On this subject, Lenin once stated:

> Lastly, the entire experience of the post-Congress struggle compels us to give thought to the juridical position of the minority (any minority) in our Party. That experience shows, we are convinced, that it is necessary to include in the Party Rules guarantees of minority rights, so that the dissatisfactions, irritations and conflicts that will constantly and unavoidably arise may be diverted from the accustomed philistine channels of rows and squabbling into the still unaccustomed channels of a constitutional and dignified struggle for one's convictions.[57]

(5) **The Principle of Procedure**

The principle of procedure refers to the legal procedures and rules to be followed in the establishment and operation of the representative system. In the practice of the representative democracy, only when all activities are carried out in accordance with certain procedures can the election of members or representatives and the exercise of functions and powers of the representative bodies be guaranteed in a normal and orderly manner, and thereby bring various functions of the representative system into full play. Without stable and complete procedures, not only will the representative system not work, but even the establishment of representative bodies is problematic. Given the legal provisions and political practice, the principle of procedure of the representative system is mainly reflected in two aspects: one concerns the process of members' or representatives' elections, and the other is the process of the deliberative activities of the representative bodies. The former is usually stipulated by the electoral law, while the latter is expressed by rules of procedure.

The election of members or representatives plays a fundamental part in organizing a representative body and establishing a representative system. Under the hierarchical system of representation in the Middle Ages, the selection of "representatives" was entirely designated by the monarch or hereditary, so there was no legal generation procedure at all. Whereas, in modern democratic political life, members and representatives must be elected through a fixed procedure. The reason why deputies are called representatives of popular will and representative bodies are called organs of

[54] Mill, J. (1982) *Daiyizhi zhengfu* [Representative Government], trans. Wang X., Beijing: The Commercial Press, p. 102. cf. Mill, J. (1861/2008) *Considerations on Representative Government*, London: The Electric Book Company, p. 131.

[55] Cf. Attlee's Speech to the Business Association after the British general election during WWII.

[56] Luxemburg, R. (1940) *The Russian Revolution*, trans. Bertram Wolfe, New York: Workers Age Publishers. www.maxists.org/archive/Luxemburg/ [last accessed 5 June 2021].

[57] *Liening quanji* [Lenin Collected Works] (1959), Beijing: People's Publishing House, vol. 7, pp. 444–445. cf. Lenin, V. (1904) What We Are Working For (To the Party).

public opinions is that these deputies are the trustees of the people, elected by them according to their own will in accordance with legal procedures. The democratic election procedures and even the democratic nature of the representatives would be greatly flawed if such procedures were absent or incomplete. According to the electoral laws and election practices in different countries, in the process of electing members or representatives, the following procedures must be carried out in general: establishment of electoral agencies, division of constituencies, registration of voters, nomination of candidates, organization of election campaigns or introduction of candidates, primary election, formal voting, announcement of results, etc.

The procedures prescribed in the process of deliberation guarantee the representative body's effective exercise of its functions and powers. Although the constitutions and laws of all countries stipulate that the representative body should be the center of the state organ system and endow it with great powers of legislation, finance and supervision, without corresponding procedures and systems, these powers would be nothing more than an abstract declaration through legal provisions. Therefore, in order to ensure that the functions and powers of the representative body can be fully exercised and its due status can be truly secured, all countries in the world have established and improved a set of systems and procedures to guarantee the deliberative activities on the basis of summarizing previous experiences and lessons. In terms of systems, there are mainly assembly systems, conference systems, session period systems, legislative assistant systems, hearing systems, information openness systems, voting systems and interpellation systems. As for procedures, there are generally four steps observed in the working process, namely, introducing a bill, deliberating on a bill, voting and passing a bill and releasing a bill. C. Schmitt noted that debate is one of the main principles of the parliament,[58] but I tend to believe that debate is merely a part of activities in the process of observing the principle of procedure, and a way for ideological confrontation between proponents and opponents on a given issue. Therefore, instead of singling out debate as a major principle of the parliament, we might as well emphasize the principle of procedure and raise our awareness of it.

(6) The Principle of Publicity

The so-called democratic politics in modern sense also refers to the politics of public opinion, in which the state affairs rest with popular will and policies are attributed to popular support. Much as the people are the masters of the country and social life, due to all kinds of subjective and objective limitations, they are not yet able to manage the state affairs in person, but only govern the country in the form of the representative system. Therefore, in order to realize the will and interests of the people, there must be a mechanism to guarantee that the people have an effective means to restrict and supervise the establishment and operation of the representative system. However, restriction and supervision are premised upon understating, on the basis of which people could correctly evaluate and judge whether the public's

[58] Cf. Schmitt, C. (1985) *The Crisis of Parliamentary Democracy*, Cambridge, Massachusetts and London: The MIT Press, p. 2.

opinions have been satisfied only when they acquire the sufficient knowledge of all aspects of the representative system in terms of its establishment and operation. Implementing the principle of publicity is an important process and effective means to achieve this goal. Hence, some scholars take publicity as a major principle of the parliament.[59] In this regard, Lenin also argued that "'the broad democratic principle' presupposes the two following conditions: first, full publicity, and secondly, election to all offices. It would be absurd to speak of democracy without publicity.... Since the entire political arena is as open to the public view as is a theatre stage to the audience", for political activists, " their every move could be examined universally or universally in real sense."[60] Karl Marx explained, "The representative constitution is a great advance, for it is the open, genuine, consistent expression of the condition of the modern state."[61]

In light of theory and practice, two aspects have to be illustrated concerning the publicity principle of the representative system: first, the process of electing members or representatives should be open to all. Second, the deliberative activities of the representative bodies should be disclosed. As for the election process, since the deputies are elected to represent the people, if the people know nothing about them, how can we call them representatives? Therefore, only when the people adequately know and actively participate in the election of candidates, the registration of voters and the specific election results, can the generation of the representative bodies have a real foundation of the popular will, and such representative bodies are qualified to discuss the state affairs on behalf of the people. In this sense, deliberative activities are the focus of the publicity principle implemented in the representative system. However, the understanding and interpretation of the so-called open deliberations in the representative bodies differ considerably in the practices of various countries. For example, in France, open deliberation means that the people are allowed to listen in and journalists are allowed to publish records, so that the public can monitor whether their elected members have fulfilled their obligations, and understand the government policies through the consultation of the members and the reply of the government. Meanwhile, in Germany, publicity means that the committee meetings are open to all members of the houses, whether they belong to the committee or not, and the representatives of the government and the senate can also attend as nonvoting delegates. However, the general public and journalists are not allowed to attend, but the participants can describe the details of meetings to the outside public and news media. In general, open deliberation includes the release of meeting agendas, the publication of the records and permission to sit in on meetings, etc. In addition, with the development of the modern democratic politics, governments all over the world have placed more attention on open deliberation through specific provisions in their

---

[59] Cf. Schmitt, C. (1985) *The Crisis of Parliamentary Democracy*, Cambridge, Massachusetts and London: The MIT Press, p. 2.

[60] *Liening quanji* [Lenin Collected Works] (1959), 1st edition, Beijing: People's Publishing House, vol. 5, p. 449. cf. Lenin, V. (1902) *What Is To Be Done?*

[61] *Makesi Engesi quanji* [Marx and Engels Collected Works] (1965), Beijing: People's Publishing House, vol. 1, p. 338. cf. Marx. K. (1843) *Critique of Hegel's Philosophy of Right.*

constitutions and laws. According to a survey of the 61 constitutional countries in Asia and Europe, 34 of them have established the system of open deliberations in their representative bodies, accounting for 55.7% of the total.

However, the very nature of the capitalist state powers determines that the implementation of the publicity principle in the representative system is bound to be constrained by capital. Although in the actual political life, the bourgeoisie often creates some spectacular "scenes of democracy", the privilege of capital is bound to limit the degree of publicity. However, the nature of the socialist state, with people being masters of their own countries determines that it is both necessary and possible to thoroughly implement the publicity principle. When it comes to the difference between Soviet regime and the old regime, Lenin once said, "It was an authority open to all, which carried out all its functions before the eyes of the masses, and was accessible to the masses." "The new authority maintained itself and could maintain itself solely because it enjoyed the confidence of the vast masses, solely because it, in the freest, widest, and most resolute manner, enlisted all the masses in the task of government. It concealed nothing, it had no secrets, no regulations, no formalities."[62]

1.4.2 Distinctive Principles of Capitalist Parliamentary System

The bourgeoisie has declared that the general principles mentioned above must be implemented in the process of establishing and operating the representative system, but some distinctive principles as well must be adopted due to the nature of its capitalist state power. They are chiefly the principles of separation of powers and checks and balances and the principle of representation of all citizens.

(1) **The Principles of Separation of Powers and Checks and Balances**

The principles of separation of powers and checks and balances are the organizational and operational principles for capitalist countries to establish their state organs centered on their representative bodies. Separation of powers refers to the division of the state power into several parts, independently exercised by several state organs. Checks and balances mean that these state organs maintain a mutual check and balance relationship in the process of exercising their powers.

The idea of power separation can be traced back to Aristotle in ancient Greece, who divided the government power into three parts: deliberative, executive and judicial. In the Roman period, Polybius advocated the theory of "mixed government", believing that the Roman government should be checked and balanced by three forces, i.e. the Consul representing the monarch, the Senate representing the aristocracy, and the people's assembly representing the people. In modern times, Locke refocused attention to the separation of powers that further developed by Montesquieu. In order to

[62] *Liening quanji* [Lenin Collected Works] (1958), Beijing: People's Publishing House, vol. 10, pp. 214–215. cf. Lenin, V. (1920) A Contribution to the History of the Question the Dictatorship.

justify constitutional monarchy, Locke and Montesquieu based their ideas of separation of powers on the reality of the British constitutional monarchy and the theories of the modern natural law school combined with the social contract theory, specifically, the concepts of natural rights, principles of natural law and human rationality in the natural law theories, as well as the social contract theory and the state purpose theory. However, two points need to be highlighted. For one thing, the thought of "separation of three powers" is not synonymous with the term "separation of powers and checks and balances" because the former appeared far earlier than the latter. For another, significant differences exist between the doctrine of Locke's power separation and that of Montesquieu's. Firstly, Locke emphasizes "power separation among social classes", while Montesquieu stresses the rational allocation of the state power on the whole. Secondly, Locke's so-called "three powers" actually only have "two powers", because he holds that both the power of execution and that of diplomacy can be exercised by the government. Thirdly, Locke does not involve the doctrine of checks and balances at all in his theory of separation. Moreover, in terms of the relationship between the legislative power and the executive power, Locke believes that the former has superiority over the latter, and the latter is derived from the former. As a result, it is in fact implicated "unity of legislative and executive powers". Therefore, we cannot confuse the doctrine of Locke with that of Montesquieu when analyzing the development of the theory of separation of powers and checks and balances. It follows that in modern times, Locke initiated the theory of separation and Montesquieu developed and completed it.

The principle of separation of powers and checks and balances was established during the bourgeois revolution in the seventeenth and eighteenth centuries by the bourgeoisie in accordance with the modern doctrines of separation of powers, and it guided the establishment of the bourgeois representative system to replace the feudal autocratic system after the bourgeois revolution. According to this very principle, the U.S. Constitution of 1787 stipulated that the organization and operation of the state organs should center on the representative body. The French *Declaration of the Rights of Man and of the Citizen* states that a society, in which neither the people's rights are assured nor the separation of powers is established, has no constitution at all. Influenced by France and the United States, the principle of separation of powers and checks and balances have been echoed in the constitutions of capitalist countries in different forms.

In view of the political practice of the capitalist countries, the principle of separation of powers and checks and balances has indeed played a very important role in establishing and consolidating the bourgeois democracy and promoting the bourgeois representative system for the benefit of the propertied class. For example, US president Nixon was forced to resign, which was the result of the internal conflict among the bourgeois monopoly groups. And more importantly, the class nature of the capitalist countries is concealed by this illusion of separation of powers and checks and balances. In fact, just as Engels pointed out, this kind of separation of powers was nothing more than a division of routine tasks for the purpose of simplifying and supervising the state organs. Additionally, it has been a universal fact that the executive power expands while the legislative power diminishes day after day in the capitalist countries.

(2) **The Principle of Representation of All Citizens**

Concerning the relationship between representatives and electors, bourgeois scholars have put forward three general theories. The first is the trustee theory of representation, which holds that it is too difficult to exercise direct democracy due to large populations and the vast territories of modern nations, so representatives are elected to form a legislative body and are entrusted to exercise the legislative power on behalf of the electors. Consequently, the relationship between the representatives and the electors is equivalent to the so-called "the trust relationship" in civil law, and the relationship between the electors and the legislature is also the trust relationship between the electors and the elected. The second is the delegate theory of representation, which holds that the legislature represents all the people of the country and has a special, close relationship with the people. In other words, the legislature belongs to all the people, not to any part of the people. No single elector can be regarded as a trustee of any individual member of the legislature. Hence, the will of the legislature is equivalent to that of the whole society, and the legislature as a whole has a delegate relationship with the electors. The third is the institution theory of representation, in which both the parliament and the electoral body are taken as state organs and their functions are prescribed by laws. It is believed that the job of the people is to elect, while the job of the parliament is to legislate and supervise the administration. There is neither trust relationship nor delegate relationship between them.

The delegate theory is the most influential of the three, and it has actually become the guiding principle of the bourgeois parliamentary system. In political practice, it manifests itself as the so-called principle of representation of all citizens, that is to say, a member of the parliament is not a representative of an individual constituency or elector, but that of all citizens. This principle is deemed by the bourgeois scholars as "the negation of Imperatives Mandat of the Estates General in the Middle Ages" and "a general rule of the modern parliaments".[63]

In the United Kingdom, the idea of representation of all citizens was recognized early in the middle of the sixteenth century. In this regard, Algernon Sydney (1622–1683) made an early elaboration on the representation of all citizens in his *Discourses Concerning Government*.[64] An equally zealous advocate of the contract theory, John Locke, the British bourgeois enlightenment thinker, insisted that "The power that every individual gave the society when he entered into it can never revert to the individuals again, as long as the society lasts, but will always remain in the community."[65] In fact, the idea of representation was implicated in his statement. In his famous speech addressed to the electors in the Bristol constituency, Edmund Burke,

[63] Satou, I. (1984) *Bijiao zhengzhi zhidu* [Comparative Political Institutions], trans. Liu Q. L. and Zhang G. B., Beijing: Law Press· China, p. 36.

[64] Bogdanor, V. (1985) *Representatives of the People?* Gower, England, p. 3.

[65] Locke, J. (1982) *Zhengfu lun (II)* [On Government (II)], trans. Qu J. L. & Zhang G. B., Beijing: Law Press China, pp. 150–151. cf. Locke, J. (1690/1988) *Two Treatises of Government*, London: Cambridge University Press, p. 427.

an eighteenth century British politician, also elaborated this principle systematically in detail. He said that "when you have chosen him, he is not a member of Bristol, but a member of Parliament."[66] According to John Stuart Mill, he also believed that men of higher intelligence and talent should be chosen to Parliament and that their decisions would naturally contain more opinions of right than those of lower intelligence, and hence, a member of the legislature should not make commitment to nor be bound by his constituents. "It follows that the electors will not do wisely, if they insist on absolute conformity to their opinions, as the condition of his retaining his seat."[67] Some western scholars argued that the principle represented by Burke's speech indicated that the Member of Parliament's (M.P.) responsibility to the nation took priority over his responsibility to his constituents, and that his duty was to promote the national interests rather than to promote sectional interests.[68] And they believed that Burke's speech had confused the following two questions: Firstly, whether the M.P. was to act as a representative bound by "delegation" and "instructions" or as a trustee who has the freedom to decide on affairs? Secondly, as an M.P., should he focus on the interests of his constituents or the interests of the whole nation in his legislative actions?[69] However, in the actual operation of the British parliamentary system, this principle has been applied to the utmost, which was thoroughly expressed by Baku in his well-known letter to the voters of his constituency.[70]

In continental Europe, this principle was established during the French Revolution. After the revolution, the French Constitution of 1791 stipulated that "The representatives elected in the departments shall not be representatives of a particular department, but of an entire nation, and no mandate may be given them."[71] This was the public expression of this idea. In addition, the Weimar Constitution stipulated that "The deputies shall be representatives of the entire people. They are subject only

[66] Burke, E. (1866) *Works* (II), Boston: Little, Brown Company, pp. 95–96.

[67] Mill, J. (1982) *Daiyizhi zhengfu* [Representative Government], trans. Wang X., Beijing: The Commercial Press, Chapter 12. cf. Mill, J. (1861/2008) *Considerations on Representative Government,* London: The Electric Book Company, p. 222.

[68] Cf. Birch, A. (1971). *Representation*, London: Pall Mall Press Ltd., p. 79.

[69] Cf. Eulau, H., Wahlke, J., Buchanan, W. and Ferguson, L. (1959) The Role of the Representative: Some empirical observations on the theory of Edmund Burke, *American Political Science Review* 53(3):744.

[70] Baku wrote, "It shall be considered beatific and glorious for a senator to have the most intimate contact and the most prevalent communication with his voters.... However, he should never compromise his unbiased opinion, his sophisticated judgment and clear conscience for the voters or any individual or group.... The parliament is not a place for the representatives of different stakes to advocate their respective interest or to oppose other deputies of other stakes, but rather a collegiate bench of the people of unanimous stakes. Moreover, because it is not an institution designed for local needs, rather than a place for local bias, it is a collegiate bench that operates by the universal reason of all the citizens. Please remember that, once the senator has been elected, he would be not only a senator of the Bristol constituency, but also a senator of the parliament of the United Kingdom.".

[71] Cf. *The Constitution of 1791* (French), Sect. 3 of Chap. 1.

to their conscience and are not bound by instructions."[72] Further, this principle is clearly stated in Article 43 of the Japanese Constitution, too.

From the claims of bourgeois scholars and the practice of the principle in the capitalist countries, there is no institutional relationship between representatives and voters except for a regular election every few years. Just as Rousseau pointed out in criticizing the British parliamentary system, voters were only free when electing members of parliament, but after that they were no more than slaves. As a result, once elected, members were totally divorced from their voters. To this defect, some bourgeois scholars expressed similar disillusionment. For example, Sa Mengwu, a scholar from Taiwan, China believes that in this way "it is no surprise that the parliament cannot represent the will of the people."[73] The parliament produced by such a system is bound to become a ruling institution that isolates and oppresses the people. For some bourgeois scholars, "only in this way can the M.P.'s freedom of action and status be effectively guaranteed",[74] but their so-called freedom of action is only the freedom to serve the propertied class. Although the principle satisfies the need of the bourgeoisie to dress up the parliament as representing the interests of all citizens, this charming theory hardly reflects the political practice of capitalist countries. In the book *American Parties and Elections*, the contemporary American scholars Harold F. Gosnell et al. demonstrated that U.S. elections are manipulated by the two major bourgeois parties, and the occasional emergence of some small parties representing the interests of other political groups is always short-lived, just like a flash in the pan, and that the campaign expenses are mostly donated by special interest groups, and the reason why the donors are so generous to the candidates and the parties is that they expect returns from the politicians in the future. Just as Lenin pointed out, "Every few years a decision must be made about who of the ruling class should suppress and oppress the people in the parliament—this is the real nature of the bourgeois parliamentary system."[75] Therefore, the principle of representation of all citizens is simply a tool for abstraction of the relationship between the representatives and the electors by the bourgeoisie.

Nevertheless, with the change of the social class power balance and the progress of the bourgeois democracy in theory and practice, the principle of representation of all citizens is gradually being replaced. "Once the political individualism was established, the focus of representation thought had been shifted, and the delegation mode proposed by Burke had gradually been abandoned. It followed that the doctrine of representatives being responsible to and subject to their constituencies emerged."[76]

---

[72] Cf. *Weimar Constitution*, Article 21, Second Chapter of Part One.

[73] Sa, M. W. (1986) *Zhengzhi xue* [Political Science], Taipei: San Min Book Co., Ltd., p. 170.

[74] Satou, I. (1984) *Bijiao zhengzhi zhidu* [Comparative Political Institutions], trans. Liu Q. L. and Zhang G. B., Beijing: Law Press ·China, p. 36.

[75] *Liening xuanji* [Lenin Selected Works] (1995), Beijing: People's Publishing House, vol. 3, p. 150. cf. Lenin, V. (1917) *The State and Revolution*.

[76] Miller, D. and Bogdanor, V. (eds) (1992) *The Blackwell Encyclopedia of Political Science*, New York: Wiley-Blackwell, p. 646.

1.4.3 Distinctive Principles of Socialist People's Representative System

The socialist people's representative system, due to the socialist public ownership of the means of production and the nature of the socialist state power, must adopt principles distinct from those of the bourgeois parliamentary system, specifically, the principle of democratic centralism and the principle of supervision and removal.

(1) **The Principle of Democratic Centralism**

From the perspective of historical development, the organizational and operational principle of the socialist state power organs has undergone a transitional process from the unity of legislative and executive powers to democratic centralism.[77] The principle of unity of legislative and executive powers means that the people's representative organs are in charge of both legislation and administration, while the democratic centralism refers to "the combination of centralism built on the basis of democracy with democracy under centralized guidance."[78] As the initial organizational and operational principle of the socialist state power organs, the principle of unity of legislative and executive powers is not only a result of the experience accumulated in the process of the proletarian regime construction, but also is determined by the nature and the mission of the proletarian dictatorship.

The Paris Commune of 1871 was the first proletarian regime in history. In the Commune, the people directly elected representatives to form ten Commune committees, equivalent to government departments. Members of the Commune, who were also members of the committees, led the administrative departments to enforce the decrees of the Commune. Therefore, the proletarian regime of the Paris Commune is fundamentally different from the bourgeois regime established in accordance with the principle of separation of powers and checks and balances in that the former actually combines the legislative power with the executive power. In summing up the experience of the Paris Commune, Karl Marx formally articulated the principle unity of legislative and executive powers on the basis of the facts of the Paris Commune and his theories such as the Theory of State, Theory of the Proletarian Dictatorship and the Theory of Smashing the Old State Machinery. He noted "The Commune was to be a working, not a parliamentary body, executive and legislative at the same time."[79]

After the victory of the Russian October Socialist Revolution, Lenin developed the historical experience of the Paris Commune in the process of establishing the Soviet regime. Considering that the Paris Commune was only a political power organization founded by the French working class in the city of Paris with relatively small area of jurisdiction and simple structure of organization, and that it needed

[77] Some scholars hold these two are parallel, but I consider them to be the same in nature while the latter is more sophisticated.

[78] *Mao Zedong xuanji* [Selected Works of Mao Tsetung] (1991), Beijing: People's Publishing House, vol. 3, p. 1057.

[79] *Makesi Engesi xuanji* [Marx and Engels Selected Works] (1995), Beijing: People's Publishing House, vol. 3, p. 55. cf. Marx, K. (1871) *The Civil War in France.*

to deal with various affairs with urgency due to extremely fierce struggle between the revolutionists and anti-revolutionists at that moment, therefore, it was of vital significance for the Commune to enact and enforce decrees and laws all by itself. However, since the Russian revolution was a triumph in an entire country, a national regime was badly needed. Moreover, the class struggle between the revolutionists and the counter-revolutionists was not as intense as it had been during the Paris Commune after a time period. In this case, it was not only unnecessary, but also impossible, to copy the principle of unity of legislative and executive powers adopted by the Paris Commune, and to integrate the missions of law-making and law implementing into one in the people's representative body. Therefore, under these circumstances, Lenin changed the practice of unity of the representative organ and the executive organ elected by the people during the Paris Commune, and separated the above two organs beginning in 1918 on the premise of ensuring the plenipotentiary status of the Soviet Congress. According to the 1918 Soviet Russian Constitution, the highest organ of state power was the All-Russian Soviet Congress and its permanent body the All-Russian Soviet Central Executive Committee, and the highest executive organ was the People's Committee. However, the people's Committee was responsible to the All-Russian Soviet Congress and the All-Russian Soviet Central Executive Committee. According to the 1936 Constitution of the USSR, the highest organ of state power of the Soviet Union was the Supreme Soviet, and the Soviet Council of Ministers, the executive organ of the Supreme Soviet, was the highest administrative organ of the Soviet Union, which was generated by, responsible for and reported to the Supreme Soviet. When the Supreme Soviet was not in session, the Soviet Council of Ministers was responsible to and reported its work to the permanent body, the Presidium of the Supreme Soviet.

Why did the early proletarian regime adopt the principle of unity of legislative and executive powers rather than that of separation of powers and checks and balances? According to classical Marxist writers, the reason is that it is determined by the nature of the proletarian regime and the need to develop the proletarian democracy.[80] First of all, since it is stipulated that all power belongs to the people in the proletarian regime, in the execution of power, we must choose and adopt a principle that best suits the status of the people as masters. Secondly, it is also an important procedure to develop the proletarian democracy. According to Lenin, "it is a huge progress with historic significance all over the world in the development of democracy"[81] to concentrate the state power in the hand of the Soviet which is closely related to the people and to combine the functions of legislation and law enforcement mediated through the responsible people's representatives elected.

Nevertheless, with the in-depth development of the theory and the practice of the socialist state regime construction, the principle of "unity of legislative and executive

[80] *Makesi Engesi xuanji* [Marx and Engels Selected Works] (1995), Beijing: People's Publishing House, vol. 3, pp. 58–60; see also Xu, C. D. & He H. H. (1987) 'Sanquan fenli yu yixing heyi de bijiao yanjiu' [A Comparative Study of Separation of Powers and Combination of Legislative and Executive Powers], *Faxue pinglun* [Law Review], (5). cf. Marx, K. (1871) *The Civil War in France.*

[81] *Liening xuanji* [Lenin Selected Works] (1995), Beijing: People's Publishing House, vol. 3, p. 296.

powers" has increasingly been challenged. Although the practice of this principle was recognized by the classical Marxist writers, the arguments of the revolutionary tutors should not be understood in isolation from the specific historical context in which they arose because their views were aimed at the state regime construction during the period of seizing and consolidating the political power, so this principle could not be regarded as a universally applicable guidance that must be followed for the construction of the socialist state regime. As mentioned above, the concept of "unity of legislative and executive powers" underwent changes in actual political practices different from its original sense since the 1918 Soviet Russian Constitution and the 1936 Constitution of the USSR. Thus, some scholars insisted that the legislative and executive should not be combined.[82] So, what is the organizational and guiding principle of the socialist state power organs? The answer is definitely the system of democratic centralism, which is affirmed in the constitutions of various socialist countries and the theoretical explanations of the socialist scholars, but the key problem is that no consensus has been reached as to the relationship between "unity of legislative and executive powers" and "democratic centralism". Consequently, while it is agreed that the democratic centralism must be observed in the socialist constitution and political practice on the one hand, but disputes over the principle of unity of legislative and executive powers never stop on the other. In my view, the principle of democratic centralism is the inheritance and development of the principle of unity of legislative and executive powers, and the reasons are as follows:

First, both principles emphasize that the people are masters of the country. Under the principle of unity of legislative and executive powers, the legislative organ and the executive organ are integrated into one, which reflects the master status of the people, while under the principle of democratic centralism, although the legislative organ and the executive organ are separated, the latter is derived from the former, and is also responsible to and supervised by the former, thus the people's master status is also reflected. If the principle of unity of legislative and executive powers is believed to be perfectly applicable to the urban regime construction such as the Paris Commune, the principle of democratic centralism is designed for making up its inadequacies in a national regime construction. Since the two principles are consistent in the aspects of intrinsic attributes and basic contents, it also makes sense to interpret the regime built up on the basis of the principle of democratic centralism as a reflection of the principle of unity of legislative and executive powers.

Second, the principle of democratic centralism practiced in the regime construction of socialist countries is the application of the organizational and guiding principle of the proletarian parties in the construction of a state regime. Neither Marx nor Engels definitely put forward the concept of "democratic centralism", but they laid the

---

[82] Cf. Lan, W. Q. (1989) Dui 'Yixing heyi' de zairenshi [Re-Examination of Combination of Legislative and Executive Powers, *Zhengzhixue yanjiu* [Journal of Political Science], (5); Wang, Y. M. (1989) 'Yixing heyi bushi woguo guojia jigou de zuzhi yuanze' [Combination of Legislative and Executive Powers Is Not Organizational Principle of China's State Organs], *Zhongguo renmin daxue baokan fuyin ziliao: Faxue* [Periodical Literatures Reprinted by China Renmin University: Law], (8).

foundation for it.[83] In mid-December of 1905, the first assembly of the Russian Social Democratic Labor Party passed a resolution, in which the concept of "democratic centralism" was explicitly used for the first time. In the article "Terms of Admission into Communist International" published in July 1920, Lenin stressed that "Parties belonging to the Communist International must be organized on the principle of democratic centralism".[84] Afterwards, democratic centralism has been universally accepted as the organization and action principle by the proletarian parties of all countries. With the rational understanding of the principle of democratic centralism deepened and the practical experience accumulated by proletarian parties, and especially due to the dilemma that the principle of unity of legislative and executive powers faces in the actual regime construction, the democratic centralism has naturally been adopted by the proletarian parties as the organization and action principle, which is clearly stipulated in their constitutions. For these reasons, the principle of democratic centralism is considered in this book as one of the distinctive principles of the socialist people's representative system, and it is also a concrete reflection of the procedural principle in the socialist people's representative system, so to speak.

According to the constitutions and the political practices of the socialist countries, the principle of democratic centralism is manifested in three aspects in the socialist people's representative system. Firstly, the people's representative organ is produced by democratic election, responsible to the people and supervised by the people. Secondly, the administrative, judicial and procuratorial organs are all elected by the people's representative organ, to which they are responsible and by which they are supervised. Thirdly, the division of functions and powers between the central and local state organs follows the principle of giving full play to the initiative and enthusiasm of the local governments under the unified leadership of the central government.

(2) The Principle of Supervision

In terms of the relationship between representatives and electors, the socialist people's representative system has adopted a totally different principle from that of the bourgeois parliamentary system in that it completely discards the so-called "principle of representation of all citizens" in the bourgeois parliamentary system and holds that representatives are responsible to electors and report their work to electors, and that representatives are supervised by electors and can be removed anytime according to law. These points mentioned above are the main contents of the principle of supervision in the socialist people's representative system, but it is not the whole story. Additionally, the principle of supervision, I think, also includes the supervision of electors and representatives over the whole representative organ system, especially the administrative and judicial organs. The following discussion mainly focuses on the first aspect of the principle of supervision.

[83] Cf. *Makesi Engesi xuanji* [Marx and Engels Selected Works] (1995), Beijing: People's Publishing House, vol. 4, p. 395, and vol. 3, p. 226.

[84] *Liening xuanji* [Lenin Selected Works] (1995), Beijing: People's Publishing House, vol. 4, p. 254. cf. Lenin, V. (1920) Terms of Admission into Communist International.

The principle of supervision in terms of the relationship between electors and representatives was also created by the Paris Commune, the first regime of proletarian dictatorship. As Marx once put it, "The Commune was made up of the municipal councillors elected by universal suffrage in all arrondissements of Paris, and these councillors should take responsibility and could be removed anytime."[85] This is a fundamental property of the political form in the Paris Commune, and can also be taken as a thorough denial to the bourgeois parliamentary election system. As mentioned above, members of parliaments in capitalist countries are also elected, but they are not responsible to the electors in their constituencies and only act according to their own "conscience". Accordingly, since they are representatives of all citizens instead of the constituencies, they accept neither delegation from their constituencies nor supervision from their electors. However, according to the supervision principle of the Paris Commune, representatives were not only required to be responsible to their electors, but also subject to effective supervision by electors, that is, those representatives elected could be removed at any time. In other words, removal can be regarded as an extension and guarantee of the supervision. And that is why Engels pointed out, "the Commune made use of two infallible expedients. In this first place, it filled all posts—administrative, judicial, and educational—by election on the basis of universal suffrage of all concerned, with the right of the same electors to recall their delegate at any time."[86] Therefore, removal of the representatives by electors at any time was the fundamental mark that signified distinction between proletarian electoral system and the bourgeois electoral system, and was also the key to complete denial of the bourgeois parliamentary system by the Paris Commune. It is in this sense that Lenin said, "No elective institution or representative assembly can be regarded as being truly democratic and really representative of the people's will unless the electors' right to recall those elected is accepted and exercised. This fundamental principle of true democracy applies to all representative assemblies without exception, including the Constituent Assembly."[87]

This principle, initiated by the Paris Commune, has been accepted by later socialist countries as an important democratic principle to guide their establishment and improvement and aid the operation of the socialist people's representative system. The principle has been explicitly stipulated in the constitutions of all socialist countries. According to Article 107 in the 1977 Constitution of the USSR, "Deputies shall report on their work and on that of the Soviet to their constituents, and to the work collectives and public organizations that nominated them," and "Deputies who have not justified the confidence of their constituents may be recalled at any time by decision of a majority of the electors in accordance with the procedure established

[85] *Makesi Engesi xuanji* [Marx and Engels Selected Works] (1995), Beijing: People's Publishing House, vol. 3, p. 55. cf. Marx, K. (1871) *The Civil War in France.*

[86] *Makesi Engesi xuanji* [Marx and Engels Selected Works] (1995), Beijing: People's Publishing House, vol. 3, pp. 12–13. cf. Engels, F. (1891) An Introduction to *The Civil War in France.*

[87] *Liening xuanji* [Lenin Selected Works] (1995), Beijing: People's Publishing House, vol. 3, pp. 12–13. cf. Lenin, V. (1917) Draft Decree on the Right of Recall.

by law."[88] According to Article 8 in the 1972 Constitution of the DPRK, "Deputies to the organs of state power at all levels are accountable to their constituents."[89] According to Article 77 in the 1982 Chinese Constitution, "Deputies to the National People's Congress are subject to the supervision of the units which elected them. The electoral units have the power, through procedures prescribed by law, to recall the deputies whom they elected."[90]

By implementing the principle of recall, the socialist countries not only guarantee that the elected are real representatives and public servants of the electors, which thus eliminates the phenomenon that the elected and the electors are divorced from each other in the bourgeois parliamentary system, but also effectively ensure the realization of the true democracy and the implementation of the universal suffrage. Japanese Scholar Isao Satou once noted, "In a sense, it is a revival of the mandatory appointment system that once existed. But here we can find the difference between Soviet representatives and members of parliament in the capitalist countries, that is, the former has the people as its real foundation."[91] In my view, the principle of supervision is an extension of the principle of universal suffrage. The reason why the bourgeois principle of universal suffrage is no more than "the freedom at the moment of election" is that the indispensable part of the supervision is lost.

References

Beetham, D. (1989). *Makesi Weibo yu xiandai zhengzhi lilun* [Max Weber and the Theory of Modern Politics] (H. B. Xu, J. H. Xu, & L. W. Kang, Trans.). Zhejiang People's Publishing House.

Benton, W. (Ed.). (1929/1964) *Encyclopedia Britannica.* Encyclopedia Britannica, Inc.

Birch, A. (1971). *Representation.* Pall Mall Press Ltd.

Bogdanor, V. (1985. *Representatives of the people?* Gower, England.

Brett, S. (1929). *The story of the British constitution.* Blackie & Son Limited.

Brett, S. (1936) *Yingguo xianzhengshi tan* [On the History of the British Constitution] (S. D. Chen, Trans.). The Commercial Press.

Burke, E. (1866). *Works (II).* Little, Brown Company.

Cao, P. L., et al. (1993). *Bijiao zhengfu tizhi* [A Comparison of Government System]. Fudan University Press.

Easton, D. (1965). *A systems analysis of political life.* Wiley.

Easton, D. (1989). *Zhengzhi shenghuo de xitong fenxi* [A Systematic Analysis of Political Life] (P. Q. Wang, Trans.). Hua Xia Publishing House.

Engels, F. (1884). *The origin of the family, private property and the state.*

Engels, F. (1891). *An introduction to the civil war in France.*

Eulau, H., Wahlke, J., Buchanan, W., & Ferguson, L. (1959). The role of the representative: Some empirical observations on the theory of Edmund Burke. *American Political Science Review, 53*(3), 744.

[88] The 1977 Constitution of the USSR, Article 107.

[89] The 1972 Constitution of the DPRK, Article 8.

[90] The 1982 Constitution of PRC, Article 77, Section 1.

[91] Satou, I. (1984) *Bijiao zhengzhi zhidu* [Comparative Political Institutions], trans. Liu Q. L. & Zhang G. B., Beijing: Law Press ·China, p. 252.

Gu, B. X. (1988). *Minquan zhuyi minzhu zhengzhi lun* [On Principle of Civil Rights in Democratic Politics]. San Min Book Co., Ltd.
He, H. H. (1992). *Renmin daibiao dahui zhidu de lilun yu shijian* [Theory and Practice of People's Congress System]. Wuhan University Press.
Herodotus. (1959). *Lishi (II)* [Histories (II)] (Y. Z. Wang, Trans.) The Commercial Press.
Huang, D. Q., et al. (1993). *Shehui zhuyi minzhu: kuashiji de chensi* [Socialist Democracy: Millennium reflection]. China Renmin University Press.
Iwai, T. (1990). *Lifa guocheng* [Legal Process] (W. Li, Trans.). The Economic Daily Press.
Jianming zhengzhixue cidian [Concise Dictionary of Political Science] (1986). Henan People's Press.
Jianming zhengzhixue cidian [Concise Dictionary of Politics] (1985). Jilin People's Press.
Lan, W. Q. (1989). Dui 'Yixing heyi' de zairenshi [Re-Examination of Combination of Legislative and Executive Powers. *Zhengzhixue yanjiu* [Journal of Political Science], (5).
Lenin, V. (1902) *What is to be done?*
Lenin, V. (1904). *What we are working for (To the Party).*
Lenin, V. (1916). *Imperialism, the highest stage of Captitalism.*
Lenin, V. (1917). *Draft decree on the right of recall.*
Lenin, V. (1917). *The state and revolution.*
Lenin, V. (1920). Terms of admission into communist international.
Liening quanji [Lenin Collected Works] (1956). People's Publishing House (Vol. 29).
Liening quanji [Lenin Collected Works] (1959). People's Publishing House (1st ed., Vol. 5).
Liening quanji [Lenin Collected Works] (1959). People's Publishing House (Vol. 7).
Liening Xuanji [Lenin Selected Works] (1995). People's Publishing House (Vol. 3).
Liening xuanji [Lenin Selected Works] (1995). People's Publishing House (Vol. 4).
Lipset, S. (1960). *Political Man: The social bases of politics.* Doubleday & Company Inc.
Lipset, S. (1993). *Zhengzhi ren* [Political Man] (G. M. Liu & R. Nie, Trans.). The Commercial Press.
Locke, J. (1690/1988). *Two treatises of government.* Cambridge University Press.
Locke, J. (1982). *Zhengfu lun (II)* [On Government (II)] (J. L. Qu & G. B. Zhang, Trans.). Law Press China.
Luxemburg, R. (1940). *The Russian revolution* (Bertram Wolfe, Trans.). Workers Age Publishers. Retrieved June 5, 2021, from www.maxists.org/archive/Luxemburg/
Makesi Engesi Quanji [Marx and Engels Collected Works] (1959). People's Publishing House.
Makesi Engesi quanji [Marx and Engels Collected Works] (1965). People's Publishing House (Vol. 1).
Makesi Engesi Xuanji [Marx and Engels Selected Works] (1995). People's Publishing House (Vol. 4).
Makesi Engesi xuanji [Marx and Engels Selected Works] (1995). People's Publishing House (Vol. 3).
Mao Zedong xuanji [Selected Works of Mao Tsetung] (1991). People's Publishing House (Vol. 3).
Marx, K., & Engels, F. (1850). *Review of latter-day pamphlets* (Thomas Carlyle, Ed.).
Marx, K. (1871). *The civil war in France.*
Marx. K. (1843). *Critique of Hegel's philosophy of right.*
Mayo, H. B. (1960). *An introduction to democratic theory.* Oxford University Press.
Meiguo baike quanshu [The Encyclopedia Americana] (Vol. 2).
Miliband, R. (1982). *Capitalist democracy in Britain.* Oxford University Press.
Miliband, R. (1988). *Yingguo ziben zhuyi minzhuzhi* [Capitalist Democracy in Britain] (Q. Bo & D. Xiang, Trans.). The Commercial Press.
Mill, J. (1861/2008). *Considerations on representative government.* The Electric Book Company.
Mill, J. (1982). *Daiyizhi zhengfu* [Representative Government] (X. Wang, Trans.) The Commercial Press.
Miller, D., & Bogdanor, V. (Eds.). (1992). *The Blackwell encyclopedia of political science.* Wiley-Blackwell.

Montesquieu. (1777). *The spirit of laws*, The Online Library of Liberty © 2004 Liberty Fund, Inc.
Montesquieu. (1982). *Lun fa de jingshen* [The Spirit of Laws] (Y. S. Zhang, Trans.). The Commercial Press.
Qiu, D. H. (1993) *Zhongguo minzhu zhengzhi lun* [On Chinese and Western Democratic Politics]. China Worker Press.
Rawls, J. (1988). *Zhengyi lun* [A Theory of Justice] (H. H. He, B. G. He, & S. B. Liao, Trans.). China Social Sciences Press.
Raws, J. (1971/1999). *A theory of justice*. The Belknap Press of Harvard University Press.
Sa, M. W. (1986). *Zhengzhi xue* [Political Science]. San Min Book Co., Ltd.
Satou, I. (1984). *Bijiao zhengzhi zhidu* [Comparative Political Institutions] (Q. L. Liu & G. B. Zhang, Trans.). Law Press·China.
Schmitt, C. (1985). *The crisis of parliamentary democracy*. The MIT Press.
Shijie yihui cidian [Dictionary of World Parliaments] (1987). China Radio & Television Publishing House.
Tatsukichi, M. (1927). *Xianfaxue yuanli* [Principles of Constitutional Law] (Z. Y. Ou & Z. L. He, Trans.). The Commercial Press.
The Encyclopedia Americana (1829/1985). Grolier Incorporated (Vol. 23).
Thucydides. (2005). *Boluobennisa zhanzhengshi* (II) [The Peloponnesian War (II)] (D. F. Xie, Trans.). The Commercial Press. cf. https://www.globalgreyebooks.com/history-of-peloponnesian-war-ebook.html, p. 59.
Wang, Y. M. (1989). 'Yixing heyi bushi woguo guojia jigou de zuzhi yuanze' [Combination of Legislative and Executive Powers Is Not Organizational Principle of China's State Organs], *Zhongguo renmin daxue baokan fuyin ziliao: Faxue* [Periodical Literatures Reprinted by China Renmin University: Law], (8).
Wang, Z. H. (1989). *Minzhu yu zhongguoren* [Democracy and Chinese People]. China Radio & Television Publishing House.
Wilson, W. (1990). *Guohui zhengti* [Congressional Government] (X. L. Xiong & D. B. Lv, Trans.). The Commercial Press.
Wison, W. (1885/2011). *Congressional government*. Houghton Mifflin Company.
Wisti, F. (1990). *Beioushi minzhu* [Nordic Democracy] (Z. Q. Zhao, Trans.). China Social Sciences Press.
Xu, C. D., & He H. H. (1982). *Xianfa yu minzhu zhidu* [Constitution and Democratic System]. Hubei People's Press.
Xu, C. D., & He, H. H. (1987). Sanquan fenli yu yixing heyi de bijiao yanjiu [A Comparative Study of Separation of Powers and Combination of Legislative and Executive Powers], *Faxue pinglun* [Law Review], (5). Marx, K. (1871). *The civil war in France*.
Zhang, G. B. (1984). *Xianfa lun* [On Constitution]. Jilin People's Press.
Zhao, C. F. (1986). *Zhengzhixue xinlun* [New Theory of Politics]. Northeast Normal University Press.
Zhengzhixue changjian mingci qianshi [A Brief Explanation of Common Terms in Political Science]. People's Publishing House.
Zhongguo da baikequanshu: Faxue [Encyclopedia of China: Law] (1984), Encyclopedia of China Publishing House.

Chapter 2
History of Representative System

The history of democracy, in terms of its forms, is in fact a history of the alternative development of direct and indirect democracy. Lenin pointed out that "ever since the rudiments of democracy first appeared in antiquity, its forms notably changed over the centuries as one ruling class replaced another. Democracy assumed different forms and was applied in different degrees in the ancient republics of Greece, the medieval cities and the advanced capitalist countries".[1] However, different forms of democracy do not result from people's subjective wishes. As Engels suggested, "… the final causes of all social changes and political revolutions are to be sought, not in men's brains, not in men's better insights into eternal truth and justice, but in changes in the modes of production and exchange."[2] That is to say, all political forms are subject to various social relations determined by economy. The best explanations are provided by Marx's creative findings of three development forms of human society in *Economic Manuscripts of 1857–1858*.[3] In the study of the representative system, only when we get to know the origin of the system can we scientifically assess its position and its functions in the development of human society, determine the differences and relationships between the socialist people's representative system and the capitalist parliamentary system, scientifically predict the historical trend of the representative system and thereby deduce its laws of development.

---

[1] *Liening xuanji* [Lenin Selected Works] (1995), Beijing: People's Publishing House, vol.3, p.699. cf. Lenin, V. (1919) Speech at the Opening Session of the First Congress of the Communist International delivered on March 2.

[2] *Makesi Engesi xuanji* [Marx and Engels Selected Works] (1995), Beijing: People's Publishing House, vol.3, pp.617–618. cf. Engles, F. (1880) *Socialism: Utopian and Scientific*.

[3] Marx holds that the development of human society will experience three forms, respectively, the initial social form on the basis of the dependence on people, the second major form on the basis of the dependence on things, the third major form with the association of free people as the main feature. Different social forms inevitably require different political forms corresponding to them.

Y. Zhou, *A Comparative Study of Representative Systems*,
https://doi.org/10.1007/978-981-15-4186-5_2

2.1 Historical Review of Democratic Forms in Pre-capitalist Society

Democracy, according to Huang Daqiang, "as a common management method, originated in the primitive society, was often manifested as habits of the day. As the primitive clan system collapsed, democracy, as a state institution, which acknowledged the minority was subordinate to the majority, emerged in the class society. In the capitalist society, democracy began to become a combination of "popular sovereignty" and state institution, and obtained the constitutional status."[4] It is true that there isn't a clear divide on the issues of democracy, especially its form in different stages of historical development of human society. In some sense, it is by carrying forward and further developing on past experience that democratic forms mature and improve. Generally speaking, although a fundamental difference exists between ancient democracy and modern democracy, the pre-capitalist stage is also an important period in the development of democratic forms.

2.1.1 Democratic Forms in Primitive Society

In 1989, Elisabeth Comber, a Chinese-British writer, gave a lecture titled "Democracy and Its History" at Nankai University. She said:

> It is a misconception that democracy is ready-made and belongs to the western world. Actually, it's not necessarily so. Now we approach the history of democracy. It is said that the word "democracy" first occurred in Greece. In fact, before the word appeared, democracy had existed not only in Greece, but also in other European, Asian and African countries, to a different extent. I am a scholar of African history, and I find that democracy existed in the South African tribes where all issues were required to be discussed by all people of the tribes, who were healthy men and women. If one was unhealthy, he/she would be excluded and eliminated. Why? As these tribes often changed places, and the destination and path were only decided through joint efforts, all the qualified people should discuss together. It is a kind of democracy.[5]

This sort of democracy is a primitive one. In Engels' words, it is a "naturally developed ancient democracy".[6] From a historical perspective, primitive democracy consisted of two parts, i.e. the clan and the military.

(1) **Clan Democracy**

Due to low productivity in primitive society, individuals felt helpless in fighting against nature and increasingly complicated production and life. Thus, people

---

[4] Huang, D. Q. (ed.) (1993) *Shehui zhuyi minzhu: Kuashiji de chensi* [Socialist Democracy: A millennium reflection], Beijing: China Renmin University Press, p.1.

[5] Huang, D. Q. (ed.) (1993) *Shehui zhuyi minzhu: Kuashiji de chensi* [Socialist Democracy: A millennium reflection], Beijing: China Renmin University Press, p.12.

[6] *Makesi Engesi xuanji* [Marx and Engels Selected Works] (1995), Beijing: People's Publishing House, vol.4, p.103. cf. Engels, F. (1884) *Origins of the Family, Private Property and the State.*

required an organization in pursuit of their interests and survival. With the introduction of the clan commune as the primary management organization, clan democracy emerged. The clan commune was divided into the matriarchy and the patriarchy, and the matriarchal and the patriarchal democracies came into existence accordingly. The matriarchal democracy boasted two specific organizations, namely, the clan council where all men and women participated, and a chieftain was elected by the council. From the barbarian period when the clan institution came into being to the civilized time, the council remained a major feature of ancient societies in Asia, Europe and the Americas. "It was a democratic assembly because every adult male and female member had a voice upon all questions brought before it. It elected and deposed its sachem and chiefs."[7] Engels spoke highly of it, "And a wonderful constitution it is, this gentile constitution, in all its childlike simplicity! No soldiers, no gendarmes or police, no nobles, kings, regents, prefects, or judges, no prisons, no lawsuits—and everything takes its orderly course.... All are equal and free—the women included."[8]

Compared with the matriarchal democracy, the patriarchal democracy also kept a chieftain and a clan council. However, there were two differences between them. One was the inequality between men and women in the patriarchal democracy, under which membership on the council was confined to men. The other was that a new council, also called a council of chiefs, was established among the chieftains and the clan council. As Lewis Henry Morgan said:

> The council [of chiefs] had a natural foundation in the gentes of whose chiefs it was composed.... As the gens was represented by its chiefs, so the tribe was represented by a council composed of the chiefs of the gentes. It was a permanent feature of the social system, holding the ultimate authority over the tribe. Called together under circumstances known to all, held in the midst of the people, and open to their orators, it was certain to act under popular influence. Although oligarchical in form, the government was a representative democracy.[9]

Accordingly, he continued, "A council of Indian chiefs is of little importance by itself; but as the germ of the modern parliament, congress, and legislature, it has an important bearing in the history of mankind."[10]

---

[7] Morgan, L. (1992) *Gudai shehui (I)* [Ancient Society (I)], trans. Yang D. C., Ma Y. & Ma J., Beijing: The Commercial Press, p.82. cf. Morgan, L. (1877/1985) *Ancient Society*, Chicago: Charles H. Kerr & Company Co-operative, p.85.

[8] *Makesi Engesi xuanji* [Marx and Engels Selected Works] (1995), Beijing: People's Publishing House, vol.4, p.95. cf. Engels, F. (1884) *Origins of the Family, Private Property, and the State.*

[9] Morgan, L. (1992) *Gudai shehui (I)* [Ancient Society (I)], trans. Yang D. C., Ma Y. & Ma J., Beijing: The Commercial Press, p.113. cf. Morgan, L. (1877/1985) *Ancient Society*, Chicago: Charles H. Kerr & Company Co-operative, p.118.

[10] Morgan, L. (1992) *Gudai shehui (I)* [Ancient Society (I)], trans. Yang D. C., Ma Y. & Ma J., Beijing: The Commercial Press, p.116. cf. Morgan, L. (1877/1985) *Ancient Society*, Chicago: Charles H. Kerr & Company Co-operative, p.121.

(2) **Military Democracy**

Military democracy similarly existed in the transition period from barbarism to civilization. After the collapse of clanship, it maintained the elements of the clan democracy to some extent, but ultimately expanded the individual power of military chiefs. "[This democracy was called] military, since war and organization for war have now become regular functions of national life."[11]

Under military democracy, there were three kinds of organs, "the assembly of the people, the council of chiefs, and the military leader seeking the real kingship".[12] Originally, a military chief was elected. However, with frequent wars and growing individual power, the hereditary system was gradually established. It was anti-democratic because chiefs were only from the few privileged families. There were two democratic organs, i.e. the popular assembly to which all males had access, and the council. Different from the patriarchal democracy of the gens, the military democracy clearly stated the relationship between the popular assembly and the council. Morgan pointed out:

> The council of chiefs, which still remained, found it necessary, no doubt through popular constraint, to submit the most important public measures to an assembly of the people for acceptance or rejection; ... This assembly did not originate measures. It was its function to adopt or reject, and its action was final. From its first appearance it became a permanent power in the government. The council no longer passed important public measures, but became a pre-considering council, with power to originate and mature public acts, to which the assembly alone could give validity.[13]

In its infancy, the assembly and the council discussed and decided great issues of clan interest, so they still had an important role. As the individual power of military chiefs grew, the council became the domain of the privileged, and the assembly was of little significance and was even discarded. For this reason, the appearance of military democracy meant the end of primitive democracy and primitive society.

From the clan democracy and the military democracy, we can observe that although direct democracy was dominant, indirect democracy gradually came into being in primitive democracies. Though I disagree with Morgan's view that the council of chiefs is "the representative system of democracy", one cannot utterly deny his notion that the council of chiefs be regarded as the germ of the modern parliament, because similarities exist between them in terms of discussing issues through the medium of representatives. Therefore, Bertrand Russell's expression

---

[11] *Makesi Engesi xuanji* [Marx and Engels Selected Works] (1995), Beijing: People's Publishing House, vol.4, p.164. cf. Engles, F. (1884) *Origins of the Family, Private Property and the State.*

[12] *Makesi Engesi xuanji* [Marx and Engels Selected Works] (1995), Beijing: People's Publishing House, vol.4, pp.145–146. cf. Engles, F. (1884) *Origins of the Family, Private Property and the State.*

[13] Morgan, L. (1992) *Gudai shehui (I)* [Ancient Society (I)], trans. Yang D. C., Ma Y. & Ma J., Beijing: The Commercial Press, p.116. cf. Morgan, L. (1877/1985) *Ancient Society*, Chicago: Charles H. Kerr & Company Co-operative, p.122.

that "In antiquity, the representative system [was] unknown"[14] and Godwin's argument that "the ancients were unaccustomed to the idea of deputed or representative assemblies"[15] are rather arbitrary. Of course, it must be made explicit that "The primitive democracy just represented a kind of person-to-person relations and organizations, concerning human activities. It did not connote the distribution of power among certain interest groups, nor did it definitively state the ownership of political authority."[16] Technically, essential differences, both theoretical and practical, existed between primitive democracy and the democracies in all forms of class societies. However, "Mankind owe a debt of gratitude to their savage ancestors for devising an institution able to carry the advanced portion of the human race out of savagery into barbarism, and through the successive stages of the latter into civilization."[17] Although the primitive democracy as such was extremely backward, its influence on later democracy cannot be underestimated. For this, even Morgan confirmed, "...out of the ancient council of chiefs came the modern senate; out of the ancient assembly of the people came the modern representative assembly, the two together constituting the modern legislature."[18]

2.1.2 Democratic Forms in Slave Society

Morgan pointed out that "When property had become created in masses, and its influence and power began to be felt in society, slavery came in."[19] Indeed, the primitive democracy came to the end of the line on account of the germination and development of private ownership, the divide between the rich and the poor, and the emergence of class. It is worth pondering why democracy still existed in slave states to a certain extent, given that the slave economy as a whole was incompatible with the essence of democracy and fundamentally negated slaves' entire political and economic rights. Two points should be considered: first, most states where the slave democracy existed were city-states (i.e. poleis); second, the advanced form of

---

14 Russell, B. (1991) *Quanli lun* [On Power], trans. Wu Y. S., Beijing: The Commercial Press, p.138. cf. Russell, B. (1938/2004). *Power*, New York: Routledge, p.157.

15 Godwin, W. (1991) *Zhengzhi zhengyi lun* [On Political Justice], trans. He M. L, Beijing: The Commercial Press, p.393. cf. Godwin, W. (1793/1976) *Enquiry Concerning Political Justice and Its Influence on Morals and Happiness*, Penguin Classics, p.178.

16 He, X. M. (1991) *Gudian minzhu zhengti lun* [On Classic Democratic Regimes], Lanzhou: Lanzhou University Press, p.29.

17 Morgan, L. (1992) *Gudai shehui (II)* [Ancient Society (II)], trans. Yang D. C., Ma Y. & Ma J., Beijing: The Commercial Press, pp.337–338. cf. Morgan, L. (1877/1985) *Ancient Society*, Chicago: Charles H. Kerr & Company Co-operative, p.350.

18 Morgan, L. (1992) *Gudai shehui (II)* [Ancient Society (II)], trans. Yang D. C., Ma Y. & Ma J., Beijing: The Commercial Press, p.338. cf. Morgan, L. (1877/1985) *Ancient Society*, Chicago: Charles H. Kerr & Company Co-operative, p.351.

19 Morgan, L. (1992) *Gudai shehui (II)* [Ancient Society (II)], trans. Yang D. C., Ma Y. & Ma J., Beijing: The Commercial Press, p.338. cf. Morgan, L. (1877/1985) *Ancient Society*, Chicago: Charles H. Kerr & Company Co-operative, p.351.

the slave democracy was radically dependent on the prosperity of the commodity economy.

The earliest slave states, such as ancient Greece, Rome and the ancient Orient, were all comprised of small poleis or city-states with small populations. In other words, the slave polis was an early necessary stage for all slave states. The polis, with a city as the center, was formed by combining several kindred or neighboring gentes, tribes and communes, a process of unified mixing. On one hand, since poleis originated from gentes and tribes, they bore the stamp of the primitive democracy to varying degrees. Under the slave economy, although the wage slaves were so crushed by poverty that they could not be bothered with democracy and politics, they created property and leisure time necessary for the slave owners and civilians to participate in politics.[20] Therefore, the slave economy provided conditions for the development of primitive democracy and slave democracy. However, one cannot help but ask, why Athens and Sparta, both slave poleis, were so different in terms of democratic development? For this question, the commodity is the key. Specifically, the growth of the commodity economy exerted a profound effect on Athens. The principle of exchange at equal value not only widely cultivated citizens' sense of equality in Athens, but also forged an important political force – the industrial and commercial stratum (including slaveholders and civilians). Thus, the commodity economy and its anthropomorphized representative were major impetuses for the development of democracy in Athens.

Although from the traditional perspective, Athens of ancient Greece, is regarded the birthplace of democracy, recent research has shown that democracy actually originated from the ancient Orient. As early as about 3000 B.C., the earliest city-states, such as Eridu, Ur, Uruk, Lagash, and Kish, emerged in the ancient Sumerian region of the southern Tigris and Euphrates. Herein, the polis system lasted for four to five centuries. However, in the literature, the word "king" could not be found, while an "archon" as the head in a polis, a noble council, a concilium plebis, and other systems often appeared. Therefore, though the advanced form of the slave democracy was in ancient Athens, the initial form stemmed from the Orient.

What was the basic regime structure of the slave polis? Generally, the regime consisted of three major parts: first, a polis leader, called archon, having evolved from a military chief in the age of the military democracy; second, a noble council or senate, out of a council of clan and tribal elders or a council of chiefs; third, an ecclesia or comitia, derived from a clan council. The council of elders and the clan council had great influence in the transition period from the clan democracy to the slave democracy. In this regard, the earliest historical record dated back to the council of elders in Uruk depicted in the Sumerian epic *Gilgameš and Akka.* Under the threat of Akka, king of Kish, Gilgameš, king of Uruk, first convened a council of elders to determine how to deal with enemy threats, peace or war? The council of elders advocated surrender. Gilgameš convoked an ecclesia again. The ecclesia advocated for continued war against the enemy, negating the decision of the council of elders.

---

ning xuanji [Lenin Selected Works] (1995), Beijing: People's Publishing House, vol.3, p.159.
n, V. (1917) *The State and Revolution.*

Sumerian scholars held that it was the earliest "bicameralism" (a coexistence of two councils) in history[21]. According to this epic, the ecclesia with the involvement of all male citizens was the state's supreme body, empowered with the right to decide war, peace and other major affairs in the polis. Similar to the ancient Sumerian region, ancient Assyria, in the northern part of the Tigris and Euphrates basin, also witnessed the ecclesia control over the body of supreme state power where citizens could speak freely, as well as discuss and decide major national activities. So far, the above mentioned are insufficient to demonstrate the essence of the slave democracy, so I will elaborate further on democracy in Athens.[22]

From Draco's reform which marked the beginning of democratization in Athens, through an array of reforms by Solon, Cleisthenes, Pericles, etc., slave democracy in Athens proliferated. The basic contents manifested themselves in three major aspects:

The first was the ecclesia as the supreme power body. The ecclesia was composed of male citizens over 20 years old with Athens as their ancestral home and had the right to deal with all major issues in Athens: passing and enacting laws and decrees; electing the board of ten strategoi and other senior military officers; reviewing reports on work of the state senior public officers; discussing the state fiscal matters and formulating national budgets; dealing with criminal cases and determining the list of exiles; deciding diplomatic issues such as war, peace and alignment; conducting affairs related to the naturalization of aliens, etc. The ecclesia was convened regularly, one time every nine days, 40 times every year. In particular, subordinate to the ecclesia were all other state bodies, such as the boule, the jury court, the noble assembly, the board of ten strategoi, and archons. This structure showed, as Morgan put it, that "The human race is gradually learning the simple lesson that the people as a whole are wiser for the public good and the public prosperity, than any privileged class of men, however refined and cultivated, have ever been, or by any possibility, can ever become".[23]

The ecclesia represented direct democracy in terms of its formation and its operational procedure. Conferees could speak freely and discuss proposals in the assembly. Every Athenian citizen was entitled to appraise current policies, measures, and any public officers, and expressed their own opinions. The ecclesia adopted the rule of

---

[21] Ri, Z. (ed.) (1989) *Gudai chengbangshi yanjiu* [A Study of History of Ancient Polis], Beijing: People's Publishing House, p.37.

[22] In the Roman Republic there appeared successively four kinds of people's assemblies, namely, the Comitia Curiata, the Comitia Centuriata, the Comitia Plebis Tributa or Concilium Plebis, and the Comitia Populi Tributa. Although the Comitia Centuriata was the nominally supreme power body, the senate was composed of elders of the gens and former consuls played a decisive role. For this, the then Roman Republic was in fact the dictatorship of aristocratic slaveholders. Then this book takes democracy in Athens as the typical example. If readers want to know more about the people's assembly in ancient Rome, you can refer to Wang, N. X. (1994) 'Guluoma renmin dahui ruogan wenti bianxi' [Analysis on Comitia in Ancient Rome] in the first issue of *Qiu Shi* [Seeking Truth].

[23] Morgan, L. (1992) *Gudai shehui (II)* [Ancient Society (II)], trans. Yang D. C., Ma Y. & Ma J., Beijing: The Commercial Press, p. 332. cf. Morgan, L. (1877/1985) *Ancient Society*, Chicago: Charles H. Kerr & Company Co-operative, p.351.

voting by openly raising hands and the majority rule. Except the election of ten strategoi, all public officers were elected by secret ballot.

The second was the boule. The boule was formed by electing 50 citizens of each tribe from male citizens over 30 years old through drawing lots. The term of office was one year. The boule's functions were to prepare proposals for discussion in the ecclesia, define the convening time, and arrange the agenda. When the ecclesia was not in session, the boule executed its resolutions, safeguarded Athens, controlled and managed the state financial matters, conducted diplomatic affairs, restored and prepared to build public buildings and temples, held celebrations, etc. In this sense, the boule was actually the highest executive organ, responsible for the state administration. Hence, "the combination of legislative and executive powers" was basically put in place in Athenian polis.

The third was the jury court, which consisted of 6000 jurors. Every tribe elected 600 citizens from those who were over 30 years old and willing to assume office, by drawing lots. Jurors must take the oath of office,[24] from which we can see that the jury court had an important political function in addition to hearing cases. Hence, the jury court was not only an important part of democracy in Athens, but also a major organ to safeguard the democracy. The court was divided into 10 judicial committees, each composed of 500 jurors and 100 candidates. To prevent bribery, the rule of drawing lots was employed to assign jurors and cases to different committees.

The elaboration of the basic content shows that the Athenian polis did not only ensure in the abstract that political affairs were "decided by the people"[25] and that "everyone took his turn as the ruler and the ruled",[26] but established a complete set of basic systems to realize democracy. For example, the ecclesia held a vote of confidence annually on the archon, generals and senior officers; the male citizens over the age of 20 had the right to vote; the male citizens over 30 enjoyed equal opportunities to assume public office; every official, archon or officials in the lowest ranks, was elected. Meanwhile, during the execution of administrative power, the functions of council, administration and judiciary were gradually separated. As mentioned above, the ecclesia, where proposals were discussed, generated administrative and judicial organs. This system was like "the combination of legislative and executive powers", which fully proved a state organizational improvement in Athens. In addition, although the Boule implemented the governmental function, with regard to its origins, it was actually a form of indirect democracy, inherited and further developed after the council of chiefs in the primitive democracy. In essence, Athenian democracy was mainly a typical direct democracy as far as its main contents were concerned. However, although Athen's direct democracy could reflect public opinion, many defects also existed. Take the ostracism for example. The state could exile not only those harmful to democracy, but also those without faults. What's more,

[24] *Demositini* [Demosthenes] (XXIV), p.149.

[25] Herodotus (1959). *Lishi* (III) [History (III)], trans. Wang, Y. Z., Beijing: The Commercial Press, p.82.

[26] Aristotle (1983). *Zhengzhixue* [The Politics], trans. Wu S. P., Beijing: The Commercial Press, p.312.

as Lenin put it, "The slave-owning state could be a monarchy, an aristocratic republic or even a democratic republic. In fact the forms of government varied extremely, but their essence was always the same: the slaves enjoyed no rights and constituted an oppressed class; they were not regarded as human beings."[27] In this sense, the democracy in Athens, be it contents or forms, was in essence a democracy of slave-owners. Because it carried the nature of slavery, and contained historical limitations and insurmountable contradictions, its decline was inevitable.

2.1.3 Democratic Forms in Feudal Society

The feudal society, based on the natural economy, employed the system of enfeoffment instead of democracy. However, this does not imply that democratic forms were not found in the feudal society. For example, in medieval Europe, there appeared democratic forms of republics in several cities in northern Mediterranean Italy.

With favorable geographical conditions and easy transportation, Venice, Florence, Genoa and other cities in Italy enjoyed fast growth in handicrafts and commerce. At that time, Italy had not yet realized unification and these cities abolished serfdom earlier than others. The above economic and political conditions facilitated the emergence of city republic or city democracy. With urban autonomy and independence, the commune, a new type of city organizational system, came into existence. To some extent, some traditions from the polis system in ancient Greece revived. Specifically, at the initial stage, the citizen assembly, where all members of the commune participated, was a major organ for the city commune. The assembly was of importance due to its power to enact laws and elect the municipal chief. The elected municipal chief was in power, while the municipal assembly composed of the nobility served as an adversary organ for assisting the chief exercising power. With the passing of time, the city democracy evolved into two different forms, namely, the aristocratic republic and the democratic republic.

Generally speaking, in cities where commerce was more advanced than handicraft manufacture, aristocratic oligarchy was employed. For example, the regime in Venice was early in the hands of the nobility of merchants who made their fortunes through foreign trade. In the twelfth century, the influence of the citizen assembly on political life completely disappeared, and the great assembly composed of the urban nobility became a primary organ with the power to enact laws and elect all officials. From the thirteenth century, membership of the great assembly was determined through inheritance from the most powerful families rather than election. The great assembly generated a subordinate council, a senate, to conduct diplomatic and business affairs. Later, a council of ten members was established to surveil governmental organs and the common citizens. Therefore, Venice embodied the aristocratic republic.

[27] *Liening quanji* [Lenin's collected Works] (1995), Beijing: People's Publishing House, vol.4, p.33. cf. Lenin, V. (1919) The State: lecture delivered at the Sverdlov University on July 11, 1919.

Florence was then the most democratic city republic. In general, its manufacture of handicrafts was more developed, most of citizens were engaged in the manufacture of handicrafts and they were strong enough to suppress the nobility all contributing to the development of its democracy. In 1293, the democratic leader Gino Bella led citizens from the craft guild in Florence to completely defeat the nobility, directly hold the city regime, and enact *The Ordinances of Justice*. As the city's supreme body, the elder council consisted of seven members, elected from seven major guilds, i.e. lawyer, banking, pharmaceutical, wool merchants, fur merchants, and wool fabric makers. Later, the council added two seats, elected from 14 small guilds like blacksmiths. The term of office was two months. The elder council had subordinate officials like 12 "solons" and 16 "standard-bearers" to conduct daily political and military affairs. Both of them were recommended by guilds, through examination, and then generated by drawing lots. Their term of office were 3 and 4 months respectively. This enabled guild members to engage widely or frequently in administration, in a sense, avoiding individual dictatorship. It should be clarified that although this democracy carried the capitalist feature to some extent, it remained a feudal democracy in essence. However, in form, the democracy in Florence had the rudiment of the representative democracy in some sense. From the history of the representative system, "Hierarchical Conference" or "Estates General" that emerged in some countries at the end of the feudal society was also significant in the development of the representative system. With regard to this issue, this book will elaborate in the next section.

2.2 Emergence and Development of Capitalist Parliamentary System

The forms of indirect democracy in the pre-capitalist society cannot be regarded as the representative system in modern sense, but they have a certain historical connection with the initial forms of the representative system, namely, the capitalist parliamentary system. To some extent, the trajectory of development could be generalized as "Council of Chiefs–Boule–Municipal Council–Hierarchical Conference—Parliament". If indirect democratic forms in the pre-capitalist society were simply confined to limited areas, they took a qualitative leap when entering the historical stage of the capitalist society after withstanding the millennium-long dark rule of the Middle Ages. What are the social and historical conditions for this leap? How did process unfold?

2.2.1 Reasons for Emergence of Representative System

Concerning the reasons for the emergence of the representative system, opinions among scholars in China and in the west vary. As mentioned at the beginning of this chapter, the ultimate cause of any political change must be explored in changing of the means of production and of exchange. For me, the primary reason for the emergence of the representative system is due to the emergence and development of the capitalist commodity economy. According to the Marxism, any social phenomenon is attributable to the resultant of various forces towards different directions with different sizes. This is the case for the representative system. In this sense, the capitalist commodity economy plays a decisive role in the emergence of the representative system, which mainly manifests itself in the following aspects:

(1) **Formation of Nation States**

The feudal society in Europe, particularly in the initial stage of the Middle Ages, was divided into many small principalities and states. A king had very limited power, often only nominal, beyond his own manor; instead feudal lords were the real rulers in their own manors. By the end of the feudal society, the development of productive forces brought about the age of handicraft workshops, a rapid growth of the monetary economy, and a dramatically expanding commodity market, which evolved into a national market. However, under the feudal separation, feudal lords arbitrarily imposed and levied import and transit duties, which were serious obstacles for economic growth. Expanding a national market and boosting economic growth required the end of feudal separation and the establishment of a unified nation with highly centralized power. With the support of the rising capital class, many European countries under the feudal separation was transformed into feudal centralized states, i.e. unified nation states. Engels pointed out, "one of the most important indicators of the Middle Ages' advance is the increasingly obvious trend and awareness of establishment of nation states."[28] One of the most far-reaching effects brought about by this transformation was "the shift of the locus of democracy from the small scale of the city state to the large scale of the modern nation state." Meanwhile, "the consequences of this shift in scale and location, from democracy as appropriate to the small scale of the city state to democracy as appropriate to the large, even gigantic, scale of the nation state, were momentous."[29] Specifically, the significance of this change manifested itself in three aspects:

First, a new type of representation was established. Basically, the nation states featured vast territories and large populations. Although these features provided favorable conditions for the development of the national market and the production and exchange of capitalist commodity, it set up barriers for public involvement in political life. The fact that a large number of citizens lived scattered around the nation

---

[28] *Makesi Engesi quanji* [Marx and Engels Collected Works] (1965), Beijing: People's Publishing House, vol.21, p.452.

[29] Miller, D. and Bogdanor, V. (eds) (1992) *The Blackwell Encyclopedia of Political Science*, New York: Wiley-Blackwell, p.188.

state made it impossible for them to get together to realize direct rule, so they needed to elect representatives to exercise their supreme power instead. As such, the representative system would become a legitimate democratic system. Thomas Paine pointed out, "By ingrafting representation upon democracy, we arrive at a system of government capable of embracing and confederating all the various interests and every extent of territory and population."[30]

Second, since nation states were vast with large population, it was hard to form a relatively homogenous citizen group united by the common emotional attachment to their cities, languages, race and history. Instead, political contradictions or conflicts caused by differentiated interests were inevitable in the political life. What's more, political theories and practices tend to acknowledge that conflicts are a formal, not abnormal, feature. Seymour Martin Lipset argued that "The breakdown of a traditional society exposed to general view for the first time the difference between society and the state. It also raised the problem: How can a society face continuous conflict among its members and groups and still maintain social cohesion and the legitimacy of state authority?"[31] As representatives came from different interest groups, the representative system with the representative organ as the core was the best approach for nation states to mitigate and solve various political contradictions and conflicts.

Third, in the process of administrative democratization of nation states, their issues and conditions, far more complicated than those in a polis, led to a totally new structure composed of various political institutions and practices. The balance between democracy and objective restrictions of territory and population determined the representative system as the most fundamental part of the new structure.

(2) **Outbreak of Bourgeois Revolution**

Although the formation of nation states provided external conditions for the development of the capitalist commodity economy, it did not fundamentally resolve contradictions between the new productive forces and the old production relations. With continued growth of the capitalist commodity economy, this pair of contradictions intensified and was finally resolved only by the bourgeois revolution. Therefore, the bourgeois revolution facilitated the emergence of the representative system as it was in two aspects.

First, it led to the dualization of politics and economy, also known as the dualization of political state and civil society.[32] One major feature of the pre-capitalist society was the integration of politics and economy, especially in the feudal society of the Middle Ages, where politics permeated economy, causing a prolonged decline

[30] Paine, T. (1982) *Panen xuanji* [Selected Works of Thomas Paine], trans. Ma Q. H., Beijing: The Commercial Press, p.246. cf. Paine, T. (2005) *Common Sense and Other Writings*, London and New York: Barnes & Noble Books, p.218.

[31] Lipset, S. (1993) *Zhengzhi ren* [Political Man], trans. Liu G. M. & Nie R., Beijing: The Commercial Press, p.9. cf. Lipset, S. (1960) *Political Man: The social bases of politics*, New York: Doubleday & Company, Inc., p.22.

[32] Rong, J. et al. (1988) *Minzhu lun* [On Democracy], Shanghai: Shanghai People's Publishing House, p.79–86.

in the economy. In the feudal society, social economy was attached to politics and could not be separated from political control to become independent and develop based on its own law, on account of personal attachment and ultra-economic coercion. Consequently, both economic growth and political development were confined. For this reason, the primary objective of the bourgeois revolution for developing the commodity economy was to separate the economy from politics and arrive at the dualization of political state and civil society. At last, the bourgeois class "completed the transformation of the political classes into social classes, in other words, made the class distinctions of civil society into merely social distinctions, pertaining to private life but meaningless in political life. With that, the separation of political life and civil society was completed."[33]

During the dualization of politics and economy, the society handed the political administrative function over to the state, while the latter returned social and economic functions to the former. As a result, on the one hand, the manor natural economy, strongly fortified and widely pervasive in the Middle Ages, quickly disintegrated; the capitalist free economy fully developed; and the society in regard to economic sphere finally got rid of the coercion of feudal politics, and even obtained the right of self-operation after casting off state control. On the other hand, such a separation helped the society evolve from hierarchy to representation, and then enabled the capitalist "political state" to be continually perfected. In the Middle Ages, inequality in the civil society was also that in the political state, and vice versa. When the civil society was separated from the political state, inequality that existed in the former was accompanied by formal equality occurring in the latter. The inequality in the practices of economic life could be superficially manifested as equality in the political state, where representation was the only approach to realize equality. Meanwhile, in the case of separation between civil society and political state, citizens needed a medium, i.e. legislative power, to participate in political affairs. Herein, a council that represented the legislative power became the plenipotentiary of the civil society in the political state. Just as Marx pointed out, "The Estates (parliaments, the author notes) are civil society's deputation to the state."[34]

Second, a triangle balance of power among "kingship, citizens, and vassal"[35] was created by the bourgeois revolution. At the end of the era of feudal societies in Europe, "citizens" referred to the emerging bourgeoisie, "vassal" stood for the aristocratic forces under the feudal separation, and "kingship" embodied the unified feudal government. The convergence and antagonism of the interests amongst the three different forces often led a pair-wise alignment against the other in the struggle. In the process of abolishing the feudal separation and promoting the emergence and development of the national market, the bourgeoisie supported consolidating and joining

---

33 *Makesi Engesi quanji* [Marx and Engels Collected Works] (1965), Beijing: People's Publishing House, vol.1, p.344. cf. Marx, K. (1843) *Critique of Hegel's Philosophy of Right*.

34 *Makesi Engesi quanji* [Marx and Engels Collected Works] (1965), Beijing: People's Publishing House, vol.1, p.327. cf. Marx, K. (1843) *Critique of Hegel's Philosophy of Right*.

35 Cf. Jin, G. T. et al. (1985) *Xifang shehui jiegou de yanbian* [Evolution of Western Social Structure], Chengdu: Sichuan People's Publishing House, pp.169–226.

the kingship against aristocratic forces; when the bourgeoisie was strong enough to threaten the kingship, the king would align with aristocratic forces against the bourgeoisie; while the king's power was expanding, the bourgeoisie and aristocratic forces would then join together to limit the king.

> The possible pair-wise alignment made it impossible that any force would reign alone by its own force. The balance of power was the only choice. At that time, there was a need for a new institution, a new system, which showed the balance of power and exercised the function of containment. Obviously, such an institution was created, that is, the parliamentary system of monarchy.[36]

As the bourgeoisie's economic and political power strengthened day by day, the barons were too weak to maintain the tripartite balance of power, and the kingship was soon overthrown by the bourgeois revolution. Thus, the parliament as an important arena, where citizens involved in the state politics and boosted economic growth, was firmly held in the hands of the bourgeoisie. Besides, the parliament continued to improve its practices as it accumulated experience. In this sense, we argue that the emergence of the capitalist parliament had a positive effect on the development of the capitalist productive forces to some extent. Whether the parliament became more bourgeois as in Britain through a protracted political struggle, or through reestablished parliaments after the victory of bourgeois revolution in France, America, and other countries, they all represented the interests of the bourgeoisie to limit, disempower and get rid of the kingship. Then the hierarchical conference designed to levy taxes for the king was changed to the constitutional conference which established the rule of the bourgeoisie; out of conferences which served the feudal ruling class came institutions which advanced economic and political interests of the bourgeoisie; and representatives of civilians who were controlled by the king evolved into political gravediggers for the feudal aristocracy.

(3) **Summary of Governing Experience**

Ruling a country means administering it. While any ruling class would spare no effort to maintain its own interests once in power, it also faces the issue of administrative efficiency from the perspective of management. In other words, the efficiency of the state regime can be brought into full play for serving the ruling class only when it finds the optimal methods, measures and procedures of governance. With regard to this issue, two aspects are decisive: one is the degree of awareness of administrative experience; the other is the objective conditions of the state. Generally, political practices must be implemented on the basis of awareness of the objective conditions combined with the past experience. Considering the experience of state governance in the pre-capitalist society and especially the political reality of the nation states, the representative system is the best approach to effective management for nation states.

First, economic equality and freedom advocated in the capitalist commodity economy are bound to be reflected in political equality and freedom. Therefore,

[36] Jin, G. T. et al. (1985) *Xifang shehui jiegou de yanbian* [Evolution of Western Social Structure], Chengdu: Sichuan People's Publishing House, pp.193–194.

in the process of governing, nation states, which came into being accompanied by the capitalist commodity economy, will necessarily abandon the dictatorial system based on the feudal economy and be replaced by the democratic system with political equality and freedom as its core. That is to say, the citizens' will and interests must be fully and equally reflected in the process of state governance. And only when the citizens' will can be well expressed freely and the will of the majority of people can be transformed into that of the state through legal procedures, would the policies of the state be carried out accurately and properly and be understood and supported by the general public, thus yielding the optimum efficiency in state governance activities. As mentioned above, the fact that a nation state is vast with a large population made it impossible for citizens to directly participate in state affairs, "so the issue of representation appeared as the issue of political and social participation in a modern way."[37]

Second, the existence of differences in politics, economy, culture, etc. necessarily results in the formation of various organizations and groups, which exert their influence on the reign and governance of the state in various ways to secure their interests and needs. If no channels are provided for coordinating and compromising between them, their contradictions and conflicts will intensify in the process of each advocating for their respective interests and needs. Therefore, the parliament, as a platform where different political forces can express their wills, plays a very important role in this regard.

Third, from the perspective of management science, generally, the practice of state administration is not easy, rather it is a complex task that requires versatile skills and relatively high quality participants. Successful administration can only be accomplished by people of relatively high abilities. Moreover, political and cultural differences brought about by economic disparity determine that only a few people are competent for this job. Under such circumstances, the state can only be governed by the minority representing the majority. As we have stated before, the slave economy in Athens provided economic guarantee and leisure time for slave-owners and civilians to participate in political affairs. However, under the capitalist commodity economy, "most electors had to devote much time and energy to making a living", so it was difficult for them to directly participate in political affairs, and they had to entrust representatives to administer the state.

Fourth, since the parliament is composed of only a limited number of representatives from various political factions, it is convenient for the ruling class to control their activities and then establish an effective monitoring mechanism. Specifically, it is much easier for the ruling class to control the parliament by controlling the limited number of parliament members, so as to finally control the whole state power and secure its status and role.

---

[37] Mastellone, S. (1992) *Ouzhou zhengzhi sixiang shi: Cong shiwu shiji dao ershi shiji* [History of European Political Thoughts: From 15th Century to 20th Century], trans. Huang, H. G., Beijing: Social Sciences Academic Press, p.186.

(4) Development of Modern Capitalist Democratic Thought

Historical development is a process which determines that the establishment of the representative system cannot be realized overnight. The development of modern capitalist democratic thoughts is the precondition for the formation and establishment of a complete system of representation. In order to satisfy the needs of the capitalist commodity economy and reflect the political demands of the capitalist class, the modern bourgeoisie engaged in revolutionary reform in the field of political thought. This "reform mainly manifested itself in two ways: on one hand, politics was liberated from moral pressure and recovered its independence; on the other hand, humanity replaced divinity, which reconstituted the starting point of politics."[38] Since these reforms, the capitalist theories and practices of democracy emerged. Machiavelli argued it was necessary to establish a forceful centralized state power and to endow the monarch with supreme power in order to cater to the great trend of the formation of European nation states. Later, Hobbes, Locke, Montesquieu, Rousseau, Mabry, Paine, Kant, Hegel, etc., fully elaborated on the origin of the state, the source of state power, and state institutions, and put forward various theories on democracy, freedom, equality, rule of law, human rights, and the like in a systemic way. Among those theories, popular sovereignty was the core. However, there was a divergence of opinions among these Enlightenment thinkers on the issue of establishing ancient democratic republics, and that of realizing popular sovereignty through the representative republics still in their nascent state. "Obviously, if the sovereignty had only been exercised directly by all the people, just the small ancient poleis would have made it, rather than the modern, unified nation states. The ideal kingdom would never be put into practice."[39] For this reason, most bourgeois thinkers advocated the idea of representative democracy, under which the bourgeoisie adopted this realistic path in their democratic practices. On the basis of the representative forms of the medieval hierarchical conference, which were gradually transformed into the representative system compatible to the capitalist production relations represented by the bourgeoisie, the hierarchical system of representation was changed into the representative system generated by the general election, which was the best political shell for the rule of the bourgeoisie. John Stuart Mill argued, "the ideally best form of government is that in which the sovereignty, or supreme controlling power in the last resort, is vested in the entire aggregate of the community."[40]

---

[38] Rong, J. et al. (1988) *Minzhu lun* [On Democracy], Shanghai: Shanghai People's Publishing House, p.88.

[39] Cao, P. L. et al. (1993) *Bijiao zhengfu tizhi* [A Comparison of Government System], Shanghai: Fudan University Press, pp.1–2.

[40] Mill, J. (1982) *Daiyizhi zhengfu* [The Representative Government], trans. Wang X., Beijing: The Commercial Press, p.43. cf. Mill, J. (1861/2008) *Considerations on Representative Government*, London: The Electric Book Company, p.56.

The emergence of the representative system, as discussed above, points to three basic conclusions. First, the representative system was the best political shell for the emerging bourgeoisie to cover up the essence of capital exploitation of employed labor in the process of developing the commodity economy, and thus a covert way of political rule created to conceal the exploitation by the bourgeoisie. Second, the representative system was a breakthrough in the development of the direct democracy deployed in ancient polis. Without the representative system, ancient democracies, which originated from the primitive society and evolved through the Greek democratic republics to at best several medieval European city republics, would not have formed unified nation states. Therefore, the representative system, as a result of the development of democracy itself, marked tremendous progress from ancient to modern democracy in the history of world civilization. Third, under the situation in which economic status was unequal and the economic gap was the principal contradiction in the society, the representative system was the best administrative approach to adapt to the political and cultural disparities caused by the economic gap. Accordingly, we can infer that the foundation of the representative system is bound to be shaken when disparities in economy, politics and culture are increasingly narrowed, thereby strenghtening, the status and role of direct democracy.

2.2.2 Development Process of Capitalist Parliamentary System

During the process of the emergence and development of the representative system, its earliest form was manifested as the capitalist parliamentary system. Britain, with the reputation of "Mother of Parliaments",[41] was the first country that established the parliamentary system in a systemic way. Although opinions vary as to when the English parliament originated,[42] it is generally agreed that it stemmed from the hierarchical conference under the feudal dictatorship in the Middle Ages. As

[41] Of course, the parliament existed long ago as far as the pure sense of representative organs was concerned. For example, the Icelandic parliament established in 930 was one of the oldest parliaments in the world (cf. *Dictionary of World Parliaments*, p.279). Before the unification of Spain, the parliaments of the Kingdom of Aragon and the Kingdom of Castile were respectively established in 1071 and 1137 (ibid, p.423). However, these parliaments did not carry the feature of modern parliaments in essence. The first organ which could be described as a parliament appeared in 1188 under the reign of the Kingdom of Leon. In this organ, the king should promise to "follow the advice from his bishop, the nobility and solons", "no matter in peace or war" (Antonio Marongiu, *Medieval Parliaments*, p.62). However, it was only a hierarchical conference without effect on the modernization.

[42] William Stubbs, the originator of the constitutional history in Britain, believed that the parliament came into being in 1295; Sayles, a current expert in legal history, held that the parliament started from the mid-1200 s when the term appeared in official literatures of the Supreme Court; most Soviet and Chinese scholars argued that the parliament occurred in 1265 or 1295; Liu Xincheng thought that the parliament stemmed from the time of political reforms in the 1320 s. cf. Liu, X. C. (1991) 'Zaiyi yingguo yihui de qiyuan' [The Origin of British Parliament Revisited], *Shijie lishi* [World

Anthony Harold Birch said, "Only in England has the parliamentary assembly had a continuous history from the Middle Ages to the present time".[43] In form, the British parliament could date back to "the Witan" and "the Great Council" respectively in the ages of the Anglo-Saxons and of the Normans. According to recorded literature, from the middle of the eighth century, the Witan emerged as the central assembly where the king summoned the archbishop, the nobility, and courtiers to participate on a non-scheduled basis. The earliest assembly was held in the Kingdom of Mercia.[44] In addition to recommending heirs to the throne, the Witan had extensive rights. Almost all the king's major decisions would be realized only after consultation with and approval by the Witan.[45] Strictly speaking, there was no organizational inheritance relationship between the Witan and the parliament, but at least some "nebulous continuity of political habit".[46] After the House of Normandy came to power in 1066, the Witan evolved into the Great Council. From 1135 to 1154, the forces of feudal separatism tended to surpass those of kingship, and the nobility launched an insurgence. In response, Henry II aligned with civilians to fight against feudal lords under the support of burgesses and knights, and the alignment with civilians was later fixed in the form of law. This directly resulted in "the Great Council"[47] where the king, citizens, and barons participated. In 1199, King John succeeded to the throne, and continued to expand the kingship with the help of the bureaucracy. He craved greatness and success, and used all his armed might to indulge in wars of aggression. However, he was defeated by Philip II, the French king, in a territorial war and lost again in the conflict with Pope Innocent III. After these failures, he directly transferred the state financial burden to barons and citizens, and acquired funds by confiscating barons' lands, arbitrarily levying taxes, etc. to expand the power of bureaucracy and the kinship. For these reasons, the nobility, with the support of knights, industrialists, businessmen and citizens, forced King John to sign *Magna Carta Libertatum* (Great Charter) in 1215, which recognized the power of "the Great Council", and prohibited the king from levying extra temporary duties and additional tax on feudal lords without the approval of the Council. Besides, *Magna Carta* stated that the king must observe the law, otherwise, the subjects had the right to force him to adhere. In 1254, Henry III decided to summon the Great Council to fund the military. Besides the nobility and the clergy, each shire assigned two knights to attend. It was decreed that the elected knights were empowered to speak for the whole county and promised to be bound by the consent of the whole county.[48]

History], (3); see also Shen, H. et al. (1991) *Yingguo yihui zhengzhishi* [British Parliamentary and Political History], Nanjing: Nanjing University Press, pp.36–38.

[43] Birch, A. H. (1971) *Representation*, London: Pall Mall Press Ltd., p.26.

[44] Jiang, M. Y. (1988) *Yingguoshi* [The History of Britain], Beijing: China Social Sciences Press, p.59.

[45] Cf. Shen, H. et al. (1991) *Yingguo yihui zhengzhishi* [British Parliamentary and Political History], Nanjing: Nanjing University Press, pp.3–4.

[46] Spufford, P. (1967) *Origins of the English Parliament*, London, p.3.

[47] Wang, R. T. (1983) 'Luelun yingguo yihui de qiyuan' [On Origins of the English Parliament], *Shixue yuekan* [Journal of Historical Science], (4).

[48] Birch, A. (1971) *Representation*, London: Pall Mall Press Ltd., p.27.

In 1258, Henry III again summoned the Great Council, this time to ask the barons to support his youngest son's bid to ascend the throne in Sicily. The barons, however, attended the council armed to the teeth, insisting on the expulsion of foreigners and political reform, and forced the king to accept *Provisions of Oxford* approved by the council. According to *Provisions of Oxford*, the king could not arbitrarily confiscate, allot and hold lands, nor go out to a battle, without the permission of the Great Council. Meanwhile, the Oxford conference handed powers to the Great Council composed of 15 barons. The king could not make any decision without the approval of the Great Council. In addition, a 12-member committee with legislative power was elected. The council was to meet three times a year to discuss state affairs and was later called the "Mad Parliament." The organizations above were already important organs of authority in 1263 when a civil war broke out in Britain and some barons, under the leadership of Simon de Montfort and the support of knights and citizens, captured King Henry III and his heir Edward. In 1265, Montfort summoned the council attended by nobility and clergy. In addition, it was the first time for knight and citizen representatives assigned by each shire and city to participate in the council. Unfortunately, in the years following this parliament, assigning representatives to parliament was not fixed as an institution. In November, 1295, King Edward I summoned the parliament which included members of "elected" citizen representatives (2 per city) and knight representatives (2 per shire), besides the clergy and the nobility. Actually, this was the rudiment of the English parliament. Since then, this organizational form has gradually been fixed as an institution for a long time. Capitalist historians called it the "Model Parliament", and Edward I "the Monarch of English Parliament". With the development of the British capitalism since the 1340 s, the parliament was gradually split into two forces based on different interests. One consisted of great noblemen and the clergy which later became the House of Lords, or the Upper House. The other was composed of knights and burgesses, which later evolved into the House of Commons, or the Lower House. So, the English parliament was transformed from one house to two houses, which changed the balance of power between "common" representatives and members of the House of Lords. In other words, the status of the "common" representatives was promoted in the parliament, which strengthened the power of the parliament to some degree. In 1365, the judge in England announced that the parliament represented the whole kingdom. However, the parliament at that time was still a feudal, hierarchical assembly where royalty and nobility remained dominant. By the seventeenth century, as British capitalist relations further developed, contradictions intensified between the bourgeoisie and bourgeoisified nobility and the king, and a bourgeoisie-led opposition faction emerged in the parliament. On one hand, they abhorred the feudal system restraining capitalist development, and attempted to overthrow the rule of the feudal dynasty. On the other hand, they were in fear of the people and did not dare to depend on them against feudalism. So, the bourgeoisie took the parliament as the major position to fight against the king. After the bourgeois revolution broke out in 1640, the "Long Parliament" became the organizational core of the revolution, and once became the supreme state body during the civil war. After the Glorious Revolution in 1688, the bourgeoisie and the feudal nobility mutually compromised to share the power of the state. In 1689 and 1701, *The Bill of Rights* and *The Act of Settlement* were successively passed, confirming that the parliament was the supreme legislative body overriding the king, and enjoyed the power of deciding heirs to the throne, setting the financial budget, supervising the government, etc. Later, the parliament also obtained the power of selecting candidates and the convening of the cabinet. Therefrom, the capitalist parliamentary system was established.

Although the French monarchy was a typical feudal autocracy, the king would make some temporary compromises and concessions for his own interests under certain historical conditions. And the Estates-General was the product of such compromises. In 1302, the first Estates-General in the history of France was convened by King Philip IV, in order to earn the support of those of all walks of life against the church. In 1308, King Philip IV convoked the Estates-General again to outlaw the Knights Templar. Attending the assembly were three estates: the first was senior clergy, the second secular nobles, and the third affluent citizens. The Estates-General was designed mainly to approve new taxes with less restriction on the kingship, so the king could convene and dismiss it at will.[49] In this regard, "in theory, the Estates-General was a supervising organ within the autocratic monarchy in France",[50] but in practice, it was just a consultative body to the king, and it was not in session once for 175 years afterwards. In 1789 when the bourgeois revolution smoldered in France, King Louis XVI was forced to summon the Estates-General, where he still followed the old practice of holding meetings and voting separately according to the different estates. This discrimination and inequality aroused great indignation among the representatives of the third estate, so that they, under the support of the vast masses, declared themselves the National Assembly representing all people with the mission of enacting a new constitution. Louis XVI was reluctant to give up the right to rule, and attempted to expel the assembly by force. This move provoked the people in Paris to rise in revolt and the regime was forced to transfer power from the royal to the assembly. Afterwards, the constitutional activities in 1791, 1793, and 1795 helped to establish the capitalist parliamentary system in France.[51]

Unlike Britain and France, America neither experienced feudal society nor hierarchical monarchy. In the U.S., the capitalist parliamentary system evolved from the feudal parliament during the colonial period. Before the American War of Independence, the representative system was successively established in the North American colonies, conforming to "the representative tradition brought by migrants from Britain."[52] During the War of Independence, the American bourgeoisie convoked the Second Continental Congress, ratified *The Declaration of Independence* in 1776,

---

[49] Zhang, Z. L. (ed.) (1989) *Faguo jianshi* [A Concise History of France], Beijing: Peking University Press, p.62–63.

[50] Mastellone, S. (1992) *Ouzhou zhengzhi sixiang shi: Cong shiwu shiji dao ershi shiji* [History of European Political Thoughts: From 15th Century to 20th Century], trans. Huang, H. G., Beijing: Social Sciences Academic Press, p.179.

[51] Jin, G. T. et al. (1985) *Xifang shehui jiegou de yanbian* [Evolution of Western Social Structure], Chengdu: Sichuan People's Publishing House, p.187.

[52] Jiang, J. S. (1992) *Meiguo guohuishi* [The History of the United States Congress], Hainan: Hainan Publishing House, p.7.

and drafted *The Articles of Confederation* in 1777, which stated the Confederation Congress would be a consultative organ of all sovereign states. In 1787, the American constitution confirmed, based on the principle of separation of powers, that the Congress composed of the Senate and the House of Representatives would be the supreme legislative body; the president would be the chief executive who enjoyed all the executive and military power; and the Supreme Court would be the supreme judicial organ. Hence the American capitalist parliamentary system was officially established.

From the process by which the capitalist parliamentary systems in Britain, France and America emerged, we can observe that although all the parliamentary systems possessed the same class nature, the parliaments of different countries took different forms with different features attributable to different class power relations, historical and cultural traditions, national psychology, etc. Among those differences, the most important one lies in: the English parliament was the supreme state body, while the French and American parliaments were just the supreme legislative organ. In the operation of the capitalist parliaments, the ruling classes from various countries adapted to changes in their own social and historical conditions, and correspondingly improved and perfected[53] their parliamentary systems, thus arriving at an advanced state. In addition, the practices of the parliamentary system in the three countries provided different models for other capitalist countries. With the successive acquisition of power by the bourgeoisie in many countries, the parliamentary system was generally established in various capitalist countries, and thus gained further opportunities to develop.

2.3 Emergence and Development of Socialist People's Representative System

The emergence of the socialist people's representative system is a step of great historical significance in the development of the representative system. However, before every major social change, theoretical breakthroughs always play an important role.

[53] In terms of parliamentary reforms, British was the most prominent. It mainly started with the capitalist democratization on political structures in the post-industrial revolution (cf. Shen, H. *Yingguo yihui zhengzhishi* [The History of British Parliament and Politics], Chapter 6). France and America also made adjustments to the parliamentary system many times (cf. Hong, B. *Faguo zhengzhi zhidu bianqian* [The Changes of the French Political System], Chapter 3–4; Jiang, J. S. *Meiguo guohuishi* [The History of the United States Congress], Chapter 14, etc.).

2.3.1 Theoretical Exploration by Classical Writers of Marxism-Leninism

Long before socialism was first realized men of insight had envisioned it. Only after the birth of Marxism did socialism develop "from fantasy to science". This was the case for the democratic form in future ideal societies. Scholars had made valuable explorations of democracy, such as Thomas More who argued that the assembly of the people and its standing organ were the supreme bodies of Utopia, Gerrard Winstanley who held that the parliament was "the supreme justice body", Etienne Cabet who proposed that the supreme power body should be the national people's congress, composed of 2000 representatives. However, restricted by historical conditions and subjective factors, those theories of the utopian socialists were flawed in theoretical strength, for their lack of understanding the law of social development, and in practical effect, for guiding political practices. Therefore, this historic task was left unaccomplished until the time of the classical writers of Marxism. Herein, this issue will be discussed from the following two aspects.

(1) **Criticism of Capitalist Parliamentary System**

After the capitalist parliamentary system was established, bourgeois rule was usually manifested in the form of the parliament. As a legislative body, the parliament was elected by the people, which marked a great progress in the history of social development, compared to the feudal monarchy. However, the bourgeoisie boosted the parliament as a people's representative body for it superficially reflected the public opinions and represented the sovereignty of the people. Therefore, it is of special importance for socialist thinkers to reveal the true nature of the capitalist parliamentary system.

According to the classical writers of Marxism, the capitalist "parliamentary forms were only attachments to the administrative power for deception",[54] and could only represent the bourgeoisie's will and interests. Through debate and voting in the parliament, the bourgeoisie pretended their will as that of all the people. Therefore, they regarded the parliament as "a place for idle talk", and held that the heated debate in the parliament was in reality a competition between various capitalist groups for their own interests, but did not change the nature of parliament serving the bourgeoisie. "Any state with the parliamentary system, the United States of America, Switzerland, France, Britain, Norway, etc., dealt with the true 'state' affairs behind the scenes through departments, government offices, and headquarters. The parliament was full of idle talk to fool 'the common people'. It was absolutely true."[55] Apparently, "the parliamentary democracy" was just a decoration to the capitalist states in essence. What really ruled according to Marx was "property, which enabled the aristocracts to control representative elections in agricultural areas and small cities, which made it possible for merchants and factory owners to exert influence on

[54] *Makesi Engesi xuanji* [Marx and Engels Selected Works] (1995), Beijing: People's Publishing House, vol.3, p.94. cf. Marx. K. (1871) *The Civil War in France.*

[55] *Liening xuanji* [Lenin Selected Works] (1995), Beijing: People's Publishing House, vol.3, p.151. cf. Lenin, V. (1917) *The State and Revolution.*

representative elections in large cities and some small cities, and which allowed the aristocrats, merchants and factory owners to strengthen their power through bribery. The rule of property was confirmed by the reform act which passed the stipulation of property qualification."[56] Thus, "To decide once every few years which members of the ruling class is to repress and crush the people through parliament – this is the real essence of bourgeois parliamentarism, not only in parliamentary-constitutional monarchies, but also in the most democratic republics."[57]

It must be clarified that although classical writers of Marxism explicitly revealed the class essence of the capitalist parliamentary system, they did not deny the system was a great progress in the history of national institutions. As Marx and Engels pointed out, "the bourgeoisie eliminated all old differences among existing estates within a country, and abolished all privileges and immunities obtained by tyranny. They had to take the principle of election as the ruling basis. In other words, they recognized equality in principle."[58] It follows that under the capitalist parliamentary system, the capitalist had to allow the common people to be involved in political activities in form. Compared to the absolutism in the Middle Ages, it was a great advance. More than that, the bourgeois democracy with the parliament as its core objectively provided favorable conditions for the proletariat to grow and fight against the bourgeoisie within certain confines. Lenin noted, "The more radical the democratic reform of the bourgeois revolution, the more beneficial to other classes outside the bourgeoisie. The more thorough the bourgeois revolution, the more certain the proletariat and peasants would benefit from the democratic revolution."[59] He added, "Without parliamentarism, without an electoral system, this development of the working class would have been impossible."[60] Hence, "The bourgeois republic, parliament, universal suffrage – all represent great progress from the standpoint of the development of world society."[61]

(2) **Theoretical Generalization of the Proletarian Representative System**

The classical writers of Marxism were concerned with how the proletariat established the national regime after they came to power. In *The Communist Manifesto*, Marx and Engels argued that "the first step in the revolution by the working class is to raise the proletariat to the position of the ruling class to win the battle of democracy."[62] Herein,

---

[56] *Makesi Engesi quanji* [Marx and Engels Collected Works] (1965), Beijing: People's Publishing House, vol.1, p.687. cf. Engles, F. (1844) *The Condition of England.*

[57] *Liening xuanji* [Lenin Selected Works] (1995), Beijing: People's Publishing House, vol.3, p.150. cf. Lenin, V. (1917) *The State and Revolution.*

[58] *Makesi Engesi quanji* [Marx and Engels Collected Works] (1957), Beijing: People's Publishing House, vol.2, p.647. cf. Engels, F. (1846) *The Condition of Germany.*

[59] *Liening quanji* [Lenin Collected Works] (1959), Beijing: People's Publishing House, vol.9, p.36.

[60] *Liening quanji* [Lenin Collected Works] (1956), Beijing: People's Publishing House, vol.29, p.442. cf. Lenin, V. (1919) The State: A lecture delivered at the Sverdlov University.

[61] *Liening quanji* [Lenin Collected Works] (1956), Beijing: People's Publishing House, vol.29, p.442. cf. Lenin, V. (1919) The State: A lecture delivered at the Sverdlov University.

[62] *Makesi Engesi xuanji* [Marx and Engels Selected Works] (1995), Beijing: People's Publishing House, vol.1, p.272. cf. Marx, K. and F. Engels (1848) *Manifesto of the Communist Party.*

the notion of the proletariat dictatorship was first proposed. Later in *Critique of the Gotha Programme*, Marx further pointed out that "Between capitalist and communist society there lies the period of the revolutionary transformation of the one into the other. Corresponding to this is also a political transition period in which the state can be nothing but the revolutionary dictatorship of the proletariat."[63] How would the working class realize this end? With regard to this issue, Marx proposed the famous principle of smashing the old state machinery. In the book *The Eighteenth Brumaire of Louis Bonaparte*, Marx posited, after examining the actual progress of the French revolution, that "All revolutions perfected this machine instead of breaking it."[64] In *The Civil War in France*, he summarized the experiences and lessons of the Paris Commune and further pointed out that "the working class cannot simply lay hold of the ready-made state machinery, and wield it to achieve its own purposes."[65] The reason is that "the political tool enslaving them could not be used as the emancipatory tool".[66]

Since the proletarian revolution must smash the old state machinery, the capitalist parliamentary system as the core of the capitalist democracy should certainly be destroyed. However, the classical writers of Marxism did not take a simplistic attitude towards this issue. In their opinions, countries with the proletariat as the masters would not copy the capitalist parliamentary system which was the tool for the bourgeois dictatorship, but could still adopt the form of the representative system. Lenin held that "The way out of parliamentarism is not, of course, the abolition of representative institutions and the elective principle, but the conversion of the representative institutions from talking shops into "working" bodies."[67] When the proletariat came to power, the parliamentary system, a special system of capitalism, would not exist, but "Representative institutions remain", because "We cannot imagine democracy, even proletarian democracy, without representative institutions."[68] For this reason, in the process of establishing their own regime, the proletariat must not only fundamentally deny the capitalist representative system, namely, the essence of the capitalist parliamentary system, but also borrow the form of the capitalist representative system.

In the *Letter to Paul Lafargue*, Engels wrote that "A republic, ... is the ready-made political form for the future rule of the proletariat... But a republic, like any other form of government, is determined by what composes it; so long as it is the

[63] *Makesi Engesi xuanji* [Marx and Engels Selected Works] (1995), Beijing: People's Publishing House, vol.3, p.314. cf. Marx, K. (1875) *Critique of the Gotha Programme.*

[64] *Makesi Engesi xuanji* [Marx and Engels Selected Works] (1995), Beijing: People's Publishing House, vol1, p.675. cf. Marx, K. (1852) *The Eighteenth Brumaire of Louis Bonaparte.*

[65] *Makesi Engesi xuanji* [Marx and Engels Selected Works] (1995), Beijing: People's Publishing House, vol.3, p.52. cf. Mark, K. (1871) *The Civil War in France.*

[66] *Makesi Engesi xuanji* [Marx and Engels Selected Works] (1995), Beijing: People's Publishing House, vol.3, p.117. cf. Mark, K. (1871) *The Civil War in France.*

[67] *Liening xuanji* [Lenin Selected Works] (1995), Beijing: People's Publishing House, vol.3, p.151. cf. Lenin, V. (1917) *The State and Revolution.*

[68] *Liening xuanji* [Lenin Selected Works] (1995), Beijing: People's Publishing House, vol.3, p.152. cf. Lenin, V. (1917) *The State and Revolution.*

form of bourgeois rule, it is quite as hostile to us as any monarchy whatsoever (save in the forms of that hostility). Hence it is a gratuitous illusion to treat it as an essentially socialist form; to trust it whilst it is dominated by the bourgeoisie, with socialist tasks."[69] Here, Engels clearly stated that the bourgeois republic could never realize the contents of socialism and only the democratic republic with socialist nature could realize the political form enabling the proletariat to be masters of their country. Likewise, the capitalist representative system could not realize the contents of socialism, and only the representative system with socialist nature could achieve the basic form of the proletarian democracy. At the same time, this also proved that the proletariat could modify and utilize the representative forms of the capitalist parliamentary system, just as they could with the democratic republic forms of the bourgeois democratic republic.

In addition to the general principles of the proletarian representative system, classical writers also had many discussions about the socialist people's representative system, combining the proletarian revolution and regime construction. As to this issue, we turn to the next section.

2.3.2 *Socialist People's Representative System: Further Development of Representative Democracy*

23 years after *The Communist Manifesto* was published, the proletariat across the world entered a new stage of historical development. From the Paris Commune to the Soviet, the representative system had undergone a qualitative leap and the socialist people's representative system was finally established.

(1) **Paris Commune: Initial Experiment of Proletarian Representative System**

In 1871, the proletariat in Paris staged an uprising, and overthrew the capitalist regime. They not only created the first political form enabling the proletariat to be the masters of their country, but also established the first proletarian representative system in history. Although the Commune existed only for 72 days, it also provided us valuable experience and principles in the establishment of the proletarian representative system in Paris.

First, the principles of general election and supervision. Marx expressed that "The Commune was formed of the municipal councilors, chosen by universal suffrage in the various wards of the town, responsible and revocable at short terms."[70] After the success of March 18th uprising, the Commune immediately released an announcement, and prepared for elections. Although the hurried election in led to a fatal error

[69] *Makesi Engesi xuanji* [Marx and Engels Selected Works] (1995), Beijing: People's Publishing House, vol.4, p.735. cf. Engels, F. (1894) 'To Paul Lafargue at Le Perreux'.

[70] *Makesi Engesi xuanji* [Marx and Engels Selected Works] (1995), Beijing: People's Publishing House, vol.3, p.55. cf. Marx, K. (1871) *The Civil War in France.*

for the Commune, the election itself fully reflected the true democracy of the proletariat. There was no limitation on electoral rights, enabling the working people to fully enjoy the right of general election. What's more, most civil servants of the government offices needed to be elected, including three categories of: Commune councilors; officers of the People's Armed Forces; and factory managers and workshop directors, etc.. Meanwhile, the principle required that representatives should be responsible for their constituency and must accept supervision by voters in an effective way and that electors could remove their representatives at any moment in order to prevent social servants from being masters of the society. Engels pointed out, "From the outset the Commune was compelled to…safeguard itself against its own deputies and officials, by declaring them all, without exception, subject to recall at any moment."[71] This kind of removal system was the key factor differentiating the socialist representative system from the capitalist counterpart. As Lenin described, "No elective institution or representative assembly can be regarded as being truly democratic and really representative of the people's will unless the electors' right to recall those elected is accepted and exercised. This is the fundamental principle of true democracy."[72]

Second, the principle of workers' government. The Commune council was the supreme power body of the Paris Commune. "The majority of its members were naturally working men, or acknowledged representatives of the working class."[73] Of 86 councilors, more than 20 members were capitalist liberals. Although these liberals were elected on March 28th, they withdrew from the Commune in early April. And all the positions in the Commune, including administration, jurisdiction and national education, etc., were given to those elected in the general election. In this way, all the offices were taken by workers and the Commune became a workers' government in a real sense.

Third, the principle of combining legislative and executive powers. Marx stated that "The Commune was to be a working, not a parliamentary body, executive and legislative at the same time."[74] During the bourgeoisie revolution, the parliament, as the capitalist legislative organ, once played a positive role against the feudal dictatorship. However, when the bourgeoisie came to power, the parliament became a "talking shop" for deceiving the people. Totally different from the parliament, the Commune was not only a legislative organ with the power to enact law and make resolutions on all the Commune's matters, but also an administrative organ, assigning sub-committees to implement and supervise its resolutions. Besides, many members of the Commune directly engaged in the leadership of sub-committees. So, the Paris Commune implemented the principle of combining legislative and executive powers.

---

[71] *Makesi Engesi xuanji* [Marx and Engels Selected Works] (1995), Beijing: People's Publishing House, vol.3, p.12. cf. Engels, F. (1891) *On the 20th Anniversary of the Paris Commune.*

[72] *Lening quanji* [Lenin Collected Works] (1959), Beijing: People's Publishing House, vol.26, p.314. cf. Lenin, V. (1917) *Draft Decree on the Right of Recall.*

[73] *Makesi Engesi xuanji* [Marx and Engels Selected Works] (1995), Beijing: People's Publishing House, vol.3, p.55. cf. Marx, K. (1871) *The Civil War in France.*

[74] *Makesi Engesi xuanji* [Marx and Engels Selected Works] (1995), Beijing: People's Publishing House, vol.3, p.55. cf. Marx, K. (1871) *The Civil War in France.*

Fourth, the principle of low salary. The proletarian regime was radically different from others in that government officials were turned into people's public servants. How was this realized? The Paris Commune made valuable explorations in this respect. Besides the effective supervision, which was a must, the principle of low salary was also a very important means creating people's public servants. Engels pointed out that preventing the state and its organs from changing the role of social servants to social masters… it paid all government officials, no matter what positions they hold, the salary same with that of workers… in this way, the commune could be confident to prevent officials from winning promotion and getting rich even if it did not limit the power of the representatives. So, the Commune council and all other public servants could only earn the salary, equivalent to that of workers. Their wage was 12 pounds a month, and the highest wage was just 240 pounds a year. Huxley, a British professor, estimated that such a salary was just over 1/5 of that of a secretary from the Education Bureau of London. Therefore, the Paris Commune made the catch word of "cheap government" a reality, which was impossible for the bourgeoisie.

The classical Marxist writers spoke highly of the Paris Commune because it left to the proletariat an abundant legacy in the process of building the proletarian representative system and creating the genuine proletarian regime. Marx pointed out, the true secret of the Commune was this: "It was essentially a working-class government, the product of the struggle of the producing against the appropriating class, the political form at last discovered under which to work out the economical emancipation of labor."[75] This claim was proved to be true later in the practice of the proletarian regime building.

(2) **Soviets of Workers', Peasants' and Soldiers' Deputies: First Socialist People's Representative System**

The October Socialist Revolution of 1917 shattered the weakest link of the imperialist system, materializing socialism in one country for the first time. When leading the proletarian revolution in Russia, Lenin summarized the experience and lessons from international communist movements since the Paris Commune and finally found that the Soviet was the practical form to enable the proletariat to establish its rule. If the Paris Commune took the first epoch-making step in the development of the proletarian dictatorship and was the bud of the socialist people's representative system, "'the Soviet Regime' took the second step of global historical significance in the development of the proletarian dictatorship",[76] and "was the direct continuance of the Paris Commune."[77]

[75] *Makesi Engesi xuanji* [Marx and Engels Selected Works] (1995), Beijing: People's Publishing House, vol.3, p.55. cf. Marx, K. (1871) *The Civil War in France.*

[76] *Liening quanji* [Lenin Collected Works] (1956), Beijing: People's Publishing House, vol.28, p.409. cf. Lenin, V. (1919) Thesis and Report on Bourgeois Democracy and the Dictatorship of the Proletariat.

[77] *Liening quanji* [Lenin Collected Works] (1958), Beijing: People's Publishing House, vol.27, p.171. cf. Lenin, V. (1919) Thesis and Report on Bourgeois Democracy and the Dictatorship of the Proletariat.

The word "Soviet" was the transliteration of the Russian word "COBET", meaning council. During the first Great Russian Revolution of 1905, some new forms of organizations were created by the people, such as Soviet of Workers' Deputies, Soviet of Soldiers' Deputies and Soviet of Peasants' Deputies. Among them, the most prominent was the Soviet of Workers' Deputies, consisting of worker representatives from factories and workshops. At first, the Soviet of Workers' Deputies was just an organization for leading the workers' strikes and later it developed into an institution responsible for guiding various revolutionary struggles of the masses, and finally it became a revolutionary organ of insurgence, independently exercising certain functions of state power. It once announced the eight-hour day, conducted anti-tax activities, organized the court to maintain the revolutionary order, and issued newspapers to materialize the freedom of publication, etc. Although it attempted to align with all the other Soviets, it failed due to the loose and casual organizational framework to group its members. However, Lenin attached great importance to the Soviets voluntarily organized by the people, and further argued that the Soviet of Workers' Deputies should be regarded as the embryo of a provisional revolutionary government,[78] and "marked the beginning of seizing the regime"[79] by the people. In February of 1917, under the leadership of Lenin, the Bolshevik integrated the Soviet of Workers' Deputies and the Soviet of Soldiers' Deputies into the Soviet of Workers' and Soldiers' Deputies. In April, 1917, Lenin first proposed to take the Soviet as the organizational form of the state power in *The April Theses*, and pointed out that "the Soviets of Workers' Deputies are the only possible form of the revolutionary government",[80] and came up with the slogan of "the entire state power to the Soviets". After the victorious October Revolution in 1917, the Second All-Russian Congress of Soviets officially confirmed that the Soviet was the new organ of state power. At that time, the Soviets of Workers' and Peasants' and Soldiers' Deputies were established from the central to local governments. Meanwhile, the Second All-Russian Congress of Soviets elected the All-Russian Central Executive Committee as its standing organ, and established the Council of People's Commissars as the executive organ. The 1918 Soviet Russian Constitution as the basic law confirmed the Soviet on behalf of workers, peasants, and soldiers as the people's representative organ of Russia. From then on, the proletarian representative organ with supreme power was established. Correspondingly, the first socialist people's representative system with the representative organ as the core in the history of mankind came into existence.

As the result of the specific historical conditions of Russia, the Soviet regime had its own distinctive features. Both Lenin and Stalin generalized the features respectively in *The Bolshevik Must Assume State Power* and *The Basis of Leninism* in a

[78] *Liening quanji* [Lenin Collected Works] (1958), Beijing: People's Publishing House, vol.10, p.213. cf. Lenin, V. (1905) Our Tasks and the Soviet of Workers' Deputies.

[79] *Liening quanji* [Lenin Collected Works] (1959), Beijing: People's Publishing House, vol.16, p.165.

[80] *Liening xuanji* [Lenin Selected Works] (1995), Beijing: People's Publishing House, vol.3, p.15. cf. Lenin, V. (1917) The Tasks of the Proletariat in the Present Revolution.

systematic way.[81] From the perspective of the representative system, their main points can be summarized as follows. First, compared to the former institutions, the Soviet was more democratic since its members were to be elected and replaced based on public opinion. In addition, it promised to have extremely close ties with the masses or most of the people and assimilate labors' organizations to be frequently involved in the state administration without preconditions. Second, it guaranteed functioning of the proletarian vanguard in mobilizing, educating, training and leading the masses. Third, it ensured to take in both the advantages of the parliamentary system and those of the direct democracy, that is to say, the functions of legislation and law enforcement were to be combined under elected the people's representatives and the workers and the ordinary people were to be associated with the state administrative organs.

From the above-mentioned features, we can observe similarities and differences between the Soviet and the Paris Commune in terms of the representative system. Their nature and some basic principles were the same. For example, the representatives were elected, responsible to their electorates and could be removed anytime; both of them implemented the principle of combining legislative and executive powers. Meanwhile, differences also existed between them as follows due to their different historical conditions. First, the Soviet was led by the Bolshevik who mobilized the masses to materialize proletarian dictatorship through the Soviet. Therefore, the Bolshevik particularly highlighted the close ties between the Soviet and the masses and stressed giving full play to the people's initiative, enthusiasm and creativity. These features were closely related to national conditions in Russia. At that time, Russian capitalism was not developed, and the number of workers was not the majority, so the alignment of workers and farmers was a must. By comparison, the Paris Commune emphasized that the people directly became the masters of their countries on account of the lack of leadership of Marxist political parties and the misalignment of workers and farmers. Second, although the representatives both from the Soviet and the Paris Commune were elected and responsible to their electors, and would be replaced anytime, other public servants of the Soviet were not elected nor replaced at any moment, and the salaries of the public servants were not the same with those of ordinary workers because the state organs were not yet streamlined and different posts had different requirements of competence.

Since the socialist people's representative system was established in the Soviet Russia in 1918, it was affirmed and perfected through the Soviet Constitution of 1924 and that of 1936, with the progress of the political, economic, and cultural achievements. After World War Two, the socialist people's representative system found its applications and development in those countries, where socialist state regimes were newly established.

---

[81] *Liening xuanji* [Lenin Selected Works] (1995), Beijing: People's Publishing House, vol.3, pp.308–309; *Sidalin quanji* [Stalin Collected Works] (1956), Beijing: People's Publishing House, vol.6, pp.107–108. cf. Lenin, V. (1917) *The Bolshevik Must Assume State Power?*

References

Aristotle. (1983). *Zhengzhixue* [The Politics] (S. P. Wu, Trans.). The Commercial Press.
Birch, A. (1971). *Representation.* Pall Mall Press Ltd.
Cao, P. L. et al. (1993) *Bijiao zhengfu tizhi* [A Comparison of Government System]. Fudan University Press.
Engels, F. (1846). *The Condition of Germany.*
Engels, F. (1891). *On the 20th Anniversary of the Paris Commune.*
Engels, F. (1894). To Paul Lafargue at Le Perreux.
Engles, F. (1844). *The Condition of England.*
Engles, F. (1880). *Socialism: Utopian and Scientific.*
Engles, F. (1884). *Origins of the Family, Private Property and the State.*
Godwin, W. (1793/1976). *Enquiry Concerning Political Justice and Its Influence on Morals and Happiness.* Penguin Classics.
Godwin, W. (1991). *Zhengzhi zhengyi lun* [On Political Justice] (M. L. He, Trans.). The Commercial Press.
He, X. M. (1991). *Gudian minzhu zhengti lun* [On Classic Democratic Regimes]. Lanzhou University Press.
Herodotus. (1959). *Lishi* (III) [History (III)] (Y. Z. Wang, Trans.). The Commercial Press.
Huang, D. Q. (ed.). (1993). *Shehui zhuyi minzhu: Kuashiji de chensi* [Socialist Democracy: A millennium reflection]. China Renmin University Press.
Jiang, J. S. (1992). *Meiguo guohuishi* [The History of the United States Congress]. Hainan Publishing House.
Jiang, M. Y. (1988). *Yingguoshi* [The History of Britain]. China Social Sciences Press.
Jin, G. T. et al. (1985) *Xifang shehui jiegou de yanbian* [Evolution of Western Social Structure]. Sichuan People's Publishing House.
Lenin, V. (1905). Our Tasks and the Soviet of Workers Deputies.
Lenin, V. (1917). The Tasks of the Proletariat in the Present Revolution.
Lenin, V. (1917). *Draft Decree on the Right of Recall.*
Lenin, V. (1917). *The Bolshevik Must Assume State Power?*
Lenin, V. (1917). *The State and Revolution.*
Lenin, V. (1919). Thesis and Report on Bourgeois Democracy and the Dictatorship of the Proletariat.
Lenin, V. (1919). Speech at the Opening Session of the First Congress of the Communist International delivered on March 2.
Lenin, V. (1919). The State: lecture delivered at the Sverdlov University on July 11, 1919.
Lening quanji [Lenin Collected Works] (1959). People's Publishing House (Vol. 26).
Liening quanji [Lenin Collected Works] (1956). People's Publishing House (Vol. 29).
Liening quanji [Lenin Collected Works] (1956). People's Publishing House (Vol. 28).
Liening quanji [Lenin Collected Works] (1958). People's Publishing House, (Vol. 27).
Liening quanji [Lenin Collected Works] (1958). People's Publishing House, (Vol. 10).
Liening quanji [Lenin Collected Works] (1959). People's Publishing House (Vol. 9).
Liening quanji [Lenin Collected Works] (1959). People's Publishing House (Vol. 16).
Liening quanji [Lenin's collected Works] (1995). People's Publishing House (Vol. 4).
Liening xuanji [Lenin Selected Works] (1995), Beijing: People's Publishing House, vol.3.
Lipset, S. (1993). *Zhengzhi ren* [Political Man] (G. M. Liu, & R. Nie, Trans.). The Commercial Press.
Lipset, S. (1960). *Political Man: The social bases of politics.* Doubleday & Company, Inc.
Liu, X. C. (1991) 'Zaiyi yingguo yihui de qiyuan' [The Origin of British Parliament Revisited], *Shijie lishi* [World History], (3).
Makesi Engesi quanji [Marx and Engels Collected Works] (1957). People's Publishing House (Vol. 2).
Makesi Engesi quanji [Marx and Engels Collected Works] (1965). People's Publishing House (Vol. 21).

Makesi Engesi xuanji [Marx and Engels Selected Works] (1995). People's Publishing House (Vol. 3).

Makesi Engesi xuanji [Marx and Engels Selected Works] (1995). People's Publishing House (Vol. 4).

Makesi Engesi xuanji [Marx and Engels Selected Works] (1995). People's Publishing House (Vol. 1).

Makesi Engesi xuanji [Marx and Engels Selected Works] (1995), Beijing: People's Publishing House, voll. Marx, K. (1843) *Critique of Hegel's Philosophy of Right.*

Marx, K. (1852). *The Eighteenth Brumaire of Louis Bonaparte.*

Marx, K. (1871). *The Civil War in France.*

Marx, K. (1875). *Critique of the Gotha Programme.*

Marx, K., & Engels, F. (1848). *Manifesto of the Communist Party.*

Mastellone, S. (1992). *Ouzhou zhengzhi sixiang shi: Cong shiwu shiji dao ershi shiji* [History of European Political Thoughts: From 15th Century to 20th Century] (H. G. Huang, Trans.). Social Sciences Academic Press.

Mill, J. (1861/2008). *Considerations on Representative Government.* The Electric Book Company.

Mill, J. (1982). *Daiyizhi zhengfu* [The Representative Government] (X. Wang, Trans.). The Commercial Press.

Miller, D., & Bogdanor, V. (Eds.). (1992). *The Blackwell Encyclopedia of Political Science.* Wiley-Blackwell.

Morgan, L. (1877/1985). *Ancient Society.* Charles H. Kerr & Company Co-operative.

Morgan, L. (1992). *Gudai shehui (I)* [Ancient Society (I)] (D. C. Yang, Y. M, & J. Ma, Trans.). The Commercial Press.

Morgan, L. (1992). *Gudai shehui (II)* [Ancient Society (II)] (D. C. Yang, Y. Ma, J. Ma, Trans.). The Commercial Press.

Paine, T. (1982). *Panen xuanji* [Selected Works of Thomas Paine] (Q. H. Ma, Trans.). The Commercial Press (p. 246).

Paine, T. (2005). *Common Sense and Other Writings.* Barnes & Noble Books.

Ri, Z. (ed.). (1989). *Gudai chengbangshi yanjiu* [A Study of History of Ancient Polis]. People's Publishing House.

Rong, J. et al. (1988). *Minzhu lun* [On Democracy]. Shanghai People's Publishing House.

Russell, B. (1938/2004). *Power.* Routledge.

Russell, B. (1991). *Quanli lun* [On Power] (Y. S. Wu trans.). The Commercial Press.

Shen, H. et al. (1991). *Yingguo yihui zhengzhishi* [British Parliamentary and Political History]. Nanjing University Press.

Sidalin quanji [Stalin Collected Works] (1956). People's Publishing House (Vol. 6).

Spufford, P. (1967). *Origins of the English Parliament.*

Wang, N. X. (1994). Guluoma renmin dahui ruogan wenti bianxi [Analysis on Comitia in Ancient Rome] in the first issue of *Qiu Shi* [Seeking Truth].

Wang, R. T. (1983). Luelun yingguo yihui de qiyuan [On Origins of the English Parliament], *Shixue yuekan* [Journal of Historical Science], (4).

Zhang, Z. L. (ed.). (1989). *Faguo jianshi* [A Concise History of France]. Peking University Press.

Chapter 3
Representative System and Popular Sovereignty

Since the representative system emerged, it quickly spread to various countries in the world and become an important part of the political systems of different countries, despite different objective historical reasons for its emergence. However, the representative system is not necessarily equal to democracy. "Only when the representative system has succeeded in ensuring that the government acts in accordance with the will and demands of the people, is it justifiable to call it a representative democracy."[1] Therefore, the representative system is often criticized by people both in theory and in practice. Taking a survey of different views, we find that the key problem lies in how to understand and deal with the relationship between the representative system and popular sovereignty.

3.1 Does Representative System Contradict Popular Sovereignty?

With the formation of nation-states came the issue of sovereignty. With the social and economic development of Western Europe, a unified domestic market was required to be established, nation-states began to take shape, and the centralization of political power intensified. According to the above historical conditions, Jean Bodin, the French political philosopher, formulated a systematic theory of sovereignty. He argued that sovereignty is the supreme power over citizens and subjects and shall not be limited by the law. It must be perpetual. So, to whom should this absolute, supreme and perpetual power belong on earth? In opposing the separation of the feudal lords, Bodin called for the a monarchical sovereignty based on the divine power. Thomas Hobbes, the British bourgeois thinker, insisted on centralization and absolutism of

[1] Law Institute of Shanghai Academy of Social Science (ed.) (1982) *Constitution*, Shanghai: Knowledge Press, p. 148.

Y. Zhou, *A Comparative Study of Representative Systems*,
https://doi.org/10.1007/978-981-15-4186-5_3

state power and advocated the sovereignty of the monarch in accordance with the theories of "natural law" and "social contract", though he was resolutely opposed to "divine sovereignty". In order to consolidate the political power obtained by the bourgeoisie in struggling against feudalism, John Locke proposed parliamentary sovereignty instead of the monarchical sovereignty. Afterwards, Rousseau further developed the bourgeois sovereignty theory and put forward the idea of popular sovereignty.

3.1.1 Historical Evolution of Popular Sovereignty Principle

(1) **Review of Popular Sovereignty Theories**

Generally speaking, popular sovereignty means that the majority of citizens of a state enjoy supreme power. As a matter of fact, the concept of popular sovereignty has long existed in the history of human society. During the English bourgeois revolution, Algernon Sidney, an independent representative, argued for the principle of popular sovereignty. In his opinion, there is only one legitimate ground for sovereignty, which is a free agreement that people made for their own purposes. In establishing state power, people ought to limit their own freedom according to some essential rules in order to safeguard common interests, but they have the right to establish or overthrow a government. George Lawson, another political thinker, believed all political power should belong to people. Power can be granted to a government only when it is in the interest of all people and can carried out only by the consent and expression of its people. Jean-Jacques Rousseau, a great Enlightment thinker, was a master of popular sovereignty theories. Based on the theories of the "state of nature" and "social contract", he assumed that sovereignty is the expression of the general will, which represents the supreme power. For him, people are the source of the supreme power of a state, which is a product of the social contract agreed upon by free people, so the power of government is endowed by people. In this sense, the master of a state is not a monarch, but its people since sovereignty is simply exercised by the people through their elected representatives. So, the sovereignty can only belong to the people.

The emergence of popular sovereignty theories marked a great progress in the history of the development of the theory of state, and became a sharp ideological weapon for the bourgeois revolution against the feudal autocracy. It dealt a heavy blow to the theory of "divine right of kings" popular then in Europe, and immediately disarmed the monarch spiritually and in the meantime armed revolutionary people ideologically. However, popular sovereignty theories, proposed during the rise of the bourgeoisie, had some inevitable limitations of their own. The first is the issue concerning the class nature of the "people". For the Enlightenment scholars, the people often refer to all the people in both their concepts and formulations. However, the founders of Marxism noted that the concept of the people for the Enlightenment scholars actually referred to the capitalist class only. Second, the argument of the popular sovereignty theorists is idealistic because their argumentation is based on the theories of the "state of nature" and the "social contract" that are impossible to verify. As the basis of popular sovereignty theory, the historical starting point of the social contract theory is also a conjecture that does not conform to the historical facts, an aesthetic illusion of the Robinsonades, and rather an anticipation of "civil society", making giant strides towards maturity.[2] Therefore, a state is not established according to contracts, but a product or representation of the irreconcilable class contradiction. The so-called state of reason established under the banner of popular sovereignty was no more than the idealized kingdom of the bourgeoisie,[3] and the so-called eternal reason advocated by enlightenment ideologists is not that of all human beings, but the idealized perception of the middle class citizens who are becoming capitalist. What's more, the so-called popular sovereignty advocated by those theorists only involves the aspect of political power without mentioning that of social and economic power, the much more important areas.

Although the notion of popular sovereignty has many limitations, its historical value cannot be underestimated, because some of its principles exceed far beyond its progressive role in opposition against the feudal autocracy: First, sovereignty belongs to people and powers of government come from people, hence, the establishment of a government should be agreed upon by the people, and the powers of government should be supervised by the people. As for the relationship between the government and the people, the people are masters while state organs and their staff are trustees. This is the core concept of popular sovereignty, and it is this core concept that gives popular sovereignty significance beyond just anti-feudalism. Besides, it provides the possibility for the proletariat to make use of it to fight against the bourgeois government, and to assimilate its rational part through criticism and transformation so as to truly realize the ideal of people being masters of the country under the circumstance of socialist democracy. Second, since the powers of government come from the people, the people have the right to ask for the government to serve them. This idea was used by the bourgeois revolutionists to make demands on the feudal government, which played a powerful role in fighting against the feudalism. However, the bourgeois government proper cannot truly fulfil the function of serving the people. Hence, the masses of working people can oppose it in the similar way according to the popular sovereignty theory, and assimilate its rational part during the process of establishing a government in which the proletariat are in power, so as to achieve a real people's government.

Engels once pointed out, "From the moment when the bourgeoisie emerged from feudal burgherdom, when this estate of the Middle Ages developed into a modern class, it was always and inevitably accompanied by its shadow, the proletariat."[4] The

[2] *Makesi Engesi quanji* [Marx and Engels Collected Works] (1962), Beijing: People's Publishing House, vol. 12, p. 733. cf. Marx, K. (1857) *Grundrisse: Foundations of the Critique of Political Economy (Rough Daft).*

[3] *Makesi Engesi xuanji* [Marx and Engels Selected Works] (1995), Beijing: People's Publishing House, vol. 3, p. 356. cf. Engels, F. (1880) *Socialism: Utopian and Scientific.*

[4] *Makesi Engesi xuanji* [Marx and Engels Selected Works] (1995), Beijing: People's Publishing House, vol. 3, p. 447. cf. Engels, F (1877) *Anti-Dühring.*

same is true of the requirement for sovereignty. Although the proletariat was the spearhead in the anti-feudalism bourgeois revolution, the capitalist system did not allow them to hold power but madc them even poorer. This cruel reality made them clearly recognize that "compared with the splendid promises of the philosophers, the social and political institutions born of the 'triumph of reason' were bitterly disappointing caricatures."[5] Therefore, they proposed their own idea of popular sovereignty, and the utopian socialists and communists became their ideal spokesmen. For example, during the period of the British Bourgeois Revolution, the Diggers represented by Gerald Winstanley believed that though the kingship was abolished, oppression still existed and the poor masses still could not see the sunlight of freedom. Hence, Winstanley advocated that the supreme power of a nation should belong to the people and he called on the people not to believe in kingship and governance of the parliament. He deemed that the political organization should be established on the principle of absolute democracy, all public officials must be elected by general election, and supreme legislative power, supreme executive power as well as the top leadership of economic activities should all belong to the parliament elected by general election. What's more, the people would make their own comment on law. Gabriel Bonnot de Mably, a French utopian communist, considered that every citizen should have the right to change his government since the people are the only source of supreme power. He advocated all the legislative powers be concentrated in the people's representative organs, all government officials be elected, the executive organ of the supreme political power be elected by the people's representative organs and the power of executive organ be restricted by legislative institution. In addition, François-Noël Babeuf, Robert Owen, Étienne Cabet and others were all advocates of popular sovereignty, so were the classical Marxists. They not only equipped themselves with the ideology of popular sovereignty to fight against the feudal autocracy as well as the bourgeois governments, but also fully absorbed the essence of popular sovereignty and transformed it into the theory of the popular sovereignty of the proletariat.

(2) The Embodiment of Popular Sovereignty Principle in the Constitutions of Countries

The popular sovereignty theory is the core concept of the Bourgeois democracy and one of the revolutionary theoretic bases for people to fight against the feudal monarchy and overthrow the feudal autocracy under the leadership of the bourgeoisie. Therefore, since the American *The Declaration of Independence* announced that human rights endowed by the Creator are unalienable in 1776, and *The Declaration of the Rights of the Man and of the Citizen* announced that "The Nation is essentially the source of all sovereignty" in 1789, western countries have generally acknowledged the popular sovereignty in theory and regarded it as the first principle of bourgeois democracy. Besides, the constitutions clearly stipulated that the sovereignty resides with the people. For instance, *the Constitution of the Fifth*

[5] *Makesi Engesi xuanji* [Marx and Engels Selected Works] (1995), Beijing: People's Publishing House, vol. 3, p. 607. cf. Engels, F. (1880) *Socialism: Utopian and Scientific*.

Republic of France stipulated the "sovereignty belongs to the people"; *The Constitution of Japan* in 1964 declared that "This is proclaimed that sovereign power resides with the people"; *The Basic Law for the Federal Republic of Germany* stipulated that sovereignty belongs to the people, etc. However, these written stipulations do not mean that the people have already enjoyed the right of being masters of their countries in the actual political practices of modern capitalist countries.

However, in the constitutions in socialist countries, there are no such regulations of sovereignty belonging to the people as in the capitalist constitutions, but the principle that "all power belongs to the people." So, what is the relationship between the notion that "all power belongs to the people" and popular sovereignty? In my opinion, "all power belongs to the people" is a creative application and development of the popular sovereignty principle based on the critical inheritance of the bourgeois democratic ideas when the proletariat established its regime. Hence, the essence of "all power belongs to the people" implies that sovereignty is in the hands of the people.

Firstly, Let's look at the attitudes of the classical Marxist writers towards popular sovereignty. Engels pointed out, modern socialism "in its theoretical form, originally appears ostensibly as a more logical extension of the principles laid down by the great French philosophers of the 18th century."[6] And popular sovereignty is one of the principles for the progress and development of the modern socialism. In fact, Marx once used the ideology of popular sovereignty as a weapon against the feudal despotism in criticizing Hegel's philosophy of monarchical sovereignty. He said "The sovereignty of the people is not derived from the sovereignty of the king but the basis of it."[7] When he referred to the rights of the national parliament of Germany, he wrote: "The National Assembly, as such, has no rights; the people has merely entrusted it with the defense of its own rights. If the Assembly does not act in accordance with the mandate it has received, then this mandate lapses. The people then takes the stage itself and acts on its own authority .... If the Crown makes a counter-revolution, the people has the right to reply with a revolution."[8] Engels used to quote the expression of Rousseau about popular sovereignty in an affirmative tone as he talked about the dialectics: "It is an incontestable fact, and the fundamental principle of all public law, that the peoples set up their chieftains to safeguard their liberty and not to enslave them." And from this he drew a conclusion: "... before the despot all are equal—equally ciphers."[9] The above fully indicate the attitude of the founders of Marxism towards popular sovereignty.

After Marx and Engels, Lenin also used the theory of popular sovereignty in his revolutionary struggle against feudal despotism. In the outline of *Three Constitutions*

[6] *Makesi Engesi xuanji* [Marx and Engels Selected Works] (1995), Beijing: People's Publishing House, vol. 3, p. 119. cf. Engels, F. (1880) *Socialism: Utopian and Scientific*.

[7] *Makesi Engesi quanji* [Marx and Engels Collected Works] (1956), Beijing: People's Publishing House, vol. 1, p. 279. cf. Marx, K. (1843) *Critique of Hegel's Philosophy of Right*.

[8] *Makesi Engesi quanji* [Marx and Engels Collected Works] (1961), Beijing: People's Publishing House, vol. 6, p. 305. cf. Marx, K. (1849) Speech at The Trial of the Rhenish District Committee of Democrats.

[9] *Makesi Engesi xuanji* [Marx and Engels Selected Works] (1995), Beijing: People's Publishing House, vol. 3, p. 482. cf. Engels, F. (1877) *Anti-Dühring*.

or Three Systems of Government, Lenin discussed the significance of the democratic republic and pointed out: "(1) No independent power for either the police or the officials, and they are completely subordinate to the people; (2) No privileges for either the capitalists or landlords; (3) All power—wholly, completely and indivisibly—in the hands of the whole people."[10] Here, Lenin clearly stated the nature of democratic republic, i.e. "All power is completely in the hands of the whole people", which became a sharp weapon for Lenin to oppose the Czarist absolutism and also a creative development for popular sovereignty theory.

The attitudes of the classical Marxist writers towards the popular sovereignty indicated that they did not totally discard it, but that they transformed, utilized and developed it.

Secondly, to observe from the practice of the political power construction in socialist countries, the socialist state power, like any other state powers, also faces such issues as the ownership of the supreme power and the relationship between the government and the people, which are the key issues to be solved for socialist democracy. In fact, the Paris Commune, the first dictatorship of the proletariat, already settled these problems effectively and provided experience for later construction of socialist political power. After the victory of the armed uprising, the Paris proletariat established the Commune Council, which controlled both the executive and legislative functions, by universal suffrage. It was stipulated that councillors should be responsible to voters and that electors have the right to recall the elected at any time; all the public servants should be paid for the same wages as other workers regardless of positions.[11] These measures ensured that supreme power belonged to the proletariat of the Paris Commune and secured the correct relationship between the government and the people so as to prevent the public servants transforming from "the servants of the people" into "the masters of the people". It was based on the summary of the Paris Commune experience that Marx and Engels advanced to establish a people's government in which workers were absolute masters and public servants should be responsible for the society after the victory of the proletarian revolution. Just like the Paris Commune, the relationship between this type of government and the people should be a relationship between "civil servant" and "social master." It fully demonstrated that the core of the popular sovereignty theory is that the supreme power belongs to the people and the relationship between the people and the government should be a relationship between client and trustee. Obviously, the popular sovereignty theories of capitalist enlightenment thinkers became the basic democratic principle of the socialist regimes after they had been modified and utilized by the classical Marxist writers from their generalization in the process of the proletarian political power construction.

Thirdly, considering the relationship between sovereignty and state power, I think the state power of a country contains various aspects. Vertically, there are the highest

[10] *Liening quanji* [Lenin Collected Works] (1959), Beijing: People's Publishing House, vol. 8, p. 524. cf. Lenin, V. (1905) 'Three Constitutions or Three Systems of Government'.

[11] *Makesi Engesi xuanji* [Marx and Engels Selected Works] (1995), Beijing: People's Publishing House, vol. 2, p. 13. cf. Marx, K. (1871) *The Civil War in France.*

state power, central state power and local state power; horizontally, there are legislative power, executive power and judicial power. What is the relationship between them? I believe that the supreme power of a country is the sovereignty that is a generalization or aggregation of the general powers of a state, while the general powers are derived from the sovereignty. Since "all the power belongs to the people", it necessarily follows that the supreme power of a state belongs to the people. It is ridiculous to admit that "all power belongs to the people", but object to the popular sovereignty principle. If the people do not have the supreme power, how can they have all the powers of the state? However, some scholar as C. scharf considered that the popular sovereignty and the state power are considered contradictory. "History reveals that the power of the state has always been used to exploit and repress the majority of the people."[12] However, it is only a result of the divorce between the sovereignty of the people and the power of the state in the class exploiting countries. In the socialist countries, "The executive organs of government are married to the assemblies of popular representation, forming the centerpiece of the new 'socialist democracy'. In this way, it becomes theoretically possible to strengthen both state power and popular sovereignty simultaneously."[13] Hence, the two are fundamentally consistent in the socialist countries.

3.1.2 Political Participation: Realization of Popular Sovereignty

If the substantial difference between democratic politics and autocratic politics in terms of the source of state power is whether the state power is to satisfy the general will and interests of the society or those of the minority or even some individuals, the establishment of the popular sovereignty principle makes the difference more prominent and provides a fundamental guiding principle for democratic politics. However, the principle itself does not produce objective practical effectiveness. The popular sovereignty principle relies on various forms and measures. Although "people being masters" involves various aspects of social life such as politics, economy and culture, for democratic politics, the so-called popular sovereignty means the will and interests of the majority play a leading role in the political life of a country. Then, how can the will and interests of the majority be reflected and realized in the political life of a country? The fundamental way to address this question is to achieve universal

[12] Scharf, C. (1988) *Minzhu deguo de zhengzhi yu biange* [Politics and Change in East Germany], trans. Qin G., Beijing: Chunqiu chubanshe [Spring and Autumn Publishing House], pp. 37–38. cf. Scharf, C. (1984/2019) *Politics and Change in East Germany*, New York: Routledge, p. 36.

[13] Scharf, C. (1988) *Minzhu deguo de zhengzhi yu biange* [Politics and Change in East Germany], trans. Qin G., Beijing: Chunqiu chubanshe [Spring and Autumn Publishing House], p. 38. cf. Scharf, C. (1984/2019) *Politics and Change in East Germany*, New York: Routledge, p. 36.

political participation of all citizens. In this sense, we consider that political participation is a basic approach to achieve the popular sovereignty, which fundamentally settles the question of whether state power originates from the people.

Political participation means that the citizens directly and indirectly decide or influence the state policies and supervise the activities of the state organs and their staff members through various ways. Its main features are as follows: first, political participation is an independent political behavior chosen by a citizen himself through his own analysis and judgment. Citizens can either express the same opinions and take the same political actions on the same issues, or voice different views and choose different political actions. Second, political participation is a self-conscious political behavior in which a citizen participates actively and voluntarily as a master. In other words, it is "I want to participate in" rather than "I am required to participate in". Third, political participation is a legitimate political behavior, which determines and influences the political process of the country within the law, aiming to make the national policies meet the interests and will of the people to the maximum extent.

In the western political science, Aristotle, Rousseau and John Stuart Mill all investigated political participation. Just like some scholars point out, "Participation is a key concept in both theoretical and empirical studies. It plays an extremely important role in the analysis of democracy."[14] Modern western scholars have continued to focus on the role and function, the pattern, and the effect of political participation. For instance, Huntington regarded broad political participation as one of the three most basic elements of political modernization. He argued that citizens in all the modern countries are already involved in and directly affected by various political affairs. Hence, broad participation in politics "may enhance control of the government by the people."[15] Sheldon A. Eliason pointed out, "One of the foundations of democratic politics in northern European countries is the active participation of citizens in the political decision-making processes."[16] Some other scholars have analyzed the functions of political participation in the aspects of its instrumental, developmental and communicative natures. The instrumental nature means that the aim of participation is to promote or to defend the rights of the participants. Whether people participate or not will depend on their assessment of the expected benefits and costs as well as on their own power to achieve their goals; The developmental nature means that the political participation will improve the general moral, social and political awareness of the participants; And the communicative nature means that political participation

[14] Miller, D. and Bogdanor, V. (eds) (1992) *The Blackwell Encyclopedia of Political Science*, New York: Wiley-Blackwell, p. 563.

[15] Huntington, S. (1988) *Biange shehui zhong de zhengzhi zhixu* [Political Order in Changing Societies], trans. Li S. P., Hua Xia Publishing House, p. 35. cf. Huntington, S. (1968) *Political Order in Changing Societies*, New Haven: Yale University Press, p. 35.

[16] Wisti, F. (ed.) (1990) *Beioushi minzhu* [Nordic Democracy], trans. Zhao, Z. Q. et al., Beijing: China Social Sciences Press, p. 121.

can contribute to opinion exchange and the formation and protection of the public interest.[17]

Political participation also occupies an important place in the Marxist democratic theories. Marx refuted Hegel's view that direct participation by all in the deliberation of and deciding on political matters of general concern admits the democratic element without any rational form into the organism of the state, and pointed out, "The democratic element should be, rather, the actual element that acquires its rational form in the whole organism of the state."[18] The reason is that only when all the citizens have the right to directly participate in the state affairs can the "rational form" of the state system be truly established, otherwise, the extremely irrational content will be included in the rational form, like bourgeois representative democracy. Therefore, Marx attached great importance to the direct participation of the people in state political life. He said, "Posed correctly, the question is simply this: Does a people have the right to give itself a new constitution? The answer must be an unqualified 'yes!' because the constitution becomes a practical illusion the moment it ceases to be a true expression of the people's will."[19] With the strengthening of the socialist democracy and the construction of the legal system during the current stage of development in China, people have become more and more aware of the importance of the political participation. Wang Zhenhai, a Chinese scholar even affirmed, "The hope of democracy is in the vitality of social individuals, i.e. the number and quality of enthusiasts and participants for democracy. In general, the more participants there are and the higher quality they are, the more developed the democracy is. Therefore, the key to democracy development lies in expanding the number of participants in democracy."[20]

However, one thing must be clarified. Although political participation is extremely important, its realization must be based and premised on popular sovereignty. If someone radically negates popular sovereignty but pursues the monarchical sovereignty instead, then there is no political participation at all. Or even if popular sovereignty is superficially acknowledged but in fact the sovereignty only belongs to the minority of property holders, it is similarly impossible to have authentic political participation. Thus, we can say that popular sovereignty is the premise and basis of political participation, and political participation is the fundamental way to realize popular sovereignty.

In political practice, in all countries, there are two forms of political participation: direct and indirect. The former includes popular initiative, referendum and the later includes representative systems, etc. For instance, political participation in the

---

[17] Yamaguchi, Y. (1991) *Zhengzhi tizhi* [Political System], trans. Han, T. Y., Beijing: The Economic Daily Press, pp. 62–63; cf. Miller, D. and Bogdanor, V. (eds) (1992) *The Blackwell Encyclopedia of Political Science*, New York: Wiley-Blackwell, p. 564.

[18] *Makesi Engesi quanji* [Marx and Engels Collected Works] (1956), Beijing: People's Publishing House, vol. 1, pp. 389–390. cf. Marx, K. (1843) *Critique of Hegel's Philosophy of Right*.

[19] *Makesi Engesi quanji* [Marx and Engels Collected Works] (1956), Beijing: People's Publishing House, vol. 1, p. 316. cf. Marx, K. (1843) *Critique of Hegel's Philosophy of Right*.

[20] Wang, Z. H. (1989) *Minzhu yu zhongguoren* [Democracy and Chinese], Beijing: China Radio Film & TV Press, p. 75.

northern European countries mainly covers two important aspects. One is the activity of individuals, which more or less directly influences the candidates and behaviors of the government, and the other is the collective political activities of interest groups or other organizations in the society, which mostly affect the government indirectly.[21] Due to subjective and objective factors, people's political participation in modern countries is mainly in the indirect form. There are two ways of indirect participation, i.e. voting and supervision. Karl Marx noted, "The vote is the actual relation of actual civil society to the civil society of the legislature, to the representative element. In other words, the vote is the immediate, the direct, the existing and not simply imagined relation of civil society to the political state. It therefore goes without saying that the vote is the chief political interest of actual civil society. In unrestricted suffrage, both active and passive, civil society has actually raised itself for the first time to an abstraction of itself, to political existence as its true universal and essential existence."[22] That is to say, it is only in the thorough unlimited election system that the citizens can participate in the political life in the country, so that the state power is produced in accordance with the social general interests, and that the officials become public servants. Of course, the political form a country adopts at a certain historical period is supposed to be determined by the specific historical conditions and the balance of class forces in different countries, not decided by people's subjective assumptions. For example, Rousseau, a bourgeois enlightenment scholar, while championing the popular sovereignty, also discussed in depth the forms to achieve it. However, the forms of political participation he proposed finally became fantasy under various historical restrictions.

Here, I will make a brief comment on the "public participation system."[23] As aforesaid, citizens in modern countries participate in politics mainly through indirect forms. However, many western scholars have recently called for direct participation in their works. For example, in the United States, a country with vast territory and large population, some scholars also call for the public participation system with direct participation as its core. The guiding principle of public participation is: People whose lives are affected by a certain decision should be involved in the process of such a decision-making. And people's direct participation in the activities of initiative, referendum and recall enables the political system to be more responsive to the needs of the people. In their view, with the progress of science and technology, revolutionary changes have taken place in communication tools, and the knowledge and political literacy of voters have been greatly improved with the advent of universal education, so that voters can immediately know what the representatives know by sharing information in an instant. Under such conditions, it is relatively

---

[21] Wisti, F. (ed.) (1990) *Beioushi Minzhu* [Nordic Democracy], trans. Zhao, Z., Beijing: China Social Sciences Press, p. 121.

[22] *Makesi Engesi quanji* [Marx and Engels Collected Works] (1956), Beijing, People's Publishing House, vol. 1, p. 396. cf. Marx, K. (1843) *Critique of Hegel's Philosophy of Right*.

[23] Cf. Pan, H. F. (1987) *Dangdai shijie zhengzhi sichao* [Contemporary World Political Thoughts], Harbin: Heilongjiang People's Publishing House, pp. 36–39.

simple to practice public participation if the administrative units could be divided into smaller ones.

In my view, the rise of the democratic idea of public participation in the western countries is of great positive significance. This is reflected in the following two points. First, the western capitalist parliamentary system appears to be in crisis. In some developed capitalist countries in the contemporary western world, the power of some representative organs has been gradually transferred to the administrative organs. The representatives in the legislature find it increasingly difficult to know the will of the small constituencies they represent, and "the lobby groups" or "the political pressure groups" find it more and more hard to conduct intricate deals and bargains with the legislature. If these trends continue, the theory of parliamentarism as a political broker will go bankrupt, and thus necessary to combine law making directly by the legislature with law making directly by voters. Second, the bourgeois two-party system has shown sign of crisis. People feel unsatisfied with and distrustful of the two major bourgeois political parties that dominate the election and monopolize the legislature and other government organs, so they would like to participate in the affairs concerning their own lives and future, which is a reflection of people's political awakening and their dissatisfaction with the status quo.

Despite the positive aspects of the democratic ideas of public participation system discussed above, and the fact that quite a few western countries have attempted to implement the system in political practice, the propositions above can never be fully realized and will remain a formality to some extent because they are based on the privilege of capital.

3.1.3 Dilemma: Direct Democracy or Representative System?

Ever since the formation of popular sovereignty theory, there has been a dispute between the direct democracy and the representative system concerning the issue of how to achieve popular sovereignty. We mentioned the fact that there are two types of political participation: direct form and indirect form, and the political form that should be adopted in a country at a certain historical period depends on the objective social and historical conditions. However, we have neither made an in-depth discussion theoretically on such issues as the relationship between popular sovereignty and direct democracy and that between popular sovereignty and representative system, nor have we come up with our own ideas to eliminate people's misunderstandings and disputes on these issues. Then which one, direct democracy or indirect democracy, can better facilitate the realization of popular sovereignty?

(1) **Direct Democracy: The Ideal of Rousseau**

Generally, the direct democracy is a system of democracy in which citizens can, in person, participate in such activities as making laws, supervising the government and determining other state affairs. Just as I stated in the second chapter, the ancient

Greek city-state of Athens practiced a typical type of direct democracy. "The US Town Meeting in the 17th and 18th century offered us a recent example. The direct democracy still exist in places where the political units are small enough to practice the direct democracy, such as the parish meeting held in England and Wales with less than 30 residents, the town meeting held in those smaller cities and towns in Connecticut and Rhode island of New England in the United States, and the town meeting in the small towns in the five small states and sub-states of the east and middle of Switzerland."[24] Similarly, the initiatives and referendums practiced in some countries are all specific forms of direct democracy.

In intellectual history, there are quite a number of people advocating for direct democracy, among whom Rousseau, the French bourgeois Enlightenment scholar, is the most active in the discussion of this issue in detail. He argued, "Sovereignty cannot be represented for the same reason that it cannot be alienated; it consists essentially in the general will, and the will cannot be represented; it is itself or it is something else; there is no middle ground."[25] Therefore, Rousseau was an opponent of the representative system and an advocate of direct democracy. He argued for an ideal world of a small country with few people where each citizen has the right to directly participate in the discussion and decision-making of the political affairs of the government, and listed a series of the advantages of direct democracy: protecting the individual interests, ensuring the service of the government for citizens, making each man his own master in politics, improving people's political awareness, and strengthening the sense of social responsibility of an individual for his behaviour through the process of direct participation. In addition, Rousseau laid special emphasis on the importance of people's direct participation in enacting laws. He expected the territory and population of a country to be as small as possible so that everybody could represent himself and directly participate in the making of the laws. However, in Rousseau's theory, we cannot find the answer to how people could realize their legislative power. Therefore, his theory was called idealism or "rational democracy" by the Italian scholar Sardori. That is to say, the direct democracy is the most ideal form to achieve the true democracy, i.e. "the people being masters of the country".

It should be clarified that, in methodology, the idealistic democracy adopts its way of thinking about democracy from a rational point of view. And the question it tends to address is to find the ideal form of democracy from the definition and connotation of democracy as the point of departure. According to Lei Jingxuan, there are three major contents discussed in idealistic democracy: popular sovereignty, equality and autonomy. Among the three, the popular sovereignty is the basis of the whole framework, which affirms that the state power belongs to the people definitively by answering questions such as "what is democracy?" and "what is true democracy?"

---

[24] Miller, D. and Bogdanor, V. (eds) (1992). *The Blackwell Encyclopedia of Political Science*, New York: Wiley-Blackwell, p. 204.

[25] Rousseau, J. (1982) *Shehui qiyue lun* [The Theory of Social Contract], trans. He Z. W., Beijing: The Commercial Press, p. 116. cf. Dunn, S. (ed.) (2002) *The Social Contract and First and Second Discourses* by Jean-Jacques Rousseau, New Haven and London: Yale University Press, p. 221.

and then the conclusion can be naturally derived that the power should be held equally in the hands of each individual. Then, since each individual has equal power, there cannot be, and should not be a power above the people to govern them, thus leading to the natural conclusion of people's autonomy.[26] Therefore, the general tendency of this democratic thought is to arrive at the establishment of a form of direct democracy, which aims to eliminate the intermediary agent between the people and the power and seeks to establish a system in which people could directly control and exercise the power. In short, it pursues a democracy in which people could govern themselves.

Despite the fact that idealistic democracy, which concerns such abstract issues as its definition, connotation and ideal conditions, exerts great influence on the establishment of specific political systems, it has a fatal weakness as we have mentioned before, that is, it is not practicable. Aside from the constraints of location, population, traffic and quality of citizens, the practice of direct democracy still faces three other key weaknesses. The first is the trend of pan-politicization. People must participate in political activities regularly since the power is exercised by themselves. There is a conception of the popular sovereignty in the direct democracy that if you do not take the initiative to directly exercise power, others will do it for you, and thus become rulers of you, or, if others have the freedom to govern you, you are deprived of the freedom from not being governed. Then, everything is haunted by political life and people have to attend various political activities. Secondly, the direct democracy is prone to give rise to unrest and disorder. Since each individual has and can exercise power, and no authority above the people is acknowledged or allowed to issue orders, once conflicts and disputes arise among the people, no authority of arbitration and mediation would be accessible. If the two parties in conflict could not compromise, they might resort to violence, leading to unrest and disorder. Thirdly, the system of direct democracy may easily be turned into dictatorship. In a specific system, it is hard to create an effective approach to guarantee that everybody can participate in and exercise power. So, "in political life, the government and the people are a pair of opposites that are inevitably associated."[27] For this reason, Rousseau once stated, "There has never existed, and never will exist, a true democracy, in the strict sense of the term democracy. It is contrary to the natural order that the majority should govern and that the minority should be governed."[28] Here, we can find the inherent contradiction in Rousseau's theory: he opposes the representative system on the one hand, and holds that it is against the natural order for the many to govern the few on the other. In addition, there are still two questions: First, what does Rousseau's direct democracy really entail? and how can it be realized? Second, is there any inherent relationship between direct democracy and popular sovereignty? In other words, is direct democracy the only way to achieve popular sovereignty?

[26] Lei, J. X. (1989) *Xuanju zhidu* [Electoral System], Taipei: Taiwan Dongcha Press, p. 18.

[27] Lei, J. X. (1989) *Xuanju zhidu* [Electoral System], Taipei: Taiwan Dongcha Press, pp. 19–20.

[28] Rousseau, J. (1982) *Shehui qiyue lun* [The Theory of Social Contract], trans. He Z. W., Beijing: The Commercial Press, p. 88. cf. Dunn, S. (ed.) (2002) *The Social Contract and First and Second Discourses* by Jean-Jacques Rousseau, New Haven and London: Yale University Press, p. 201.

On the first question, so-called direct democracy for Rousseau does not require everyone to govern in person, but rather calls on the rulers to administer the country based on the "general will" of the people. In other words, direct democracy here only refers to the fact that the content and formation of the "general will" must result from people's personal involvement. The execution of the "general will", however, could be delegated to others. As Rousseau pointed out, "The laws being nothing but the declaration of the general will, it is clear that in their legislative capacity the people cannot be represented; but they can and should be represented in the executive power, which is only force applied to law."[29] Hence, the key of Rousseau's opposition to the representative system lies in the question: what is the relationship between the "general will" or the legislative power and the representative system? As for the second question, as we have already discussed above, what kind of political form a country will adopt for achieving the popular sovereignty cannot be necessarily deduced from the popular sovereignty principle itself. Actually, it is determined by the specific historical conditions and class power balance in different countries. Otherwise, why do all claim to advocate the popular sovereignty, but the forms they adopt to realize it are so varied in political practice? Emmanuel-Joseph Sieyes (known as Abbey Sieyes), an active advocate of the French Bourgeois Revolution, once fiercely attacked direct democracy though he championed the principle of popular sovereignty. On the eve of the French Revolution, Abby Sieyes addressed the national assembly: "An extremely harmful misconception is prevailing that people should not delegate to others whatever rights they are able to exercise themselves, and they believe that this is the principle that guarantees freedom. However, this is just like saying to someone who is sending a letter to Bordeaux that he should reserve the right to carry it himself in order to better guarantee freedom. Why? Because he can do it himself without entrusting it to a public facility that handles postal services. Who can admit such a clumsy idea is a true principle?"[30] Therefore, he believed it didn't make sense to say that direct democracy is the only way to achieve popular sovereignty.

(2) **General Will Cannot Be Represented: True or False?**

To understand why Rousseau opposes the representative system and to comment on his conception, we can only start with the "general will" and the relationship between the "general will" and the representative system. The "general will"[31] is the core concept in Rousseau's political and moral philosophy. Then, what is the "general will"? In Chapter 3 (Volume 2) of his book *The Social Contract*, titled "Whether the General Will Can Err", Rousseau pointed out, "There is often a great

---

[29] Rousseau, J. (1982) *Shehui qiyue lun* [The Theory of Social Contract], trans. He Z. W., Beijing: The Commercial Press, p. 118. cf. Dunn, S. (ed.) (2002) *The Social Contract and First and Second Discourses* by Jean-Jacques Rousseau, New Haven and London: Yale University Press, p. 222.

[30] Kawamura, M. (1934) *Zhijie minzhu zhengzhi* [Direct Democracy], Tokyo: Nippon Hyoron Sha Co. Ltd., p. 395.

[31] Miller, D. and Bogdanor, V. (eds) (1992) *The Blackwell Encyclopedia of Political Science*, New York: Wiley-Blackwell, p. 563.

deal of difference between the will of all and the general will; the latter regards only the common interest, while the former has regard to private interests, and is merely a sum of particular wills; but take away from these same wills the pluses and minuses which cancel one another, and the general will remain as the sum of the differences."[32] In Chapter 1 of Volume 5 titled "That The General Will Is Indestructible", he noted, "As long as a certain number of men consider themselves to be a single body, they have but one will, which relates to the common security and to the general welfare. In such a case all the forces of the State are vigorous and simple, and its principles are clear and luminous; it has no confused and conflicting interests; the common good is everywhere plainly clear and only good sense is required to perceive it."[33] From these two quotations, we can see that the so-called "will of all" refers to the "embroilments or conflicts of interests", which is a kind of will reflecting the specific, current, and private interest of individuals or small groups; while the "general will" indicates "the common interests" shared by people, which is an abstract will aiming at collective interests and focusing on the majority of people in the long run.

Therefore, we can draw a conclusion that is the most fundamental and most significant: "Will" is an abstract concept, but it contains tangible contents. That is to say, "will" is in fact a demand or a desire, which aims at the pursuit of various interests. Everyone has his own will which, as a kind of personal spiritual activity, cannot be represented, but when the will is manifested as an interest requirement or an interest desire, it can completely be represented by others. As previously mentioned, "Sovereignty" is the supreme power of a nation and "is composed of the common will" in an abstract sense, as Rousseau pointed out, but the concrete manifestation of the common will is actually the unanimous fundamental interest of the people. Hence, it is untenable to let one individual represent the "common will", which may lead to the imperiousness of representatives. However, "how does the common will come into being?" Undoubtedly, it is not a natural formation, but a result of the cancellation of positive and negative interests through communication and integration of the "embroilments or conflicts of interests". The essence of the representative system is that the unanimous fundamental interests are reached by the spokespersons (representatives) of various partial interests through expression and compromise. Hence, in my opinion, Rousseau's criticism of the representative system is flawed because he confused the common will with the process of its formation.

Two related questions have to be addressed. First, does the operation of the representative system imply the transfer of sovereignty? Rousseau pointed out,

[32] Rousseau, J. (1982) *Shehui qiyue lun* [The Theory of Social Contract], trans. He Z. W., Beijing: The Commercial Press, p. 39. cf. Dunn, S. (ed.) (2002) *The Social Contract and First and Second Discourses* by Jean-Jacques Rousseau, New Haven and London: Yale University Press, p. 172.

[33] Rousseau, J. (1982) *Shehui qiyue lun* [The Theory of Social Contract], trans. He Z. W., Beijing: The Commercial Press, p. 135. cf. Dunn, S. (ed.) (2002) *The Social Contract and First and Second Discourses* by Jean-Jacques Rousseau, New Haven and London: Yale University Press, p. 227.

"Sovereignty, being nothing but the exercise of the general will, can never be alienated, and that the sovereign power, which is in fact a collective being, can be represented only by itself; power indeed can be transmitted, but not will."[34] In other words, in Rousseau's opinion, sovereignty cannot be transferred and can only "be represented by the sovereign himself". If the representative system is implemented, it will inevitably lead to the transfer of sovereignty. Is that really the case? Generalization here is not posssible. That is to say, it is not simply a "yes" or "no" question but requires concrete analysis in the specific situations. In other words, since sovereignty is the supreme power of a nation, then the key to judge whether the representative system would transfer the sovereignty lies in whether people could exercise the ultimate power of control, that is, whether the supreme power of a nation is held by people in the end, so as to "ensure that the actions of the *pars principans* are in fact kept fully under the ultimate control of the sovereign body of the people."[35] In theory, implementing the representative system in a popular sovereignty state, "[people] only delegate and never alienate it [sovereignty], and thus... no legitimate ruler can ever enjoy a higher status than that of an official appointed by, and capable of being dismissed by, his subjects."[36] In this way, there is no transfer of sovereignty as long as the representatives or members of an assembly are elected and dismissed by people at any time.

Therefore, the reason why Rousseau opposes the representative system is that sovereignty for him is the enforcement of the general will, which is nontransferable. In addition, there are other important reasons, i.e. the drawbacks of the British Parliamentary System. As we know, The United Kingdom was once a nation that pursued "Parliamentary Supremacy", whose guiding principle is Locke's "parliamentary sovereignty". "If we say that Locke has idealized the British political system, under which all the legislative power is handed over to the Parliament, then Rousseau's attitude towards this was totally negative."[37] From the practice of the British parliament, Rousseau found that the parliament often did not represent the people, and he pointed out: "The English nation thinks that it is free, but is greatly mistaken, for it is so only during the election of members of Parliament; as soon as

---

[34] Rousseau, J. (1982) *Shehui qiyue lun* [The Theory of Social Contract], trans. He Z. W., Beijing: The Commercial Press, p. 135. cf. Dunn, S. (ed.) (2002) *The Social Contract and First and Second Discourses* by Jean-Jacques Rousseau, New Haven and London: Yale University Press, p. 170.

[35] Skinner, Q. (1989) *Xiandai zhengzhi sixiang de jichu* [The Foundations of Modern Political Thought], trans. Duan S. W., Beijing: Qiushi Chubanshe [Truth Seeking Publishing House], p. 66. cf. Skinner, Q. (1978) *The Foundations of Modern Political Thought: The Renaissance*, London: Cambridge University Press, p. 63.

[36] Skinner, Q. (1989) *Xiandai zhengzhi sixiang de jichu* [The Foundations of Modern Political Thought], trans. Duan S. W., Beijing: Qiushi Chubanshe [Truth Seeking Publishing House], p. 67. cf. Skinner, Q. (1978) *The Foundations of Modern Political Thought: The Renaissance*, London: Cambridge University Press, p. 65.

[37] Bernadiner, B. (1981) *Lusuo de shehui zhengzhi ahexue* [Social and Political Philosophy of Rousseau], trans. Jiao, S. A. & Che, M. Z., Beijing: China Social Sciences Press, p. 152.

they are elected, it is enslaved and counts for nothing."[38] Because Rousseau found, from the practice of the British parliament, that people didn't truly take over the ultimate power of control after the implementation of the representative system and that the popular sovereignty was actually turned into parliamentary sovereignty, he firmly opposed the representative system. However, I hold that Rousseau's way of thinking is one-sided in denying the representative system's fundamental value of existence just because of some flaws during its operation. The problem is that he focused on one point while ignoring the overall picture. Actually, the emergence of "parliamentary sovereignty" or the so-called transfer of sovereignty is not a necessary result of the representative system itself, but an artificial consequence brought about by those who utilize and transform the representative system. More specifically, it is the result of the British bourgeoisie that attempts to make parliament its battlefield for seizing the power from the feudal aristocracy during its revolution against them. Therefore, it is groundless to assume that the representative system will inevitably lead to the transfer of sovereignty. In this respect, the argument of Kawamura Yuusuke, a Japanese scholar, is worthy of reference:

> Only when the parliament reflects the general will can parliamentary sovereignty be treated as equal to popular sovereignty. But if the the general will which serves as the origin of sovereignty conflicts with parliament, the former should be given priority. Of course, the citizens needn't handle all things in person. However, when the so-called representatives can't represent the general will, people should still have control measures to express their own will. Although it is unnecessary for a citizen to bring a letter to Bordeaux in person, even if one wants to do this himself, he still needs to entrust a post office, then he is not a sovereign at all. When the parliament takes actions against his will, such as deciding whether the letter should be sent or what content should be written in it, he has no way to remedy the situation and can only obey. Under such a circumstance, he couldn't be called a sovereign.[39]

Then, how should one understand "the supreme organ of state power"? China's constitution stipulates all power of the state belongs to the people, that is, sovereignty is held by the people. But in the meantime, the constitution of China states the National People's Congress is the supreme organ of the state power. How should we explain this phenomenon? To my understanding, the three concepts of *sovereignty*, *sovereign* and *sovereign authority* are mutually related but distinct. "Sovereignty" refers to the supreme power of the state, a "sovereign" is the owner of the supreme power of the state, and "sovereign authority" indicates organizations or organs which engage in certain activities on behalf of the sovereign within limits. The sovereign authority, though relatively independent during the process of exercising certain powers, is not the sovereign, and the ultimate power of control is in the hands of the sovereign. That is to say, the same sovereign can choose and organize different sovereign authorities. Obviously, the National People's Congress, as the supreme organ of the state power, is the sovereign authority of China, while the sovereign

---

[38] Rousseau, J. (1982) *Shehui qiyue lun* [The Theory of Social Contract], trans. He Z. W., Beijing: The Commercial Press, p. 125. cf. Dunn, S. (ed.) (2002) *The Social Contract and First and Second Discourses* by Jean-Jacques Rousseau, New Haven and London: Yale University Press, p. 221.

[39] Kawamura, M. (1934) *Direct Democracy*, Tokyo: Nippon Hyoron Sha Co. Ltd., p. 397.

are the vast working people. So, under this political system in China, similarly, sovereignty transfer can definitely not be on the stage.

Second, is the "general will" the source of state power or the basis of state rule? Rousseau noted:

> The first and most important consequence of the principles established above is that the general will alone can direct the forces of the State according to the object of its founding, which is the common good; for if the opposition of private interests has rendered necessary the establishment of societies, it is the concord of these same interests that has rendered it possible. That which is common to these different interests forms the social bond; and unless there were some point in which all interests agree, no society could exist. Now, it is solely with regard to this common interest that the society should be governed.[40]

Rousseau's conclusion is correct in terms of the basic connotation and requirements of the popular sovereignty principle. Since the supreme state power belongs to people, the implementation of state power should be in accordance with the will and interests of the people. As mentioned above, the interests, will and demands of various groups or individuals are naturally different. If state power is exercised only in line with individual or partial interests, social conflicts will arise. Hence, it is perfectly right to govern the country with the guidance of people's "common interests" or "common will", i.e. the so-called "general will" as Rousseau proposed. As Georg Jelinek pointed out, the representative organ is subordinate to the people's will, which is the indispensable source of all power in the state.[41] However, from the traditional Liberals' perspective, the foundation of state rule is the "consent of the people" based on "contract", the so-called 'two Cs'. Leonard Trelawney Hobhouse commented that "the contract theory" though fictional, is following a right direction to seek the foundation of state rule from the people who constitute the state. But the problem is that the foundation of state rule is not "people's consent" on the basis of a "contract", but the "common will" of people who constitute the state. He holds that a nation is composed of individuals and cannot exist without individuals. Thus its overall interest is above that of individuals. All members of a nation will have their own particular interests and their individual will to express these interests. After numerous contradictions and offsetting, there remains a common interest shared by the majorities and "the common will" to express it. And this kind of "common will" is the foundation of state rule. He pointed out, "The function of the state then is to secure the common ends which recommend themselves to the general will and which cannot be secured without compulsion."[42]

---

[40] Rousseau, J. (1982) *Shehui qiyue lun* [The Theory of Social Contract], trans. He Z. W., Beijing: The Commercial Press, p. 35. cf. Dunn, S. (ed.) (2002) *The Social Contract and First and Second Discourses* by Jean-Jacques Rousseau, New Haven and London: Yale University Press, pp. 277–278.

[41] Cf. Mastellone, S. (1992) *Ouzhou zhengzhi sixiang shi: Cong shiwu shiji dao ershi shiji* [History of European Political Thoughts: from 15th Century to 20th Century], trans. Huang, H. G., Beijing: Social Sciences Academic Press, p. 449.

[42] Hobhouse, L. (1935) *Shehui jinhua yu zhengzhi xueshuo* [Social Evolution and Political Theory], trans. Liao K. S., Beijing: The Commercial Press, p. 215. cf. Hobhouse, L. (1911/1922) *Social Evolution and Political Theory*, New York: Columbia University Press, p. 196.

Since "general will" or "common will" is the foundation of state rule, such a position rooted in people's will and reliant upon people's interests still encounters two difficulties in political practice. One is its abstraction. The larger a population is, the more abstract their will and interests will be. This makes it more difficult to create an effective way to express their will and interests, and in the end they usually resort to the rulers' intuition and the ability of persuasion. The other is the inconsistency of the will and interests of the people. There can be numerous wills concerning the same issue and multiple interests that conflict and contradict with each other. Even if the rulers would really like to act in accordance with the people's wills and interests, they could only make choices among all the conflicting wills and interests. However, the establishment and operation of the representative system can solve these two problems. As mentioned before, members of the representative organs are generally representatives from various social classes and strata representing different interests, and their responsibility is to generalize, summarize and express the particular interests of the class and stratum they represent. Therefore, the activities of the representatives are the processes of reifying the people's will and interests. On the other hand, the essence of the representative system lies in a certain shared fundamental interest that can be formed through expression and compromise by the spokespersons (i.e. representatives) of various partial interests. As a result, the operation of the representative system can eliminate conflicts of interests to arrive at the "common will", though there are different wills and interests among people. Moreover, through legislative activities, representative organs will transform the "common will" into the will of the state, which fundamentally guides state rule and regulation of the state power operation.

(3) **Representative System: Compromise or Progress?**

We have mentioned that the representative system marked great progress in the history of world civilization from ancient democracy to modern democracy and it is not an overstatement to say that there is no democracy in a nation-state without the representative system. Robert A. Dahl once stated:

> Without a system of representation, effective popular participation in large-scale government was impossible.... Even if the idea of representation was not democratic in origin, it is no wonder that in the late eighteenth century, when advocates of popular government realized that representation might be joined with the democratic process to bring about democracy on the giant scale of an entire country, they saw this astounding new combination as among the greatest political inventions of all time.[43]

Therefore, the representative system should be understood as a compromise of the idealistic democracy, but it is an impetus to the democratic system in the progress of democracy.

Meanwhile, we have repeatedly stressed that whether a country today or in a different period of time should adopt the direct democracy or the indirect democracy with the representative system as its core in the process of realizing the popular

[43] Dahl, R. (1989) *Duoyuan zhuyi minzhu de kunjing: zizhi yu kongzhi* [(1982). *Dilemmas of Pluralist Democracy: Autonomy VS. Control*, New Haven and London: Yale University Press, p. 9.

sovereignty mainly depends on the objective historical conditions and the power relations between different classes. Therefore, I reckon that the key to determining the relationship between the representative system and popular sovereignty is to make clear whether the representative system is an impetus or an impediment to the conditions of achieving the popular sovereignty. Specifically, this issue can be analyzed from the following aspects.

First, let's start with the emergence of the representative system. For some western scholars, the representative system arises mainly due to the fact that "the huge territory and large population in contemporary and modern countries create great difficulties in the implementation of direct democracy."[44] This view, I think, is only half right, but it at least tells us that there is no better way to achieve the popular sovereignty than the representative system under these objective conditions in modern and contemporary times. In addition, the need for the class rule, consisting of both the revolutionary and anti-revolutionary aspects caused the rise of the representative system. The so-called revolutionary aspect indicates that the ruled and oppressed classes will attempt to take advantage of the representative system to overthrow the old regime and establish a new one, similar to how the representative system was established in the United Kingdom as discussed in Chapter Two. And the anti-revolutionary aspect refers to the fact that the emergence of exploiting class, after establishing its own regime, will suppress the oppressed classes through the control of the representative organs by means of limiting the status and role as well as the number of members of each institution. Therefore, from its emergence and process of establishment, the representative system is indeed an impetus to the realization of popular (i.e. bourgeois) sovereignty.

Similarly, the birth and establishment of the proletariat representative system resulted from objective historical conditions and the demands of the ruling class. While the former reason is not significantly different from that of the bourgeois representative system, the latter is. The reason why the proletariat need the representative system is to establish a country with the proletariat as the masters of the country so as to realize the interests, desires and requirements of the working people. The consistency of the fundamental interests of the working people with the purpose of the representative system provides possible conditions for the implementation of the system. Therefore, the need for class rule by the proletariat is to satisfy the feasibility and adequacy of the people being masters of the country. In this sense, we can draw the same conclusion that the emergence of the proletarian representative system promotes the realization of the popular sovereignty.

Second, whether the representative system is an impetus or an impediment to the realization of the popular sovereignty depends on the objective effects of its operation. If its operation truly guarantees the realization of the interests and desires of the people, then it is an impetus rather than an impediment. Since the bourgeois and the proletarian representative systems belong to two fundamentally different types, there must be fundamental differences in their class natures, class purposes and service

---

[44] Cf. Pan, H. F. et al. (eds) (1987) *Dangdai shijie zhengzhi sichao* [Contemporary World Political Thoughts], Harbin: Heilongjiang People's Publishing House, p. 17.

objects. The bourgeois representative system, due to the nature of its economic base and of the state power, determines that it can only be a significant approach to realization of the sovereignty of the propertied class. In a sense, it impedes the achievement of the sovereignty of the people (i.e. the masses of the working people). In contrast, the nature of the proletarian representative system determines that it is an important form to truly realize the majority of the working people as masters of the country. In other words, the proletarian representative system is, in essence, an impetus for popular sovereignty. The generalization put forth by Sa Mengwu, a Chinese scholar from Taiwan, is quite reasonable if we define the "people" here definitely as the broad masses of the working people. He said, "In order for a parliament to represent the will of the people, the members of the parliament and the people they represent must remain homogenous…. Since the representatives and the represented are homogenous, they surely have some common interests and identical propositions concerning some certain issues."[45] Otherwise, popular sovereignty can only be alienated. The reason why the bourgeois representative system impedes the achievement of the popular sovereignty of the working people is that the members of the bourgeois parliament and the broad masses of the working people are heterogeneous instead of homogenous. However, the proletarian representative system is just the opposite.

Third, although some western scholars have successively pointed out the existential crisis of the representative system, the aim of public participation they proposed is to correct and remedy the defects of the representative system rather than to abandon it completely. Further, both the direct democracy and the representative system are only different means, approaches and methods to achieve democracy, and that the combination of the two is the best system to realize popular sovereignty where there are not the conditions to fully implement direct democracy. Which system dominates for any given period mainly depends on the objective demands and historical conditions of the time. According to the present situation, we still have to take the representative system as the most appropriate form of democracy. Therefore, the representative system is and will be the major form for the realization of popular sovereignty at present and into the foreseeable future.

In conclusion, whether the representative system is an impetus or an impediment to the realization of popular sovereignty should be analyzed according to specific conditions. But there is a common rule: if the representatives are homogeneous with the voters, the representative system plays a progressive role; if heterogeneous, it will be an impediment.

[45] Sa, M. W. (1986) *Zhengzhi xue* [Political Science], Taipei: San Min Book Co., Ltd., pp. 168–169.

3.2 Capitalist Parliamentary System and Popular Sovereignty

Regardless of what comments people made on the representative system, the form of representative democracy is irreplaceable both in terms of social management and the development of democracy. This is because class rule in the class society cannot bypass the historical stage of the representative system before the realization of the direct democratic management of the society.

The emergence and development of the representative system in the capitalist countries has fully demonstrated that the representative system is not only the best political shell for the rule of the bourgeois states but also the only practical democratic form that adapts to the development needs of the modern nation states. So, how well does the capitalist parliamentary system function in the process of realizing the popular sovereignty? To this question we cannot answer in a general and simple way, as we have pointed out before. Rather, discussion of popular sovereignty with reference to the foundations and political practices of the capitalist parliamentary system is necessary.

3.2.1 Foundations of Capitalist Parliamentary System

The survival and development of any political system is fundamentally dependent on the given social and historical conditions, otherwise, a political system is just like a castle in the air, which not only does not change the social reality, but is also necessarily short-lived. In other words, the foundations of any political system fundamentally determines its actual operation, the same goes for the capitalist parliamentary system. Therefore, we should take its foundations of existence as the logical starting point if we want to investigate the impact of the capitalist parliamentary system on the realization of popular sovereignty. Although there are many social and historical conditions for the existence of the capitalist parliamentary system, they mainly fall into three aspects as follows.

(1) **Private Ownership of Capitalist Means of Production Is the Economic Foundation of Capitalist Parliamentary System**

The capitalist commodity economy not only hastened the appearance of a unified national market, the formation of nation states and the emergence of the representative system, but also is the root cause for stimulating the contradiction between the new productive forces and the old production relations, which eventually provoked the bourgeois revolution. One of the significant consequences of the bourgeois revolution was the complete elimination of feudal super-economic coercion and the creation of the social and historical conditions for the free development of the commodity economy out of control of any political power. Therefore, although the capitalist economy, like the slave and feudal ones, is an economy of private ownership, it differs operation. Under the condition of private ownership in slave and feudal societies, slave owners and slaves or feudal lords and serfs were openly unequal in their political, economic and social status due to the existence of personal and hereditary privileges. However, under the condition of capitalist private ownership, the economic operation was no longer subject to political manipulation, but dominated by the "invisible hand" of the law of value, and the principles of equivalent exchange and free competition in the commodity economy radically denied any possibility of economic privileges and formed a kind of superficial "equality" and "freedom" between workers and capitalists. In other words, the transformation of the mode of economic operation or the mode of exploitation of the exploiting class necessarily requires the adjustment of the form of state rule. In contrast with the outward exploitation in slave and feudal countries, which requires the corresponding overt form of rule, the capitalist countries require a covert form of rule in correspondence with their invisible means of exploitation. The capitalist parliamentary system is the covert political form that best reflects the free and equal relationship between wage labor and capital in the market. Under this system, workers enjoy gradually expanded universal suffrage, exercise their "natural rights" and become the masters of the country. Just as one is "free" to choose some certain capitalists by which he is exploited in the market, one is also "free" to elect some certain rulers from the bourgeois class by which he is ruled. Seemingly, the so-called human rights, equality, freedom and democracy are highly consistent here economically and politically. Therefore, from the economic point of view, the capitalist parliamentary system is the inevitable outcome of the socialized mass production on the basis of the capitalist private ownership. Moreover, the function of the economic basis of the capitalist private ownership is also reflected in different practices of the parliamentary system for the bourgeoisie at different historical stages.

As stated previously, the capitalist parliamentary system is actually a means of political rule adopted by the bourgeoisie to satisfy the needs of its economy. Lenin once insightfully remarked on the ruling methods of the bourgeois class. He noted:

> As a matter of fact, in every country the bourgeoisie inevitably devises two systems of rule, two methods of fighting for its interests and of maintaining its domination, and these methods at times succeed each other and at times are interwoven in various combinations. The first of these is the method of force, the method which rejects all concessions to the labour movement, the method of supporting all the old and obsolete institutions, the method of irreconcilably rejecting reforms.... The second is the method of "liberalism", of steps towards the development of political rights, towards reforms, concessions, and so forth.[46]

He also said:

> The bourgeoisie passes from one method to the other not because of the malicious intent of individuals, and not accidentally, but owing to the fundamentally contradictory nature of its own position. Normal capitalist society cannot develop successfully without a firmly

---

[46] *Liening xuanji* [Lenin Selected Works] (1995), Beijing: People's Publishing House, vol. 2, p. 276. cf. Lenin, V. (1910) Differences in the European Labour Movement.

> established representative system and without certain political rights for the population, which is bound to be distinguished by its relatively high "cultural" demands.[47]

The method of "liberalism" was mainly adopted by the bourgeoisie during the stage of liberal capitalism in the rising period of capitalism. As we know, the main feature of a liberal capitalist economy is free competition, which is reflected in the demand for political freedom, but during this period, feudal hierarchical privilege that hindered freedom and thus equality was inevitably demanded. Freedom and equality are rights expressed in law, while democracy is the form and guarantee for the realization of these rights. Therefore, freedom, equality, rights and democracy are the real needs of the bourgeoisie in the period of the liberal capitalism, but cannot simply regarded as deceptive slogans. Since the representative body is also known as the organ of public opinion, the parliamentary system, which embodies the bourgeois democracy, plays an important role in the realization of political rule, and exercises the legislative power to ensure people's freedom and equal rights through legislative activities. That is why Karl Marx and Frederick Engels called it the committee of managing the common affairs for the bourgeois class.

(2) The State Power of Bourgeois Dictatorship as the Political Basis of Capitalist Parliamentary System

The victory of the bourgeois revolution elated the bourgeoisie, for their economic strength rapidly increased. However, their political status was not immediately improved. Although the state power was established, consolidating it was extremely arduous task for the bourgeoisie. The new bourgeois regime needs not only to prevent return of feudal forces, but also to guard against the outbreak of the workers' and peasants' revolution. In addition, it has to train the outstanding talents of its own class for the rule and governance of the country at the same time. Fortunately, the capitalist parliamentary system provides the best way to solve these problems. In order to prevent restoration of feudal forces, it is not only necessary to unite all the forces that can be united to strengthen the anti-feudal allies, but also to establish a new system superior to the feudal one so as to attract people, and the capitalist parliamentary system successfully promotes people's solidarity to defeat the feudal forces in concerted effort through the system in which people can enjoy equal participation both formally and superficially. With regard to the workers' and peasants' revolution, democracy, freedom and equality advocated by the capitalist parliamentary system will not only result in a vague understanding among people, but also alleviate the contradictions between the bourgeoisie and the workers and peasants and paralyze their revolutionary morale through the propaganda that the parliament is a "representative organ for all people." As for cultivating bourgeois administrative talents, the parliament, proposed by Max Weber, is the training ground for political leaders. Therefore, the capitalist parliamentary system plays a very important role in consolidating the bourgeois regime. In other words, the state power of bourgeois

[47] *Liening xuanji* [Lenin Selected Works] (1995), Beijing: People's Publishing House, vol. 2, p. 276. cf. Lenin, V. (1910) Differences in the European Labour Movement.

dictatorship provides the political preconditions for the existence and development of the capitalist parliamentary system, and to some extent, the economic basis of the private ownership functions through the political basis of the bourgeois regime.

(3) **Theories of Democracy, Freedom, Equality and Human Rights Proposed by Bourgeois Enlightenment Scholars as Ideological Bases of Capitalist Parliamentary System.**

The principles of freedom and equality in the capitalist commodity economy are naturally reflected in people's political ideology. In order to meet the demands of the advent and development of the capitalist commodity economy, the bourgeois enlightenment scholars came up with theories of natural human rights and popular sovereignty, as well as slogans of liberty, equality and fraternity, and the founding plans of a democratic republic under the rule of law in the struggle against feudalism. These theories, slogans and founding plans not only encouraged the workers and peasants to participate in the revolutionary struggle of the bourgeoisie against feudalism and promoted the victory of the bourgeois revolution, but also made these concepts more popular among the people, thus forcing the bourgeoisie to establish a democratic system to guarantee the people's freedom, democracy and equality after victory. Therefore, the capitalist parliamentary system not only met the demand of realizing democracy in the nation-states, but also provided formal assurance of citizens' rights of equality and freedom through universal suffrage and political party system.

3.2.2 Popular Sovereignty Under Capitalist Parliamentary System

As stated before, after the victory of the bourgeois revolution, sovereignty in the people was stipulated in most subsequent constitutions, where the "divine rights" were completely denied by the "popular sovereignty" both in words and in institutions. However, the basis of existence for the capitalist parliamentary system fully indicated that the bourgeois revolution resulted from the capitalist commodity economy is not the final form of human emancipation because it fails to eliminate class antagonism and the private ownership of the means of production, but rather presupposes class antagonism and private ownership for its existence. Therefore, the bourgeois revolution at large is only "part of civil society emancipating itself and attaining general domination."[48] And its limitation determines that the capitalist parliamentary system has not achieved the real goal of democracy, i.e. people being masters of the country.

As mentioned before, although the bourgeois revolution freed the commodity economy from the control of political power and endowed it with the right of free

---

[48] *Makesi Engesi quanji* [Marx and Engels Collected Works] (1956), Beijing: People's Publishing House, vol. 1, p. 463. cf. Marx, K. (1843) Introduction to *Critique of Philosophy of Right.*

development, private ownership of the means of production still remains. The operation of capitalist private ownership is bound to result in the differentiation of social classes, some of which are deprived of the ownership of the means of production, thus losing their economic autonomy, and have to become the objects of exploitation by the classes that possess it. Based on the ownership of means of production, "Society as a whole is more and more splitting up into two great hostile camps, into two great classes directly facing each other—Bourgeoisie and Proletariat."[49] And so, the private ownership and the class antagonism that resulted from it will inevitably lead to new social inequality, which although markedly different from that of the feudal hierarchy in that the latter maintains the economic differences entirely through the political hierarchy while the former is the product of negating the feudal political privileges, they are identical in terms of permitting inequality. Therefore, the political equality of citizens advocated by the bourgeois class in the process of establishing the parliamentary system does not actually destroy the economic inequality. In other words, when the capitalist countries declare the non-political distinctions of birth, class, educational level and occupations and that everyone is an equal participant in popular sovereignty regardless of all these distinctions, they only eliminate the differences in form. Actually, the capitalist states are "far from abolishing these real distinctions, the state only exists on the presupposition of their existence".[50] So, the conflict between the formal political equality and the practical economic inequality is the new contradiction of capitalist private ownership. This contradiction is the root of disconnection between the ideal of popular sovereignty and the reality of inequality in capitalist countries.

Political power is closely related to the economic relations and always goes to the economically dominant class, whose primary task is to protect the fundamental interests of its own and suppress the resistance of the oppressed class, as is the case in capitalist countries. The bourgeoisie ruthlessly exploit the surplus value of the employed workers by way of appropriating the private ownership of the means of production and seizing the vast majority of the social property for free, which enables them to manipulate politics with money. Frederick Engels pointed out, "...the power of the bourgeoisie is entirely derived from money, so they have to make money the only criterion for measuring people's legislative capacity if they want to obtain the political power. And they must integrate all the feudal privileges and political monopolies of the past dynasties into one great monetary privilege and monopoly. That is why the political rule of the bourgeoisie is under the cloak of liberalism."[51] Therefore, even though the bourgeoisie took measures to eliminate the distinctions among all social classes and seemingly attempted to establish universal political equality, their fundamental purpose is to replace all the personal and hereditary privileges in

[49] *Makesi Engesi xuanji* [Marx and Engels Selected Works] (1995), Beijing: People's Publishing House, vol. 3, p. 213. cf. Marx. K and Engels, F. (1848) *Manifesto of the Communist Party*.

[50] *Makesi Engesi quanji* [Marx and Engels Collected Works] (1956), Beijing: People's Publishing House, vol. 1, p. 427. cf. Marx, K. (1844) 'On the Jewish Question'.

[51] *Makesi Engesi quanji* [Marx and Engels Collected Works] (1957), Beijing: People's Publishing House, vol. 2, p. 647. cf. Engels, F. (1846) *The Condition of Germany*.

the past with money privilege, that is to say, "money, the alienated empty abstraction of property, has become the ruler of the world, and man is thus no longer a slave to man, but a slave to things."[52] By making full use of their economic advantage, the bourgeoisie are in the position to manipulate elections and politics, and ultimately control the state power. Therefore, Engels believed that the political equality advertised by the bourgeoisie "is the equality under the premise of inequality between the rich and the poor, that is, the equality limited within the scope of the current major inequality. In brief, inequality is simply distorted into equality."[53] In capitalist countries, the interest of the state, nominally as the real interest of the people, is only a kind of formal existence and becomes a decoration, a formality and condiment for people's lives. It is obvious that as long as the bourgeoisie still takes the protection of private ownership as their fundamental purpose, the capitalist parliamentary system can hardly get rid of the manipulation of property, and it can only achieve the sovereignty of man of property. However, for the vast majority of laborers, popular sovereignty is simply an ideal and abstract principle. Thus we conclude that popular sovereignty under the capitalist parliamentary system is only the sovereignty of capital or "the sovereignty of dollar", and the capitalist parliamentary system is by no means an institution representing the will of the people, but only an easy tool maneuvered by the bourgeoisie. The specific manifestations are as follows:

Firstly, the vast majority of members of the capitalist parliament are industrial and commercial capitalists, big ranchers, bankers, lawyers, politicians, etc. and few of them are from working people. Even though the constitutions and laws of capitalist countries stipulate that all citizens enjoy the rights to vote and stand for election, high campaign expenses and restrictions on property qualifications exclude the vast majority of citizens from the ranks of parliamentarians, and thus capital has become the only ladder to enter the parliament. In the United States, "…candidates who are the bigger spenders may not always win but they usually do, as has been the case over the last fifteen years in more than 80 percent of House and Senate races…better-funded candidates won 75 percent of the time."[54] This, in fact, determines the composition and nature of the parliament. For example, almost half of the representatives and nearly 1/3 of the senators in the 96th, 97th, 98th U. S. Congress (1979–1986) were lawyers or from the legal profession, and the number from the business and banking community were also substantial, with close to 1/3 in each chamber. In the United States, the major clients of lawyers are corporations and many agents of the corporations.

> The members of the congress from the above-mentioned circles account for 4/5 of all senators and 3/4 of all representatives. And those from agriculture (ranchers), education, the press and other sectors are also leading figures in their fields (about 1/4 of the representatives and

[52] *Makesi Engesi quanji* [Marx and Engels Collected Works] (1956), Beijing: People's Publishing House, vol. 1, p. 664. cf. Engels, F. (1844) *The Condition of England.*

[53] *Makesi Engesi quanji* [Marx and Engels Collected Works] (1957), Beijing: People's Publishing House, vol. 2, p. 648. cf. Engels, F. (1846) *The Condition of Germany.*

[54] Parenti, M. (1991) *Meiguo de minzhu* [American Democracy], trans. Han J. Z et al., Zhengzhou: Henan People's Publishing House, p. 215. cf. Parenti, M. (1974/2011) *Democracy for the Few*, Wadsworth: Cengage Learning, p. 186.

> 1/5 of the senators). But members from the working class are as few as morning stars. The composition signified that the congress is just an institution representing the interests of the bourgeoisie.[55]

For another example, between 1971 and 1972, there were 627 members in the British House of Commons, among whom there were 375 serving or concurrently serving as chairman of the board, 870 board members, 194 managers, 101 lawyers, and 154 journalists, let alone the House of Lords, where members were often hereditary aristocrats appointed by the monarch. How could such a parliament of rich tycoons, apart from defending the interests of their own and their bosses, work out a legislation that benefits the working people?

Secondly, the capitalist parliamentary system is closely related to the party system, and the majority of the seats in the parliament are held by the bourgeois parties. Lenin pointed out, "This so-called bipartisan system prevailing in America and Britain has been one of the most powerful means of preventing the rise of an independent working-class, i.e., genuinely socialist, party."[56] In the United States, the Democratic Party and the Republican Party not only established corresponding party organizations in both Houses of the Congress, but also actually manipulate the legislative activities, personnel appointment and removal, and congressional election in both Houses. Sometimes the two parties do quarrel with each other in Congress, which is only a reflection of the conflicts between the different capitalist groups representing different interests, but they never quarrel on behalf of the interests of the working people.

Thirdly, since the voters have no right to recall the members of the parliament, the working people have no way to effectively supervise them. As mentioned above, the capitalist parliamentary system generally upholds the principle of representing all the people of the nation, so members of parliament are generally not responsible to the voters in their constituencies. In turn, voters have no right to recall unsatisfactory members. Even if a member is to be removed from parliament, the deposing process is undertaken by the propertied class. In the United States, for example, the removal of any member of either House shall be approved by over 2/3 majority of that house. In countries with a cabinet system, such as Britain and Japan, presidents or prime ministers can announce the dissolution of the parliament once unsatisfied. Therefore, the parliament can only be manipulated by the monopoly bourgeoisie.

One more question must be addressed. Since, in capitalist countries, it is the propertied class who possess sovereignty, then why do the majority of working people still enjoy some partial democratic rights? The answer mainly involves two aspects. The first concerns the relationship between state power and civil rights. Although people have different understandings of the relationship between the two, generally, civil rights are the goal of state power, and state power is the guarantee of civil rights. Since sovereignty is the highest power of the state, under the condition

[55] Li, D. K. (1990) *Meiguo zhengfu he Meiguo zhengzhi* [American Government and American Politics], Beijing: China social Sciences Press, p. 334.

[56] *Liening quanji* [Lenin Collected Works] (1959), Beijing: People's Publishing House, vol. 18, p. 398. cf. Lenin, V. (1912) The Results and Significance of the U.S. Presidential Elections.

of capitalist private ownership, the so-called sovereignty of the propertied implies that the property owners control the highest power of the state. Therefore, under such a power structure, even if the majority of citizens are legally endowed with certain rights, these kinds of legal rights are difficult to be realized because they are not guaranteed by the state power which the majority of citizens do not have. The second concerns the law of mutual change of quality and quantity between state sovereignty and civil rights. There exists a corresponding relationship between power and rights. In a sense, sovereignty is the sum of a certain amount of power and a certain amount of rights. Although power is a means to obtain rights in terms of their relationship, different changes between the two will lead to different political structures. In other words, if the amount of civil rights accounts for only a small part of the total sovereignty, the bourgeois sovereignty would not be threatened of course, instead, the class contradictions and conflicts could be appeased, thus consolidating the regime of the bourgeoisie. That is why limited civil rights are allowed to exist. Nevertheless, if the amount of civil rights takes up a dominant part in the total amount of the bourgeois sovereignty, a qualitative change will result, which the bourgeoisie will absolutely not allow to happen. As far as the current situations of modern capitalist countries are concerned, the whole state power is put under control of the bourgeoisie because the private ownership occupies a fundamental position in the national political power, and it is also completely understandable that citizens are endowed with certain rights by the bourgeois countries in the form of law due to the changes in the balance of class power under the struggle of the vast majority of the working people.

In addition, after hundreds of years of development, the capitalist parliamentary system has increasingly improved in terms of its system, procedure and form. This perfected system in form, on the one hand, consolidates the sovereignty of the propertied, and at the same time, provides certain favorable conditions for the vast majority of working people participating in politics; on the other hand, it conceals the essence that the propertied class monopolizes the state sovereignty through the superficial illusion of democracy, in which the rule of the bourgeoisie can be maintained.

3.3 Socialist People's Representative System and Popular Sovereignty

In *The Communist Manifesto*, Marx and Engels pointed out, "The development of Modern Industry, therefore, cuts from under its feet the very foundation on which the bourgeoisie produces and appropriates products. What the bourgeoisie therefore produces, above all, are its own grave-diggers. Its fall and the victory of the proletariat are equally inevitable."[57] The victory of the proletarian revolution and the establishment of proletarian regime have proven the prophecy of Marx and Engels.

[57] *Makesi Engesi xuanji* [Marx and Engels Selected Works] (1995), Beijing: People's Publishing House, vol. 1, p. 284. cf. Mark, K. and Engels, F. (1848) *Manifesto of the Communist Party.*

Then what impact did these earthshaking changes bring to the representative system and popular sovereignty?

3.3.1 Foundations of Socialist People's Representative System

Generally speaking, although the socialist people's representative system and the capitalist parliamentary system are different in nature, they share something identical or similar in form. So, why do similar forms lead to opposite results? This must be also analyzed from the foundations of the establishment and operation of the socialist people's representative system.

(1) **Socialist Public Ownership of Means of Production as the Economic Foundation of the Socialist People's Representative System**

According to the classical Marxist writers, the most fundamental prerequisite for establishment of a new proletarian democratic system is to abolish private ownership of the means of production and establish a socialist public one. To be specific, once the majority of the working people have obtained the means of production in society, they have also mastered their independent rights to labor, thus ending the long standing situation in history where the working people are separated from means of production, as well as establishing an equal relationship in the economic field and the status of the broad masses of the people as masters of the country. Therefore, on the basis of socialist public ownership, it is also imperative to build a corresponding political superstructure. Likewise, the master status of the broad masses and their all-round equal relationship in the economic field must be reflected in the political field. In other words, the socialist public ownership, by eradicating economic inequality caused by the private ownership, succeeded in eliminating political inequality. Therefore, establishing a political system with the realization of the people being masters as its fundamental content is bound to become the basic requirement of the socialist public ownership and the broad masses of the people. Only in this way can the general will of the broad masses be expressed in the form of the state will, so that their fundamental interests could be effectively protected rather than infringed by political forces. As Lenin pointed out, "But while being based on economics, socialism cannot be reduced to economics alone. A foundation—socialist production—is essential for the abolition of national oppression, but this foundation must also carry a democratically organized state, a democratic army, etc."[58] Moreover, under public ownership, by extending the democratic rights of the working people obtained as a result of their political emancipation to the economic field, the economic democracy, which is impossible to achieve under the system of exploitation, has been realized. Therefore, the establishment of socialist public ownership and the development of the socialist economy not only unify both the economic and

[58] *Liening quanji* [Lenin Collected Works] (1958), Beijing: People's Publishing House, vol. 22, p. 319. cf. Lenin, V. (1916) 'The Discussion on Self-Determination Summed Up'.

political rights of the working people, but also provide necessary material conditions to ensure the realization of these rights. In a certain sense, the broad masses of the people can jointly possess the means of production, and enjoy different rights of its ownership and control, which is not only the fundamental point for the growth of a socialist democratic country with the core content of the people as masters of the country, but also for the development of the socialist democracy with the socialist people's representative system as the core.

However, although the socialist public ownership provides a decisive basis for the masses of people to become the masters of the country through the socialist people's representative system, its superiority has not been given full play with the constraints of the traditional economic system. Under the traditional economic mode, the socialist public ownership is mainly practiced in the form of state ownership. Although state ownership has played an irreplaceable role in the socialist transformation of the private ownership of means of production, it is sure to have the following negative effects that cannot be ignored on the long-term development of the socialist economy and politics. First, under state ownership, there is no direct ownership between the members of society and the means of production because the state possesses the means of production fully on behalf of all the people. "This objectively results in a phenomenon of 'absence' of the subject of ownership and an antinomy of the possession of the means of production by everyone and direct possession by no one."[59] Second, on the basis of the state ownership, a highly centralized economic system must be implemented, where the state interferes in all economic activities. Consequently, a highly centralized economic system will definitely lead to a highly centralized political system. In this way, the state ownership not only fails to give full play to the great superiority of public ownership, but also fails to really ensure the status of people as masters of the country. So, people are still dependent on the country and dominated by the forces they entrusted themselves to. Just for these reasons, most socialist countries have embarked on successive reforms to such economic and political systems and made remarkable achievements recognized worldwide. With the deepening of the reforms, the role of the socialist public ownership has increasingly been given full play in the process of realizing the status of people as masters of the country.

(2) The State Power with People as Masers as the Political Foundation of Socialist People's Representative System

Lenin pointed out, "The dictatorship of the proletariat alone can emancipate humanity from the oppression of capital, from the lies, falsehood and hypocrisy of bourgeois democracy—democracy for the rich—and establish democracy for the poor, that is, make the blessings of democracy really accessible to the workers and poor peasants"[60] That is to say, the proletariat can only win victory and rise to the ruling

---

[59] Rong, J. et al. (1998) *Minzhu lun* [On Democracy], Shanghai: Shanghai People's Publishing House, pp. 273–274.

[60] *Liening quanji* [Lenin Collected Works] (1956), Beijing: People's Publishing House, vol. 28, p. 350. cf. Lenin, V. (1918) "Democracy" and Dictatorship.

class through revolution and struggle, and gain hold of state power by breaking up the old state machinery, so as to exercise dictatorship over a small number of exploiters. Only in this way can they establish the socialist people's representative system, guaranteed by state power, and truly realize the goal that the masses of the people become masters of their own country in all aspects of politics, economy and culture. As Marx and Engels pointed out, "...the first step in the revolution by the working class is to raise the proletariat to the position of ruling class".[61] If money controls the state power due to the capitalist private ownership of means of production, which transforms the various rights of the broad masses of the people stipulated in law into nothing more than unachievable abstract principles, then socialist public ownership, by contrast, makes the people become masters of the state power and all their rights stipulated in law are truly transformed into various social relations in the political reality. Therefore, from the political point of view, the establishment and operation of the socialist people's representative system are determined by the state power of the people being the masters.

(3) State Theories of Marxism-Leninism as Theoretical Bases of Socialist People's Representative System

The State Theories of Marxism-Leninism, fundamentally in opposition to the western bourgeois political theories, serve as the theoretical bases for the construction of the socialist state power. By means of systematically analyzing the basic contradictions in the capitalist societies, summarizing the basic laws governing the emergence and development of a state, and in particular, unveiling the nature of the bourgeois democracy, the classical Marxist writers have explicitly indicated that only by abolishing private ownership, smashing the old state apparatus, taking over the state power and establishing an effective form of state governance can the proletariat really stand up to be masters of their own fate. This points out the direction for the revolution and struggle of the proletariat. As we have elaborated in Chap. 2, the classical Marxist writers not only profoundly criticized the nature of the bourgeois democracy, but also systematically summarized the experiences and lessons in the construction of the proletarian regimes from the Paris Commune to the Soviet. Moreover, they not only proposed that the proletariat must criticize and transform the form of the bourgeois parliamentary system, but also provided a series of principles for the establishment and operation of the socialist people's representative system. Hence, if the practice of socialist democratic politics shows that the socialist people's representative system is the optimal form to install people as masters of the country, then there is no doubt that it is the result of effective operation of the state theories of Marxism-Leninism in the practice of the socialist state power construction.

---

[61] *Makesi Engesi xuanji* [Marx and Engels Selected Works] (1995), Beijing: People's Publishing House, vol. 1, p. 293. cf. Marx, K. and F. Engels (1848) *Manifesto of the Communist Party.*

3.3.2 *Popular Sovereignty Under Socialist People's Representative System*

In discussing the difference between bourgeois democracy and the parliamentary system and proletarian democracy, Lenin stated:

> By and large, the difference between bourgeois democracy and parliamentarism on the one hand, and Soviet or proletarian democracy on the other, boils down to this: the centre of gravity of the former is in its solemn and pompous declarations of numerous liberties and rights which the majority of the population, the workers and peasants, cannot enjoy to the full. Proletarian, or Soviet, democracy, on the contrary, has transferred the centre of gravity away from the declaration of rights and liberties for the entire people to the actual participation of none but the working people, who were oppressed and exploited by capital, in the administration of the state, the actual use of the best buildings and other premises for meetings and congresses, the best printing-works arid the biggest warehouses (stocks) of paper for the education of those who were stultified and downtrodden under capitalism.[62]

In other words, the theory and practice of popular sovereignty in a socialist country are not divorced from each other as in a capitalist country, but exist in organic unity of ideal and reality. After leading the broad masses of the working people to occupy the position of the ruling class through revolution and struggle, "The proletariat will use its political supremacy to wrest, by degree, all capital from the bourgeoisie, to centralize all instruments of production in the hands of the State, i.e., of the proletariat organised as the ruling class; and to increase the total productive forces as rapidly as possible."[63] In this way, the broad masses of the people, who make up the overwhelming majority of the society, become not only the masters of the means of production, but also of their own destiny, and this also provides a fundamental guarantee for them to express and defend their own rights and interests. Therefore, the existing basis of the socialist people's representative system determines that the broad masses of the people are masters not only in law and principle, but also in political reality in the actual operation of the representative system. The specific manifestations are as follows:

First, the members of the socialist people's representative organs are the representatives elected from all classes, strata, and all walks of life by the people, so they can fully reflect the nature of the state power in which the people are masters of the country. In accordance with the provisions of the constitutions and electoral laws of all socialist countries, all citizens of legal age, except those deprived of political rights by law, are endowed with the right to vote and to be voted, regardless of their nationalities, races, genders, occupations, family backgrounds, religious beliefs, educational levels, property status and lengths of residence. In this way, money plays no role in the process of electing representatives into the socialist people's representative organs, and the main factors determining the candidates to be elected are the political morality and capability. Hence, the representatives are elected according to the

---

[62] *Liening quanji* [Lenin Collected Works] (1956), Beijing: People's Publishing House, vol. 29, p. 87. cf. Lenin, V. (1919) Draft Programme of the R.C.P (B).

[63] *Makesi Engesi xuanji* [Marx and Engels Selected Works] (1995), Beijing: People's Publishing House, vol. 1, p. 293. cf. Marx, K. and F. Engels (1848) *Manifesto of the Communist Party.*

will of the people, who are assigned to the people's representative organs and trusted by the people. For instance, the deputies to the Chinese representative organ cover a wide range of professions. Among the 2970 representatives to the 7th National People's Congress, there are 687 ordinary workers and peasants (23% of the total), 697 intellectuals (23.4%), 733 cadres (24.7%), 267 from People's Liberation Army (9%), 49 returned-overseas Chinese (1.6%), 540 members from democratic parties (18.2%). From these figures and percentages, we can see that workers, peasants and intellectuals were the major forces in the socialist construction of China, which fully indicates the nature of the Chinese state power that the people are the masters of the country.

Second, the powers or authorities of the socialist people's representative organs come from being entrusted by the broad masses of the people, which indicates the unity between the power of the state and the power of the people. Generally, the constitutions of socialist countries not only stipulate that all power of the state belongs to the people, but also that the people's representative organs are institutions through which the people exercise state power. Therefore, different from the parliaments of capitalist countries, such as the United States, France, Britain and Germany, the people's representative organs of socialist countries are in fact organs of the state power. The current Chinese constitution prescribes that "All power in the People's Republic of China belongs to the people. The organs through which the people exercise state power are the National People's Congress and the local people's congresses at different levels." According to the 1972 Constitution of the Democratic People's Republic of Korea, "The power of the Democratic People's Republic of Korea belongs to workers, peasants, soldiers and working intellectuals. The working people exercise their power through their own people's representative organs, the Supreme People's Assembly and the local people's assemblies at various levels." And the 1977 Constitution of the Soviet Union states that "all power in the Soviet Union belongs to the people and through the People's Soviet, the political foundation of the Soviet Union, the people exercise their state power." It can be concluded that the socialist people's representative organs are all the state power institutions that are entitled with the power to decide on all major state affairs, and all their powers come from the entrustment by the people. In other words, they are the plenipotentiary organs that exercise the state power on behalf of the people.

Third, the socialist people's representative organs must be responsible to and supervised by the people. Lenin once pointed out that "No elective institution or representative assembly can be regarded as being truly democratic and really representative of the people's will unless the electors' right to recall those elected is accepted and exercised."[64] The key reason why the socialist people's representative organs can truly ensure the people to be masters of the country is that the people enjoy the power of supervision and removal. For example, According to the 1982 Constitution of China, "the National People's Congress and the local people's congresses at different levels are instituted through democratic election. They are responsible to

[64] *Liening quanji* [Lenin Collected Works] (1959), Beijing: People's Publishing House, vol. 26, p. 314. cf. Lenin, V. (1917) Draft Decree on the Right of Recall.

the people and subject to their supervision." In the 1977 Constitution of the Soviet Union, it was stipulated that "Representatives who fail to live up to the trust of the voters may be recalled at any time in accordance with the decision of the majority of the voters and of the procedures prescribed by law.", etc. Obviously, although the power of the people is entrusted to their elected representatives, the supreme power of the state remains in the hands of the people.

Of course, it must be made clear that the popular sovereignty, as the fundamental principle of the socialist democracy, generally has four basic requirements: (1) the people are the only subject to exercise the state power; (2) the people enjoy the supremacy to exercise state power; (3) the people exercise the state power fully; (4) the people exercise the state power consistently. By analyzing the political practice of socialist countries on the basis of these requirements, we find that even though we assume that the socialist people's representative system truly unifies the ideal and the reality of the people being masters of the country, this unity has not reached the ideal state due to various subjective and objective reasons. This is not only reflected in the need to further improve the electoral system for representative generation and people' supervision over the representatives, etc., but also in the need to further promote the ability and authority of the socialist people's representative organs to exercise their functions and powers. Hence, strengthening the construction of the socialist people's representative system is still the most important task in the building of democratic politics of socialist countries.

References

Bernadiner, B. (1981). *Lusuo de shehui zhengzhi ahexue* [Social and Political Philosophy of Rousseau] (Jiao, S. A. & M. Z. Che, Trans.). China Social Sciences Press.

Dahl, R. (1989). *Duoyuan zhuyi minzhu de kunjing: zizhi yu kongzhi* [(1982). *Dilemmas of Pluralist Democracy: Autonomy VS. Control*. Yale University Press.

Dunn, S. (Ed.). (2002). *The Social Contract and First and Second Discourses* by Jean-Jacques Rousseau. Yale University Press.

Engels, F. (1877). *Anti-Dühring*.

Engels, F. (1844). *The Condition of England*.

Engels, F. (1846). *The Condition of Germany*.

Engels, F. (1877). *Anti-Dühring*.

Engels, F. (1880). *Socialism: Utopian and Scientific*.

Hobhouse, L. (1911/1922). *Social Evolution and Political Theory*. Columbia University Press.

Hobhouse, L. (1935). *Shehui jinhua yu zhengzhi xueshuo* [Social Evolution and Political Theory] (Liao K. S., Trans.). The Commercial Press.

Huntington, S. (1968). *Political Order in Changing Societies*. Yale University Press.

Huntington, S. (1988). *Biange shehui zhong de zhengzhi zhixu* [Political Order in Changing Societies] (Trans.). Hua Xia Publishing House.

Kawamura, M. (1934a). *Direct Democracy*. Nippon Hyoron Sha Co., Ltd.

Kawamura, M. (1934b). *Zhijie minzhu zhengzhi* [Direct Democracy]. Nippon Hyoron Sha Co., Ltd.

Law Institute of Shanghai Academy of Social Science, (Eds.). (1982). *Constitution*. Knowledge Press.

Lei, J. X. (1989). *Xuanju zhidu* [Electoral System]. Taiwan Dongcha Press.

Lenin, V. (1905). 'Three Constitutions or Three Systems of Government'.
Lenin, V. (1910). 'Differences in the European Labour Movement'.
Lenin, V. (1912). 'The Results and Significance of the U.S. Presidential Elections'.
Lenin, V. (1916). 'The Discussion on Self-Determination Summed Up'.
Lenin, V. (1917). 'Draft Decree on the Right of Recall'.
Lenin, V. (1918). "Democracy" and Dictatorship.
Lenin, V. (1919). Draft Programme of the R.C.P (B).
Li, D. K. (1990). *Meiguo zhengfu he Meiguo zhengzhi* [American Government and American Politics]. China social Sciences Press.
Liening quanji [Lenin Collected Works]. (1956). People's Publishing House (Vol. 28).
Liening quanji [Lenin Collected Works]. (1956). People's Publishing House (Vol. 29).
Liening quanji [Lenin Collected Works]. (1958). People's Publishing House (Vol. 22).
Liening quanji [Lenin Collected Works]. (1959). People's Publishing House (Vol. 8).
Liening quanji [Lenin Collected Works]. (1959). People's Publishing House (Vol. 18).
Liening quanji [Lenin Collected Works]. (1959). People's Publishing House (Vol. 26).
Liening xuanji [Lenin Selected Works]. (1995). People's Publishing House (Vol. 2).
Makesi Engesi quanji [Marx and Engels Collected Works]. (1956). People's Publishing House (Vol. 1).
Makesi Engesi quanji [Marx and Engels Collected Works]. (1957). People's Publishing House (Vol. 2).
Makesi Engesi quanji [Marx and Engels Collected Works]. (1961). People's Publishing House (Vol. 6).
Makesi Engesi quanji [Marx and Engels Collected Works]. (1962). People's Publishing House (Vol. 12).
Makesi Engesi xuanji [Marx and Engels Selected Works]. (1995). People's Publishing House (Vol. 3).
Makesi Engesi xuanji [Marx and Engels Selected Works]. (1995). People's Publishing House (Vol. 2).
Makesi Engesi xuanji [Marx and Engels Selected Works]. (1995). People's Publishing House (Vol. 1).
Marx, K. (1843). *Critique of Hegel's Philosophy of Right*.
Marx, K. (1843). Introduction to *Critique of Philosophy of Right*.
Marx, K. (1844). 'On the Jewish Question'.
Marx, k. (1849). 'Speech at The Trial of the Rhenish District Committee of Democrats'.
Marx, K. (1857). *Grundrisse: Foundations of the Critique of Political Economy (Rough Daft)*.
Marx, K. (1871). *The Civil War in France*.
Marx, K., & Engels, F. (1848). *Manifesto of the Communist Party*.
Mastellone, S. (1992). *Ouzhou zhengzhi sixiang shi: Cong shiwu shiji dao ershi shiji* [History of European Political Thoughts: From 15th Century to 20th Century] (Trans.). Social Sciences Academic Press.
Miller, D., & Bogdanor, V. (Eds.). (1992). *The Blackwell Encyclopedia of Political Science*. Wiley-Blackwell.
Pan, H. F. (1987). *Dangdai shijie zhengzhi sichao* [Contemporary World Political Thoughts]. Heilongjiang People's Publishing House.
Pan, H. F., et al. (Eds.). (1987). *Dangdai shijie zhengzhi sichao* [Contemporary World Political Thoughts]. Heilongjiang People's Publishing House.
Parenti, M. (1974/2011). *Democracy for the Few*. Cengage Learning.
Parenti, M. (1991). *Meiguo de minzhu* [American Democracy] (Han, J. Z. et al., Trans.). Henan People's Publishing House.
Rong, J., et al. (1998). *Minzhu lun* [On Democracy]. Shanghai People's Publishing House.
Rousseau, J. (1982). *Shehui qiyue lun* [The Theory of Social Contract] (He, Z. W., Trans.). The Commercial Press.
Sa, M. W. (1986). *Zhengzhi xue* [Political Science]. San Min Book Co., Ltd.

Scharf, C. (1984/2019). *Politics and Change in East Germany*. Routledge.
Scharf, C. (1988). *Minzhu deguo de zhengzhi yu biange* [Politics and Change in East Germany] (Qin, G., Trans.). Chunqiu chubanshe [Spring and Autumn Publishing House] (pp. 37–38).
Skinner, Q. (1978). *The Foundations of Modern Political Thought: The Renaissance*. Cambridge University Press.
Skinner, Q. (1989). *Xiandai zhengzhi sixiang de jichu* [The Foundations of Modern Political Thought] (Duan S. W., Trans.). Qiushi Chubanshe [Truth Seeking Publishing House].
Wang, Z. H. (1989). *Minzhu yu zhongguoren* [Democracy and Chinese]. China Radio Film & TV Press.
Wisti, F. (Ed.). (1990). *Beioushi minzhu* [Nordic Democracy] (Zhao, Z. Q. et al., Trans.). China Social Sciences Press.
Yamaguchi, Y. (1991). *Zhengzhi tizhi* [Political System] (Trans.). The Economic Daily Press.

Chapter 4
Representative System and Electoral System

If the representative system is an inevitable outcome of the realization of democracy in modern nation-states, then the electoral system is the necessary prerequisite for the realization of the representative system. As such, the so-called electoral system in modern times, which appeared with democratic thought and the democratic system, is the fundamental means to establish and realize democracy. "If a government is elected, it will be regarded as democratic and thus legitimate in people's minds. If it is not constituted by election but rather coup or usurpation, it will be regarded as undemocratic, and its legitimacy will often be questioned."[1] Therefore, the electoral system is not only an important part of the democratic system of a country, but also a basic way to realize democracy for the ruling class.

4.1 Electoral System as Foundation of Representative System

The practice of election has a long history. When describing the customs within the Iroquois tribes, Engels mentioned the issue of electing a sachem in his book *The Origin of the Family, Private Property and the State*: "All voted in the elections, both men and women."[2] However, the selection of people responsible for public affairs by means of election originated in the ancient Greek city-states, such as the election of the Gerousia (Council of Elders) and the Council of Five Hundred People. Throughout the Middle Ages, the electoral system played little role in the political life, but the city councils in some commercial and handcraft industrial cities were nevertheless elected by citizens. Nonetheless, the so-called "elections" mentioned

[1] Lei, J. X. (1989) *Xuanju zhidu* [Electoral System], Taiwan: Dongcha Press, p.3.

[2] *Makesi Engesi xuanji* [Marx and Engels Selected Works] (1995), Beijing: People's Publishing House, vol.4, p.84. cf. Engels, F. (1884) *The Origin of the Family, Private Property and the State.*

Y. Zhou, *A Comparative Study of Representative Systems*,
https://doi.org/10.1007/978-981-15-4186-5_4

above are different from the modern electoral system in terms of both function and scope.

4.1.1 An Overview of Electoral System

In order to accurately understand the influence of the electoral system upon the representative system, we must first clarify the notion of the electoral system itself. Generally speaking, although there are many differences in the establishment and operation of electoral systems in countries around the world, it can be analyzed from the following points.

(1) **Significance of Electoral System**

Electoral system is a general term for various subsystems concerning the election of representatives to the representative organ and public officials of the state by the ruling class of a country according to law, and it is also an important means and a set of procedures for the ruling class to select representatives and outstanding figures of its own class to enter the state organs for the realization of the state power. As a crucial part of the modern democratic system, the electoral system is not only the product of the application of the theories of natural rights and popular sovereignty proposed by the bourgeois scholars in bourgeois political practice, but also the result of bourgeois opposition to the feudal hierarchy. Compared with the electoral activities in primitive, slave and feudal societies, the modern electoral system has the following three characteristics: (1) Those who stand for election are usually representatives or members of the representative organs; (2) Formal universal suffrage is adopted; (3) There is a relatively complete set of legal regulations for guidance. And in political practice, although there are fundamental differences between the electoral systems with different class nature in terms of the object, purpose, etc., their functions are similar in form. As far as the generation and operation of the representative organs are concerned, the functions of the electoral system are as follows:

First, the electoral system provides an institutional guarantee for voters to elect their trusted representatives to constitute the state institutions, where the transfer of the state power is achieved. Therefore, the electoral system is the basic approach to connect the civil society with the political state in modern times. As mentioned above, popular sovereignty is the most fundamental principle of a democratic state in modern times, that is to say, all power of the state belongs to the people. But even in the most direct democracy, it is impossible to make all people direct rulers. In this sense, the power of the state can only be exercised by a few, which results in the separation between the owners and exercisers of state power and the contradiction between the minority of leaders and the majority of the led, and the electoral system is the fundamental way to solve such problems. Since representatives or members of the parliament are elected by citizens according to their own will, and the state organs and their staff obtain their functions and powers delegated by voters through election, those who exercise power, though endowed with the legal status of a representative, they are only the medium and bridge to help the true power owners to achieve power. Therefore, although the power exercisers are relatively independent, such a peaceful power delegation or power transfer cannot change the status of the power owners, instead, with the help of other relevant systems, the will of the power owners can be better realized. Moreover, in political practice, since the status of power exercisers are legitimized by election, "the electoral system becomes a justifiable legitimate institution for the contemporary usurpers with the promotion of its theory. In the past, the dictator, who seized power by force, could only get legitimacy through religious coronations or marriage to princesses. However, today he resorts to referendums or manipulated elections." And of course, "the electoral system actually is nothing more than a window dressing."[3]

Second, the electoral system provides an important way for the voters to supervise the power exercisers and replace them under certain conditions. The delegation relationship between the electorate and the power exercisers determines that the latter must be responsible to the former. Although there is a division between collective responsibility and individual responsibility in the political practice, the same basic principle must be observed that the voters will judge whether the power exerciser conforms to their will according to his or her specific performance, and if the power exerciser violates the will of the voters, he or she will be held accountable for his or her actions. Gabriel Almond once pointed out:

> The basic concept of a modern democratic political system is that citizens can control elites through periodic elections. On the one hand, the citizens can choose among competing candidates, selecting those whose preferences are most like their own or in whom they have the most trust. On the other hand, the existence of the elections enhances elite responsiveness through the anticipation of electoral sanctions.[4]

If the voters withdraw their "delegation" to the power exerciser, then the power exerciser will lose legitimacy as well as the basis for his or her existence, continuation and power. In such circumstances, the voters can re-elect a new power exerciser under their own will through democratic processes. As stated in *The Declaration of Independence*, "… governments are instituted among men, deriving their just powers from the consent of the governed. That whatever any form of government becomes destructive to these ends, it is the right of the people to alter or to abolish it, and to institute new government…."[5] This requires those who exercise power to insist on serving the voters and keep in mind the idea of being responsible to the voters.

Third, the electoral system is an important means to promote the formulation and expression of the popular will, as well as the democratic awareness of the voters.

[3] Duvergey, M. (1987) *Zhengzhi shehuixue* [Political Sociology], trans. Yang, Z. G. and Wang, D. D., Beijing: Hua Xia Publishing House, p.129.

[4] Almond, G. et al. (1987) *Bijiao zhengzhixue* [Comparative Politics], trans. Cao P. L. et al., Shanghai: Shanghai Translation Publishing House, p.130. cf. Almond, G. et al. (1911/1978) *Comparative Politics: System, Process, and Policy*, Boston: Little, Brown, p.111.

[5] *The Declaration of Independence*, cited in Xie D. F. et al. (1962) *1765–1917 nian de Meiguo* [The United States of 1765–1917], Beijing: The Commercial Press. cf. *The Declaration of Independence*: http://uscode.house.gov/download [12 December 2021].

And both the governance of the country and the management of the society must be in accordance with the popular will. An election, as the way of formulating and expressing public opinions, is not just a simple selection of candidates, but actually an expression of the basic requirements for those who exercise power imposed by voters on the one hand, and the basic opinions of what policies should be implemented in terms of governance of the state and the society, on the other. Moreover, the exchange and compromise of different opinions in the process of election leads to the formulation of opinions that are acceptable to all. Seymour Martin Lipset said that "voting is the key mechanism of consensus in democratic society."[6] Therefore, the electoral system plays a very important role in the formation and expression of public opinions, and at the same time it can also enhance the democratic awareness of the voters by way of participating in electoral activities. To what extent voters attach importance to and participate in the electoral activities is influenced by many factors, such as historical traditions, national customs, religious beliefs and educational levels, though the election itself is also an essential factor. By participating in elections, voters not only have a clearer understanding of their own status and role, but also enhance their ability to analyze and judge political phenomena and issues, so as to actively participate in the discussion and governance of state affairs.

Fourth, the electoral system is also an important measure to alleviate social contradictions, relieve social crises and maintain social stability. After all, social conflicts and crises, such as economic depression, inflation, political unrest and fierce conflicts of group interests, are important factors affecting the order of state governance and social stability, as mentioned earlier. Elections are one of the most important democratic approaches to solve these conflicts or crises in a democratic system, though there are many other ways involved. Further, elections not only help to build closer connections both between the voters themselves and between the voters and the representatives, but also can gather various opinions and policy options for discussion, so as to find a reasonable and acceptable solution for various social problems. Lipset even referred to elections as "the expression of the democratic class struggle".[7]

(2) Basic Principles of Electoral System

According to the constitutions, laws and electoral practices in various countries, some basic principles are mostly affirmed and observed in their electoral systems. If the electoral system is the necessary condition for the implementation of the representative system that ultimately guarantees the realization of democracy in a modern democratic state, then these basic principles are the prerequisites for the democratization of the electoral system and realization of the representative organ as an organ of public opinions, so as to safeguard the representative system as a basic form to achieve democracy. Although each country has its own way of defining

---

[6] Lipset, S. (1993) *Zhengzhi ren*, trans. Liu G. M. & Nie R., Beijing: The Commercial Press, p.16. cf. Lipset, S. (1960) *Political Man: The Social Bases of Politics*, New York: Doubleday & Company, Inc., p.30.

[7] Lipset, S. (1993) *Zhengzhi ren* [Political Man], trans. Liu M. G. & Nie R., Bejing: The Commercial Press, Chapter 7 and 8. cf. Lipset, S. (1960) *Political Man: The Pocial Bases of Politics*, New York: Doubleday & Company, Inc., p.265.

and implementing the basic principles, there are generally four major principles as follows:

First, the universality principle of suffrage. Specifically, this refers to the wide range of subjects who enjoy the right to vote and the principle of universal right for voters without other qualification restrictions, except for nationality, age, mental illness and deprivation of political rights according to law. In terms of its theoretical origin, the principle of universal suffrage is the concrete application of the popular sovereignty principle. Since the people are the masters of the country and all power of the country belongs to the people, it is natural that the people have the right to select those who exercise the power of state and social administration on their behalf. Thus, some Western scholars hold that suffrage is the inherent right of citizens. In terms of its historical development, "universal suffrage" is the slogan first put forward by the bourgeoisie to mobilize the broad masses of the people to participate in the struggle against the feudal autocracy, but the privilege of capital makes this right of universal suffrage difficult to achieve in capitalist countries. As a matter of fact, capitalist countries have generally gone through the process of gradual elimination of such restrictions on suffrage as direct property and property-related residence, educational level, gender, ethnicity and race. However, the electoral systems of socialist countries have established their own principle of universal suffrage on the basis of criticizing and reforming the capitalist "principle of universal suffrage". Under the public ownership of means of production and the political power with its nature of the people being masters of the country, the range of citizens who really enjoy the right of election has fundamentally expanded in socialist countries. However, this does not mean that all citizens in socialist countries have the right to vote. In other words, on the issue of universal suffrage, socialist countries also have to go through a process from the restriction on the hostile classes to the gradual reduction and elimination of this restriction.

Second, the equality principle of suffrage. Ideally, this means that all voters can only vote once in only one place, and that all votes are equally valid. The equality principle of suffrage involves two aspects: (1) Equal opportunity for each voter to vote, i.e. each voter can only vote once; (2) Equal weight for each vote, i.e. each vote has the same effect. In theory, the equality of suffrage originates from the bourgeois slogan of freedom, equality and fraternity and the thought of opposing feudal privilege, but in practice, it has also undergone a process of development in history. In the Western capitalist countries, it has experienced the property-centered plural voting system and hierarchical voting system, and it was not until recent decades that such an overtly expressed privilege of capital was abolished. For example, at the beginning of the twentieth century, in the election to the lower house of Prussia, the voting power of voters was in proportion to the amount of tax they paid, that is, the number of people represented by the members of parliament elected by the voters who paid less tax was several times or dozens of times more than the number of people represented by the members elected by the voters who paid more tax. For another example, in the British Lower House elections before 1918, those who owned houses in several constituencies were entitled to several votes. In addition, voters with university degrees could often enjoy two or more votes. Obviously, a system in which people with special status due to property, residence, education, and other factors could be entitled to several votes, or even only one vote was allowed, but its effect was greater than that of others was harmful to the equality principle of suffrage. In socialist countries, the distinction between workers and peasants has been removed in terms of the actual electoral efficacy, but such a privilege still exists in some countries.

Third, the principles of direct and indirect elections. Direct election refers to the electoral means by which voters elect in person their deputies or members of the parliament to the representative organs, and the public officials to other state organs. In contrast, the indirect election is the method by which voters first select the electors or electoral groups, who in turn elect the deputies or members of the parliament to the representative organs, and the public officials to other state organs. Generally, the direct election is a more democratic form of election than the indirect election. It is not only beneficial for the voters to directly select people they are familiar with and trust to control the organs of state power to exercise the power of managing the state affairs on their behalf, so that voters can directly express their opinions and demands to the deputies or members of the parliament and supervise their activities, but also helpful for the deputies and members of the parliament to listen to the opinions and demands of the voters. In this way, the direct election facilitates both the enthusiasm of the voters in political participation and the sense of responsibility of the deputies and members of the parliament. Therefore, quite a number of countries in the world adopt direct elections, whereas, many other countries take the form of indirect election due to their vast territory, large population, poor transportation and relatively low level of economic and cultural development, etc. In practice, the application of the indirect election is also different in various countries. For example, in some countries, voters are required to elect the primary candidates first, and then the primary candidates elect the deputies or members to the parliament; in some other countries, the deputies or members of the parliament are elected to the national representative organs by the local representative organs. Generally, in the representative organs of the Western countries, members of the lower houses are directly elected by voters, but for the election of members of the upper houses or the president, either direct or indirect election is adopted in different countries. China adopts the principle of the combination of both direct and indirect election in practice. That is, the deputies to the local people's congresses at the county-level or below are directly elected, while the deputies to the National People's Congress or the local congresses above the county levels (excluding county levels) are elected indirectly by the congresses at the next lower levels in turn. From the perspective of historical development, the indirect election will shrink gradually and the direct election will expand continuously in terms of the scope and levels, but this is a rather slow and long-term process.

Fourth, the principle of a secret ballot. The secret ballot, as opposed to open ballot, is a voting procedure in which voters write their votes in person and put them into a sealed ballot box without signature. At present, secret ballot voting is carried out in most countries in the world, but in the past, open ballot voting was practiced in both capitalist and socialist countries. Generally, open ballot voting has four types in form, including voice vote, cheering vote, show of hands vote and registered ballot vote. In these types of voting, the will of the voters cannot be freely expressed without any pressure because their vote is not a secret. However, a secret ballot has the advantage of keeping a secret so as to ensure the voters to express their own will freely without personal concern and consideration of "face". Therefore, the secret ballot is more advisable in ensuring a fair election to select the right people without any possible external pressure on or intimidation and bribery of the voters. China, like many others, has gone through a historical process from open to secret. For example, the Electoral Law of 1953 stipulated that the grassroots general election and the election of township deputies to the county people's congresses could be conducted either by show of hands or by secret ballot, which is a feasible and practical, but a transitional democratic method suitable for the specific historical conditions, such as the fact that there were still a large population of illiteracy among the electorate in the early days of the People's Republic of China. Since the enactment of the Electoral Law of 1979, secret ballot is utlized everywhere in China.

(3) **Electoral Procedure**

Although basic principles constitute the basis and premise of the electoral system, which are increasingly democratized in modern countries, whether such democratic principles can be truly put into practice depends heavily upon the electoral procedure. In a sense, the electoral procedure is even decisive to the implementation of the electoral principles. For example, in some Western countries, the division of constituencies is decided according to so-called Electoral Geography, which results in unequal votes, and thereby undermines the equality principle of suffrage. Moreover, the electoral guaranty money system actually disqualifies many candidates and violates the universality principle of suffrage. Therefore, the electoral procedure occupies a pivotal position in the electoral system. In a sense, the electoral procedure is in fact the key factor that affects the composition of the representative organs, and consequently influences the generation and operation of the representative system. According to the laws and the electoral practices in various countries, the electoral procedure mainly involves such processes as the establishment of electoral bodies, constituency division, voter registration, candidate nomination, election campaign or candidate introduction, voting by ballot, and announcement of election results.

First, electoral bodies, which are usually set up in countries with different names, are the working institutions that organize and handle election matters. For instance, according to the Constitution and laws of China, the standing committees of the people's congresses above the county level (excluding the county level) are the electoral authorities that preside over the election of deputies to the congresses at the corresponding levels, while an election committee shall be set up to hold the election of deputies to the corresponding congresses at the county level or below. In Western countries, in addition to the electoral authorities established by the government, political parties also set up electoral bodies to raise election expenses and run campaign activities.

Second, the constituency division. This refers to the regional division of electoral units for voting. Whether it is for the election of the people's deputies in a socialist country or the members of parliament in a capitalist country, the constituency division must be made before the election, so that people can vote in a certain electoral district. However, the ways of division vary from country to country. For example, in some countries, the division of constituencies is consistent with that of the administrative districts, while others are not. In some countries, the electoral districts must not be changed in accordance with the law, but in others, the division of constituency may be determined by the administrative authorities when needed at each election according to "administrative discretion". Since the number of members elected from different constituencies varies, there is also a division between "great constituency system" and "small constituency system." A small constituency system exists where only one member can be elected from each electoral district, but a great constituency system exists where multiple members can be elected. Judging from the political practices in capitalist countries, the division and change of constituencies directly serves the needs of bourgeois dictatorship, and in the meantime, reflects the contradictions and struggles among the bourgeois parties. The division of constituencies in socialist countries, however, emphasizes the convenience for the majority of voters to participate in the voting and understand and contact the representatives, so as to actually guarantee the voters to exercise their right to vote.

Third, the voter registration involves electoral bodies reviewing the electoral qualifications of citizens according to law. The purpose of the voter registration process is to confirm and guarantee the suffrage of the voters, to prevent the citizens without suffrage from voting, and to protect the citizens with suffrage from being deprived of the right to participate in the election. This is because a person who is legally qualified to vote may not necessarily obtain the suffrage. No voter can get a ballot to participate in voting unless he or she is registered and has received an electoral certificate. Therefore, the voter registration is the primary condition for the voters to realize their right to vote and is an important process to ensure the smooth running of elections.

Fourth, the candidate nomination refers to the system by which candidates are nominated by relevant institutions, organizations, groups and citizens for the selection of the voters. Superficially, the proletariat and other working people in capitalist countries have the right to enter the parliament and rise to the "throne" of the presidency, in fact, whether they can be elected as members of the parliament or public officials of the state mainly depends on whether they are favored by the monopoly capital groups. In addition, although all political parties and nonpartisans are legally entitled to nominate candidates, the voters have no right to interfere in nomination for the majority of candidates are usually controlled by the major bourgeois political parties. Therefore, the dominance of the monopoly capital groups over the government and parliament is guaranteed not only by their control over the bourgeois political parties, but also by the selection of their own loyal agents as members of parliament and president. However, in socialist countries, not only the Communist Party but also other political parties and social organizations such as trade unions and the Communist Youth League have the right to nominate candidates. In addition, a certain number of voters may also propose candidates jointly. Most importantly, the electoral theories and practices of socialist countries emphasize that the candidates proposed by all political parties, groups and voters should have equal status. This provides a protection for the majority of the working people to choose their own satisfactory representatives.

Fifth, election campaign refers to the activities launched by candidates competing for votes in order to be elected before voting for the deputies or members of the parliament and other public officials of the state to the representative organs. In Western countries, an election campaign is a very important process in the election. Generally speaking, as the general election begins, each political party introduces its own candidate. Afterwards, the candidate organizes his electoral institutions, publishes his election program, raises campaign funds and runs the election campaign through radio, television, newspaper etc. Although election campaigns appear extremely lively on the surface, they are actually a means for the bourgeoisie to maintain its dominant position by exploiting the concepts of "popular sovereignty" and "political competition", and a tool for the monopoly capital groups to manipulate the election. However, in socialist countries, there are no legal provisions for such activities, but it is stipulated in law that political parties, people's organizations, voters and representatives may give information about backgrounds of the candidates they nominate at group meetings of voters. In addition, the electoral committees should also introduce candidates to voters. However, it is quite necessary to introduce a competitive mechanism for the democratization of the electoral system.

Sixth, voting is a process by which voters or electors formally express their opinions for or against the candidates. According to the legal provisions and electoral practices of a given government, there is a distinction between the so-called "free voting system" and "compulsory voting system". The free voting system exists where suffrage is exercised by voters freely without intervention of the state, and the compulsory voting system where the state imposes sanctions on voters if they give up the right to vote with no reason. Generally, most of the countries in the modern world have adopted a free voting system. And as for the voting methods, there are open voting and secret voting.

Seventh, election results refers to the tallying of votes according to the electoral system and announcing the results. Since the purpose of election is to select deputies or members of the parliament to the representative organs as well as other public officials of the state, the election methods are quite important. In Western countries, several electoral methods are generally adopted as follows: The first is the majority election system and proportional representation system. It is called a majority election system in which the party with most votes holds all the seats in a constituency. The majority election system can be further divided into relative majority election and absolute majority election. The relative majority election refers to an election in which the parties or candidates who get relatively more votes will be elected or hold all the seats available in the constituency, and the absolute majority election means that the parties or candidates participating in the election can be elected or hold all the seats available in the constituency only if they obtain a majority of the votes in the first-round election, otherwise, the second-round election will be held. The proportional representation system refers to the allocation of seats in the parliament according to the proportion of the total number of votes obtained by each political party. On the basis of the great constituency system, the proportional representation system, combined with the party-list system, can lead to the result in a single round of voting. The second is the one majority alliance system, which means that several political parties are allowed to form alliances to participate in the election in a constituency. As long as an alliance obtains more than half of the votes, it will take all the seats in the constituency. If no election alliance or party wins more than half of the votes, the seats will be assigned among the alliances and parties in proportion to the number of votes they receive, and no further election is required. This system is implemented in countries with both a multi-party system and a great constituency system. The third is the two-round majority election system, which means that in the first round of an election, the absolute majority system is adopted, so that candidates can be elected only when they receive more than half of the valid votes in the constituency, otherwise, a second-round of election will be held. In the second-round, the relative majority system is adopted, in which the candidate who gets the most votes is elected. This system is also applied in the multi-party countries. However, socialist countries mainly adopt the majority election system. In the light of the legal provisions and electoral practices in countries around the world, the institutions in charge of the election will check and count the votes immediately after the polls are closed, and then confirm and announce the election results according to their respective electoral systems.

4.1.2 Electoral System: Precondition of Representative System

The reason why we have taken such pains to introduce the electoral system is that it is exceedingly important to the representative system. Without appreciating the fundamentals of the electoral system, one could never understand the representative system; without the electoral system, the representative system, as the basic form of democracy, would no longer exist. Therefore, the operation of the electoral system directly affects the composition and functioning of the representative system. In short, the electoral system is the precondition of the representative system.

(1) **Formation and Development of Electoral System and Representative System**

As mentioned earlier, the so-called representative system in modern times has evolved from the medieval hierarchical conference, and is the result of the emerging bourgeoisie absorbing and transforming the form of representation in the hierarchical conference. In the Middle Ages, some sorts of parliaments whose members were mainly royalty, aristocrats and landowners, and ecclesiastics existed, such as the Witenagemot (assembly of wise men) and the Great Council in England, whose members were mainly royalty, aristocrats and landowners, and ecclesiastics. In addition to acting as the king's advisory body, they also collected taxes. With the development of productivity, towns and cities took shape in some countries of Western Europe whose main economic activities were no longer land-based agricultural farming, but handicraft industry, manufacturing, commercial trade, finance, service industry, etc. In this way, capital and profits gradually became the major means and objectives of economic activities of the urban residents, and hence the emerging bourgeoisie came into being. Since the eleventh century, emerging towns and cities in some countries, such as those in England, gradually gained autonomy, and administrative organizations were elected by the urban residents. By the fourteenth century, with the continued growth of the economic power of the emerging bourgeoisie, the royal family, when facing financial difficulty, naturally sought the help of the bourgeoisie. As a result, the representatives of the urban residents obtained opportunities to enter the King's Parliament.

Unlike the landlords and aristocrats who were qualified to attend the parliament according to their hereditary status, the urban residents, i.e. the emerging bourgeoisie, lacking the noble blood ties and status of the landlords, could only select their delegates to the parliament through elections. For example, since the twelfth century, the United Kingdom stipulated that all the freemen from each town could have two seats selected to the parliament by themselves. At the beginning, no serious technical problems occurred since both the electors and qualified candidates participating in the election were few in number due to the small population of freemen. However, as the economic power of town representatives continued to grow, their influence in the parliament became increasingly important. Early on, they gained the fiscal and budgetary powers related to taxation and state expenditure. And during the period from the sixteenth century to the middle of the seventeenth century, the bourgeoisie, i.e. the town representatives, fiercely competed for power with the feudal landlords and the royal family, through which the emerging bourgeoisie gradually gained the upper hand. This was mainly manifested in the following two aspects. First, the bourgeoisie became more powerful in the parliament. With the increasing number of representatives elected by the bourgeoisie, the Lower House was established, in which various powers were increasingly vested. Second, the parliament gradually took power from the royal family. By the middle of the 17th, the parliament became a formal legislative body. By the middle of the eighteenth century, a parliament-centered representative system was finally established in the United Kingdom, and the parliament gradually became the center of political activities and power in the country. Therefore, the method of selecting town representatives became an important issue. With the ongoing progress of political practices in various countries, especially the continuous reflections on the electoral problems from theory to practice, a comprehensive electoral system has been established including electoral qualifications, constituency division, assignment of representatives and voting method. Obviously, the electoral system in the modern sense emerged and developed along with the representative system. In other words, without the electoral system, there would be chaos in the process of representative selection, and the establishment and operation of the representative system would be impossible.

(2) **Prerequisite of Representative System**

The representative system is by no means an abstract concept or principle, but a concrete political system consisting of a series of specific constituents. The deputies or members of the parliament and the representative organs constitute the most basic components of the representative system. Without such basic components, there could be no representative system at all. Therefore, the selection of representatives is the top priority in the process of establishing the representative system. Although there have been many ways to select representatives in history, such as by appointment and inheritance, election is the most important and far-reaching one. In this sense, we can say that election, a means of representative selection, is the prerequisite for the establishment and operation of the representative system.

On the other hand, if representatives are selected by other means than election, then the representative system will not be regarded as the basic form of democracy. As I have pointed out several times, when human history transcended the period of direct democracy in a small country with few people, the minority governing the majority has become the normal pattern of political administration, regardless of its difference in class nature or in external forms, and such a pattern will not be abolished unless the appropriate conditions emerge through the development of history. In this case, democracy can only be achieved through the representative system. The function of the representative system lies in that it can transform the will of the majority into the authority of the minority who control the power of political administration. As far as democratic principles are concerned, the essence of the representative system is that it is a kind of power transfer, that is, the power is transferred from the people who own it to the delegates, members of the parliament and other public officials who exercise it. However, the representative system does not equal democracy. Only when the power of the people is really entrusted to the representatives, can the representative system become the basic form of democracy. Montesquieu once wrote:

> There can be no exercise of sovereignty but by their suffrages, which are their own will: now, the sovereign is the sovereign himself. The laws, therefore, which establish the right of suffrage, are fundamental to this government. And indeed it is as important to regulate, in a republic, in what manner, by whom, to whom, and concerning what, suffrages are to be given, as it is, in a monarchy, to know who is the prince, and after what manner he ought to govern.[8]

Therefore, if the representatives are not selected by election but by other means such as appointment or inheritance, then they are not entrusted with the power by the people, and the so-called representative system thus formed is by no means a basic form to democracy, and the regime will remain autocratic. James E. Anderson, an American political scientist, pointed out:

---

[8] Montesquieu (1982) *Lun fa de jingshen* [The Spirit of Laws], trans. Zhang Y. S., Beijing: The Commercial Press, p.8. cf. Montesquieu (1777) *The Spirit of Laws*, The Online Library of Liberty © 2004 Liberty Fund, Inc., p.53.

> The most conspicuous difference between authoritarianism and democratic regimes is that in democratic regimes citizens choose their top policymakers in genuine elections. Some political scientists speculate that voting in genuine elections may be an important method of citizen influence on policy not so much because it actually permits citizens to choose their officials and to some degree instruct these officials on policy, but because the existence of genuine elections puts a stamp of approval on citizen participation. Indirectly, therefore, the fact of elections enforces on proximate policy makers a rule that citizens' wishes count in policy-making.[9]

Max Weber even believed that any systems that do not have general election are not compatible with contemporary systems.[10]

(3) **Formation and Operation of Representative Organs**

In modern democratic politics, the representative organs, i.e. the public opinion organs, are organizations that represent the common interests and reflect the common will of the vast majority of members of the society. However, can such a theoretical consideration be transformed into concrete political practice? In other words, can the representative organs of a country in a certain historical period be truly the public opinion organs? Only by analyzing the internal composition of the representative organs can we approach the correct answer. If the representative organs can only represent a very small number of members of the society, they are by no means the public opinion organs. However, if their members come from all social classes, strata and groups, representing an overwhelming majority of social members, they are sure to be the public opinion organs. Therefore, election is a key factor in determining the member composition of the representative organs. Gabriel A. Almond et al. pointed out, "The complexities of electoral laws in linking voting outcomes to legislative and executive representation cannot be quickly summarized. But three features of such laws are of particular importance and affect both the immediate legislative outcomes and the long-range encouragement and discouragement of parties to run and to offer alternatives to voters."[11] He then systemically elaborated the impact of election upon the assignment of parliamentary seats and the composition of the parliament from three aspects: the restrictive provisions of the legislative representatives, the number of representatives in each constituency, and the proportional representation system and plurality voting system.[12]

---

[9] Anderson, J. (1990) *Gonggong Juece* [Public Policy-Making], trans. Tang L., Beijing: Hua Xia Publishing House, p.57. cf. Anderson, J. (1978/2010) *Public Policy-Making*, Boston: Cengage Learning, 7th edition, p.69.

[10] cf. Beetham, D. (1989) *Makesi Weibo yu xiandai zhengzhi lilun* [Max Weber and the Theory of Modern Politics], trans. Xu, H. B., Xu, J. H. and Kang, L. W., Hangzhou: Zhejiang People's Publishing House, p.109.

[11] Almond, G. et al. (1987) *Bijiao zhengzhixue* [Comparative Politics], trans. Cao P. L. et al. Shanghai: Shanghai Translation Press, p.252. cf. Almond (1911/1978) *Comparative Politics: System, process, and policy*, Boston: Little, Brown, pp.213–214.

[12] Cf. Yamaguchi, Y. (1991) 'Lun xuanju zhidu dui zhengquan goucheng de yingxiang' [On the Impact of Political Regime by Electoral System], in Yamaguchi, Y. (ed.) *Zhengzhi tizhi* [Political Regime] (1991), trans. Han, T. Y., Beijing: The Economic Daily Press, pp.171–177.

Relevant to its influence on the composition of the representative organ, elections also exert a profound impact on the functioning of the representative organ and the operation of the representative system with the representative organ as the center. In modern countries, the representative organ is generally the legislative body. John Rawls indicated that "it [positive liberty] requires that all citizens are to have an equal right to take part in, and to determine the outcome of, the constitutional procedures that establish the laws with which they are to comply."[13] However, there are still many restrictions on direct participation of the citizens in such a process due to various subjective and objective factors, so citizens can only influence the legislative process through the elected representatives. At the same time, to ensure the implementation of the laws of the state, it is not only required that the laws reflect the common will of all members of the society, but also that the representatives and members of the parliament participating in the legislative process must be highly qualified. However, such problems can only be solved in the process of election by starting with the quota assignment of representatives and formulation of the criteria of selecting representatives. Moreover, the representative organs in some countries are not only the center of political activities of the state, but also the center of state power. Therefore, how representative system with the representative organ as the core functions and operates politically depends directly on the actual operation of elections. When analyzing why members of the parliament are always so enthusiastic about the electoral system, Lei Jingxuan pointed out, "There must be a very important reason behind it: different electoral systems will lead to different outcomes. In other words, an electoral system is by no means neutral, but rather, has its orientation and tendency. In other words, by controlling and modifying the electoral system, different results and effects can be produced."[14]

4.2 Capitalist Parliamentary System and Electoral System

Although in general, the electoral system is the premise and foundation of the representative system, their specific manifestations often vary from country to country in terms of the nature of state power, the balance of class forces, historical and cultural traditions, etc. Lei also noted, "Different electoral systems will exert different impacts and can be deliberately designed by people to achieve a specific purpose."[15] Therefore, in the study of the representative system and the electoral system, it is necessary for us to understand the specific impacts exerted by the two different types of electoral systems upon the representative system.

---

[13] Rawls, J. (1988) *Zhengyi lun* [A Theory of Justice], trans. He H. H., He B. G. and Liao S. B., Beijing: China Social Sciences Press, p.211.

[14] Lei, J. X. (1989) *Xuanju zhidu* [Electoral System], Taipei: Dongcha Press, p.120.

[15] Ibid, p.121.

4.2.1 *Critical Analysis of Capitalist Electoral System*

The capitalist electoral system, as a significant part of the capitalist democratic system, was established by transforming and gradually improving upon the electoral system in the feudal society after the victory of the bourgeois revolution. Although the development process of the electoral system differs in capitalist countries, the general trend is: the development from restrictive election to universal suffrage, from an unequal to a formally equal electoral system, from an indirect to a direct electoral system, and from an open ballot to a secret ballot. In other words, the capitalist electoral system has increasingly democratized and its democratic principles are constantly improving. At the same time, in the process of development and change, the right to vote has been expanded not only within the bourgeoisie, but also among the proletariat and the working masses. Early after the founding of the capitalist electoral system, the bourgeoisie established various legal and institutional barriers to prevent the working masses from exercising the right to vote, but later, the bourgeoisie turned to improve its electoral system by gradually abolishing some barefaced restrictions, which enabled the broad masses of the people to enjoy the universal and equal right to vote at least in form. What are the reasons for this development and change? There are three main reason for the shift.

The first is due to the struggle of the broad masses of the people. Although various ideas and principles such as democracy, freedom, equality and human rights were proposed by the bourgeoisie during the bourgeois revolution, they turned out to be empty promises for the broad masses of the people in practice. As a result, the broad masses of the people continued to struggle against the bourgeoisie for universal and equal suffrage. For example, before the eve of the electoral system reform in the United Kingdom in 1832, the National Union of the Working Class was founded, which demanded "the right to vote for all adult males, annually elected Parliaments, vote by secret ballot, abolition of the property qualifications for membership, and protection of social rights of the working class".[16] After the passage of the Reform Act of 1832, the working class democrats severely attacked the limitations of the reform on the one hand, and demanded further political democratization centered on universal suffrage on the other, which resulted in the famous Chartist Movement. Just as Shen and Liu stated, "By combining the thorough bourgeois democratic program with the social demands of the working class, the Chartists pushed forward the development of the parliamentary reform and the democratic movement in the United Kingdom."[17] The same is true of the acquisition of suffrage for the women and blacks in the United States. For example, it was the revolutionary waves of the African-American Civil Rights Movement, Student Movements and the American Antiwar Movement after World War II, especially in the late 1960s and early 1970s that

[16] Shen, H. and Liu, X. C. (1991) *Yingguo yihui zhengzhishi* [British Parliamentary and Political History], Nanjing: Nanjing University Press, p.275.

[17] Shen, H. and Liu, X. C. (1991) *Yingguo yihui zhengzhishi* [British Parliamentary and Political History], Nanjing: Nanjing University Press, p.290.

forced the American government to successively cancel the restrictions on suffrage, including the "poll tax" and "literacy test".

The second is that democracy has become a trend in world history. Although democratization has varied manifestations in different historical periods of development, its general development trend is irresistible. With the continuous expansion of the world market and intensified competition, the mobile and open social environment and the technological revolutions, etc. that emerged became important conditions for the development of democratic politics. Moreover, the market economy, as an insurmountable development stage of human society, has an inevitable internal connection with democratic politics. Therefore, in general, all countries in the modern world, regardless of their class nature, will explicitly advocate democratization in form. In addition, the existence of two different social systems has also greatly facilitated the development of democratization. The German Weimar Constitution of 1919 illustrates how a socialist constitution affects a capitalist democratic system. It is driven by the continuous democratization of the bourgeois electoral system.

The third is due to the adjustment of governance by the bourgeoisie. Frederick Engels pointed out that "the propertied class rules directly by means of universal suffrage."[18] Compared with overt and naked exploitation and oppression, universal suffrage is more deceptive. Early when the bourgeoisie set up such a covert way of governance, it was overtly unequal and undemocratic. However, with the growth of the working class and an improvement in their political awareness, the bourgeoisie realized that they must reconcile with the proletariat and satisfy some demands of the working class in order to consolidate their dominant position on the premise of maintaining the basic system, that is, the bourgeoisie paid more attention to the use of conciliatory strategies in their style of governance. And in their view, it is the most favorable thing to attract the struggle of the proletariat against the bourgeoisie into the election campaign because quarrels over election in the parliament are much safer than armed uprisings. Lenin once pointed out that "… in all the circumstances and the entire situation of parliamentary struggle and elections the strength of the oppressed classes is less than the strength they can actually develop in civil war."[19] The abolition of unequal and undemocratic forms in the electoral system were the "conditions and circumstances" set by the bourgeoisie for the oppressed class.

Accordingly, the democratic development of the capitalist electoral system is also the product of various objective historical conditions. However, such formal democratization does not mean that the nature of the capitalist electoral system has changed. As a matter of fact, the capitalist electoral system is still an important means for the bourgeoisie to maintain its governance since property remains the decisive factor to determine whether one can be elected as a member of the parliament or the president. Specifically, there are two aspects to be further illustrated. One is the so-called election deposit. For example, in the United Kingdom a candidate has to submit a

[18] *Makesi Engesi quanji* [Marx and Engels Collected Work] (1956), Beijing: People's Publishing House, vol.21, p.197. cf. Engels, F. (1884) *The Origin of the Family, Private Property and the State.*

[19] *Liening quanji* [Lenin Collected Works] (1959), Beijing: People's Publishing House, vol.26, p.16. cf. Lenin, V. (1917) *The Russian Revolution and Civil War.*

deposit of 150 pounds (roughly $185), which will be forfeited to the Treasury if he fails to receive 1/8 of the total votes; In France, the deposit will be 1,000 francs, and 100,000 yen (roughly $800) in Japan. The second is the high campaign expenses. Generally, election campaigns often involve a contest of capital and money. Li Dakui noted, "Money can be transformed to political power through elections, thus affecting the candidates, political parties, procedure of policy-making, and government policies."[20] In this sense, elections are only the exercise of suffrage within the scope designated by others for the broad masses of the people. This sort of procedure with only formal meaning does not undermine the essence of the bourgeois regime. Lenin noted, "When parties and elections are financed not by public funds but by private contributions, the political forum is so constrained by the wishes of the dominant interests that the basic measures needed to establish just constitutional rule are seldom properly presented."[21] Therefore, taken to the extreme, the essence of the capitalist electoral system is to decide once every few years which particular members of the ruling class is to repress and crush them in parliament.[22]

4.2.2 Electoral Procedure: Major Control of the Bourgeoisie Over the Parliament

Since the electoral system is the basis of the representative system, the control of elections is the basic means for the bourgeoisie to control the parliament and even the entire state power. The assignment of the seats in the parliament through election can not only ease the contradictions within the ruling class, but also consolidate its class rule. However, as previously discussed, the capitalist electoral system, after hundreds of years of development, has not only gradually established in its democratic principles, but also increasingly improved its form. In turn, the bourgeoisie has shifted its focus from principles and forms to the procedure of controlling the parliament through elections. As discussed, apart from controlling candidate selection and manipulating election campaigns through money, the bourgeoisie controls election activities in several ways.

First, the bourgeoisie controls election activities by manipulating election results through constituency division. The so-called "Electoral Geography" in capitalist countries is mainly concerned with the study of this issue. Since the division of constituencies is directly related to the interests of all parties, all political parties, especially the dominant ones, will strive to adopt the method of division most favorable to their own parties. Through division, the voters who do not support the party

---

[20] Li, D. K. (1990) *Meiguo zhengfu he Meiguo zhengzhi* [American Government and American Politics], Beijing: China Social Sciences Press, p.244.

[21] Rawls, J. (1988) *Zhengyi lun* [A Theory of Justice], trans. He H. H., He B. G. and Liao S. B., Beijing: China Social Sciences Press, p.216.

[22] *Liening quanji* [Lenin Selected Works] (1995), Beijing: People's Publishing House, vol.3, p.150. cf. Lenin, V. (1917) *The State and Revolution.*

are deliberately dispersed to different constituencies, so that they cannot form a majority in each constituency, or they are concentrated in one single constituency, so that candidates of the party can be elected successfully in other constituencies. For example, suppose 6 members of the parliament would be elected out of a certain region, where both Party A (the ruling party) and Party B have 300,000 supporters respectively. If the constituencies are divided fairly, each party may hold 3 seats. However, Party A may deliberately assign the majority of the 300,000 supporters of Party B into one single constituency, so as to ensure its advantage in the other five constituencies. As a result, Party B may receive only one seat. For example, in 1958, in order to prevent the French Communist Party from being elected in big cities with large population of workers such as Marseilles, Charles de Gaulle divided the big cities into smaller districts, with the naturally formed areas being deliberately separated. As Lei Jingxuan noted that "since voters from different classes and occupations have different political orientations and they may live in a concentrated area, it is rather feasible to affect the election through constituency division. For example, it is more favorable for the Left to be elected where residents are mainly workers, while it is more favorable for the Right to be elected where residents are mainly merchants and employers."[23] As a result, the proportion of voters and members of the parliament is extremely uneven across regions. For example, in 1974, the proportion of voters and members of the parliament in various parts of the United Kingdom was like this: one member representing 51,927 voters in Scotland, 55,798 in Wales, 64,634 in England, and 86,377 in North Ireland.[24]

Similarly, whether they will adopt the "great constituency system" or the "small constituency system", the bourgeois political parties inevitably account their own interests. For example, the small constituency system is often implemented in countries where the two-party system is adopted, such as the United Kingdom and the United States. Since the voters tend to select one of the two candidates nominated by the two major parties, it is much easier for the major parties to win more seats in the parliament, while other small parties can hardly win any seats in the campaign. The great constituency system is generally practiced in countries where the multi-party system is applied, such as Germany and Italy, so that all major parties may have a certain number of candidates to be elected to the parliament and jointly rule and govern the country, and in the meantime, they can also ease contradictions among them and suppress minor parties together.

Second, the bourgeoisie controls election activities by controlling the size of the electorate through voter registration. Voter registration confirms the qualifications of voters. With the establishment of universal suffrage, formal restrictions on the qualifications of voters have been gradually reduced. In the past, citizens needed to meet certain qualifications, including property, knowledge level, religious belief, length of residence, race, age, and status as functionaries or servicemen requirements if they wanted to be voters. Now, all these restrictions have been greatly reduced,

[23] Lei, J. X. (1989) *Xuanju zhidu* [Electoral System], Taipei: Dongcha Press, p.71.

[24] Beloff, M. and G. Peele (1980) *The Government of the United Kingdom: Political Authority in a Changing Society*, London: Weidenfield and Nicolson, p.133.

and "in general, voter qualification is heading to the unrestricted universal suffrage of 'one person, one vote'."[25] Therefore, it does not make sense any longer to control the size of the electorate simply through voter qualification, but what kind of system that is adopted for voter registration in political practice matters much. If voter registration is obligatory for the electorate and the government makes great efforts to encourage voters to register, the proportion of registered voters must be very high. In some countries, "even 95% of eligible voters are registered."[26] However, in countries where voter registration is voluntary, either de facto (such as the United Kingdom) or legally (such as the United States), many eligible citizens do not register to vote. "Around 10% in France and 1/3 in the United States of eligible voters are not registered."[27] Some western scholars, as Miller and Bogdanor, pointed out that "though, in western countries at present, no major groups will be deprived of their right to vote except foreigners, there are still obstacles to the electoral system, of which voter registration is the key issue."[28] Thus, concerning the issue of voter registration, the capitalist countries have shifted their strategies from imposing legal and formal restrictions on voters to requiring voters to register voluntarily in actual practice.

Third, the bourgeoisie controls election activities by controlling the assignment of parliamentary seats through the vote counting system. The vote counting system, in fact, refers to a calculation method by which tens of thousands or even hundreds of thousands of votes are converted into a limited number of seats. Before the end of the nineteenth century, people did not pay enough attention to this, and the simple majority election system was often applied. However, with the development of certain election practices, the bourgeoisie gradually realized that different vote counting systems would bring about very different results for the assignment of seats in the parliament. Furthermore, in political practices, the bourgeois political parties would always decide on a vote counting system based on their own interests. For example, in order to combat the French Communist party and the Rally of the French People in the French National Assembly election in 1951, the then centrist political parties decided to adopt a new form of joint election system on the basis of the original proportional representation system. It stipulated that the list of candidates could be jointly designated by parties for election. If the list of candidates received an absolute majority of votes, the parties would win all the seats in the district. Because the French Communist party and the Rally of the French People were hostile to each other, the centrist political parties achieved their desired outcome in the election. In the end, if the old vote counting system was applied, the French Communist party should have won 180 seats in the parliament instead of only 101. Similarly, the Rally of the French People should have won 144 seats instead of 117,

---

[25] Lei, J. X. (1989) *Xuanju zhidu* [Electoral System], Taipei: Dongcha Press, p.60.

[26] Miller, D. and Bogdanor, V. (eds) (1992) *The Blackwell Encyclopedia of Political Science*, New York: Wiley-Blackwell, p.778.

[27] Miller, D. and Bogdanor, V. (eds) (1992) *The Blackwell Encyclopedia of Political Science*, New York: Wiley-Blackwell, p.778.

[28] Ibid.

and the centrist political parties should have had around 300 seats instead of 400. According to Jacques Chapsal, "in fact, it is a trick specially designed to combat the Communist Party."[29] In the election of the National Assembly of the French Fifth Republic in 1958, Charles de Gaulle changed the vote counting system and applied "small constituency two-round majority voting system", the Union for the New Republic won 196 seats in the National Assembly while the French Communist Party won only 10 seats even though it had more votes nationwide than the Union for the New Republic. In another example, the British Conservative Party won 260,000 more votes than the Labor Party in the United Kingdom's 1974 general election, though the latter had 5 more seats than the former since the distribution of seats in the parliament was not decided by the total number of votes obtained, but by the elected candidates in various electoral districts. About this, Vernon Bogdanor pointed out, "One of the results for this fact is that not only the majority parties in parliament that adopts the plural and the majority method in democracies, but also the majority parties in most of democracies are factitious majority parties. That is to say, the majority of the legislative body does not represent the majority of the electorate."[30]

From the discussion above, we can see that the bourgeoisie not only fundamentally control the election and eventually control the parliament and state power through the property, but also specifically manipulate the relevant electoral procedures, so that their representatives can enter the parliament to serve their political and economic interests.

4.3 Socialist People's Representative System and Electoral System

The fundamental reason why the socialist people's representative organ truly represents the will and interests of the people and guarantees the realization of people's right to be the masters of the country is that its representatives and the electorate are homogeneous in nature. In other words, under the socialist people's representative system, the owners and the exercisers of state power have achieved real unity. Socialist public ownership of the means of production ultimately forms the basis that determines this unity or homogeneity, and the fundamental economic unity is politically manifested through the electoral system. Therefore, the socialist electoral system plays a crucial role in the process of enabling the broad masses of the people to be the master of the country through the people's representative system.

[29] Chapsal, J. (1981) *1940 yilai de Faguo zhengzhi shenghuo* [French Political Life Since 1940], trans. Quan, K. K. et al., Shanghai: Shanghai Translation Publishing House, p.183.

[30] Miller, D. and Bogdanor, V. (eds) (1992) *The Blackwell Encyclopedia of Political Science*, New York: Wiley-Blackwell, p.220.

4.3.1 *Critical Analysis of Socialist Electoral System*

The socialist electoral system is the application and development of the proletarian electoral system of Paris Commune in socialist countries. In 1871, the French proletariat in Paris established the first proletarian regime in human history and implemented the proletarian electoral system. In order to ensure the dominant position of the representatives of the workers and the laboring people in the Commune, the Central Committee of the National Guard broke the old tradition of equal representation in each constituency and established the principle that the representatives are proportional to the number of residents in each constituency. By doing so, the communards, most of whom were workers or recognized workers' representatives and the laboring people truly enjoyed a universal democratic right for the first time. Therefore, the Commune "was essentially a working class government, the product of the struggle of the producing against the appropriating class, the political form at last discovered under which to work out the economical emancipation of labor."[31]

After the victory of the October Revolution in 1917, under the leadership of Lenin and the Bolshevik Party, the electoral system was specially prescribed in the Russian Constitution of 1918. The Constitution not only removed all previous restrictions on the qualifications for election, but also clearly stipulated that all citizens of the Russian Soviet Federative Socialist Republic, regardless of their gender, beliefs, ethnic groups, and length of residence, etc. have the right to vote and to be elected, as long as they reached the age of 18 years old before the election day, except those who exploited others. According to the 1936 Soviet Constitution, all Soviet representatives of workers, including those of the Supreme Soviet of the USSR, the Supreme Soviet of the Autonomous Republic, and local soviets at all levels, were elected by voters on an equal, direct and secret ballot. All Soviet citizens who reached the age of 18 were entitled to participate in the election, regardless of their race, nationality, gender, belief, educational level, length of residence, social origin, property status, and past activities, except those who were diagnosed with psychosis or deprived of the right to vote by courts. All Soviet citizens who reached the age of 23, regardless of their race, nationality, gender, educational level, length of residence, social origin, property status, and past activities, had the right to be elected as representatives of the Supreme Soviet of the USSR. The socialist electoral system was basically implemented in those socialist countries established after the victory of the Second World War. As stated in the 1948 Constitution of the Democratic People's Republic of Korea, the Supreme People's Assembly should be composed of members elected by secret ballot in accordance with the principles of universal, equal, and direct election. After the founding of the People's Republic of China, the Electoral Law of 1953, the Constitution of 1954 and their subsequent amendments not only clearly affirmed the basic principles of universality, equality, combination of direct and indirect election, and secret ballot, but also improved the socialist electoral procedures. In this way, a relatively complete socialist electoral system was established.

[31] *Makesi Engesi xuanji* [Marx and Engels Selected Works] (1995), Beijing: People's Publishing House, vol.3, p.59. cf. Marx, K. (1871). *The Civil War In France.*

The historical development of the socialist electoral system highlights the following points. First, the socialist electoral system has confirmed from the very beginning, without exception, that the representatives of the broad masses of the working people should be placed in an advantageous position in the people's representative organs. For this reason, the democratic principles of the electoral system have not only been legally confirmed, but also completely implemented from the electoral procedures to the systems concerned in the electoral practices. Although the electoral system of capitalist countries also confirms these democratic principles legally and formally, the bourgeoisie have made them an abstract content that cannot be fulfilled for the broad masses of the people by imposing various restrictions. However, the socialist electoral system guarantees the realization of these principles without restrictions, so that the electoral system can be confirmed legally and carried out practically in reality at the same time.

Second, the socialist public ownership of the means of production determines that the socialist electoral system is not only the instrument for reflecting the will of the broad masses and protecting the democratic rights of the people, but also the basic processes for the broad masses of the people to participate in the state administration and to be the masters of the country. The reason why the democratic principles of the electoral system in capitalist countries are divorced from reality is determined by the private ownership of the means of production, because "property enables the aristocracy to control the election of deputies for rural areas and small towns; property enables the merchants and manufacturers to choose the members for the large and to some extent also for the small towns; property enables both to increase their influence by bribery".[32] Therefore, under the private ownership of the means of production, it is impossible for the broad masses of the people to become their own masters through the electoral system. However, the socialist public ownership of the means of production enables the broad masses of the people to be masters not only in social and economic life, but also in political life with the guarantee of this material basis. Different from the capitalist countries that only formally stipulate the rights of citizens without paying attention to the conditions for realizing these rights, the socialist countries "do not put emphasis on declarations of the rights and freedom of all people, but truly ensures that … the working people can actually participate in state administration".[33] Therefore, "in none of the most democratic bourgeois states have the working masses ever been able to enjoy the electoral rights formally granted them by the bourgeoisie (who actually hinder their enjoyment) anywhere near as extensively, frequently, universally, easily and simply as they are enjoyed under Soviet power."[34]

[32] *Makesi Engesi quanji [Marx and Engels Collected Works]* (1956), Beijing: People's Publishing House, vol.1, p.687. cf. Engels, F. (1844) *The Condition of England.*

[33] *Liening quanji* [Lenin Collected Works] (1959), Beijing: People's Publishing House, vol.29, p.87. cf. Lenin, V. (1919) 'Draft Programme of the R.C.P.(B.)'.

[34] *Liening xuanji* [Lenin Selected Works] (1959), Beijing: People's Publishing House vol.3, p.723. cf. Lenin, V. (1919) 'Draft Programme of the R.C.P.(B.)'.

Third, as we have indicated in Chapter One, the socialist people's representative system has a unique principle of supervision. Specifically, for the socialist electoral system, it is mainly reflected in the removal and recall of the representatives by the voters at any time. This is a key aspect to guarantee that the representatives and voters remain 'homogeneous', and that the broad masses of the people can be the masters of the country through the people's representative system. In capitalist countries, the election of parliamentarians is mostly a "one-shot deal". The voters can only send their representatives to power, but have limited power to dismiss them. In socialist countries, however, if the elected representatives are incompetent and fail to live up to the expectations and trust of the electorate, they can be replaced at any time in accordance with legal procedures. As Lenin pointed out:

> No elective institution or representative assembly can be regarded as being truly democratic and really representative of the people's will unless the electors' right to recall those elected is accepted and exercised. This fundamental principle of true democracy applies to all representative assemblies without exception, including the Constituent Assembly.[35]

Therefore, socialist electoral system regards the recall of representatives at any time as a critical part and even materializes and institutionalizes it through legislation.[36]

4.3.2 Electoral Procedure: Realization of People as Masters of the Country Through People' Representative System

If the separation between the principles of the capitalist electoral system determined by the private ownership of means of production and reality is caused by the capitalist electoral procedure, then the unity between the principles of the socialist electoral system determined by the public ownership of means of production and reality is accomplished through the socialist electoral procedure. Therefore, the socialist electoral procedure is the basis for the people to become the masters of their country under the people's representative system. Looking through the legal provisions and election practices of all socialist countries, this is mainly reflected in the following aspects.

First, through strengthening the function and independence of the electoral bodies, the elections can be conducted in a fair and orderly manner. In the process of parliamentary elections in capitalist countries, the electoral bodies set up by each political party play a leading role. Since all electoral bodies carry out election activities in the interests of their own parties, "fairness" in elections is out of the question. However, in the process of electing the people's representatives in socialist countries, the electoral bodies are not set up by various political parties, but by the permanent body of

---

[35] *Liening quanji* [Lenin Collected Works] (1959), Beijing: People's Publishing House, vol. 26, p.314.cf. Lenin, V. (1917) 'Draft Decree on the Right of Recall'.

[36] Cf. Topornin, B. (1986) *Shehui zhuyi zhengzhi zhidu* [Socialist Political System], trans. Huang, Z. H., Beijing: The Masses Publishing House, p.131.

the peoples' representative organs or the specially established electoral commission. Just as B. H. Topornin has pointed out that "the functions of electoral commission can never be reduced to counting votes, but will lead the operation of election, supervise the practice of the electoral law, register candidates, organize voting, announce the results of voting, and solve many other problems."[37] That is to say, the electoral commission of socialist countries or the permanent body of the people's representative organs play a leading role in administering elections, which not only helps elections operate smoothly, but also plays a crucial role in maintaining the fairness of elections.

Second, through the division of electoral districts and the allocation of representative quotas, it is ensured that the composition of the representatives to the people's representative organs fully reflects the nature of the regime, in which the people become the masters of the country. The basic motivation for the constituency division in socialist countries is to facilitate voter registration and voting, and fully guarantee that voters exercise their rights to vote. The Electoral Law of the People's Republic of China stipulates that constituencies can be divided according to the residential distribution, or on the basis of production units, public institutions, and work units. This principle of constituency division makes it convenient for voters to select the people they know and trust as representatives and to participate in electoral activities nearby, so as to maximize the participation of the electorate. Moreover, under this principle, the representatives can easily contact with, be monitored by, and be responsible to the electorate. On the contrary, in capitalist countries, the division of constituencies can be adjusted at will by the bourgeoisie according to their own interests. At the same time, although the regulations are not identical in socialist countries in terms of the representative assignment, for instance, it is stipulated that only one representative can be elected for one constituency in some countries, while several representatives in other countries, "...this system is generally produced on the principle that the number of representatives in a certain district is determined by its population."[38] It is ensured that the broad masses of the people who account for the majority of the country's population will occupy the majority number of seats in the people's representative organs. For example, among the elected representatives of the Supreme Soviet of the USSR in 1971, 481 of them were workers, 282 were farmers from the collective farms, and 754 were intellectuals and employees. And among 5879 elected representatives of the Supreme Soviets of the Soviet republics in 1971, 1742 of them were workers, 1211 were farmers of the collective farms, and 2916 were intellectuals and employees.[39] Among all representatives in the seventh National People's Congress of the People's Republic of China, 684 were workers and farmers, and 697 were intellectuals. The composition of the representatives in

---

[37] Cf. Topornin, B. (1986) *Shehui zhuyi zhengzhi zhidu* [Socialist Political System], trans. Huang, Z. H., Beijing: The Masses Publishing House, p.130.

[38] Chirkin, S. (1988) *Xianfa yu zhengzhi zhidu* [Constitution and Political System], trans. Zhou, W. et al., Chengdu: Sichuan University Press, p.312.

[39] Topornin, B. (1986) *Shehui zhuyi zhengzhi zhidu* [Socialist Political System], trans. Huang, Z. H., Beijing: The Masses Publishing House, p.132.

the socialist people's representative organs does not only fully indicate the status of the broad masses of people in the country, but also ensures the broad masses to sufficiently exercise the right to be the masters of the country through engaging the people to participate in the activities of the people's representative organs.

Third, through voter registration, the broad masses of people can be encouraged to actively participate in election activities. In socialist countries, there are generally only two restrictions on voters for qualification: one is age; the other is that they are not deprived of political rights by law.[40] In this way, the number of eligible voters accounts for a very high proportion of the total population of the country. Moreover, since voter registration in socialist countries is carried out by the electoral bodies in an active, systematic and comprehensive way, there are no individuals eligible to vote who cannot become voters, as usually happens in capitalist countries, let alone socialist countries will publicize the list of voters in a certain period before the election day, which can be corrected if there are any mistakes or omissions.

Fourth, through candidate nomination and confirmation, the true representatives of the broad masses of the people shall be elected to the people's representative organs. Generally, candidates in socialist countries can be nominated in three ways, i.e. by each political party or organization independently; by political parties or organizations jointly; or by a certain number of voters jointly. As stipulated in the Supreme Soviet Electoral Law of the Soviet Union, candidates should be nominated by the Soviet Communist Party, the trade unions, the Communist Youth League, the cooperatives and other social groups, the labor collectives, and the General Assembly for the Military. According to The Electoral Law of the People's Republic of China, all political parties and people's organizations can nominate candidates in coalition or independently. And ten or more voters or representatives in coalition are entitled to nominate candidates. On the one hand, since the communist party is the ruling party in socialist countries, who represents the fundamental interests of the broad masses of the people and does not seek any special interests of its own, the candidates it nominates are often the faithful representatives of the people. On the other hand, since the voters themselves can also recommend candidates, and the social groups such as the trade unions and the Youth Leagues are consistent with the broad masses of the people in their fundamental interests, the candidates they nominate will similarly the people. Therefore, the candidates produced by the three ways above not only can be universally representative, but also can fundamentally represent the common interests of the broad masses of the people. In this way, the members elected to the people's representative organs are the true faithful representatives of the broad masses of the people. What's more, as the material conditions for election are secured by the state during the process of final candidate confirmation and formal voting, election will not be manipulated by money, and the voters' choice will not be bewildered by false illusions, and thus the representatives eventually elected by voters are the most reliable and satisfying ones.

---

[40] Some countries once abrogated this restriction. cf. Topornin, B. (1986) *Shehui zhuyi zhengzhi zhidu* [Socialist Political System], trans. Huang, Z. H., Beijing: The Masses Publishing House, p.129.

Fifth, the common will of the broad masses of the people is transformed into the concrete will of people's representative organs through the vote counting system. Different from the vote counting system in capitalist countries, which may be adjusted at any time according to the needs of the bourgeois political parties, the vote counting system in socialist countries is relatively stable, whose basic principle is that the elected representatives are determined according to the will of the majority voters within the limit of the representative quotas assigned on the basis of the proportion of the population. As S. I. Chirkin has summarized:

> In most socialist countries, a candidate who wins more than half of the votes is regarded as the elected. If no candidates win more than half of the votes, a second round of voting should be carried out. If the number of candidates who win more than half of the votes exceeds the number of the representatives to be elected within the constituency, the candidate who wins more votes or whose surname is ordered first is elected.[41]

It's worth noting that the greatest advantage of this vote counting system is that it can avoid such a case that the so-called "the majority of the legislative body cannot represent the majority of the electorate" in capitalist countries, so as to ensure that the representatives of the people's representative organs really become the public servants of the broad masses of the people.

However, when we say that the socialist electoral system provides the premise and basis for the majority of people to become their own masters through the people's representative system, it does not mean the socialist electoral system has already fully exercised its function. In fact, it still needs to further its process of democratization.[42] Only by improving the democracy of socialist electoral system, can the People' Representative System promote its democratization.

References

Almond, G. et al. (1911/1978). *Comparative politics: System, process, and policy*, Little, Brown.

Almond, G. et al. (1987). *Bijiao zhengzhixue* [Comparative Politics] (P. L. Cao et al., Trans.). Shanghai Translation Publishing House.

Anderson, J. (1978/2010). *Public policy-making* (7th ed.). Cengage Learning.

Anderson, J. (1990). *Gonggong Juece* [Public Policy-Making] (L. Tang, Trans.). Hua Xia Publishing House.

Beetham, D. (1989). *Makesi Weibo yu xiandai zhengzhi lilun* [Max Weber and the Theory of Modern Politics] (H. B. Xu, J. H. Xu, & L. W. Kang, Trans.). Zhejiang People's Publishing House.

Beloff, M., & Peele, G. (1980). *The government of the United Kingdom: Political authority in a changing society*. Weidenfield and Nicolson.

Chapsal, J. (1981). *1940 yilai de Faguo zhengzhi shenghuo* [French Political Life Since 1940] (K. K. Quan, et al., Trans.). Shanghai Translation Publishing House.

[41] Chirkin, S. (1988) *Xianfa yu zhengzhi zhidu* [Constitution and Political System], trans. Zhou, W. et al., Chengdu: Sichuan University Press, p.313.

[42] Zhou, Y. Z. (1992) 'Some Problems of Democratization of China's Electoral System', *Law Review*, (5).

Chirkin, S. (1988) *Xianfa yu zhengzhi zhidu* [Constitution and Political System] (W. Zhou, et al., Trans.). Sichuan University Press.

Duvergey, M. (1987). *Zhengzhi shehuixue* [Political Sociology] (Z. G. Yang, & D. D. Wang, Trans.). Hua Xia Publishing House.

Engels, F. (1844). *The condition of England.*

Engels, F. (1884). *The origin of the family, private property and the state.*

Lei, J. X. (1989). *Xuanju zhidu* [Electoral System]. Dongcha Press.

Lenin, V. (1917). *Draft decree on the right of recall.*

Lenin, V. (1917). *The Russian revolution and civil war.*

Lenin, V. (1917). *The state and revolution.*

Lenin, V. (1919). *Draft programme of the R.C.P.(B.).*

Li, D. K. (1990). *Meiguo zhengfu he Meiguo zhengzhi* [American Government and American Politics]. China Social Sciences Press.

Liening quanji [Lenin Collected Works]. (1959). People's publishing house (Vol. 26).

Liening quanji [Lenin Collected Works]. (1959). People's publishing house (Vol. 29).

Liening xuanji [Lenin Selected Works]. (1959). People's publishing house (Vol. 3).

Lipset, S. (1960). *Political man: The social bases of politics.* Doubleday & Company Inc.

Lipset, S. (1993). *Zhengzhi ren* [Political Man] (M. G. Liu & R. Nie, Trans.). The Commercial Press.

Makesi Engesi quanji [Marx and Engels Collected Works]. (1956). People's Publishing House (Vol. 1).

Makesi Engesi xuanji [Marx and Engels Selected Works]. (1995). People's Publishing House (Vol. 3).

Makesi Engesi xuanji [Marx and Engels Selected Works]. (1995). People's Publishing House (Vol. 4).

Marx, K. (1871). *The civil war in France.*

Miller, D., & Bogdanor, V. (Eds.). (1992). *The blackwell encyclopedia of political science.* Wiley-Blackwell.

Montesquieu. (1777). *The spirit of laws.* The Online Library of Liberty © 2004 Liberty Fund, Inc.

Montesquieu. (1982). *Lun fa de jingshen* [The Spirit of Laws] (Y. S. Zhang, Trans.). The Commercial Press.

Rawls, J. (1988) *Zhengyi lun* [A Theory of Justice] (H. H. He, B. G. He & S. B. Liao, Trans.). China Social Sciences Press.

The Declaration of Independence. Retrieved December 12, 2021, from http://uscode.house.gov/download.

Shen, H., & Liu, X. C. (1991). *Yingguo yihui zhengzhishi [British Parliamentary and Political History].* Nanjing University Press.

Topornin, B. (1986). *Shehui zhuyi zhengzhi zhidu* [Socialist Political System] (Z. H. Huang, Trans.). The Masses Publishing House

Xie, D. F., et al. (1962). *1765–1917 nian de Meiguo* [The United States of 1765–1917]. The Commercial Press.

Yamaguchi, Y. (1991). 'Lun xuanju zhidu dui zhengquan goucheng de yingxiang' [On the Impact of Political Regime by Electoral System]. In Y. Yamaguchi (Ed.), *Zhengzhi tizhi* [Political Regime] (1991) (T. Y. Han, Trans.). The Economic Daily Press.

Zhou, Y. Z.(1992). Some problems of democratization of China's electoral system. *Law Review*, (5).

Chapter 5
Representative System and State Structure

In modern democratic politics, popular sovereignty is a highly abstracted and generalized form of democratic content. Therefore, in my view, it is impossible to practically implement popular sovereignty until it has been transformed into civil rights and reified as the state power and the function of the state organs. Correspondingly, the representative system, as the basic system for the realization of democracy, is also a highly abstracted and generalized form of the indirect democracy, which, by extension, contains practical contents of the political life of democracy. In other words, only when the representative system is reified as various institutions and organizations, and by coordinating the relationship between them, can it truly be a basic approach to the realization of the popular sovereignty. Therefore, if popular sovereignty can only be realized through the process of decomposition and transformation, the same is true for the effective operation of the representative system. Therefore, discussion of the relationship between the representative system and the state structure reveals how the representative system is transformed and decomposed into specific organs and organizations.

5.1 Government System, Organizational Form of State Power and the Representative System

As analyzed in Chap. 2, the representative system is the product of modern society. Nevertheless, with the emergence of private ownership, classes and states, the political power has become the most important force in the management of human society. That is to say, when human beings progress from barbarism to civilization, they inevitably face the problem of how to use the political power to realize the power of the state. The representative system is a specific manifestation of political power construction during a certain historical period of human society. Moreover, since the representative system is an abstraction of indirect democratic forms, it does not

Y. Zhou, *A Comparative Study of Representative Systems*,
https://doi.org/10.1007/978-981-15-4186-5_5

include all forms of democracy. Moreover, democracy does not comprise all issues concerning the realization of power of the state and political power construction in different social forms. Therefore, I believes a concept with richer and broader connotations and denotations exists above the representative system. That is the government system.

5.1.1 The Government System and Others

(1) The Concept of Government System

To understand the concept of the government system, we have to first make clear the concept of the state system. In the history of political thought, the distinction between the state system and the government system is a product of social development at a certain stage of history. Ancient scholars, such as Plato and Aristotle, usually confused the two. It was not until in the 16th century that the French thinker Bodin first distinguished the two. According to him, a distinction should be made between the organizational form of the state, which depends on the number of sovereigns, and the management form of the state, which depends on the ways and methods of exercising power. However, Bodin "did not find a real scientific criterion to distinguish the type of state from the form of state, so he not only confused the concepts of the state system and the government system, but also failed to explicitly define the concept of the form of state."[1] Even later scholars such as Hobbes, Locke, and Rousseau failed to make substantial progress on this issue. As a matter of fact, all theories of political science and jurisprudence of the exploiting classes failed to make a clear distinction between the state system and the government system. Even though some scholars made an attempt, they still believed that the state systems of all countries were of the same nature. For example, Zhang J. J. once said, "all countries are the same without any fundamental differences in terms of their constituent elements and political nature."[2] The reason why the systems of all countries in the world are so different in form lies in their different types of government systems, so it is easy to confuse the two if we cannot differentiate them.

Only Marxism has made a clear distinction between the state system and the government system, and holds that the state system refers to the nature of the state, i.e. which classes are in the ruling position and which classes are in the ruled position in the country. In the ruling classes, if several classes jointly rule, it is still necessary to further distinguish which is the leading class and which are merely allies. However, although the concept of the state system has been generally accepted by the academic community, there are few illustrations of state systems in the whole relevant literature.

---

[1] Xu, D. T. (ed.) (1985) *Xifang zhengzhi sixiang shi* [A History of Western Political Thought], Tianjin: People's Publishing House, p. 150.

[2] Zhang, J. J. (1979) *Zhengzhixue gailun* [An Introduction to Politics], Taipei: San Min Book Co., Ltd., p. 143.

In my view, associating the concept of the state system with Bodin's theory, is somewhat suggestive. His so-called distinction between "the organizational form of the state" and "the management form of the state" does not make much sense, for both of them actually refer to the same thing, i.e. the government system, without touching upon the type of the state in a scientific sense. Nevertheless, Bodin's distinction between "ownership of sovereignty" and "exercise of sovereignty" holds some truth. Comparing the two concepts with the state system and the government system correspondingly, it is not difficult to find that the so-called state system actually concerns the issue of the ownership of sovereignty, while government system involves the exercise of sovereignty, but these concepts fall in the super-class category. However, under the Marxist method of class analysis, the state system is in fact a matter of the class attribute of sovereignty, that is, which class owns the sovereignty. Therefore, the status of various social classes in a state, I think, actually depends on the class attribute of sovereignty. In other words, the class is in possession of sovereignty determines the state system of the country. If the bourgeoisie controls the state sovereignty, then it is a state ruled by the bourgeoisie, similarly, if the proletariat holds the state sovereignty, it is a state of the proletariat. Before the birth of Marxism, political scientists and constitutional scholars had no conception of class analysis, so their understanding of the class attribute of sovereignty was vague. Accordingly, it was impossible for them to come up with a scientific concept of the state system.

Therefore, the state system refers to which class or classes the state sovereignty belongs, i.e. the class attribute or class nature of a state.

Then, what is the government system? Western scholars generally define the concept of government system in accordance with ownership of the legislative power or the number of members in the organizations of state power. The concept of a government system defined in this way is unscientific because the so-called ownership of legislative power actually belongs to the content of the state, and the changing of the number of members in the organizations of state power may be affected either by the nature of state power or by the population, regions, and complexity of state affairs. So, the instability of these variables might lead to the uncertainty and confusion of the so-called "government system". In fact, there is no consensus achieved among the proletarian scholars on the issue of the government system, they have even failed to obtain valuable conceptions of it. Although the classical Marxist writers once discussed this issue from various angles, they did not clearly define it either. Only when Comrade Mao Tse-Tung discussed the new democratic politics in his book *On New Democracy*, was distinction made clear. Mao wrote, "As for the question of 'the government system', this is a matter of how state power is organized, the form in which one social class or another chooses to arrange its apparatus of state power to oppose its enemies and protect itself. There is no state which does not have an appropriate apparatus of state power to represent it."[3] Henceforth, Comrade Mao

[3] *Mao Zedong xuanji* [Selected Works of Mao Tsetung] (1991), Beijing: People's Publishing House, vol. 2, p. 677. cf. Mao, Z. D. (1940) *Xin minzhu zhuyi lun* [On New Democracy].

Tse-Tung's words have provided a clear definition of the government system for political and constitutional studies.

In my view, the government system and the state system are a pair of relative concepts. As mentioned above, the state system refers to the class membership or class attribute of state sovereignty, while the government system is designed to realize state sovereignty for the class that possesses it. The reason why I define the government system in this way is mainly based on the following considerations: First, the mutual relationship between the state system and the government system; Second, the relevant discourses of both the Western scholars and the Marxism-Leninist writers. To my understanding, although there are fundamental differences between their views, they both attempt to briefly outline a system for the realization of the state power. Third, I agree with Professor He Huahui's view that there is a difference between the government system and the organizational form of state power.

(2) **Similarities and Differences Between Government System and Organizational Form of State Power**

According to Professor He Huahui:

> The government system and the organizational forms of state power are two different forms of realizing state power, and both of them are closely related yet differ from each other. They have different focuses with the former on the system and the latter on the organs. The system is to briefly outline the organizing processes and basic forms of state power, whereas the organizational forms of state power is to specify the organs that implement state power and the interrelationships among various organs.[4]

Moreover, the government system and the organizational forms of state power, I believe, occupy different levels. The former is the abstraction and generalization of the latter, and the latter is the specific manifestations of the former. I hold the government system to be the state power structure at the macro level, which is general and abstract. The demarcation of the government system types must be based on the most distinctive features as the criterion. In other words, the government of the same types must share the identical distinctive features. However, the organizational forms of state power are micro manifestations of the macro state power structure, which is particular and specific. Defining the types of organizational forms of state power is not necessarily based on the distinctive features. Different organizational forms of state power may belong to the same type of state system, and their differences may result in various non-distinctive features. In other words, owing to the different historical conditions in various countries, the same type of government systems will be definitely different from one another in the process of being reified into the specific organizational forms. Therefore, in my view, the government system, in a sense, is a higher level concept of state power structure, while the organizational forms is a primary and lower level concept.

---

[4] He, H. H. (1988) *Bijiao xianfa xue* [Comparative Constitution], Wuhan: Wuhan University Press, p. 144.

(3) **Organizational Forms of State Power and State Organs**

As mentioned above, the organizational forms of state power refer to the organs that realize the state power as well as the mutual relations between the organs. In this regard, the views of the theorists are basically the same. Some scholars claimed, "the organizational forms of the state power mainly refers to the arrangement of government institutions and the division of their powers, that is, the ruling class institutes the state structure in accordance with the principles stipulated by laws in order to realize its own will, maintain its own interests and consolidate its own rule."[5] Therefore, I think that the so-called organizational form of state power is actually the organizational system of the state organs, or the internal formation of the state structure. Similarly, the state structure also refers to the sum of all state organs instituted in accordance with certain principles and operating mechanisms in the country. Strictly speaking, the state structure is only a kind of static manifestation of the organizational forms of state power. However, the government system has no direct relation with the state organs and the state structure. As a matter of fact, the government system is linked to the state organs mediated through the organizational forms of state power. Therefore, we can mark the relationships between the three as the follows:

$$\text{government system} \rightleftarrows \text{organizational forms of state power} \rightleftarrows \text{state organs}$$

5.1.2 *The Representative and Organizational Systems of State Power*

(1) **Representative System Is not the Organizational Form of State Power**

In Chinese academic circles, many people not only equate the government system with organizational forms of state power, but also consider the socialist people's representative system and the capitalist parliamentary system to be all the organizational forms of state power. In their view, the representative system is nothing but the organizational forms of state power. In my opinion, this view is questionable.

Firstly, they are both different in connotations. As previously mentioned, the representative system refers to the system in which the ruling class of a country elects a certain number of members from its own class or stratum that can reflect its will and interests to form the representative organs, and decides and manages the major state affairs whether political, economical, social or other aspects of the country in accordance with the principle that the minority is subordinate to the majority. In short, the representative system is the system through which the ruling class governs the state. Whereas, the organizational forms of state power refer to the organs through

[5] Li, Z. S. (ed.) (1987) *Xin zhengzhi xue* [The New Politics], Changsha: Hunan People's Publishing House, p. 201.

which the ruling class implements the state power and their mutual relationships between the organs. In a word, the organizational forms of state power mainly refer to the organs of state power. Therefore, state power can only be realized through its organs or institutions, similarly, the representative system has to be institutionalized into its corresponding organs, through which the state power can be achieved. In addition, the representative system itself is not a state organ but the basis on which state organs are organized and produced. As we all know, the representative system gives rise to the representative organs, from which other state organs are derived. Therefore, isn't it a bit confusing for the representative system to mainly refer to the state power organs and their interrelationship?

Secondly, they are both different semantically. According to *Ci Hai* [Word-Ocean Dictionary], the word "system" has two meanings: First, it refers to the work procedure and code of conduct that everyone is required to comply with, e.g. the working system; second, it refers to an institution formulated in a given historical context, such as political, economic and cultural ones, e.g. the socialist system. However, since the word "form" indicates the shape or structure of an object, the organizational form of state power is thus its organizational structure. Obviously, "shape or structure" does not share any common ground with "work procedure or code of conduct", and then what about the relationship between "shape or structure" and "system"? A system is an integral whole composed of certain things or ideas related to one another. Therefore, the two concepts are also different in that "structure" refers to the distribution and combination of various constituent parts, rather than an integrated whole. Therefore, in the etymological sense, the representative system is also different from the organizational forms of state power in that the representative system not only concerns the distribution and combination of the state power organs, but more importantly, it involves the organization and production of them.

(2) **Organizational Forms of State Power and Organizational System**

In my opinion, it is of great significance to put forward the concept of the organizational system of state power in the studies of political science and constitutional law. The reasons are as follows: Firstly, if the ruling class of a given state wants to establish a stable state power, some principles or regulations must be followed, otherwise, the decline and demise of the state is definite. Secondly, from the history of the state power construction of all countries, past or present, there must be reasons why state power is established in a country or a country in a certain historical period adopts one state structure instead of others. In other words, different organizational forms of state power in countries definitely result from the different principles or regulations of the state power construction in different countries, which has not been generalized yet in the previous studies. Thirdly, in the past, theorists have confused the formal structure itself with the basis on which the structure is established, which is neither conducive to the construction of the state power structure nor to the exploration of the basis for a better structure. In my opinion, the organizational system of a state power is the system where the ruling class, in accordance with certain principles and methods, organizes and manages state power for consolidating its ruling position.

So, what is the relationship between the organizational system and the organizational form of the state power? In my view, the organizational system is the basis of the organizational forms in a country, and the organizational forms are the specific surface structures of the organizational system. Therefore, the former is an inherent content with a decisive influence and the latter is the structured forms of the former. Moreover, I think, the establishment of the organizational system of a state power in a country can not simply be decided on a whim by the ruling class, but in fact, it is a static and dynamic coordination mechanism adapted to the specific values chosen by the ruling class. First, the organizational system of state power must adapt to the government system determined by the state system and the objective historical conditions. Then, it must conform to the value orientation of the ruling class. Therefore, the organizational system of state power is actually the product of a fusion of state system, government system, objective historical conditions and various conflicts of interest of the ruling class. Moreover, as a system of ways or methods to realize the sovereignty of the ruling class, the government system cannot directly affect the organizational construction of the state power. In fact, what directly decides and affects the organizational construction of state power is only the organizational system of state power. Therefore, the organizational system of state power acts as a medium or bridge for the government system and objective historical conditions to affect the construction of the forms of the state power.

(3) **The Representative System as the Organizational System of State Power**

Since the representative system cannot be regarded as the organizational form of state power, then what category should it belong to? Based on our analysis of the organizational system of state power and the representative system, I argue that the representative system belongs to the organizational system of state power and thus it is a direct basis for the ruling class to build and realize state power. Moreover, if we investigate the generation and operation of the representative system in various countries, it is not difficult to find that the representative system with the representative organs at its core plays a significant role in the process of instituting the forms of the state power, whether it is in a state under the dictatorship of the bourgeoisie or the proletariat, so its manifestations are naturally different in countries that practice the separation of powers or that do not. Even in countries that implement the separation of powers, its manifestations are also different in countries that adopt a presidential-system and a cabinet-system.

In addition, from the analysis above, we can draw a conclusion that we must make some adjustments to the current theoretical system of constitutional law. In my view, the theoretical concepts relevant to the forms of state power realized by the ruling class can be hierarchically ordered in this way: government system → organizational system of state power → organizational forms of state power → state power organs. Among them, the government system and the organizational system of state power are in the category of "state system", while the organizational forms and state organs are in the category of "state structure". This distinction above apparently contradicts with the traditional one in the current academic community of constitutional theory because the organizational forms of state power belongs to "state system" in existing constitutional law, though it actually refers to the organizational system in its real sense. Therefore, due to the differences between the organizational forms and the organizational system in terms of state power, I think that it is more appropriate to make partial adjustments to them in order to keep them more coherent and scientific in discipline.

5.2 Impact of Representative System on State Structure

As the state structure is the specific organizer and executor in the process of realizing the functions and powers of the state, its organization and operation are crucial to the fulfillment of the functions and tasks of the state. Since the representative system, as an organizational system of state power, can give full play to its function only if it is reified as an organ or organization of state power, the representative system is bound to exert a significant impact on the modern state structure, i.e. the system of state organs. However, although scholars in China and abroad have conducted some case studies on the organization and operation of the state structure in various countries, studies that combine the organization and operation of the state structure and the representative system, particularly studies of the actual impacts of the representative system on the state structure, are relatively rare. This section will attempt to address this issue.

5.2.1 An Overview of State Structure

The structure of the state, also known as the state apparatus, is the sum of state organs established by the ruling class to exercise state power and fulfill the functions of the state. Throughout the historical development of human society, the existence of state structure is a common phenomenon in any social form of an existing country. So, we can say, where there is a state, there must be the structure of the state, and without the structure of the state, a state does not exist. Since the state is an organization of class rule, it is impossible for the ruling class of a country to realize its class rule without certain political organizations. Therefore, the structure of the state is not only the main carrier of the functions and powers of the state, but also the external symbol of the state form. However, in different types of countries, or in different historical periods of a country, the sizes of the state structure and the names, organizational forms, functions and powers, and methods of operation of the state organs vary from one another. In any case, the structure of the state has the following main features: First, it is the product of historical development at a certain stage. The structure of the state does not exist until the birth of the state. Only after the emergence of private ownership and class distinction and the development of irreconciliable contradictions between the exploiting and the exploited classes, did the structure of the state finally take shape. When human society develops to the stage of communism, the structure of the state will inevitably perish with the extinction of classes and states. Second, the purpose of its organization and operation is inherently characteristic of its class nature. The structure of the state refers to all organizations established independently by the dominant class in a society or jointly with its allies in order to achieve its class will for the purpose of consolidating the dominant position of the ruling class in all aspects of political, economic and social life. Therefore, its organizations are by no means representative of all members of the society. Third, it is characteristic of the organic system of its internal structure. The purpose of establishing the structure of the state determines that each component of the structure must function independently, perform its own duties, and communicate with each other to coordinate their actions, so as to establish a well-organized and unified structural system. Fourth, it is characteristic of state coercion secured by violent organizations. In the structure of the state, not only are its internal organs, such as the army, police, prisons, and courts themselves organs of violence, but other state organs also make full use of these state coercive forces backed by the organs of violence in the realization of functions and powers of the state, so that not only every member of the ruling class is required to obey the fundamental interests of the entire ruling class, but also the ruled class is compelled to abide by relevant laws so as to maintain a ruling order in favor of the ruling class.

At the same time, based on the aforementioned concepts and features of the structure of the state, we can find another two points: First, the nature of the structure of the state is determined by the nature of the state. In other words, the nature of the state gives rise to the nature of the structure of the state. More specifically, the class nature of the state is the basis for the classification of the types of the structure of the state, that is, different class natures determine different types of the state structure. The structure of the state in every country of the exploiting class is bound to be the tool for the exploiting class to maintain its private ownership of the means of production, consolidate its dictatorship and thus perform its economic exploitation and political oppression against the working people and the exploited class. In contrast, the structure of the state in a socialist country is the tool by which the proletariat and the working people maintain their public ownership of the means of production and consolidate their dictatorship of the proletariat so as to become the masters of their own. Second, the internal components of the state structure are determined by the state functions, that is, state functions prescribes the state organs to be established. For example, during the period of liberal capitalism, the bourgeois countries did not set up enormous structure of the state in order to fulfill their doctrine of "no government is the best government". With the concentration and monopoly of capital, the bourgeois countries instituted more state administrative organs, and especially increased the violent organs such as the army, police, prisons and courts, in order to reinforce their internal and external functions of the state and meet the needs of the monopoly bourgeoisie. When early socialist countries were founded, the internal function of the state was mainly to suppress the resistance of the exploiting class at home, so its primary task was to institute and strengthen its organs of suppression. With the eradication of the exploiting class, as the focus of the state task was shifted to economic construction, the establishment of the economic management organs was prioritized.

Obviously, the functions of the state are crucial and direct factors that determine the structure of the state. Moreover, from the internal composition of the structure of the state, we can find that different conditions in different countries, such as class nature, historical missions and balance of class forces, determine the simplicity or complexity of the structure of the state and the different interrelationships between its different state organs. However, the structure of a state generally includes the legislative, executive, the judicial organs, but their status and interrelationships vary in different countries.

5.2.2 How Does the Representative System Affect State Structure?

In history, the structure of the state has developed from simple to complex, from lower level to higher level, and from the mixture of various organs to the scientific and reasonable division of labor among them. Although the economic base upon which the nature of the state is built is the most fundamental factor that determines the structure of the state, the functions of the state and the organizational system of the state power are the direct factors that lead to differences in status and interrelations of various components of the structure of the state in countries or a country in different historical periods. As mentioned earlier, the change of the state function will inevitably lead to the change of the structure of the state, that is to say, the state function determines what structure of the state the ruling class is to institute. Then, what determines the status of and the interrelationships between the various components of the structure of the state? I think it is the organizational system of state power. In other words, it is the organizational system of state power that determines the mutual relationships between various state organs, that is to say, it determines the status and roles of the state organs in the whole system of the structure of the state. Especially in the management of modern states and societies, the decisive role of the representative system is even more prominent after it became the organizational system of state power in modern times. In other words, with the emergence of the commodity economy and the formation of nation states, the representative system has become the key to the development of democracy, and thus become the fundamental basis and precondition of the state and social management in democratic countries. Generally speaking, the impacts of the representative system upon the modern structure of the state are mainly manifested in the following aspects:

(1) **The Representative System as Rationale for Establishment of State Structure**

As discussed above, the organizational system of state power is the direct basis on which the ruling class of a country builds its state power so as to achieve the power of the state, while the state structure is a general term for the state organs which are established by the ruling class to exercise the power of the state and realize state functions. Just because of this, the representative system, as the organizational system of state power, is the basis for the establishment of the structure of the state in modern countries. First, representative systems of different natures will lead to different structures of the state with different natures. To be specific, the structure of the state established on the basis of the capitalist parliamentary system is necessarily a capitalist one, while the structure of the state based on the socialist people's representative system is bound to be a socialist one. Second, different representative systems will lead to the different internal compositions in the structure of a state, that is to say, under different representative systems, the interrelationships among various state organs will be different. For example, under the socialist people's representative system, the people's representative organs, also known as plenipotentiary organs or sovereign organs, are those through which the people exercise the power of the state. Therefore, the administrative, judicial and other state organs are derived from the people's representative organs. In this way, the socialist people's representative system actually becomes the basis of the structure of the state in a socialist country. Under the capitalist parliamentary system, the representative organs are only the legislatures in general, not the organs of the state sovereignty as the socialist people's representative organs. Therefore, in the structure of a capitalist state, the legislatures are generally in an equal relationship of mutual restriction with other state organs, such as administrative and judicial ones. Third, the emergence and improvement of the representative system are directly related to the improvement and development of the structure of a state. If we say that the state functions of a slave or feudal society lead to a relatively simple structure of the state and the state functions of a capitalist country give rise to an more complicated structure of the state, similarly, the emergence and development of the representative system greatly promote the development and perfection of the structure of the state for modern countries. Under the organizational system of state power in a slave or feudal society, the broad masses of the working people, who account for the vast majority of members of the society, have no right to participate in the exercise of the power of the state wither in reality or in form. Therefore, the way of exercising the state power is relatively simple, so is the establishment of the structure of the state. However, as the representative system came into being, the participation of the majority of the working people in the exercise of state power was emphasized both in form and in effect due to the pursuit of the principle of popular sovereignty. As a result, the way of exercising state power is becoming more and more complicated, and the structure of the state is bound to be more and more complex. Fourth, modern countries mostly operate under the rule of law, where the establishment of the structure of the state must be based on laws. As the representative organs are legislatures, their legislative activities directly influence the establishment and completion of other state organs.

(2) **The Representative System as Basis for Operation of State Structure**

The ruling class establishes the state structure in order to realize and satisfy its interests and wishes through the operation of the structure. As the organizational system of state power in modern countries, the representative system is not only the rationale for the establishment of the structure of the state, but also the basis for the operation of the structure. First, any state structure, after being established, must carry out its activities according to certain principles. Although there are multiple principles, the main principles are determined by the representative system. In other words, the differences in the main operational principles of the structure of the state result from the different representative systems. For example, the principle of separation of powers and checks and balances is not only the unique principle of the capitalist parliamentary system, but also the primary operational principle of the state structure in a capitalist state, and the principle of democratic centralism is the unique principle of the socialist people's representative system as well as the primary operational principle of the state structure in a socialist state. Second, state organs can function effectively only through the exercise of their functions and powers, so as to ensure the effective operation of the structure of the state. However, the scope, procedures, ways and methods of exercising the functions and powers by the state organs must be prescribed by law. Therefore, the representative system, with the representative organs as the main bodies, provides a legal basis for the exercise of the functions and powers of the state organs. Third, the representative system can also coordinate the relationship among the constituents of the structure of the state by solving the contradictions arising in its operation because different organs will inevitably produce various contradictions in their specific activities. As an organizational system of the state power, the representative system should naturally coordinate and manage contradictions, which is easy to understand under socialist people's representative system. Even under the capitalist parliamentary system, since most of the members of the capitalist representative organs are representatives from different strata and groups of the bourgeois class, once a conflict arises between the various state organs, it can be solved completely through the activities of the members in the representative organs. This has been proved in political practice. Therefore, the representative system is the basis for the operation of state organs, and its improvement is directly related to the operation of the structure of the state.

5.3 Capitalist Parliamentary System and State Structure

Generally, the representative system has an important influence on the structure of the state, and the structure of the state is in turn the reification of the representative system. However, representative systems of different countries, especially the two different types, give rise to many specific but different effects upon the structure of the state. Therefore, it is quite necessary to study the respective effects of the capitalist parliamentary system and the socialist people's representative system upon the structure of the state.

5.3.1 Critical Analysis of Capitalist State Structure

The structure of the capitalist state was established to accomplish the tasks faced by the bourgeoisie and realize various functions of the bourgeois state after the bourgeoisie won the revolution and seized the state power. Compared with the state structures in slave and feudal countries, the economic foundation on which the capitalist state structure is built is a more advanced means of production, which determines that the capitalist state structure is the most complete and highest manifestation among all types of the exploiter states. Specifically, first, in terms of the guiding ideology, the theoretical basis of the state structure in the slave and feudal countries was grounded on the autocratic political thought of "the divine right of kings" and "rex et regnum", while that of the capitalist state structure was based on the bourgeois democratic ideas and principles such as "popular sovereignty" and "separation of the three powers". Such principles represent great progress over autocracy. Second, in terms of their organization and activities, the slave and feudal states generally practiced a system of heredity and life-long tenure for the monarchs and principal officials, and more often a system of hierarchical investiture. However, in capitalist countries, the electoral system is generally adopted, and the civil service system is established and implemented based on the principles of bourgeois democracy. In this way, the capitalist countries are more advanced than the slave and feudal countries in selection of talents, and recruiting and managing officials. Third, different from the slave and feudal countries, which are ruled by individual monarchs or a small number of rulers, the capitalist countries advocate the rule of law, emphasize that the establishment and operation of the state structure must be based on law, and have established a series of systems and principles concerning the exercise of legislative power by the representative organs, judicial independence, equality, defense, jury, public trial, etc. All these set a clear course for the management of the whole state structure. Fourth, in terms of the division of functions and completeness of structures, in the slave and feudal countries, the structure of the state was rather simple with no clear functional division of its organs; with the progress of the industrial revolution and the accumulation of state governing experience, the capitalist countries have not only equipped the state organs with reasonable and clear functions, but also established a complete system of the state structure adaptable to the state organs. In this sense, the capitalist state structure marks great and historic advance in the development of the structure of the state.

It must be made clear that when we say that the state structure of capitalist countries is more advanced than that of slave and feudal countries, it does not mean that the capitalist state structure has undergone a fundamental change in its class nature. As the capitalist state structure is an important part of the superstructure of the capitalist society, which is aimed at consolidating the private ownership of the means of production and protecting and promoting the development of the capitalist mode of production, its class nature remains the same as that of the state structures in slave and feudal countries. As a matter of fact, the two types of state structures are both tools used for the ruling class to economically exploit and politically oppress the broad masses of the working people, except that the capitalist state structure is manifested in a more sophisticated and complicated way in its forms of organization. What's more, from its evolutionary process, the capitalist state structure is the product of the inheritance, utilization and development of the old state machinery, so its nature can not be completely transformed.

In terms of the internal composition of the capitalist state structure, there are generally four major differences, though many differences exist in different capitalist countries or at different stages of capitalism in historical development. First, the head of state. The head of state or chief of state is the supreme leader of a sovereign state who is responsible for the internal and external affairs on behalf of the country in reality or in form. In modern countries, there will be a head of state regardless of the nature of the state. However, only after the emergence of the head of state in capitalist countries, did the position become endowed with its modern sense and functions. In capitalist countries, the heads of state may have different names and adopt different forms. Generally, most of capitalist countries often adopt the unitary head of state system, but a few of them, such as San Marino and Switzerland, implement the collective head of state system. There are mainly two ways to select a head of state—a hereditary system and an electoral system. Correspondingly, there are two types of terms of office: life-long tenure and limited tenure. Heads of state in capitalist countries are generally vested with great powers, such as the power of promulgating laws, the power of issuing orders, the power of convening parliaments, the power of diplomacy, the power of commanding armed forces, the power of appointing and dismissing officials, the power of pardon, and the power of having the honor. Second, the legislature. The legislature is the body that has the power to enact, amend or repeal laws. In capitalist countries, the legislature is generally the parliament or congress.[6] Third, the executive authorities. The executive authorities, also called the administrative organs or governments, are the organs that exercise the state administrative power and manages the daily political life of the country. The executive authorities of capitalist countries are the most complete and comprehensive bureaucracy that has evolved from that of the slave and feudal countries. Especially at the stage of monopoly capitalism, the combination of the monopoly organizations and the executive authorities has not only made the bureaucracy increasingly large, but also made it a major instrument for the monopoly capital to rule internally and expand externally, so they are often called "omnipotent governments". However, the forms adopted for the executive authorities, especially the central executive authority, depend on the organizational system of the state power in each country. According to constitutions and laws of various countries, the executive authority of a capitalist state generally includes the following powers: the power to enforce laws, the power to participate in legislation and the power to manage the domestic, foreign and military affairs. Fourth, the judiciary. The judicial authorities are the institutions that exercise the judicial power of the state. In capitalist countries, the judiciary authorities often refer to the courts. As for the procuratorial organ, it can be a part of the executive authorities in some countries. For example, the U.S. Department of Justice also has

[6] This has been discussed in various chapters of this book, and is omitted here.

the functions of the procuratorial organs, and the U.S. Attorney General is both the head of judicial and procuratorial organs. In other cases, it can be a part of the court. For example, the Public Prosecution Service is affiliated with the British courts to perform the functions of the procuratorial organs, and so on. According to theory of "separation of powers", the court appears to be an "independent judiciary" and an "arbitrator" of the parties concerned, but the result of both the trial activities and judicial decisions of the court is that the laws representing the will and interests of the bourgeoisie are bound to be enforced and the ruling order of the bourgeoisie is bound to be maintained. Therefore, there is no essential difference between the judicial organs and other state organs of the capitalist countries, and they cooperate with each other to jointly protect the political and economic rule of the bourgeoisie.

5.3.2 Impact of Capitalist Parliamentary System on State Structure

Superficially, in a country with the typical "tripartite system", which emphasizes the separation of powers and checks and balances between the legislative, executive and judicial organs, the legislature, namely the representative organ, has no superior position compared with other state organs. Therefore, the claim that the representative system is the rationale and basis for the structure of the state seems to be untenable. The following two facts show that this is unreasonable. First, the representative system cannot be equated with the representative organ. Although the representative system takes the representative organ as its core and there is no representative system without the representative organ, the connotation and meaning of the representative system are far from the above mentioned. Therefore, it is one-sided to conclude that the representative system cannot be the rationale and basis of the structure of the state simply judging from the status of the representative organ. What's more, when we talk about the relationship between the representative system and the structure of the state, we refer to the relationship between the representative system and the structure of the state including the legislature. Second, in the history of state and social management, the representative system emerged and developed as a necessary condition for the realization of democracy in modern nation-states. It can even be said that a modern state would have no democracy without a representative system. Therefore, in modern democratic countries, the representative system is the most fundamental form of and approach to state and social management. In this sense, the representative system constitutes the basis of all the state and social administrative organs and organizations. The structure of the state, as the most basic instrument for state governance, is certainly no exception. In discussing the U.S. government system, Thomas Paine once pointed out, "The government of America, which is wholly on the system of representation, is the only real republic in character and in practice, that now exists. Its government has no other object than the public business of the nation, and therefore it is properly a republic; and the Americans have taken care that THIS, and no other, shall be the object of their government, by their rejecting every thing hereditary, and establishing governments on the system of representation only."[7] Again, Paine argued that the representative system is the denial of the monarchy and the development of simple democracy, and it is the best government system the modern nation-states can adopt. Specifically, in the United States, the American government could be established only after the representative system was confirmed as the best form of governance of the republic. Thus, on the whole, it is the universal law that the representative system constitutes the basis of the structure of the state in all modern democratic nations.

In capitalist countries, the practice of the representative system varies from country to country, as does its specific impact upon the structure of the state. As discussed above, the impact of the representative system on the structure of the state is mainly manifested in its influence on the status of the various components of the state structure and their mutual relations. According to the constitutional provisions and political practices in capitalist countries, there are three major types of impacts of the capitalist parliamentary system on the state structure[8]:

First, the British style parliamentary republic. Its main feature is that the creation, existence and dissolution of the government is based on the Parliament. To be more specific, the government (cabinet) is formed by the political party that holds the majority of seats in the Parliament and is responsible for the Parliament. In Britain, the House of Lords is the supreme judicial body, and its main judicial functions are carried out by the permanent judges of the House of Lords (or appellate trial nobility) appointed by the King, while other members of the House of Lords are not involved in judicial activities. According to the bourgeois constitutions, in a parliamentary republic, the parliament is the highest organ of state power, which enjoys the legislative power and the power to supervise the government. In terms of the relationship between the Parliament and the government (cabinet), the government is formed by the party or party alliance with the majority of seats authorized by the Parliament. The government and its cabinet members should be accountable to the Parliament. When the Parliament does not support the government's administrative policy and passes a no-confidence motion against the government, the government must resign en bloc or appeal to the head of state to dissolve the Parliament and hold a new election. If the new parliament still passes the no-confidence motion against the government, the government must resign en bloc. Obviously, in a parliamentary republic, there is a close alignment between the parliament and the government (cabinet), where the executive power and legislative power are actually integrated and the executive authorities depend on the legislature. The creation of this type of capitalist parliamentary system originated in the attempt to weaken or restrict the executive power to a large extent. The executive authorities are indispensable

[7] Paine, T. (1982) *Pan'en xuanji* [Selected Works of Thomas Paine], trans. Ma Q. H., The Commercial Press, p. 244. cf. Stade, S. (ed.) (2005). *Common Sense and Other Writings* by Thomas Paine, London and New York: Barnes & Noble Books, p. 216.

[8] This classification here is based on the relationship between parliament and government, so the following discussion will focus on the differences of the generation and organizational form of administrative organs.

components of the government system of a state and the center of the state decision-making machine. Regardless of their legal powers, the state executive authorities are typically able to and are required to formulate important state policies, and at the same time, it is naturally involved in the implementation of these policies. Just as Jean Blondel pointed out, "It is in consideration of this dominant position of the executive organ that the liberals have been trying to weaken or restrict the executive power, but this effort has only succeeded in a limited scope."[9] He continued to point out that the success of the restriction of the executive power rests more on the operational characteristics of the political system and the combination of social forces, and less on the existence of laws.[10] In this regard, the British political practice provides sufficient proof. According to the basic principles of a parliamentary republic, the existence or abolition of a government rest upon the parliament, but on the contrary, it is the government that takes control of the parliament through the majority seats of its party in the parliament in actual political practice. However, the parliamentary republic, as one of the typical forms of the capitalist parliamentary system which has an important influence on the structure of the state, plays a very significant role in the political life of capitalist countries.

Second, The American style presidential republic. Its main feature is that the government is only responsible to the president, not to the parliament. Specifically, the government is directly led by the president, and the executive authorities headed by the president operate independent of the legislature. The Federal Supreme Court is also independent of the legislature and the executive branch, though its justices are nominated and appointed by the president with the consent of the Senate and are subject to judicial review and impeachment. According to the constitutions of capitalist countries, the president of a state that implements a presidential system is elected by universal suffrage on a regular basis. The president is both the head of state and the head of government holding the real executive power. Legally, all the ministers and officials of the executive organs of the government appointed and led by the president are only responsible to the president, not to the parliament. The president should report to the parliament and is entitled to exercise a limited veto power over the laws passed by the parliament, but has no right to dissolve the parliament. The United States is a typical example of a presidential republic. The reasons why the United States has adopted this form of political system can be traced back to the entrepreneurial American forefathers. According to *Encyclopedia Americana*, "The entrepreneurial forefathers emphasized the check and balance as a means to ensure individual freedom and avoid the government tyranny."[11] In other words, in terms of the relationship between the legislative and the executive, most of the participants of the Constitutional Convention agreed to adopt the principle of "check and balance" because they were not only worried that the executive would

[9] Miller, D. and Bogdanor, V. (eds) (1992). *The Blackwell Encyclopedia of Political Science*, New York: Wiley-Blackwell, p. 241.

[10] Ibid, p. 242.

[11] Cited in Shanghai Academy of Social Sciences Institute of Law, (ed.) (1982) *Xianfa* [Constitutions], Knowledge Publishing House, pp. 182–183.

be controlled by the parliament, but also more worried that the legislative would be manipulated by the powerful executive. In this way, the executive body and the legislature are separated, that is, the executive body is not to be produced by the legislature so that they can remain independent of each other and check and balance each other. As mentioned earlier, the typical form of the state structure based on the "separation of powers" in the United States is also grounded on the premise of the representative system. In other words, the American style presidential republic is also a kind of representative government. This view is also held by the western scholars. As Richard Margain pointed out, "Parliaments of different countries may be diverse in their functions and structures. In the system of a parliamentary government, the government or the executive branch is comprised of members who are supported by a majority of the parliament, while in the system of a presidential government, such as in the United States, the 'power of separation' is prescribed by the Constitution, where the congress mainly exercises the legislative powers. However, as far as the whole system is concerned, the system of the presidential government can still be referred to as the representative government."[12] Of course, in a system with such a structure, the influence of the parliamentary system on the state structure differs from that of the parliamentary republic. In the parliamentary republic, due to the integration of the legislative power and the executive power, the influence of the parliamentary system on the state structure is manifested as a direct and clear feature, whereas in the presidential republic, where legislative and the executive are independent of each other and are mutually restricted, the influence of the parliamentary system on the state structure is mainly indirect. Specifically, in the presidential republic, the parliamentary system affects the structure of the state from two major aspects: on the one hand, the parliamentary system, as the organizational system of the state power, affects the establishment and operation of the state structure. On the other hand, the parliament, as a legislative body, affects the state structure by making laws to provide legal basis for the establishment and operation of the state structure.

Third, the Swiss style Federal Council system. The Federeal Council system refers to a system where the highest executive power is collectively exercised by the Council, also known as Collegial System. The Swiss Confederation is typical of such a system. Since the Swiss Constitution does not adopt the system of "separation of power" and the Federal Assembly is the highest organ of the state power, its functions and powers are distinctively different from those of parliaments in other countries. In fact, it has legislative, executive and even judicial functions.[13] Therefore, in the Swiss Confederation, the parliamentary system as the prerequisite and basis of the state structure is particularly prominent. According to the Swiss Constitution, the highest executive body (i.e. the government) of the Swiss Confederation is the Federal Council composed of seven members elected by the Federal Assembly from among the citizens who are qualified representatives of the Assembly. From the seven

[12] Cited in Miller, D. and Bogdanor, V. (eds) (1992). *The Blackwell Encyclopedia of Political Science*, New York: Wiley-Blackwell, p. 648.

[13] Zeng, G. Z. (1989) *Xifang guojia xianfa he zhengfu* [Western Constitutions and Governments], Wuhan: Hubei Educational Publishing House, p. 649.

Federal Federal Councilors, one president and one vice-president are elected for a maximum of one term of one year and are not allowed to be re-elected. The president (nominally the head of state) only presides over the meetings and ceremonially represents the country externally. The status of the seven Councilors is completely equal, and each of them concurrently holds a position of minister in a department. The Council decides on the important issues and exercises the highest executive power collectively. Different from the parliamentary republic and the presidential republic, the relationship between the Federal Council and the Parliament is that the Federal Assembly enjoys the legislative and supervisory powers, and the Council implements laws and resolutions passed by the Federal Assembly, but has no veto power over them, let alone the power to dissolve the Assembly. The Federal Assembly has the right to address inquiries to the members of the Council, but if the bill proposed by the Council fails to pass, no motion of no confidence is triggered and the Council does not need to resign en bloc. At the same time, the Swiss constitution stipulates that the Federal Court is the judicial organ established by the central government, and the federal judges are elected by the joint session of the two houses of the Federal Assembly from citizens who are eligible to become representatives of the Assembly. In terms of their relationship, the Federal Court is also subordinate to and is required to submit an annual judicial report to the Federal Assembly, and the Assembly shall discuss the report and point out the deficiencies in their work, but has no authority to interfere in its judicial activities. Obviously, the Swiss Federal Assembly is the top authority in the system of the state structure and exercises the state power collectively. Therefore, the system of the Swiss Federal Assembly constitutes the most typical prerequisite and basic role for the structure of the state.

In summary, the impact of the capitalist parliamentary system on the structure of the state is manifested differently in different countries, and even in some countries it is invisible, but in fact, this invisibility itself is also the result of the different operational features of the parliamentary system. In other words, as the parliamentary system in the United States has its own distinctive features compared with those in the United Kingdom and Switzerland, its power structure is naturally different from that of the other two. Accordingly, the status of various components of the state structure and their relationship are also different in different countries. Therefore, the capitalist parliamentary system, as an organizational system of a state power, has a diverse impact on the state structure.

5.4 Socialist People's Representative System and State Structure

Since the socialist people's representative system is the fundamental approach and system for the broad masses of the working people in a socialist country to achieve the status of being masters of the country, then the socialist state structure is the specific organizer and executor that performs and implements various functions and powers of the state to guarantee the working people to exercise the power to be masters of the country. Therefore, there exists a close connection between the socialist people's representative system and the state structure.

5.4.1 Critical Analysis of Socialist State Structure

Although the state structure in capitalist countries is more advanced than that of slave or feudal states, the proletariat cannot simply inherit and adopt it directly. This is because the seizure of power by the proletariat is not a simple substitution for the exploiter countries with the identical nature. What the proletariat wants to establish is a new type of country where the system of exploitation will be completely eradicated. Therefore, "the working class cannot simply lay hold of the ready-made state machinery, and wield it for its own purposes",[14] but should completely smash it. And the socialist state structure is built on the basis of the destruction of the old state machinery. In this sense, the socialist state structure which is composed of outstanding representatives of the people performing the functions and powers of the socialist state is fundamentally different from those of the bourgeoisie and all other exploiters in nature. The socialist state structure has the following three basic features: The first is simplicity. The functions of a socialist country can be divided into two major domains: the function of governance and the function of economic and cultural construction. As for the function of governance, Lenin once pointed out that the suppression of the minority of exploiters by the majority of the wage slaves of yesterday is a comparatively easy, simple and natural a task. However, "the exploiters are unable to suppress the people without a highly complex machine for performing this task, but the people can suppress the exploiters even with a very simple 'machine', almost without a 'machine', without a special apparatus."[15] According to Lenin, it would be enough to have the simple organization of the armed people, such as the Soviets of Workers' and Soldiers' Deputies. As for the function of economic and cultural construction, Lenin argued that we could not concentrate all the economic affairs in the hands of the state organs nor rely solely on administrative measures to manage the economy, but emphasized that the people should supervise production and distribution, keep account of labor and products, and use the economic means to manage the economy. The second is incorruptibility. In summing up the experience of the Paris Commune, Karl Marx wrote, "The Commune made that catchword of bourgeois revolutions—cheap government—a reality by destroying the two greatest sources of expenditure: the standing army and state functionarism."[16] Therefore,

---

[14] *Makesi Engesi xuanji* [Marx and Engels Selected Works] (1995), Beijing: People's Publishing House, vol. 3, p. 52. cf. Marx, K. (1871) *The Civil War in France.*

[15] *Liening xuanji* [Lenin Selected Works] (1995), Beijing: People's Publishing House, vol. 3, p. 192. cf. Lenin, V. (1917) *The State and Revolution.*

[16] *Makesi Engesi xuanji* [Marx and Engels Selected Works] (1995), Beijing: People's Publishing House, vol. 3, p. 58. cf. Marx, K. (1871) *The Civil War in France.*

members of the state structure in a socialist country are no longer bureaucrats or functionaries, but public servants of the people. To prevent the degradation from public servants to bureaucrats, the revolutionary tutors repeatedly mentioned the experience of the Commune that all public servants should be universally elected and can be removed at any time, their salaries should be reduced to the level of ordinary workers, and the functions of supervision and inspection should immediately be transferred to the hands of the general public. The third is high efficiency. High efficiency means that the state structure and its members make decisions and handle the state affairs correctly, properly and quickly. As the socialist state structure is a tool for serving the people, high efficiency is sure to be demanded fundamentally.

It must be made clear that the above-mentioned three characteristics of the socialist state structure are inferred from the socialist public ownership of means of production and the nature of the state state power that is based on it. In the actual operation of the socialist state structure, simplicity, incorruptibility and high efficiency have contributed somewhat to the state structure, but the improvement is far from satisfactory.

As far as the internal composition of the socialist state structure is concerned, the socialist state structure includes the following four major components: the head of state, the legislature, the executive and the judiciary. However, their significance and status as well as the systems based on them in socialist countries are different from those of the capitalist countries in many ways. As for the head of state, socialist countries usually adopt a collective head system. Due to the principle of democratic centralism, no matter what form the head of state takes, the actual functions and powers are all exercised by the supreme organ of state power and the head of state itself is also elected by this organ. As for the legislature, the legislature of a socialist country is the supreme authority of the country and the plenipotentiary body through which the people exercise the power of governance. Different from its counterpart of a capitalist country, the legislature of a socialist country shall not be constrained by any other state organs of the country, nor shall any other state organs be allowed to compete with it. Moreover, in the system of the socialist state organs, it is in the highest position and has the supreme power. As for the executive, i.e. the administrative body, it is the executive organ of the state power organ in a socialist country, so it is elected by and responsible to the organ of state power. And the judiciary of a socialist country refers to the organ that exercises the judicial power and prosecutorial power on behalf of the country in accordance with the law. Like the executive, the judiciary is elected by and is responsible to the organ of state power at the same level. Although there is little difference in the internal composition between the capitalist state structure and the socialist state structure, in fact, they not only differ greatly in their class nature, but also in their interrelationship between various components. In other words, the socialist state structure is also unique in its formal structure, as manifested in the following two aspects. First, the legislature, as the people's representative organ, is a plenipotentiary organ, which occupies a leading and dominant position in the system of state organs. Second, all other state organs are all derived from the legislature and are responsible to and supervised by it. Therefore, the people's representative organ of a socialist country is fundamentally different from the parliament of a capitalist country.[17]

5.4.2 Impact of Socialist People's Representative System on State Structure

Different from the capitalist countries, whose theoretical bases for the state power construction are diverse, socialist countries usually observe a relatively identical theoretical basis for the construction of the state power, that is, they are all guided by the Marxist state theory. Therefore, the system of the state organs established by the socialist countries does not have diversified forms in different countries, and tends to be identical with each other in both the internal composition and the interrelationship between various components. In terms of the representative system and the structure of the state, the relationship between the socialist people's representative system and the structure of the state is a typical manifestation of the interrelationship between the organizational system and the organizational form of the state power. In other words, the socialist people representative system is the basis for the establishment of the state structure, and the state structure is a concrete external form of the socialist people's representative system. Specifically, the impact of the socialist people's representative system on the structure of the state is mainly reflected in the following two aspects:

(1) **Socialist People's Representative System Is the Basis for the Establishment and Operation of State Structure**

The socialist state power is a state power in which the broad masses of the working people are the masters of the country. Therefore, the constitutions of all socialist countries stipulate that all power of the state belongs to the people, and the organs through which the people exercise the state power are the people's representative organs at all levels. In this way, according to the theory of the socialist people's representative system, the legislative, executive and judicial powers are all exercised by the people's representative organs at various levels. In other words, under the socialist people's representative system, all power of the state belongs to the people and is collectively exercised by the people's representative organs. In this sense, the state power (including legislative, executive and judicial powers) is inseparable. However, the socialist people's representative system also requires that, on the premise of the unified exercise of the state power by the people's representative organs, there must be a clear division between the executive, judicial, procuratorial and military powers. Therefore, in the process of realizing the state power, the broad masses of the working people are required to institute the people's representative organs to uniformly exercise the state power, on the premise that a complete state organ system is also to be established. Therefore, the people's representative system, as an organizational form of the state power, plays an extremely significant role in establishing the structure of

[17] It's similar to Switzerland in form.

the state. Moreover, under this very system, the broad masses of the working people have a more direct and effective influence on the establishment of the state structure. Lenin pointed out:

> The more direct influence of the working masses on state structure and administration – i.e., a higher form of democracy – is also effected under the Soviet type of state, first, by the electoral procedure and the possibility of holding elections more frequently, and also by conditions for re-election and for the recall of deputies which are simpler and more comprehensible to the urban and rural workers than is the case under the best forms of bourgeois democracy; ... secondly, by making the economic, industrial unit (factory) and not a territorial division the primary electoral unit and the nucleus of the state structure under Soviet power. This closer contact between the state apparatus and the masses of advanced proletarians that capitalism has united, in addition to effecting a higher level of democracy, also makes it possible to effect profound socialist reforms.[18]

In addition, the reason why the status, role and interrelationship of the internal components within the socialist state structure described above are different from those of the capitalist countries is that there exist fundamental difference between the socialist people's representative system and the capitalist parliamentary system. The socialist people's representative system, as the essential approach for the broad masses of people to realize the power of being masters of the country in a unified way, inevitably determines that the socialist people's representative organ is a plenipotentiary one, while other state organs are derivative ones. However, in the process of realizing state power, the capitalist parliamentary system does not have such a unity and it emphasizes the separation and balance of the state power, so the state organs established are generally independent from and parallel to each other. Therefore, the socialist representative system provides the basis for the establishment of the state structure and for the adjustment and allocation of the interrelations between its various components. Moreover, after the establishment of the state structure, the state power and functions can only be exercised and realized through its operation and activities. Therefore, the socialist people's representative system, on the premise of insisting on the unified exercise of the state power, provides a basis for the coordination of the interrelationship between the various organs of the state structure through activities of the dominant people's representative organs.

(2) Socialist People's Representative System Provides the Basis for Unity and Improvement of State Structure

Generally, the state structure of any country is the tool for the ruling class to achieve its class rule. In this sense, it is a unity in terms of class nature and purpose. However, the unity of the internal components and their operation within the state structure is subject to a certain organizational system of a state power. Since the point of departure and basic contents of the socialist people's representative system emphasize the unified exercise of the state power, the establishment and operation of the state structure is bound to be a unity. In the meantime, the realization of state power depends

[18] *Liening xuanji* [Lenin Selected Works] (1995), Beijing: People's Publishing House, vol. 3, p. 723. cf. Lenin, V. (1931) *Draft Programme of the R.C.P. (B.).*

on the full play of various state organs to their effectiveness, and the organs that exercise the state power and realize the state functions cannot be perfect from the very beginning. Therefore, only by constantly summarizing experience and perfecting the state organ system can we achieve this goal. The socialist representative system, as the fundamental approach to the realization of the state power, serves as a basis for the further improvement of the state structure.

Crucially, the impact of socialist people's representative system on the state structure is conditional. Just as the realization of the "social republic" conceived by Marx and Engels requires the mature conditions of economy, politics, ideology, etc., the impact of socialist people's representative system on the state structure also has certain conditions. First, the status and role of the socialist people's representative system must be enhanced. Second, the internal components, structure and system of the socialist people's representative system must be improved. In other words, the status quo of the socialist people's representative system is directly related to the perfection of the state structure.

References

He, H. H. (1988). *Bijiao xianfa xue* [Comparative Constitution]. Wuhan University Press.

Lenin, V. (1917). *The State and Revolution.*

Lenin, V. (1931). *Draft Programme of the R.C.P. (B.).*

Li, Z. S. (Ed.). (1987). *Xin zhengzhi xue* [The New Politics]. Hunan People's Publishing House.

Liening xuanji [Lenin Selected Works]. (1995). People's Publishing House (Vol. 3).

Makesi Engesi xuanji [Marx and Engels Selected Works]. (1995). People's Publishing House (Vol. 3, p. 52).

Mao Zedong xuanji [Selected Works of Mao Tsetung]. (1991). People's Publishing House (Vol. 2).

Mao, Z. D. (1940). *Xin minzhu zhuyi lun* [On New Democracy].

Marx, K. (1871). *The Civil War in France.*

Miller, D., & Bogdanor, V. (Eds.). (1992). *The Blackwell Encyclopedia of Political Science.* Wiley-Blackwell.

Paine, T. (1982). *Pan'en xuanji* [Selected Works of Thomas Paine] (Ma, Q. H., Trans.). The Commercial Press.

Shanghai Academy of Social Sciences Institute of Law (Ed.). (1982). *Xianfa* [Constitutions]. Knowledge Publishing House.

Stade, S. (Ed.). (2005). *Common Sense and Other Writings* by Thomas Paine. Barnes & Noble Books.

Xu, D. T. (Ed.). (1985). *Xifang zhengzhi sixiang shi* [A History of Western Political Thought]. People's Publishing House.

Zeng, G. Z. (1989). *Xifang guojia xianfa he zhengfu* [Western Constitutions and Governments]. Hubei Educational Publishing House.

Zhang, J. J. (1979). *Zhengzhixue gailun* [An Introduction to Politics]. San Min Book Co., Ltd.

Chapter 6
Representative System and Party System

The fundamental problem that the representative system faces concerns the relationship between the representation of the minority and the interests and rights of the majority. The entrustment by the people, the consent of the people, or the "general will" is the basis of power of the representative organ system with the representative organs as the core, but how does the general will affect and shape our social life through the representative organs? It is of little significance to confine our study to some concepts of the representative system. The emphasis of research should be laid on the operation of the representative system with the purpose of figuring out the dynamic mechanism and laws of its operation, and especially the relationship between its operation and democracy. According to the theories and practices of the representative system, the dynamic mechanism for the operation of the representative system mainly consists of two parts: internal and external. The former refers to the operational relationship between the various institutions within the representative organ system, i.e. the work system that absorbs and expresses the general will, while the latter refers to the operational relationship between the political groups or political organizations relevant to the representative system, i.e. the work system that reflects and delivers the general will. In previous chapters, we have discussed the relationship between the representative system and the electoral system as well as the relationship between the representative system and the state structure, which concern the issues of the internal dynamic mechanism. From this chapter on, I will discuss the most important issues concerning the external dynamic mechanism, such as the party system and interest groups.

Y. Zhou, *A Comparative Study of Representative Systems*,
https://doi.org/10.1007/978-981-15-4186-5_6

6.1 Political Parties and Democratic Politics

Kobayashi Naoki, a well-known Japanese constitutional scholar, pointed out that political parties and party system are major issues concerning the success or failure of a parliamentary system, or even of the so-called modern constitutional democracy.[1] Yang Sen even argued that there would be no representative system without political parties.[2] Although such statements are not necessarily true, the practices of modern democratic politics have clearly indicated that political parties and party system are closely related to the representative system.

6.1.1 *An Overview of Political Parties and Party System*

(1) **Concept and Features of Political Party**

A political party is a political organization composed of the key members of a certain class, stratum or group that strives to realize its political program and political propositions reflecting its political and economic interests. A political party system is a general term for various systems concerning the status and role of the party, especially those involved with how a party governs, participates in or influences the state power, which is an important constituent of a political system in a modern state. In a broad sense, a political party can be regarded as an interest group, which is also based on the interests of a certain class, social stratum or group and aims to realize its own interests as its main contents. However, in modern democratic politics, a political party bears many distinctive features different from those of an interest group. Generally speaking, the biggest difference lies in their aims: a political party mainly seeks to take and keep control of the state power, while an interest group seeks to influence the state policies. In other words, "the pressure groups usually only care about what the government does while the political parties care more about who runs the government."[3] As David Hine pointed out, "Unlike other social constituents such as interest groups (or as Max Weber famously defined, classes or status groups), political parties aim not only at influencing the legitimate constitutional authority, but also at taking up posts in it." "As a political institute, the defining characteristic of a political party is that it is a mechanism connecting the state organs with civil and social organizations."[4] Specifically, a political party has four main characteristics. First, a political party boasts a concrete and clear political program, which is one

---

[1] Naoki, K. (1981) *Xianfa jiangyi* [The Constitutional Lectures], Tokyo: Tokyo University Press, pp. 78–79.

[2] Yang, S. (1985) *Xianggang shehui gaige* [Social Reform in Hong Kong], Hong Kong: Wide Angle Press, p. 255.

[3] Cited in Miller, D. and Bogdanor, V. (eds) (1992). *The Blackwell Encyclopedia of Political Science*, New York: Wiley-Blackwell, p. 512.

[4] Cited in Miller, D. and Bogdanor, V. (eds) (1992). *The Blackwell Encyclopedia of Political Science*, New York: Wiley-Blackwell, p. 512.

of the most important features that distinguishes a political party from other social organizations. Since the primary goal of a political party is to seize and maintain the state power, in order to achieve its political goal and guide its action amid complicated political struggles, a political party must have some clear propositions about domestic and foreign issues. Once a clear political programme is formulated by a political party, "one sets up before the whole world landmarks by which it measures the level of the Party movement."[5] Second, a political party should have clear political goals. The central issue of the political struggle is in fact a matter of state political power. A political party formed in class struggle is a political organization that aims at seizing and maintaining the state political power. More specifically, the ultimate goal of a political party is to strive for and achieve the power of domination over national life. After obtaining power, the party will consolidate its rule, and at least intervene with and influence the contents and tasks, approaches and policies of the national life, so as to maintain the interests of its class, social stratum, or group it represents. All activities of a political party should serve its political goal. Third, a political party has its fixed organizational system, and a political organization is the form of existence of a political party. In political practice, political organizations, loose or tight, are sure to have an organizational system. Without one, a political party would fall into a state of disunity like a heap of sand, unable to unify the will of its class and form a collective power. Under normal circumstances, a party organization refers to a unified organizational system shaped like a pagoda, consisting of the most basic organizations at the bottom up to the central organization at the top, and it is maintained by certain organizational principles and power relations. Fourth, all political parties have their own organizational discipline. Different from state organs, a political party often limits the behaviors of its members mainly through written or unwritten organizational discipline, which guarantee the smooth operation of the party activities, though the severity and nature of the discipline varies from party to party.

(2) **Historical Development of Party System**

Based on the concept and the characteristics of a political party discussed above, a political party is not, as some bourgeois scholars claim, an organization that expresses the will of the people, nor a centralized and unified group highly organized to gain votes for the candidates it nominates, but a political organization that strives for the fundamental interests of a certain class, social stratum or group it represents. Lenin once pointed out, "In a society based upon class divisions, the struggle between the hostile classes is bound, at a certain stage of its development, to become a political struggle. The most purposeful, most comprehensive and specific expression of the political struggle of classes is the struggle of parties."[6] Therefore, class nature is the essential attribute of a political party, while a political party is an organization

---

[5] *Makesi Engesi xuanji* [Marx and Engels Selected Works] (1995), Beijing: People's Publishing House, vol. 3, p. 296. cf. Marx, K. (1875) *Critique of the Gotha Programme.*

[6] *Liening quanji* [Lenin Collected Works] (1959), Beijing: People's Publishing House, vol. 10, p. 58. cf. Lenin, V. (1905) 'The Socialist Party and Non-Party Revolutionism'.

that belongs to a certain class, social stratum or group. Nonetheless, political parties did not come into being with the emergence of the private ownership and classes, but appeared only after classes and class struggles developed into the stage of capitalism in history. In slave and feudal societies, although there were various opposing political factions or groups due to conflicts of interest, such as the Aristocrats and the Populists in ancient Rome and Greece, the Guelphs and the Ghibellines in Italy from 12th to 15th century, they cannot be counted as political parties in modern sense because they lacked a political program, an organizational system, and organizational discipline. Then, why was it impossible to have a political party in slave and feudal societies? We are going to analyze its reasons from the aspects of economy, politics and mode of class struggle. In terms of economy, in slave and feudal societies, the self-sufficient natural economy was the dominant economic structure, while the commodity economy only occupied a subordinate position, playing a complementary role. Under the natural economy, there were no unified nation states or national markets but numerous dispersed and closed economic units due to the low productive forces. Therefore, not only was it impossible for the laboring class to gather together to organize a political party for the benefit of their own economic interests for they could not get rid of their personal attachment to the propertied class, but also there was no demand for the propertied class to organize any political parties for they had little contact and competition with each other in a closed natural economy. In terms of politics, economic self-sufficiency inevitably resulted in political self-government and establishment of numerous small states, which determined that the form of political rule was bound to be an autocratic monarchy. In order to reinforce the centralized autocratic monarchy, slave owners and feudal landlords not only deprived the ruled class of the freedom of association, but did not allow members of the ruling class to enjoy the right of association. Although different factions within the ruling class often fought against each other for powers and interests, they all had to depend on the monarch. It followed that those who comply with the monarch would thrive while those who went against the monarch would perish. In this case, it was impossible to form political parties inside the ruling class not to mention inside a ruled class. In terms of the mode of class struggle, it was similarly at a lower stage in accordance with the economic and political conditions in this historical period. Specifically, on the one hand, the class struggle only happened sporadically within a limited area, which could not coalesce into a large-scale class movement, and on the other, neither slaves nor serfs were representatives of the new social production mode, so they could only take lower forms of struggle, such as destroying tools, escaping, killing their masters and uprising spontaneously. Therefore, the closed economy, fragmented political units, the autocratic system, and isolated and backward modes of class struggle together made it unnecessary and impossible to build the economic, political, and social contact beyond the limit of the city-state. Therefore, in ancient and medieval times, there were not appropriate social conditions for the formation of any political parties at the level of a nation-state, not to mention a political party in the modern sense.

However, during the capitalist stage, especially with the development of capitalist commodity economy, parliamentary struggle and thoughts of freedom and democracy, political parties in the modern sense came into being. In other words, there were generally two major conditions at the stage of capitalism, which provided for the birth of political parties. One is that, when the productive forces had developed to a certain extent, the uneven distribution of social and economic interests had become increasingly intensified, and the interest and class conflicts (including the conflict of interest within the same class) were more and more evident and overt. The other is that, with more freedom obtained, people had a growing sense of subjectivity and a stronger desire to intervene in power for their own interests economically and politically. In terms of the economic aspect, the development of capitalist commodity economy not only broke the closed economic zone, but also gave rise to a unified domestic national market. Meanwhile, "freedom" and "equality" demanded by the capitalist commodity economy inevitably resulted in the birth of capitalist parliamentary democracy, which was reflected not only in the form of universal suffrage adopted in the parliaments and other institutions of capitalist countries, but also in the free and equal rights enjoyed by all strata and groups within the bourgeoisie to organize political parties and participate in state administration through parliaments and other institutions. Under the capitalist economic system, capitalists are bound to compete fiercely for market share, raw materials and investment opportunities to maximize their profits, thus forming different strata and interest groups. As Marx once pointed out, with the social division of labor and development of productive forces, some functions of industrial capital would be separated from the sphere of circulation, and thus different capital groups were formed accordingly, such as commercial capital, loan capital, bank capital. In competition, some capital groups would unite together to acquire an economic advantage and monopoly for their common interests, which led to contradictions and conflicts between different strata and interest groups within the bourgeoisie. In order to win in the struggle, various strata and interest groups inevitably built political alliances based on their common interests and formed political parties to seek more seats in the parliament, seize more important government posts, and gain more control of the state power. In terms of the political aspect, politics always goes hand in hand with power. The bourgeoisie know well that only with the shelter of power, can they have a reliable and lasting interest, so competition for power must be another important reason for the emergence and evolution of bourgeoisie parties. Therefore, the capitalist system not only ended the feudal rule of separatism, but also established bourgeois democracy, where the basic civil rights such as freedom of association are affirmed. In this way, different strata and groups inevitably compete with each other to enter the state organs for exercising the ruling power through universal suffrage. In order to defeat their opponents, all strata and groups have to look for partners to establish a greater political power. In terms of the ideological aspect, the theories of democracy, freedom, equality and human rights proposed by bourgeois enlightenment thinkers offered the bourgeoisie a clear political program for their struggle against the feudal class, which provided an ideological basis for them to organize their own political parties. In terms of the mode of class struggle, with the formation of unified nation-states and the help of material and cultural means, such as modern means of transportation and communication and newspapers, class struggle rapidly developed from the isolated, sporadic, spontaneous, and unorganized events into the nationwide and organized economic, political, and ideological movements. Due to the conditions mentioned above, various political factions formed inside the bourgeoisie and gradually developed into different political parties in the modern sense with their own political programs, party members, party constitutions, party organizations and authoritative leading groups in the process of fighting against the feudal forces.

Historically, the bourgeois political parties originated in Britain in the 1670s with the Whigs and the Tories, which at that time were just two different political factions in the Parliament and gradually evolved into the Conservative Party and the Liberal Party in the 1830s. In the United States, the two rival factions, the Federalist Party and the Anti-Federalist Party, emerged in the 1780s, which later developed into two political parties. Whereas, the proletarian political party was the product of the combination of Marxist theory and the workers' movement during the stage of capitalism, where the workshop-based handicraft industry was replaced by the large-scale machine industry and the struggle of the proletariat against the bourgeoisie developed from the spontaneous stage to the conscious stage. The Communist League founded in 1847 was the first proletarian political party in the world under the guidance of scientific socialism. With the development of capitalism around the world, especially after the World War II, political parties have become common components of the political landscape in almost all countries.

Two more issues that must be further illustrated here. First, political parties and party systems did not arise simultaneously. As the leader of a class, stratum, or group and the instrument of political struggle, a political party can be formed before that class, stratum, or group takes control of the state power, while the party system can only be established after a certain class, stratum or group seizes the state power under the leadership of its own party. Second, in the political practices of various countries, the party system takes on different forms, but what specific form should be adopted by each country depends on the conditions of the country and the people, such as history, status quo of classes, revolutionary road, economic basis, political culture, and national tradition.

(3) **Functions and roles of Political Parties**

Since Political parties are created with adaptation to objective social and historical conditions, similarly, the functions and roles they play can also meet the demands proposed by such conditions. So, what functions and roles does a political party have? To this question, scholars hold different views. For example, according to Samuel P. Huntington, "The function of the party is to organize participation, to aggregate interests, to serve as the link between social forces and the government."[7] David Hine holds that "almost every political party seems to be the combination of two functions:

[7] Huntington, S. (1988) *Biange shehui zhong de zhengzhi zhixu* [Political Order in Changing Societies], trans. Li S. P., Beijing: Hua Xia Publishing House, p. 90. cf. Huntington, S. (1968) *Political Order in Changing Societies*, New Haven: Yale University Press, p. 91.

it acts upon the needs of the society on the one hand, and imposes control over it on the other."[8] and Klaus von Beyme categorizes the major functions of the political party into four specific aspects: setting objectives, demonstrating interests, mobilizing society, and creating and selecting elites.[9] It should be pointed out that such views held by Western scholars do make some sense, but need to be further broadened in their scope of generalization and elevated in their level of theoretical abstraction. Therefore, I agree with Professor He Huahui that the political party has two major functions: maintaining and seizing political power,[10] to be specific, forming party politics and party system for holding or participating in the state power, and governing the state and society. Of course, the functions of a political party are closely associated with its class nature, and serve the interests of the class it represents. In a capitalist democracy, the functions of a political party are to formulate, publish and promote its political program, to win support from voters to obtain seats in order to legislate and supervise the government in the parliament, and to seek leadership or participation in the government in order to make and implement its policies in the government. The functions of the proletarian party are manifested differently at different historical stages. Before seizing power, its main task is to formulate a revolutionary program in line with the will and interests of the broad masses of the people and to contact, mobilize, organize and lead the people through its party members as the backbone to carry out political struggles, mainly in the form of armed struggles, so as to overthrow the state power of the exploiting class. After seizing power, its main task is to maintain the state power, exercise the political, organizational and ideological leadership over the whole country and society, develop social productivity and improve the living standards of the people by uniting with and relying on the broad masses of the people.

With the above-mentioned functions, the emergence of modern political parties is of great historical significance in that the autocratic politics of lifetime rule by an individual ancient monarch has been changed into the democratic politics ruled by modern political parties. Consequently, the party democratic politics not only make the political life, political struggle and political decision-making open, grouped, popularized, procedural, legalized, and institutionalized, so as to give play to the collective role of the ruling group and improve its ability to govern the country and society, but also reduce and eliminate all kinds of abuses of power that endanger the country and society, so as to maintain the political and social stability as well as to promote the progress and development of the country and society.

---

[8] Miller, D. and Bogdanor, V. (eds) (1992). *The Blackwell Encyclopedia of Political Science*, New York: Wiley-Blackwell, pp. 520–521.

[9] ibid.

[10] He, H. H. (1988). *Bijiao xianfaxue* [Comparative Constitutional Law], Wuhan: Wuhan University Press, pp. 321–323.

6.1.2 Party Politics as Basic Content of Modern Democracy

James Bryce once stated, "To begin with, parties are inevitable. No free large country has been without them. No one has shown how representative government could be worked without them."[11] Hans Kelsen also claimed, "The modern democracy has been established completely based on political parties. The more democratic principles are put into practice, the greater the importance of parties are", and "Practicing democracy without political parties is either having a pipe dream or being hypocritical."[12] Therefore, he argued that political parties must be given a constitutionally recognized status, that is to say, they must have a function as a mechanism for the formation of the will of the state. In this way, modern countries can be democratized. In fact, political parties were usually subordinate to democracy historically, but in modern democratic politics, they constitute the fundamental content of democracy and even become the necessary prerequisite of democratic politics under certain circumstances.

(1) **Party System as Product of Development of Representative Democracy**

Firstly, the fundamental reason for the emergence of political parties is attributed to the development of the capitalist commodity economy, but objective economic needs are usually manifested as claims for political power. To be specific, first, the principle of equality and freedom in the capitalist commodity economy necessarily requires a democratic governance of the state and the society and the majority of members of society to participate in the political life of the country. Second, the development of the capitalist commodity economy leads to the formation of a unified national market and nation-state, in which the rights of governance can not be exercised directly by citizens as in a small city-state with few people, but can only be realized through a medium—the representatives. Third, the interest differentiation brought about by the capitalist commodity economy not only makes different classes, strata, or groups compete for the state power through representative democracy in order to realize their own interests, but also enables them to build up their own strength by seeking allies to win power. Accordingly, in a society with diversified interests, the political party becomes a form of mobilizing and organizing the members of a certain class, stratus, or group to participate in politics. Apparently, the most direct reason for the birth of political parties is the development of representative democracy itself. About a century ago, A. L. Lowell wrote in his work *Governments and Parties in Continental Europe*, "A superficial glance at the history of democracy ought to be enough to convince us that in a great nation the people as a whole do not and cannot really govern. The fact is that we are ruled by parties whose action is more or less

[11] Bryce, J. (1921) *Modern Democracies*, New York: The Macmillan Company, p. 114.

[12] Cf. Mastellone, S. (1990) *Ouzhou minzhu shi: cong Mengdesijiu dao Kaiersen* [History of Democracy in Europe: From Montesquieu to Kelsen], trans. Huang, H. G, Beijing: Social Sciences Academic Press, pp. 399–400.

modified, but never completely directed, by public opinion."[13] F. J. Goodnow also pointed out:

> ...if the government was to go on harmoniously, some means of coordinating the expression and execution of the will of the state had to be found. Such means could not be found in the governmental system, as has been shown. It had therefore to be found outside of the government in some extralegal institution. It was, as a matter of fact, found in the political party. The party took upon itself the burden of selecting, not merely the members of the body which, by the theory of the governmental system, expressed the will of the state, i.e. the legislature, but also those persons who were to execute that will, i.e. the executive officers.[14]

Harold F. Gosnell and Richard G. Smolka concluded that people fought for a long time to have a say in their government's decision making and to protect themselves against a willful government, and thereby created the democratic political party system.[15]

Secondly, in terms of ways political parties are produced. To be sure, political parties are formed on the basis of parliamentary democracy, though they have various origins. In other words, nationwide, independent political parties usually develop from various factions in the parliament. The major bourgeois political parties in the United Kingdom, the United States, and Canada are formed in this way. For example, during the era of the Stuart Restoration in Britain, two major political factions, the Whigs and the Tories, were formed in the Parliament due to the dispute over the issue of James Stuart's succession to the throne. Yet, these two factions can not be taken as modern political parties in a strict sense. As John Gollan once pointed out, "The modern party system in Britain is a result of the Industrial Revolution, the emergence of financial capital to leadership of the state and the organized political struggle of the working class."[16] After the industrial revolution, the industrial bourgeoisie and the working class, who stepped onto the political stage, strongly demanded reform of the parliamentary system of the day in order to achieve participation in the state power, so in 1832, 1867 and 1884, Britain was forced to carry out several electoral and parliamentary reforms. In order to adapt to the new situation after the reforms, political factions in the parliament vigorously established and expanded their own organizations all over the country. For instance, in 1832, the Tory Party

[13] Cited in Goodnow, F. (1987) *Zhengzhi yu xingzheng* [Politics and Administration], trans. Wang Y. & Yang B. P., Beijing: Hua Xia Publishing House, p. 8. cf. Goodnow, F. (1900/2017) *Politics and Administration: A Study in Government,* New York: Routledge of Taylor and Francis Group, p. 150.

[14] Goodnow, F. (1987) *Zhengzhi yu xingzheng* [Politics and Administration], trans. Wang Y. & Yang B. P., Beijing: Hua Xia Publishing House, p. 57. cf. Goodnow, F. (1900/2017) *Politics and Administration: A Study in Government,* New York: Routledge of Taylor and Francis Group, pp. 104–105.

[15] GosnEll, H. and Smolka, G. (1980) *Meiguo zhengdang he xuanju* [American Political Parties and Elections], trans. Fudan University International Politics Department, Shanghai: Shanghai Translation Publishing House, p. 2.

[16] Gollan, J. (1952) *Yingguo zhengzhi zhidu* [The British Political System], trans. Xi M., Beijing: People's Publishing House, p. 81. cf. Gollan, J. (1954) *The British Political System,* London: Lawrence & Wishart Ltd, p. 76.

changed its name to the Conservative Party, and established constituency associations in various constituencies to register the voters supporting the Conservative Party and organize election campaigns. After the electoral Reform Act of 1867 was passed, the Conservative Party immediately united all the constituency associations to establish "The National Union of Conservative and Constitutional Associations"[17] so as to coordinate the publicity and election campaign of the whole party. In 1870, the Central Office, an administrative body of the Conservative Party, was established to manage the party affairs. In 1886, the Conservative Party decided to establish its regional organizations, and henceforth, its organizational system was gradually completed. Generally, the evolution of the Whig Party into the Liberal Party in Britain has undergone a similar process. In the United States, the two early parties, the Federalists and Anti-federalists, also emerged in the 1st and 2nd congresses and then evolved into the Democratic Party and the Whig Party, and finally turned into the Democratic Party and the Republican Party. Obviously, "The bourgeois parties were initially created on the basis of the parliamentary system, and can be said to be the product of parliamentary activities."[18] Furthermore, the early working-class parties also originated from the capitalist parliamentary democracy by taking advantage of the parliament to organize activities fighting for the rights of the laboring people. Therefore, in a sense, the early working-class parties were also the product of the representative democracy.

(2) **Party System Facilitating Development of Modern Democracy**

The party system is not passively affected by the development of the representative democracy. Instead it has greatly facilitated the development of modern democratic politics along with the emergence of the political party and the establishment of the party system.

Firstly, as noted above, the emergence of the party system has changed the ancient autocratic politics of lifetime rule by an individual ancient monarch into the modern party democracy, which highly reflects the impact of the party system on the democratic politics. Some scholars have pointed out that the emergence of political parties set the bourgeois democratic politics on the right track.[19] In fact, this is particularly prominent in both the United Kingdom and the United States, for, in history, the earliest parliament experienced a process of development: At the very beginning, it only established some preliminary democratic principles through its struggle against the monarchy. Under the form of parliamentary system, originally it was the authoritative oligarchy that governed the parliament, where the nobility and the military still had a great power, while the elected parliament had little. From the Glorious Revolution in 1688 to the end of nineteenth century, Britain was generally under the rule of an oligarchy or the House of Lords. The same was true of the United Sates

[17] It was renamed as the Association of Conservative and Liberal Unionist Groups in 1912 and National Union of conservative and Unionist Associations in 1924.

[18] Wu, J. et al. (1991) *Minzhu yu zhengdang* [Democracy and Political Parties], Beijing: Party School Press of the Central Committee of CPC, p. 17.

[19] Wu, J. et al. (1991) *Minzhu yu zhengdang* [Democracy and Political Parties], Beijing: Party School Press of the Central Committee of CPC, p. 8.

from the War of Independence to the 1830s. With the emergence of political parties, two or more parties started to hold power in rotation. Only after the responsible government appeared did the modern democratic politics really come into being. With the birth of the working-class party, the broad masses of the working people under the leadership of the working-class party began to seize state power and finally established their own rule through their arduous struggles, thus forming their own democratic politics. Obviously, even though the working-class parties and the bourgeois parties are fundamentally in opposition to each other, they are similar in that both have facilitated the development of democratic politics.

Secondly, the party system is an important way to resolve the contradictions and conflicts among different groups in the democratic system. The differentiation of interests, which leads to interest differences, is a common phenomenon in any modern country. Therefore, it is an important content of democratic politics to reconcile and deal with the interest contradictions and conflicts caused by interest differences so as to maintain the steady development of political and social order. And the party system plays a vital role in this process. Seymour Martin Lipset once pointed out, "Inherent in all democratic systems is the constant threat that the group conflicts which are democracy's lifeblood may solidify to the point where they threaten to disintegrate society. Hence conditions which serve to moderate the intensity of partisan battle are among the key requisites of democratic government."[20] And he also argued that in every democracy, the conflicts between social groups are manifested through the party system, which is a fundamental indication of the transformation from class struggle to a democratic form.[21] In capitalist countries, although the contradictions and conflicts of different interests within the bourgeoisie are extremely fierce due to the philosophical basis of individualism, the establishment and operation of the party system enables them to be resolved on the track set by party politics.[22] In socialist countries, the fundamental interests of the vast majority of the working people are consistent due to the philosophical basis of collectivism, but interest differences and conflicts still exist. However, the proletarian parties can also resolve differences through their own effort, especially through communication and consultation with other friendly parties.

Thirdly, the state of the party system will directly affect that of democratic politics,[23] which can be best explained by the extremely unstable political situation that often arises in countries with multi-party systems. The best example is the dilemma of the Japanese Hosokawa government, which came into power in 1993, and was

---

[20] Lipset, S. (1993) *Zhengzhi ren* [Political Man], trans. Liu G. M. & Nie R., Beijing: The Commercial Press, p. 58. cf. Lipset, S. (1960) *Political Man: The social bases of politics,* New York: Doubleday & Company, Inc., p. 83.

[21] Cf. Miller, D. and Bogdanor, V. (eds) (1992) *The Blackwell Encyclopedia of Political Science*, New York: Wiley-Blackwell, p. 512.

[22] Cf. Gosnell, H. and Smolka, R. (1980). *American Parties and Elections*, trans. Fudan University International Politics Department, Shanghai: Shanghai Translation Publishing House, pp. 7–8.

[23] Cf. Huntington, S. (1988) *Biange shehui zhong de zhengzhi zhixu* [Political Order in Changing Societies], trans. Li, S. P., Beijing: Hua Xia Publishing House, Chapter 7: Political parties and political stability.

immediately replaced by Haneda regime in early 1994 due to the withdrawal of the Socialist Party from the coalition government. Moreover, under certain historical conditions, the operation of the party system is also related to the success or failure of democratic politics. For example, after the First World War and soon after the end of the Second World War, the representative governments in the West were stuck in a universal crisis, which was largely caused by the malpractice of party competition at the time, such as mutual attacks between parties, vote bribery, use of brokers.

Finally, the party system is also one of the major means to expand political participation. As mentioned above, political participation is the basic way to realize popular sovereignty, and it is thus the most important factor that affects the construction of democratic politics. Since the operation of the party system is meant to enable the representatives of a certain class, stratum or group to exert an impact on the exercise of the state power, it naturally becomes one of the crucial ways to promote political participation. Huntington once pointed out: "The principal institutional means for organizing the expansion of political participation are political parties and the party system. A society which develops reasonably well organized political parties while the level of political participation is still relatively low (as was largely the case in India, Uruguay, Chile, England, the United States, and Japan) is likely to have a less destabilizing expansion of political participation than a society where parties are organized later in the process of modernization."[24]

(3) **Party Politics Mainly Achieved Through Representative Organs**

Party politics generally refers to the form in which a country exercises its state power through political parties. Although party politics is the product of the victory of the bourgeois revolution, most of the countries in the world today, whether capitalist or socialist, often adopt party politics. However, they are fundamentally different in essence. Professor Zhang Youyu once noted, "The practice of proletarian dictatorship must be led by the Communist Party. In fact, any dictatorship in any country is achieved through the party of the ruling class, and the government of a capitalist country is made up of bourgeois parties, where the government head is often the leader of the ruling party and all its major members are also from the ruling party. And all the policies and guidelines implemented by the government are determined by the ruling class in the form of approval by the parliament, which is also manipulated by the ruling party that accounts for the majority of it. It is safe to say that no country is not governed by the ruling party."[25] In addition, from the historical and current situation of political practices in various countries, the so-called party politics are mainly achieved through representative organs. If a political party functions as a mediator between the government and the people in a certain sense, as Frank Johnson Goodnow suggested, then it also performs a similar function with the representative system in form. In other words, in a large modern country, where

[24] Huntington, S. (1988) *Biange shehui zhong de zhengzhi zhixu* [Political Order in Changing Societies], trans. Li S. P., Beijing: Hua Xia Publishing House, p. 387. cf. Huntington, S. (1968) *Political Order in Changing Societies*, New Haven: Yale University Press, p. 398.

[25] Zhang, Y. Y. (1982) *Xuexi xin xianfa* [Learning the New Constitution], Tianjin: Tianjin People's Publishing House, p. 15.

the direct democracy is not applicable, it is only through the organized activities of political parties that the scattered, multifarious individual wills can be collected to form the "public will", on which the superstructure of the state can be constructed to make the "public will" rise to the status of national will. Therefore, there exists a profound relationship between the political party and the representative organ: the representative organ is the most fundamental organizational basis upon which the representative system is established, and the political party is the most important organizer and promoter for the realization of the representative system. Specifically, in a capitalist country, the main functions of the bourgeois party can be summarized in three aspects: manipulating the election, dominating the parliament and controlling the government, but its core is to control the parliament because the manipulation of elections and control of the government heavily depend on the domination of the parliament. Therefore, the parliament is the major political arena for each party to play a role. Whoever controls the majority of seats in the parliament may, through legislative process, transform their own party programme or political views into a national law and decide on or affect the allocation of the state budget. In a country with a cabinet system, the political party that gains the majority seats also acquires the state power. The main method by which the party take control of the parliament is to establish its own parliamentary party group. As is often the case, the parliamentary party group of the majority party is in a dominant position in the parliament.

In a socialist country, although the proletarian party is the ruling party and occupies the leadership role in the social life of the country, it does not mean that the proletarian party can replace the organs of the socialist state power or issue orders to them. That is to say, the party takes the leadership of the state, but it is not equal to the state in that the functions and powers of the state can not be achieved directly by the party but rather by the state organs. Therefore, it is necessary that the party's guidelines, principles, and policies must be carried out by the state organs and the will of the party be transformed into the will of the state. Since the people's representative organs in a socialist country are both the legislatures and the bases of the whole state organ system, the leadership of the party over the country can only be achieved through the people's representative organs. Similarly, the party politics in a socialist country can only be realized through the representative organs as well.

As discussed above, the political party has a close relationship with modern democratic politics, and in a sense, it leads modern democratic politics. However, as illustrated in Chap. 2, democracy has a very long history. In fact, a sort of democracy appeared in a few city republics in ancient Greece and Rome, or during the Middle Ages. This raises the questions, how could the ancient and medieval democracy do without the leadership of political parties? In this regard, Professor Nie Yunlin has made a relatively comprehensive analysis.[26] According to him, this is actually

[26] Cf. Nie, Y. L. (1988) *Zhongguo shehuizhuyi minzhu zhidu de fazhan he xianzhuang* [The Development and Present Situation of China's Socialist Democratic System], Wuhan: Hebei People's Publishing House, pp. 191–195.

determined by certain features of the development of democracy itself. More specifically, why ancient and medieval democracy could do without the leadership of political parties was mainly determined by the following reasons. First, in ancient and medieval times, democracy was practised in a small state with a small population. In this case, even if the ruling class did not have a party as the core of leadership, it was relatively easy to achieve a unified idea, will, policy and action, so as to effectively maintain its own interests and suppress the resistance of the ruled classes. However, in ancient nation states with larger territories formed due to the need of irrigation, all the ruling classes chose to adopt the autocratic monarchy without exception. Second, the ancient and medieval democracy was a direct democracy, whose democratic procedure was relatively simple. There was neither a representative organ nor a system of universal suffrage that produced a representative body. All issues were decided by all citizens by means of raising hands or secret voting, without any intermediate procedures. In this way, there was no room for the political party to play a role. Therefore, the political party was completely unnecessary and superfluous to the direct democracy practised in city states. Third, the democracy and hierarchy went hand in hand in ancient and medieval times. In other words, the democratic rights of governing the state could only be enjoyed by the nobility of the ruling class, who stably and hereditarily led the political activities of its own class, while the state power was beyond the reach of the ruled classes. Therefore, without the leadership of political parties, the ruling class could still firmly hold the state power through democracy.

6.2 Capitalist Parliamentary System and Party System

As mentioned above, political parties came into being only after the human society had smashed the feudal autocracy and the emerging capitalist class gained its basic democratic rights. In fact, political party was an invention by the bourgeoisie in the political field. Moreover, in modern countries the party politics is generally implemented, so the party system in different countries is often manifested in different forms. In terms of the nature of a state, there are two kinds of major party systems, i.e. the party system of the capitalist countries and that of the socialist countries. The relationship between the representative system and the party system varies based on whether the party system is capitalist or socialist in nature.

6.2.1 Critical Analysis of Party System in Capitalist Countries

First of all, political parties in the capitalist countries include the bourgeois parties and the non-bourgeois parties. A bourgeois party is the political organization that represents and struggles to maintain the will and interests of the bourgeoisie, which is composed of the most politically active and energetic members of the bourgeoisie and is the most important instrument for the bourgeoisie to seize and maintain the state power, and non-bourgeois parties refer to other political parties existing in capitalist countries, other than bourgeois parties, mainly including the proletarian parties and the petty bourgeoisie parties. The classical Marxist writers once pointed out that the epoch of the bourgeoisie "has simplified class antagonisms. Society as a whole is more and more splitting up into two great hostile camps, into two great classes directly facing each other—Bourgeoisie and Proletariat".[27] In capitalist countries, the two major classes struggle to defend their own class interests through their own political parties, and the antagonism and conflict of class interests are mainly manifested in the antagonism and struggle between the two class groups. Therefore, the struggle between the two major classes is concretely manifested as the struggle between the bourgeois party and the proletarian party, which constitute the two basic types of political parties in capitalist countries. Since the ruling parties in capitalist countries are all bourgeois parties, the party system in capitalist countries mainly refers to the bourgeois parties and their systems.

The party system in capitalist countries, as far as its basic content is concerned, generally indicates that after an election campaign held every few years, one or several bourgeois parties, by occupying a majority or a certain number of seats in the parliament, take control of or participate in the state power, whose leading representatives serve as the head of the government or join the cabinet. Moreover, once the election is over, the ruling party and the opposition party will co-exist: the ruling party governs the country and society according to its election program, and the opposition party stands against it and try to replace it. However, this kind of superficial power struggle does not mean that there is a fundamental contradiction between them. As a matter of fact, both the ruling party and the opposition party share the same basic values and social goals, i.e. to maintain the capitalist system and consolidate the state power of the bourgeoisie. Therefore, amid the general election, political turmoil and social crisis, the two parties will resist each other in a limited manner, cooperate with each other in a subtle way and replace the other in a new appearance.

As to its basic form, although, with the party system built up in more countries after the Second World War,[28] some western scholars have proposed various sorts of classifications, this book still adheres to the traditional trichotomy, which divides the party system into two-party system, multi-party system and one-party system according to the number of political parties actually involved in the control of the state power. The two-party system is a system in which two major bourgeois parties take turns in power. It was first established in Britain, and then spread to countries such as America, Canada, Australia, and New Zealand. The multi-party system means that more than two bourgeois parties take power in coalition. In most capitalist countries such as France, Italy, and Germany, political parties are numerous and

[27] *Makesi Engesi xuanji* [Marx and Engels Selected Works] (1995), Beijing: People's Publishing House, vol. 1, p. 273. cf. Marx, K. and F. Engels (1848) *Manifesto of the Communist Party*.

[28] Cf. Gao, F. (1992) 'Zhengdang zhidu' [Political Party System], in *Encyclopedia of China: Politics*, Beijing: Encyclopedia of China Publishing House, pp. 477–478.

evenly matched, which makes it difficult for a certain party to hold an absolute majority in the parliamentary election. In this case, a coalition government has to be organized with one dominant party and many other parties. And the one-party system means that one political party takes power for a long time. It is mostly implemented in the fascist countries and national independent countries. It must be made clear that although there are three classifications, the two-party system and the multi-party system are often practised in most major capitalist countries.

Superficially, the basic content and form of the party system in capitalist countries seems to indicate that both the two-party system and multi-party system are very democratic. Some people even believe that the two-party system and multi-party system are not only conducive to fair competition, but also good for checks and balances of power, so they highly advocate so-called "political opposition". For example, Blackstone once stressed the function of the "parliamentary opposition", and he argued that the system of liberalism must be open to the opinions of the opposition, and the absence of opposition will lead to despotism. Therefore, it is far from enough to accept the constitution only, and the existence of the opposition group must be allowed.[29] Rawls even pointed out: "Without the conception of loyal opposition, and an attachment to constitutional rules which express and protect it, the politics of democracy cannot be properly conducted or long endure."[30] Then, are the two-party system and the multi-party system of the bourgeoisie manifested with the form of political opposition really democratic? The answer is no. Due to the philosophical basis of individualism, the interests of different capitalist groups may contradict with one another, and even oppose each other under certain conditions, for different bourgeois parties only represent the interest groups of their own, but their fundamental political tendencies are not much different. As former U.S. President Richard M. Nixon pointed out, all political parties were organizations for the purpose of gaining the state power, and it would be too dangerous if the principles of the two parties differed so much that the switch of the state power from one party to another meant a fundamental change.[31] Therefore, the bourgeois parties are, in fact, like the wheels on a car, they perform the same function, serve the same goal and head the same direction. In Karl Marx's words, "it [the bourgeoisie party] makes sure that when the political power is let down by one hand, it will be immediately held by the other in turn."[32] Even former U.S. President Harry S. Truman admitted that the two-party system in the United States was a "two party cooperative system". That is to say,

[29] Mastellone, S. (1992) *Ouzhou zhengzhi sixiang shi: cong shiwu shiji dao ershi shiji* [History of European Political Thoughts: From 15th Century to 20th Century], trans. Huang, H. G, Beijing: Social Sciences Academic Press, p. 156.

[30] Rawls, J. (1999) *Zhengyi lun* [A Theory of Justice], trans. He H. H, He B. G. & Liao S. B., Beijing: China Social Sciences Press, p. 213. cf. Rawls, J. (1999) *A Theory of Justice*, Massachusetts: Harvard University Press, p. 196.

[31] Cf. Gong, B. S. & Yang, S. W. (1990) 'Zichanjieji duodangzhi wokui: jianlun zai Zhongguo weishenme buneng gao Xifang shi de Duodangzhi' [Bourgeois Multiparty System and Why China Cannot Implement Western Multiparty System], *Politics in China* (1):101.

[32] Cf. *Makesi Engesi quanji* [Marx and Engels Collected Works] (1962), Beijing: People's Publishing House, vol. 11, p. 399.

just as the economic competition between capitalists will only result in the transfer of wealth among monopoly capitalist groups, but ultimately the wealth is still held in the hands of the bourgeoisie, the political competition between bourgeois parties will only result in the transfer of political power among different capitalist groups, but not beyond the scope of the bourgeoisie. In addition, the "dollar politics", built on the basis of the private ownership of means of production, fundamentally determines the class nature of the party system. Therefore, when Engels talked about the American two-party system, he said, "We find here two great gangs of political speculators, who alternately take possession of the state power and exploit it by the most corrupt means and for the most corrupt ends—and the nation is powerless against these two great cartels of politicians, who are ostensibly its servants, but in reality exploit and plunder it."[33] Lenin also stated, "This so-called bipartisan system prevailing in America and Britain has been one of the most powerful means of preventing the rise of an independent working-class, i.e., genuinely socialist, party."[34] At the same time, for the bourgeoisie, the bourgeois party politics can not only deceive the broad working masses with its hypocritical democratic form, but also induce them to oppose only one particular bourgeois party for its bad performance rather than the rule of the entire bourgeoisie. Therefore, the democracy built on the basis of the two-party system or the multi-party system can only be a democracy of the minority of the propertied class.

6.2.2 Complementary: Capitalist Parliamentary System and Party System

Throughout the history of the development of the party system, political parties arose on the basis of the parliamentary democracy, but they have developed a close connection with the representative system since they were born. The most prominent manifestation of this connection in capitalist countries is that, under certain circumstances, the capitalist parliamentary system and the party system integrate, facilitate and complement each other. As Cao Peilin once pointed out, "Today's representative democracy is actually a system in which political parties control elections and the citizens elect the representatives of the parties, which is different from the representative democracy in history when political parties did not yet emerge or when the party system was not yet perfected. In fact, with the development of the party system, the representative system has been further consolidated."[35]

[33] *Makesi Engesi xuanji* [Marx and Engels Selected Works] (1995), Beijing: People's Publishing House, vol. 3, p. 12. cf. Engels, F. (1891) On the 20th Anniversary of the Paris Commune.

[34] *Liening quanji* [Lenin Collected Works] (1959), Beijing: People's Publishing House, vol. 18, p. 398. cf. Lenin, V. (1912) 'The Results and Significance of the U.S. Presidential Elections'.

[35] Cao, P. L. et al. (1993) *Bijiao zhengfu tizhi* [A Comparison of Government System], Shanghai: Fudan University Press, p. 15.

(1) Capitalist Parliamentary System Dependent Upon Party System

From the perspective of the development of democracy, the representative system is a product of such factors as the development of capitalist commodity economy and the formation of a unified nation state in modern times, and it is an unavoidable historical stage in the process of democratic development. However, the purpose of the representative system is to enable different classes, strata, and groups to communicate and compromise with each other about their demands and wishes through deliberating activities by the members or representatives of the parliament, so as to form a "public will" that is widely accepted by the public and govern the state and society accordingly. It follows that both the selection of parliament members or representatives and the arrangement of their activities can not be organized without certain intermediary forces. Since the party is a political representative for the will and interests of each social class, stratum, or group, in modern democratic politics, it has become a bridge between the voters and the parliament, and the party system has thus become an important part in the organization and operation of the representative system, as is specifically reflected in the following two aspects in capitalist countries:

First, the election of parliament members, and the composition of the parliament and the government are all manipulated by political parties. If the ancient democracy is regarded as a type of democracy without a parliament, then the parliament in the Middle Ages can be seen as a parliament without democracy. The medieval hierarchical conferences were also a form of representative system, but they were essentially different from the modern parliaments in that they were not elected but appointed by the King. Although parliaments in some countries, say, the House of Lords in the United Kingdom, are not elected, such cases are extremely rare. Therefore, elections are undoubtedly the basis of modern parliaments. The election practices in capitalist countries reveal that disparities exist among countries in the specific procedures and steps concerning the election of parliament members except for one shared feature: the election of members of the parliament is inherently related to political parties, including the division of constituencies, registration of voters, nomination of candidates, election campaigns and ballot counting. In other words, it is through the bourgeois parties that the capitalist groups control various procedures in the election of parliament members, so as to place their own representatives on the political stage of the parliament. That is to say, competition among candidates is actually competition among bourgeois parties. For example, members of the British House of Commons are elected, where the two major bourgeois parties vie for seats in the lower house through election, and the party that obtains the majority of seats organizes the cabinet and holds the power of the government. In fact, the British government is, so to speak, the "party government", and the parties under the two party system are actually the "government parties". In the 1950s, S. G. Fedorov, the scholar of the former Soviet Union, proposed the concept of "nationalization of the party organs" and argued that the two-party system in the UK has become a constituent part of the state or even a government system,[36] as is not unreasonable.

[36] Fedorov, S. (1959) *Xiandai Yingguo guojia jigou zhong de liangdangzhi* [The Two-party System in Modern British State Institutions], trans. He Y. M., Shanghai: Shanghai People's Publishing House, pp. 19–20.

The features of the British party politics are summarized in *The Dictionary of World Political Parties* as the following five major aspects. First, the cabinet is composed of MPs from the majority party, and the prime minister may include non-MPs in the Cabinet in the condition that their membership must be supplemented in due time. Second, the ruling party that holds more than half of the votes in the parliament will dominate all the decisions of the parliament. In this way, the "parliamentary supremacy", in which the cabinet is nominally accountable to the parliament, becomes "the ruling party supremacy", in which the ruling party decides everything. Third, the cabinet is both the parliamentary committee for carrying out the actual work, and also the supreme decision-making body of the ruling party headed by the prime minister (the party leader). Fourth, the cabinet is collectively responsible to the parliament, and the change of the cabinet coincides with the change of the ruling party. As long as the majority vote is in hand, a vote of confidence in the parliament is nothing but a means to intimidate the cabinet. Once the control over the majority is lost, the original cabinet cannot be maintained by adjusting policies or replacing cabinet members. Fifth, the cabinet has the right to call early parliamentary elections ahead of schedule, and the date chosen depends on the conditions favorable to the ruling party.[37] As such, the parliamentary system, the cabinet system and the party system in Britain are well coordinated. In the two-party system of the United States, the ruling party takes power through victory in the presidential election rather than holding a majority of seats in Congress. As a typical country with the "separation of powers" system, in which the national legislative power is exercised by the Congress, the seats of the Congress are also fiercely contested by various parties. In the political practice, the nomination of candidates for the congressional election is controlled by the two major parties, in addition, there are many election rules only beneficial to both parties in the United States, such as the implementation of the unitary system and the relative majority system.[38] In other words, in order to successfully take the state power and realize its own rule, the American bourgeoisie will definitely manage to control the election through the two major bourgeois parties so as to manipulate the Congress. Even some bourgeois scholars admit that a political party is a signpost in the eyes of voters, an organization to recruit members and carry out election campaign for candidates, and a leading group whose purpose is to organize and control the legislative and administrative institutions of the country.[39] The function of political parties is to "provide a means of organizing and directing the struggle for political power and influencing its exercise."[40] Thus, it is obvious that in capitalist

---

[37] Xiong, F. (ed.) (1986) *Shijie zengdang cidian* [Dictionary of World Political Parties], Beijing: Hongqi Publishing House, p. 622.

[38] Cf. Gosnell, H. and R. Smolka (1992) *Meiguo zhengdang yu xuanju* [American Parties and Elections], trans. Fudan University International Politics Department, Shanghai: Shanghai Translation Publishing House, pp. 19–20. cf. Sorauf, Frank J. (1980) *Party Politics in America*, Boston & Toronto: Little, Brown and Company, p. 237.

[39] Cf. Wilson, James Q. et al. (1980) *American Government: Institutions and policies*, Boston: Cengage Learning, p. 134.

[40] Saye, Albert B., F. A. John and B. P. Merrit (1950/1990) *Principles of American Government,* Englewood Cliffs of New Jersey: Prentice Hall, p. 119.

countries, the bourgeoisie monopolizes the state apparatus by controlling the parliamentary elections mainly through its political parties on the premise of maintaining a mighty military bureaucracy.

Second, the operation of the parliament is also controlled by political parties. The purpose of manipulating the parliamentary elections, the parliament and government composition is to control the parliamentary activities so that the exercise of the parliamentary power can be brought under control by political parties. Therefore, controlling the parliamentary election and its composition is just the beginning, the key is to control parliamentary operation, that is, to control the proposal, discussion and passage of bills in the parliament. Different party systems, however, impose disparate restrictions on the behavior of their parliament members. For instance, the two major parties in the UK adopted centralism, under which the arrangement of parliamentary voting is strictly disciplined within the party. In each important vote, all party members are required to vote as a group according to their unanimously accepted instructions or decisions made by their party leaders in efforts to form a coordinated and strong group of the majority party. In contrast, the political parties in the United States are loosely organized with no rigorous discipline imposed on the members of Congress for voting, and the members have greater freedom in voting, which makes it impossible for the two major parties to have a stable majority in Congress. Nevertheless, what they have in common is to establish their party groups in the parliament, through which members of the parliament are brought under control by the party so as to ultimately control the parliament. Each parliamentary party group serves as an important leader and organizer of its party activities in the parliament. Generally speaking, each political party mainly exerts its influence on the parliament through its own parliamentary party group. Some countries even stipulate that the parliamentary party group is entitled to participate in nominating the Speaker of the parliament, organizing various committees affiliated with the parliament, negotiating parliamentary procedures and other affairs. The task of the parliamentary party group is to implement the guidelines and policies of its own party and keep its members to take an unified action in the parliament. More often than not, before formal voting in the parliament, every party has actually predetermined its own stance and attitude through its parliamentary party group. For example, the Speaker of the U.S. House of Representatives, though elected nominally by the General Assembly of the House, is de facto selected through the caucus of the majority party, and generally, the president pro tempore of the Senate is also chosen from the members of the majority party. In addition, there are a few standing committees in both houses of the Congress, each of which is often chaired by a senior member of the majority party. Some American scholars pointed out that in the Congress and the state legislatures, "...the political parties organize majority and minority power, and legislative leaders and committee chairmen are party oligarchs."[41] Although the American political parties are more loosely organized and less disciplined, and members of the Congress may vote against the guidelines of the party, in so doing, they may still "risk the punishment" and suffer

[41] Sorauf, F. J. (1968) *Party Policies in America,* Boston: Little, Brown and Company, p. 330.

from "informal pressure."[42] As a result, the leadership of both parties in Congress are called by some scholars the Establishment of Congress, which "largely determines what the Congress will do".[43]

(2) **Controlling or Affecting National Political Life Through Parliament as a Basic Way for Bourgeois Parties to Play their Roles**

The bourgeois parties come to power on behalf of the bourgeoisie by competing with each other for the control of the parliament and government. Generally, the interests of the bourgeoisie as a whole are absolutely opposite to those of the proletariat. However, there do exist various strata and groups inside the bourgeoisie, who are usually engaged in fierce struggles politically and economically in order to maximize their own interests. The struggle among bourgeois parties is a reflection of the conflict and strife between different strata and groups within the bourgeoisie. In order to control the state power and thus control or influence the political life of the country, all bourgeois parties often wage fierce battle in elections at all levels to enable their own parties to take command of the parliament and the government. Even though there are many ways for the bourgeois parties to control or influence the political life of the country, the control of the parliament and the government is a fundamental choice. Moreover, in a British-style political structure, it is of vital significance for the bourgeois parties to have a grip on the parliament given the fact that the status of the government hinges on the number of seats obtained in the parliament. Even in an American style political structure, although the status of the government has no direct relation with the number of seats of the party in the parliament, it is of equal importance for the bourgeois parties to control the legislature and legislative activities in countries that observe the principle of the rule of law. In this way, the will and interests of the party are reflected in the legal regulations enacted by the parliament. What's more, this type of American political structure is typical of separation of powers and checks and balances, where whoever controls parliament will naturally hold an important part of the state power. Therefore, the capitalist parliamentary system is a basic form for the bourgeois parties to control the state power.

6.2.3 Proletarian Parties and Capitalist Parliamentary System

As mentioned earlier, political parties in capitalist countries consist of two basic types: bourgeois parties and proletarian parties. Although the class nature of the capitalist state power determines that the capitalist parliamentary system only serves as a tool for achieving the class rule by the bourgeoisie, for the classical Marxist writers, the proletarian parties should make use of the platform of parliament as a legitimate instrument of struggle for the masses under certain historical conditions.

---

[42] Ibid, p. 335.

[43] Dye, T. R. (1980) *Shui zhangguan Meiguo* [Who is Running America], trans. Mei S. & Wang D. C., Beijing: World Affairs Press, p. 334. cf. Dye, T. R. (1934/1983) *Who Is Running America: The Reagan years*, Englewood Cliffs of New Jersey: Prentice-Hall, Inc., p. 106.

(1) Capitalist Parliamentary System Can be Utilized by Proletarian Parties

In the capitalist parliament, the struggles between various strata, groups and factions of the bourgeoisie are mainly manifested as those between different bourgeois parties. As proletariat parties continued to play an increasing role in political life since they came to being in the 1940s, the political struggles between the proletariat and bourgeoisie are mainly reflected as those between the proletarian parties and the bourgeois parties. Since the capitalist parliamentary system is the basic form for the bourgeoisie to take control of state power and parliament is the arena for bourgeois parties to compete for state power, then parliament can also be turned into a battlefield for proletarian parties to fight against bourgeois parties. In addition, capitalist "parliamentary politics" ostensibly allows for the existence of opposition parties, so the parliamentary struggle adopted by the proletarian parties are legitimate. Therefore, Marxists believe that, under certain circumstances, it is of great necessity for proletarian parties to be involved in the parliamentary struggle and exploit the forum of the parliament in a bid to expose the nature of the bourgeoisie, educate the masses and accumulate revolutionary forces. In the early days when the Third International or Communist International (known as Comintern) took shape, the German "leftist" communists adopted an absolutely negative and reckless attitude towards the bourgeois parliament, which was strongly criticized by Lenin:

> ... it undoubtedly signifies that parliamentarianism in Germany has not yet politically outlived itself, that participation in parliamentary elections and in the struggle on the parliamentary rostrum is obligatory on the party of the revolutionary proletariat specifically for the purpose of educating the backward strata of its own class, and for the purpose of awakening and enlightening the undeveloped, downtrodden and ignorant rural masses. Whilst you lack the strength to do away with bourgeois parliaments and every other type of reactionary institution, you must work within them because it is there that you will still find workers who are duped by the priests and stultified by the conditions of rural life; otherwise you risk turning into nothing but windbags.[44]

(2) Class Struggle Cannot Be Merely Confined to Parliamentary Struggle

Marx envisaged that, through the use of parliament as a tool, "workers attain their goal by peaceful means"[45] in countries with a long tradition of parliamentary democracy. Edvard Kardelj argued control of parliament alone was insufficient:

> Such a goal achieved by 'peaceful means' can on no account rest with parliament itself but with the relative strength of social consciousness, traditions, and social and class powers,

---

[44] *Liening quanji* [Lenin Collected Works] (1958), Beijing: People's Publishing House, vol. 31, p. 40. cf. Lenin, V. (1920) *"Left-Wing" Communism: An Infantile Disorder.*

[45] *Makesi Engesi quanji* [Marx and Engels Collected Works] (1964), Beijing: People's Publishing House, vol. 18, p. 179. cf. Marx, K. (1972) 'La Liberte Speech'.

> etc.. But such strength would not only come from the number of votes, but also depend on whether the working class can influence social management in a democratic manner, which, in other words, is to see whether the working class could gain the very status in the society and government so that relations of production and social economy can experience real changes. Such status will not purely be based on parliamentary forces but dominantly on the social strength of the working class, its influence on the development of production relations and democratic capabilities and on its autonomous rights and the stronger position in the social system.[46]

Consequently, while emphasizing the necessity of proletarian parties participating in the parliamentary struggle, Marxists also pointed out its limitations from the class nature of the state, and maintained that, as long as the state apparatus is still in the hands of the bourgeoisie, the bourgeois government could, by amending the electoral law, manipulate the elections for the control of the parliament, annul elections, dismiss the parliament, or even squeeze the Communists out of the parliament, declare the Communist Party illegal and oppress the people and the progressive forces by taking brutal violent means.

Therefore, when Bernstein and Kautsky vociferously preached the parliamentary approach in opposition to the violent revolution and the dictatorship of the proletariat, Lenin pointed out, "But limiting the class struggle to the parliamentary struggle, or regarding the latter as the highest and decisive form, to which all the other forms of struggle are subordinate, is actually desertion to the side of the bourgeoisie against the proletariat."[47] Lenin continued, "... only a liberal can forget the historical limitations and conventional nature of the bourgeois parliamentary system as Kautsky does.... And now that the era of revolution has begun, Kautsky turns his back upon it and begins to extol the charms of moribund bourgeois democracy."[48] "This is nothing but the purest and most vulgar opportunism: repudiating revolution in deeds, while accepting it in words."[49]

In a word, under certain historical circumstances, the capitalist parliamentary system has provided the proletariat and its parties with a form and forum for struggle. On the one hand, the proletariat can carry out legitimate struggles and get well trained and improved in the struggles by exploiting the freedom of speech, publication, assembly and association prescribed by the capitalist laws, and on the other develop its own organizations, establish its own parties, put forward its own programs and strengthen its own unity under the favorable conditions provided by capitalist parliamentary democracy so as to continuously expand the strength of the working class in an effort to seize state power at last.

---

[46] Kardelj, E. (1981) *Minzhu yu shehuizhuyi* [Democracy and Socialism], trans. Qiu Y. J. and Zhou X. B., Beijing: People's Publishing House, pp. 34–35.

[47] *Liening quanji* [Lenin Collected Works] (1957), Beijing: People's Publishing House, vol. 30, p. 241. cf. Lenin, V. (1919) The Constituent Assembly Elections and The Dictatorship of the Proletariat.

[48] *Liening quanji* [Lenin Collected Works] (1956), Beijing: People's Publishing House, vol. 28, p. 228. cf. Lenin, V. (1918) The Proletarian Revolution and the Renegade Kautsky.

[49] *Liening quanji* [Lenin Collected Works] (1958), Beijing: People's Publishing House, vol. 25, p. 476. cf. Lenin, V. (1918) *The State and Revolution.*

6.3 Socialist People's Representative System and Party System

In his book *Principles of Communism, Engels Stated*:

> In the first place, it [the proletarian revolution] will establish a democratic constitution and thus either directly or indirectly establish political rule of the proletariat. Directly in England, where the proletariat already constitutes the majority of the people. Indirectly in France and in Germany, where the majority of the people consists not only of proletarians but also of small peasants and urban petty bourgeois, who are still in a transitory period toward the proletariat and are dependent in their political interests more and more on the proletariat and therefore soon will conform to the demands of the proletariat."[50]

According to Engels, the proletariat is able to realize its political rule in both direct and indirect forms. However, from the class nature of the proletarian regime, the most ideal form is the direct exercise of political rule by the broad masses of the working people. Therefore, around the October Socialist Revolution, Lenin proposed that the people should be allowed to directly participate in the democratic construction of the whole national life in the new types of countries. In other words, Lenin's ideal was to establish a socialist direct democracy. Unfortunately, Lenin later recognized that it was impossible for the Russian laborers to undertake direct governance of the country straight away because Russia had left its people poorly educated. In his words, "The Soviet, according to its party program, was an organ that was administered by its laborers, but in reality it was managed for laborers by the advanced stratum of the proletariat instead of the working people."[51] It is obvious that in spite of the essential differences between the regime of socialist countries and that of the exploiting class, socialist countries are still must utilize the governance by the minority to rule the majority. That is, the governance of the state by the people is ultimately achieved in an indirect way by the minority entrusted by the majority under the leadership of a few elites. Then, where do these elites come from? Of course, they can only come from the working class representing the new productive forces. And, as the vanguard of the proletariat, the proletarian party, which arises from the working class representing the new productive forces, is the leader and organizer of the indirect governance of the state and society by the broad masses of the working people in socialist countries.

6.3.1 Critical Analysis of Party System in Socialist Countries

Merely considering the number of parties, it is not true that there is only one political party in a socialist country, as some people claim. In fact, in some socialist countries,

---

[50] *Makesi Engesi xuanji* [Marx and Engels Selected Works] (1995), Beijing: People's Publishing House, vol. 1, p. 239. cf. Engels, F. (1847) *The Principles of Communism.*

[51] *Liening xuanji* [Lenin Selected Works] (1995), Beijing: People's Publishing House, vol. 3, p. 770. cf. Lenin, V. (1919) 'Report on the Party Programme'.

there are several political parties, among which, regardless of the number of parties, the proletarian party must be the ruling party. Therefore, the party system in socialist countries is a type of one-party system in nature.[52] Throughout the history of class struggle, the proletariat has been the most impartial, determined and thoroughgoing revolutionary class of all. However, as depicted by Marx, "Only by organizing itself into an independent political party opposed to all the old political parties established by the propertied class can the working class operate as a class against the joint forces of the propertied class."[53] It has turned out that only under the leadership of the proletarian party can the proletariat win its liberation and the cause of the socialist revolution and construction. Therefore, the basic content of the party system in a socialist country mainly refers to the specific system and operating mechanism in which the proletarian party is in charge of the state power and other parties participate in or influence it.

Then, why can the unique one-party system be formed in the political practices of socialist countries? Fundamentally, it is a result of the revolutionary struggle of the proletariat and the specific social and historical conditions for the construction of socialist state power. As the Soviet scholar S. I. Chirkin pointed out, "The one-party system is a product of history in a socialist society".[54] Specifically, first, in the process of seizing state power, the proletarian party, i.e. the Communist Party, became the most rigorous, disciplined and effective of all political organizations after experiencing numerous failures and being thoroughly tempered in the furnace of revolution. Therefore, the Communist Party enjoys a great prestige among the broad masses of the people. Second, most socialist countries were born in relatively underdeveloped agricultural societies, so they bear an arduous task of economic construction, which inevitably demands the Communist Party to mobilize all social forces to carry out the construction for a considerable long period of time in a unified will and through a strict discipline. Third, contrary to capitalism, socialism necessarily seeks to overcome the shortcomings of capitalism and attempts to create a more equitable system. If a society is left to its natural development, polarization in wealth distribution is inevitable. Only by implementing a system of control can the Communist Party distribute social incomes in a more equitable manner to prevent polarization.[55] Moreover, although the formation of such a party system is rooted in various profound historical and social conditions, the most basic fact is that the Communist Party as the ruling party is derived from a historical choice made by the broad masses of the working people.

---

[52] Gu, X. R. et al. (1990) *Dangzhi zhi zheng* [Debate on Party Systems], Shanghai: Shanghai People's Publishing House, p. 21.

[53] *Makesi Engesi quanji* [Marx and Engels Collected Works] (1963), Beijing: People's Publishing House, vol. 17, p. 455. cf. Marx, K. (1871) 'Resolution on Working Class Political Action'.

[54] Chirkin, S. (1988) *Xianfa yu zhengzhi zhidu* [Constitution and Political System], trans. Zhou, W. et al., Chengdu: Sichuan University Press, p. 58.

[55] Gu, X. R. et al. (1990) *Dangzhi zhi zheng* [Debate on Party Systems], Shanghai: Shanghai People's Publishing House, p. 23.

6.3.2 Non-Detachable: Socialist People's Representative System and Party System

Since the socialist people's representative system is the basic form for the broad masses of the working people in a socialist country to become masters of the country, where the party politics constitutes the basic feature of the national political life, then there must be a close link between the socialist people's representative system and the party system.

(1) **Socialist People's Representative System as Basic Way for Each Party to Play a Role**

The purpose of any class, stratum or group organizing a political party is to control or influence the exercise of state power through its own activities. The same is true of political parties in socialist countries. However, in a socialist country, neither the ruling party nor the participating parties can directly exercise state power or manage the state affairs. That is to say, although the proletarian party is the ruling party in a socialist country and holds a leading position in the national life, its leadership can only be achieved through the government organs of the state and society, and the same is true for the functioning of the participating parties. Since the nature of a socialist country is that the people are masters of the country, the basic form of realizing this end is also the basic form of governing the state and society. In this way, the socialist people's representative system, as the basic form for people to be masters of the country, has become the basic form for each party in socialist countries to play a role.[56] In addition, the organization and operation of the socialist people's representative system must adhere to the leadership of the proletarian party. In a socialist country where people are the masters of the country, the status of being masters can only be realized under the leadership of the Communist Party, the vanguard of the proletariat. Since the socialist people's representative system is the most fundamental of all democratic forms for the realization of people as masters of the country, its organization and operation must naturally accept the leadership of the proletarian vanguard, i.e. the communist party. Therefore, the political, organizational and ideological leadership under the communist party must be carried out not only in the process of election, organization and exercise of functions and powers in the people's representative organs, but also in the organization and operation of the whole socialist people's representative system established on the basis of the people's representative organs. Additionally, the essence of the leadership of the proletarian party over the socialist people's representative system in the socialist countries lies in the transformation of the will of the party into the will of the state through the people's representative organs. Undoubtedly, this kind of leading role of the proletarian party must receive the majority support in the people's representative organs. Although the majority of its own party members in the representative organs is an important guarantee for the realization of its leadership, different from

[56] Cf. He, H. H. (1992) *Renmin daibiao dahui zhidu de Lilun yu shijian* [Theory and Practice of the System of People's Congress], Wuhan: Wuhan University Press, pp. 33–36.

the bourgeois party whose control over the representative organs is only secured by obtaining a majority of seats in the parliament, the ruling party in socialist countries can win a majority support even if it fails to occupy a majority of seats in the people's representative organs because the representative organs of a socialist country are the bodies that truly represent the people, and any decision made by the party can reflect the interests and will of the people. Therefore, the party representatives will certainly support its own party decisions, while the representatives outside the party will also accept and support the decisions of the communist party in the deliberation of public affairs.

It is worth mentioning that, in the socialist countries, in addition to the socialist people's representative system, in which each political party can play its own role and exert its influence by way of electing its representatives, in some socialist countries, the political consultative or national front organizations, in which each party can select its own representatives to participate, are also established. In this way, the socialist people's representative system and the political consultative system are organically combined with the party system.

(2) **Properly Handling Relationship Between the Two Systems to Improve the Socialist People's Representative System**

As discussed above, the socialist people's representative system and the party system are inseparably linked. Thus far, we have mainly focused on their highly identical ultimate goal of ensuring the people to be masters of the country. However, there are, in fact, great differences between the two in terms of nature, scope, function, etc.. Therefore, it is extremely important to correctly and properly handle the relationship between them. Nevertheless, such an issue was far from being resolved in the political practice of the socialist countries in the past, which is prominently manifested in the non-separation of the party and the government and the substitution of the government by the party. In my view, the key to an appropriate settlement of the relationship between the socialist people's representative system and the party system rests with a correct understanding and proper handling of the relationship between the ruling party and the power of the state. Specifically, the relationship is manifested in two aspects: First, the leadership of the ruling party is fundamentally consistent with the nature of the political power of a socialist country. As mentioned above, the proletarian party, i.e. the Communist party, is the political representative and vanguard of the proletariat, which in turn is the vanguard of all the working people. Therefore, the reason why the proletarian party can be in a ruling position is that the proletariat at this moment is the direct ruler and its leadership over the country can only be achieved through its own vanguard, the communist party. In the meantime, the nature of a socialist country is the socialist state power, that is, the proletariat and the broad masses of the working people hold and exercise the power of the state. Therefore, both the leadership of the Communist party and the socialist state power, whose aims are fundamentally identical, are to ensure that the proletariat and the broad masses of the people become masters of their own country. Second, huge differences do exist between the two. Specifically, as the leading force of the country, the communist party leads the people to take and exercise their own power, but does not exercise power directly in place of the people. When we say that the Communist party is in the ruling position, we mean that it has become the leading force of the state power and the guide of direct governance by the broad masses of the people. In other words, the Communist party assists the people to exercise their leading power rather than directly exercise the state power on their behalf. Therefore, in order to promote the development of the socialist people's representative system, we must properly handle the relationship between the two systems by adopting measures such as the establishment of various institutions and improvement of various systems.

References

Bryce, J. (1921). *Modern democracies*. The Macmillan Company.

Cao, P. L., et al. (1993). *Bijiao zhengfu tizhi* [A Comparison of Government System]. Fudan University Press.

Chirkin, S. (1988). *Xianfa yu zhengzhi zhidu* [Constitution and Political System] (W. Zhou, et al., Trans.). Sichuan University Press.

Dye, T. R. (1934/1983). *Who Is running America: The reagan years*. Prentice-Hall, Inc.

Dye, T. R. (1980) *Shui zhangguan Meiguo* [Who is Running America] (S. Mei & D. C. Wang, Trans.) World Affairs Press.

Engels, F. (1847) *The principles of communism*.

Fedorov, S. (1959). *Xiandai Yingguo guojia jigou zhong de liangdangzhi* [The Two-party System in Modern British State Institutions] (Y. M. He, Trans.). Shanghai People's Publishing House.

Gao, F. (1992). *Zhengdang zhidu* [Political Party System]. In *Encyclopedia of China: Politics* (pp. 477–478). Encyclopedia of China Publishing House.

Gollan, J. (1952). *Yingguo zhengzhi zhidu* [The British Political System] (M. Xi, Trans.). People's Publishing House.

Gollan, J. (1954). *The british political system*. Lawrence & Wishart Ltd.

Gong, B. S., & Yang, S. W. (1990). *Zichanjieji duodangzhi wokui: jianlun zai Zhongguo weishenme buneng gao Xifang shi de Duodangzhi* [Bourgeois Multiparty System and Why China Cannot Implement Western Multiparty System]. *Politics in China* (1), 101.

Goodnow, F. (1900/2017). *Politics and administration: A study in government*. Routledge of Taylor and Francis Group.

Goodnow, F. (1987). *Zhengzhi yu xingzheng* [Politics and Administration] (Y. Wang & B. P. Yang, Trans.). Hua Xia Publishing House.

Gosnell, H., & Smolka, R. (1992). *Meiguo zhengdang yu xuanju* [American Parties and Elections] (Fudan University International Politics Department, Trans.). Shanghai Translation Publishing House.

Gu, X. R., et al. (1990). *Dangzhi zhi zheng* [Debate on Party Systems]. Shanghai People's Publishing House.

He, H. H. (1988). *Bijiao xianfaxue* [Comparative Constitutional Law]. Wuhan University Press.

He, H. H. (1992). *Renmin daibiao dahui zhidu de Lilun yu shijian* [Theory and Practice of the System of People's Congress]. Wuhan University Press.

Huntington, S. (1968). *Political order in changing societies*. Yale University Press.

Huntington, S. (1988). *Biange shehui zhong de zhengzhi zhixu* [Political Order in Changing Societies]. (S. P. Li, Trans.). Hua Xia Publishing House.

Kardelj, E. (1981). *Minzhu yu shehuizhuyi* [Democracy and Socialism] (Y. J. Qiu & X. B. Zhou, Trans.). People's Publishing House.

Lenin, V. (1905). The Socialist Party and Non-Party Revolutionism.

Lenin, V. (1912). The Results and Significance of the U.S. Presidential Elections.

Lenin, V. (1918). The Proletarian Revolution and the Renegade Kautsky.
Lenin, V. (1918). *The state and revolution.*
Lenin, V. (1919). Report on the party programme.
Lenin, V. (1919). The constituent assembly elections and the dictatorship of the proletariat.
Lenin, V. (1920). *"Left-Wing" communism: An infantile disorder.*
Liening quanji [Lenin Collected Works] (1956). People's Publishing House (Vol. 28).
Liening quanji [Lenin Collected Works] (1957). People's Publishing House (Vol. 30).
(1958). *Liening quanji* [Lenin Collected Works] (Vol. 31). People's Publishing House.
Liening quanji [Lenin Collected Works] (1958). People's Publishing House (Vol. 31).
Liening quanji [Lenin Collected Works] (1959). People's Publishing House (Vol. 10).
Liening quanji [Lenin Collected Works] (1959). People's Publishing House (Vol. 18).
Liening xuanji [Lenin Selected Works] (1995). People's Publishing House (Vol. 3).
Lipset, S. (1960). *Political man: The social bases of politics.* Doubleday & Company Inc.
Lipset, S. (1993). *Zhengzhi ren* [Political Man] (Liu G. M. & R. Nie, Trans.). The Commercial Press.
Makesi Engesi quanji [Marx and Engels Collected Works] (1962). People's Publishing House (Vol. 1).
Makesi Engesi quanji [Marx and Engels Collected Works] (1963). People's Publishing House (Vol. 17).
Makesi Engesi quanji [Marx and Engels Collected Works] (1964). People's Publishing House (Vol. 18).
Makesi Engesi xuanji [Marx and Engels Selected Works] (1995). People's Publishing House (Vol. 1).
Makesi Engesi xuanji [Marx and Engels Selected Works] (1995). People's Publishing House (Vol. 3). Engels, F. (1891). On the 20th Anniversary of the Paris Commune.
Engels, F. (1891). On the 20th Anniversary of the Paris Commune.
Makesi Engesi xuanji [Marx and Engels Selected Works] (1995). People's Publishing House (Vol. 1).
Marx, K. (1871). Resolution on Working Class Political Action.
Marx, K. (1875). *Critique of the gotha programme.*
Marx, K. (1972). La liberte speech.
Marx, K., & Engels, F. (1848). *Manifesto of the communist party.*
Mastellone, S. (1990). *Ouzhou minzhu shi: cong Mengdesijiu dao Kaiersen* [History of Democracy in Europe: From Montesquieu to Kelsen] (H. G. Huang, Trans.). Social Sciences Academic Press.
Miller, D., & Bogdanor, V. (Eds.). (1992). *The blackwell encyclopedia of political science.* Wiley-Blackwell.
Naoki, K. (1981). *Xianfa jiangyi* [The Constitutional Lectures]. Tokyo University Press.
Nie, Y. L. (1988). *Zhongguo shehuizhuyi minzhu zhidu de fazhan he xianzhuang* [The Development and Present Situation of China's Socialist Democratic System]. Hebei People's Publishing House.
Rawls, J. (1999a). *A theory of justice.* Harvard University Press.
Rawls, J. (1999). *Zhengyi lun* [A Theory of Justice] (H. H. He, B. G. He, & S. B. Liao, Trans.) China Social Sciences Press.
Saye, A. B., John, F. A., Merrit, B. P. (1950/1990). *Principles of American government.* Prentice Hall.
Sorauf, F. J. (1968). *Party policies in America.* Little, Brown and Company.
Wilson, J. Q., et al. (1980). *American government: Institutions and policies.* Cengage Learning.
Wu, J., et al. (1991). *Minzhu yu zhengdang* [Democracy and Political Parties]. Party School Press of the Central Committee of CPC.
Xiong, F. (Ed.). (1986). *Shijie zengdang cidian* [Dictionary of World Political Parties]. Hongqi Publishing House.
Yang, S. (1985). *Xianggang shehui gaige* [Social Reform in Hong Kong]. Wide Angle Press.
Zhang, Y. Y. (1982). *Xuexi xin xianfa* [Learning the New Constitution]. Tianjin People's Publishing House.

Chapter 7
Representative System and Interest Groups

Alexis de Tocqueville, a great French philosopher in the eighteenth century, once noted, "to substitute little by little the science of public affairs for its inexperience, knowledge of its true interests of democracy for its blind instincts … such is the first of duties imposed today on those who lead society."[1] Indeed, the reason why people have ceaselessly pursued and endlessly yearned for democracy is not only for democracy itself, but also for its most fundamental goal, which drives people to seek assiduously for such an political ideal. So, what is the ultimate goal of democracy? Although de Tocqueville failed to give a detailed discussion, on the goal of democracy his so-called "knowledge of its true interests of democracy" is instructive. That is, securing interests is the ultimate goal of democracy, in a sense. Neither the expression nor the realization of interests could be achieved without certain organs or organizations. We know that, from the practice of modern democratic politics, the aforementioned state organs and political parties are the most important institutions and organizations for the expression and realization of interests, but there is also another basic form, namely, interest groups. Moreover, with the development of democracy, interest groups have become one of the most important participants in the construction of democratic politics. Since the representative system is the basic form of realizing modern democracy, its organization and operation inevitably have a close association with interest groups.

[1] De Tocqueville, A. (1988) *De la démocratie en Amérique* [The Democracy of America], trans. Dong, G. L., Beijing: The Commercial Press, vol.1, p.8.

Y. Zhou, *A Comparative Study of Representative Systems*,
https://doi.org/10.1007/978-981-15-4186-5_7

7.1 Interests, Interest Groups and Democracy

As early as in 1842, Karl Marx pointed out, "Everything that people strive for is related to their interests."[2] Later in his writings about class struggle, he claimed that class struggle "is waged for economic interests in the first place, and political power is nothing but a means to achieve them".[3] Lenin called the economic interests "the most sensitive nerve of public life",[4] and he pointed out that "interests move 'the lives of peoples'".[5] As can be seen, the classical Marxist writers attached great importance to the issue of interests. As a state system or state form, democracy is in fact the allocation and appropriation of political power and hence only a means for certain classes, social strata or groups to achieve their interests. However, the work of connecting democracy with interests wither in theory or in practice is not yet in full swing in China. Therefore, the specific relations between interests, interest groups and democracy need to be discerned before the relationship between the representative system and interest groups are discussed.

7.1.1 Interest Satisfaction as a Fundamental Driving Force for the Development of Democracy

Where there is no motive there is no human behavior, and any motive is determined by human needs, which are often manifested in the form of interests in social life. Therefore, from the perspective of the behavioral sciences, it is not so much human needs as their own interests that motivate people to engage in social activities, and in general, it is entirely tenable to regard interest satisfaction as the driving force for democracy because the core and nature of democracy rest on the people being masters of the country, the aim of which is to realize and satisfy a certain need of interests.[6] However, the key question is, why do humans adopt a democratic form of political rule in the process of pursuing and realizing their interests only when human development has reached a certain historical stage. In other words, what is after all the status and role of democracy in this process? And how do interests facilitate the development of human state and social governance?

---

[2] *Makesi Engesi quanji* [Marx and Engels Collected Works] (1965), Beijing: People's Publishing House, vol.1, p.82. cf. Marx, K. (1842) *Proceedings of the Sixth Rhine Province Assembly.*

[3] *Makesi Engesi xuanji* [Marx and Engels Selected Works] (1995), Beijing: People's Publishing House, vol.4, p.250.

[4] *Liening quanji* [Lenin Collected Works] (1959), Beijing: People's Publishing House, vol.13, p.113. cf. Lenin, V. (1907) 'The Third Duma'.

[5] *Liening quanji* [Lenin Collected Works] (1959), Beijing: People's Publishing House, vol.38, p. 86. cf. Lenin, V. (1914) *Conspectus of Hegel's Book The Science of Logic.*

[6] Cf. Huang, W. Y. (ed.) (1990) *Guoneiwai minzhu lilun yaolan* [An Overview of Democratic Theories in China and Abroad], Beijing: China Renmin University Press, p.382.

(1) An Overview of Interest

"Interest" is a very broad concept, which is easily understood as an economic interest. Superficially, people seem to be familiar with it, but it is extremely essential to deepen their understanding of the issue of interest in order to make clear the relations between interest and democracy. So, what is "interest"? Some people suggest that "interest" means the balance of contradictions between the subjects and objects of needs with a certain social relation as a medium and social practice as a means, that is, satisfaction of needs[7]; others claim that "interest refers to a certain number of objects that meet the needs of the subjects by means of human activities in a certain social form"[8]; and still others argue that "in short, interest is manifested as human self-satisfaction."[9] and so on. Although there are subtle differences in the understandings and expressions people have of interests, the view that interests are the satisfaction of needs is fundamentally shared by all. Therefore, need is not only the fundamental prerequisite for the formation of interest, but also the essential basis for differentiating different interest subjects and interest forms in the construction of an interest system.

Throughout the history of human social development, we can see that the interests of every society always constitute an integral system for the reason that "the production relations of every society form a whole".[10] Therefore, all kinds of interests conditioned by the relations of production will inevitably become a complete, organic, interconnected and mutually restricted system. However, in the case of different social forms, in different countries or different historical periods, the constituents of the interest system and their relations are of great difference. And it is such differences that determine the different forms of political rule and governance in different countries or in different historical periods of a country.

The richness and complexity of needs determine that the subjects, types and forms of interests and their relations are also extremely complicated. Accordingly, interests can be classified differently under different criteria. Here, I'd like to discuss the classification of interests mainly according to the criterion of interest subjects. The subject of interests, which is transformed from the subject of needs, can be divided into individual, collective and social interest subjects, as can the subject of needs. Correspondingly, there are three different kinds of interests: individual, collective and social interests. Individual interests refer to a certain number of objects that meet the needs of an individual in a social form. Generally speaking, among the individual, collective and social interests, the individual interests are the basis of the

[7] Wang, W. G. and Guo, B. P. (1988) *Shehui liyi lun* [On Social Interests], Beijing: People's Publishing House, p.68.

[8] Su, H. Z. (1991) *Liyi lun* [On Interests], Shenyang: Liaoning University Publishing House, p.21.

[9] Zhang, X. (1987). *Liyi Lun Jiujiang* [Nine Lectures of Interest], Beijing: China Youth Publishing Group, p.7.

[10] *Makesi Engesi quanji* [Marx and Engels Collected Works] (1958), Beijing: People's Publishing House, vol.4, pp.144. cf. Marx, K. (1847) *The Poverty of Philosophy.*

other two, and "'common interests' are produced by individuals as 'private' at any time in history",[11] but under different forms of ownership of the means of production, the nature, basis and scope of individual interests may vary. Under private ownership, both living needs and production needs for a subject are satisfied in the form of individual interests. In other words, people's living needs are almost completely satisfied in the form of personal income and personal expenditure, while their production needs are mostly realized in the form of private accumulation and investment. Under the public ownership, however, the satisfaction of production needs usually takes the form of common interests. Living needs of individuals are even partly satisfied in the form of social or collective welfare, i.e. common interests, which occupy a considerable and increasing proportion of interests.

Collective interests refer to the objects that satisfy the needs of a certain group in a certain social form. Since any form of collective cannot exist independent of the individuals that constitute it, the collective interests are premised on the existence of individual interests, yet they cannot be reduced to the simple sum of individual interests. For individuals, different from the individual interests in a narrow sense, the collective interests are also one's own interests, which represent the survival and development needs of their entire community. Moreover, since the collective interests contain elements of both social interests and individual interests, they become both the link and the contradictory focus between the two.

Social interests refer to the objects that satisfy the needs of a society in a certain social form. Although the common needs of a society do not directly appear in the form of individual needs nor are they satisfied through the form of individual interests, they mostly develop and accumulate on the basis of individual needs and individual interests. Furthermore, the features of social interests vary according to different systems of ownership. Under private ownership of the means of production, social interests bear a dual nature: on the one hand, they represent the development requirements and conditions of the entire society, with the nature of progressiveness; on the other, they are influenced by the interests of the dominant exploiting class and represent the requirements and needs of the ruling class, with the limitations of the times and classes. Accordingly, social interests only occupy a secondary position in the interest system of the time. Under public ownership, however, with the elimination of the exploiting class, a truly unified social interest has been formed and thus occupies the primary and dominant position in the interest system.

Similarly, interests can also be classified into short-term interests and long-term interests according to the time horizen in which the interest is realized, and material interests and spiritual interests according to its social functions or its domain of realization. In addition, there are so-called economic interests, political interests and so on.

It must be noted that the systematic analysis of the individual, collective and social interests above aims to, by elaborating on their respective characteristics, provide a clearer idea of the formation of different interest structures and their impacts on the

[11] *Makesi Engels quanji* [Marx and Engels Collected Works] (1960), Beijing: People's Publishing House, vol.3, pp. 275–276. cf. Marx, K. and Engels, F. (1945) *The German Ideology*.

forms of political rule. The interest structure of capitalist countries grounded on the philosophy of individualism is fundamentally different from that of socialist countries based on the philosophy of collectivism, which results in fundamental differences in the forms of political rule, especially the forms and contents of democratic politics between them.

Moreover, although interests of various kinds within an interest system or interest structure are relatively independent of each other, they are interwoven both horizontally and vertically into a differential and contradictory relationship. All these interests interact, influence and constrain each other, forming a crisscross network of interests, in which the interest contradiction plays the most stable, decisive and basic role and determines all the specific forms of interest relations.

(1) **Interest Contradiction as a Direct Driving Force for the Development of Democracy**

The satisfaction of interests is taken as the fundamental driving force of democracy from the perspective of its ultimate goal, but in fact, it is the contradiction of interests that really has a direct impact upon the development of democracy. In other words, when the contradiction of interests develops to a certain historical stage and forms a new structure of interests, while the old forms of political rule that regulate the contradiction of interests are no longer adaptable to the new historical conditions, democracy arises as a prevalent form of political rule. This direct driving force of contradiction of interests on the development of democracy can be elaborated from the following three aspects.

Firstly, in terms of the origin of democracy, it must be noted, first and foremost, that there were ancient city-state democracies and medieval city republics in the history of democratic development, but the democracy we are talking about here mainly refers to the modern democracy of the modern nation-states. To be specific, the contradiction of interests in the modern nation-states has promoted the emergence and development of modern democracies. In real life, interests always attend human condition, and have roughly undergone three major stages of development in history: interest convergence in the primitive society, interest opposition in the private-ownership society and interest differentiation in the socialist society. After the emergence of private ownership, classes and states, which ended interest convergence and brought about contradiction and conflict of interests as the major characteristics of the interest structure of a society, political superstructures, such as the state apparatus, become significant measures for the ruling class to control and achieve its interests. In turn, the ruled class attempted to alter the old pattern of interest distribution by waging political struggles and imposing restrictions and influence on the state apparatus, so as to satisfy the interest requirements of its own class. However, the characteristics of personal dependent relationship under the self-sufficient natural economic structure not only determines that the ruled class cannot truly become an independent subject of interests to impose an effective restriction on the ruling class, but also decides that the autocratic monarchy is to be the basic form of political rule in both the slave and feudal society. That is to say, in the two forms of society, the autocratic monarchy is the primary tool to strangle the interests of the ruled class and protect those of the slave owners and feudal lords. The germination and development of the new economic structure of the commodity economy determined that the form of political rule of autocratic monarchy could no longer adapt to the interest structure and interest contradictions under the new circumstances, because the social division of labor and independent interests of laborers are the necessary conditions for the existence of a commodity economy. In the meantime, the basic principles for the operation of a commodity economy as free competition, compensation of equal value and equal exchange of commodities have not only determined that the contradiction between interest subjects with equal status are the primary characteristics of the interest contradiction, but also have decided that a form of political rule must be established to equally protect the interests of participants in social and economic life. As a result, modern democracy emerges as a new way of state and social management and a new means for the state to regulate and protect people's interests. However, the very existence of capital privileges determined that the nature of democracy in capitalist countries would be an instrument to protect the interests of the minority propertied class. The case in socialist countries is quite the opposite in that the public ownership of means of production distinguishes the essence of interest contradiction in socialist countries radically from that in capitalist countries, so democracy can truly serve as a tool to reconcile the interest contradiction and secure the interests of the majority of the society.

Secondly, in terms of the nature of democracy, the central issue of democracy, as we have emphasized repeatedly, is the matter of relationship between governance of the minority and the rights and interests of the majority. This relationship is practically an issue of interest contradiction between the minority and the majority. To be specific, democracy originally means the rule of the majority, but in modern nation states, the rule of majority could only be achieved by the governance of the minority. But whether governance of the minority or the exercise of state power by the minority aims to protect the interests of the majority or just those of their own is the most fundamental contradiction of interests inherent in democracy itself. The application or realization of democracy also means the dissolution and resolution of this contradiction. On the other hand, since democracy is a form of political rule, one of the two fundamentally opposed interests between the ruling class and the ruled class is necessarily protected and promoted while the other's is restricted and deprived.

Thirdly, in terms of the source of democratic vitality, in the most general sense, democracy could be understood as both a static political structure and a dynamic political status or process. The operation of democratic politics in all countries of the world reveals that coordination of interest contradictions is the source of vitality for democratic development. First, the operational process of democratic politics is in fact the coordination process of different interests. As mentioned above, democratic politics is derived from people's need of interests, in other words, democratic politics is essentially a product of the coordination of competing interests. When discussing the essence of constitutions, Lenin once asserted, "The essence of a constitution is that the fundamental laws of the state in general, and the laws governing elections to and the powers of the representative institutions, etc., express the actual relation of forces in the class struggle."'[12] The key factor that results in the balance of forces is the need of interests. Therefore, the balance of different forces is in fact a process of making concession and compromise between different interests. Meanwhile, the fundamental principle of democratic politics is majority rule, that is, the will and interests of the minority must be subordinated to the will and interests of the majority. In addition, democratic politics values both obedience to the majority and respect and protection of the minority, neither of which can be divorced from the coordination of interests.

Moreover, the operation of democratic politics depends on the coordination of various interests. Order is the fundamental symbol of vitality for a system, and the orderly operation and development of a democratic politics directly manifest its vitality. Since democratic politics concerns all aspects of social life, it is the fundamental approach for all classes, social strata, groups and individuals in modern countries under the rule of law to fulfil their own will and interests. Therefore, the orderly operation and development of a democratic politics depend directly on the status quo of interest relations between people. Throughout history, democratic politics would operate effectively and develop vigorously when the interest relations between people were in a relatively harmonious and relaxed state, but would operate chaotically and tend to gridlock when the interest relations between people entered into a tense and confrontational situation. Consequently, the coordination of interests directly determines the operation of a democratic politics.

Although we have concluded that interest contradiction is the direct driving force for the development of democracy, this does not mean that democratic politics itself is only passive. As the American scholar Keith Graham pointed out, "To see it from the aspect of interests, the motive that human has for democracy is that democratic system could realize the interests of every individual."[13] That is to say, the reason why people pursue and apply democracy is that democracy plays an active and positive role in its own right. As a matter of fact, the operation of democratic politics leads to the resolution of interest contradictions, which also means the satisfaction and realization of certain interests. As Huang Wenyang stated:

> Assuming that people's self-interests are justifiable, the superiority of the democratic system lies in that it assures the sufficient expression and the maximum satisfaction of each individual's of interests. Perhaps, individual need of interests might be met in some non-democratic regimes as well, but only in a democracy can the interests of every individual be respected and interests of the people thus be achieved because, in a democracy, decisions are made according to the will and requirements of the people.[14]

---

[12] *Liening quanji* [Lenin Collected Works] (1959), Beijing: People's Publishing House, vol.15, p.309. cf. Lenin, V. (1909) 'How the Socialist-Revolutionaries Sum Up the Revolution and How the Revolution has Summed Them Up'.

[13] Cited in Huang, W. Y. (ed.) (1990) *Guoneiwai minzhu lilun yaolan* [An Overview of Democratic Theories in China and Abroad], Beijing: China Renmin University Press, p.382.

[14] Huang, W. Y. (ed.) (1990). *Guoneiwai minzhu lilun yaolan* [An Overview of Democratic Theories in China and Abroad], Beijing: China Renmin University Press, p.381.

7.1.2 Interest Groups as Integral Part of the Democratic Mechanism

Interest differences give rise to different interest groups. According to David B. Truman, an interest group is one that "makes certain claims upon other groups in the society on the basis of one or more shared attitudes"[15]; according to Robert A. Dahl, "Any group of people who act together to promote or defend some common interest or objective is, in the broadest sense, an interest group"[16]; Graham K. Wilson argued, "It is an organization which seeks or claims to represent people or organizations which share one or more common interests or ideals"[17]; according to Wang Weiguang and Guo Baoping, "Interest groups are social organizations which share common interests formed on the basis of interest differences",[18] and so on. Despite a degree of the nuances in specific expression, the scholars above share much the same generalization on the basic content of interest groups: first, an interest group is a collection of certain individuals; second, the individuals that gather together have the same requirements of interests or shared desires.

From the perspective of the historical development, an interest group is a historical category. Under different historical conditions, interest groups have various historical contents. Originally, initial interest groups were the primitive groups that gathered on the basis of a certain blood ties and territorial scope, such as clans, tribes and tribal alliances. With the development of the social division of labor and private ownership, the society is divided into classes, which could be subdivided into different strata and further divided into smaller interest groups, with classes and strata being the most stable interest groups in a class society. Through horizontal social connections between different classes, strata and smaller interest groups, some relatively stable super interest groups with common interests necessarily emerged, such as families, nationalities and various economic entities. Similarly, there are also various interest groups in socialist societies due to the existence of interest differences, including the two major interest groups of the working class and the peasant class. Again, the working class can be further divided into the workers' interest groups in the enterprises owned by the whole people, the workers' interest groups in collectively-owned enterprises, and the intellectuals' interest groups. In addition, there are other interest groups formed due to various features such as gender and profession.

Undoubtedly, in any country or social form, interest groups are formed to maintain and achieve their common interests through the use of collective power. In a class society, however, the interests of any class, stratum or group can be fully maintained and realized only with the backing of state power. Therefore, every class, stratum

---

[15] Truman, D. B. (1951/1962) *The Government Process: Political interests and public opinions*, New York: Alfred A. Knopf Inc., pp.33.

[16] Dahl, R. A. (1981) *Democracy in the United States: Promise and Performance*, Boston: Houghton Mifflin Company, 4th edition, p.235.

[17] Wilson, G. K. (1981) *Interest Groups in the United States*, Oxford: Clarendon Press, p.4.

[18] Wang, W. G. and Guo, B. P. (1988) *Shehui liyi lun* [On Social Interests], Beijing: People's Publishing House, p.166.

and group hopes to hold state power, or influence the exercise of it through various ways and measures. In this sense, we can say that a political party falls within the domain of interest groups in a broad sense. Therefore, an interest group we refer to in this book is neither a social group lacking a political objective nor a political party whose purpose is to seize and exercise the state power, but a group to strive for and maintain its own interests. Professor Alan Cawson pointed out, "Interest groups are organizations which attempt to influence the direction of government policy without themselves seeking to form the government."[19] Hence, being involved in national political life as well as manipulating or influencing the making and implementing of national policies is one of the major objectives of the activities of various interest groups. However, some western bourgeois theorists hold that an interest group is ultimately formed on the basis of the political rather than the economic purpose, and its key symbol is the political power status rather than the economic features. We never deny its political purpose or its characteristics of political power, and consider them as its basic means to realize and maintain its own interests, but the root cause for the formation of an interest group is the economic relationship dominated by the ownership of the means of production. Any interest group is first and foremost an economic one and then a political one. Behind a political interest group, there are always certain economic interests hidden, and every political power group is always dominated by a certain economic interest group, and engages in political activities to realize the economic interests of a certain economic group.

It must be clear that our emphasis on the economic purpose of interest groups does not mean that we deny its political purpose, but that the latter serves the former. As a matter of fact, only when interest groups are capable of fully exerting their influence in the political realm can they finally achieve their economic purposes. However, the influence an interest group has on the national political life is not unconditional, but possible only when the external conditions allow it to play a political role. Since the natural economic structure in the slave and feudal society, which the autocratic monarchy was built on, is the characteristic of personal dependence and hierarchical privilege, most of the interest groups were prohibited from taking part in political activities affecting either the economic or political life of the country, except that only a few interest groups within the ruling class could exert a limited influence. However, the democratic political system which formed with the development of commodity economy has created economic and political conditions for various interest groups to participate in the state politics. From the history of democratic politics, interest groups are tightly connected with democratic politics and actually become an indispensable part of democratic mechanism despite the fact that they have massively participated in political life for only nearly a century. In this regard, Alan Cawson pointed out:

> At one time attacked as subversive of democratic processes, interest groups became widely regarded as the essence of the system of democratic pluralism where, it was argued, they stand as a buffer between the individual citizen and the overarching state. Political theorists such as Bentley and Truman argued that groups were the fundamental building blocks of

---

[19] Cf. Miller, D. and Bogdanor, V. (eds) (1992) *The Blackwell Encyclopedia of Political Science*, New York: Wiley-Blackwell, p.295.

> the political process, and that political institutions could be seen as being driven by group pressures. Interest groups were not regarded as a threat to democratic processes because individuals were considered to be free to form groups, and as a group formed on one side of a political issue, another could arise which would redress the balance.[20]

To be specific, firstly, the commodity economy emphasizes not only free competition between participants in economic life, but also fair competition. That is to say, the commodity economy allows various economic interest subjects to freely and equally participate in the economic life. Correspondingly, in order to satisfy and achieve their own interests, these interest subjects must also engage in the national political life freely and equally. Therefore, the commodity economy determines not only that the country must adopt the form of democratic rule, but also that all interest groups are important participants in this form of political rule. Secondly, since the contradiction of interests is the direct driving force and the satisfaction of interests is the fundamental driving force for development of democracy, how can the establishment and operation of democratic politics be separated from the expression and pursuit of their own interests by various interest groups? As mentioned above, the core and essence of democratic politics is that the people are the masters of the country, which is not an abstract concept but the most concrete manifestation of interests of the majority. However, the realization of the interests of the majority depends heavily on the activities of various interest groups. According to Huang, "It is safe to say that democracy, as a system of people's rule, can ensure the realization of both individual and social interests, and thus can be accepted by people."[21] Thirdly, from the practice of democratic politics, although the participation of interest groups in democratic political life varies greatly between the capitalist countries and the socialist countries, the most basic fact is that interest groups are one of the most active factors in democratic politics. Therefore, the interest group is "a necessary and vital component of the democratic governmental process".[22] M. J. C. Vile even argued that "the interaction of groups becomes the essence of democratic government".[23] But will the transformation from interest differences to interest groups lead to pluralistic democracy? How should we correctly understand pluralistic democracy? Such questions will be discussed in Sect. 7.3 of this chapter.

---

[20] Cf. Miller, D. and Bogdanor, V. (eds) (1992) *The Blackwell Encyclopedia of Political Science*, New York: Wiley-Blackwell, p.295.

[21] Huang, W. Y. (ed.) (1990) *Guoneiwai minzhu lilun yaolan* [An Overview of Democratic Theories in China and Abroad], Beijing: China Renmin University Press, p.381.

[22] Ornstein, N. J. and Elder, S. (1978) *Interest Groups, Lobbying and Policymaking*, Washington D. C.: Congressional Quarterly Inc., p.12.

[23] Vile, M. (1988) *Meiguo zhengzhi* [American Politics], trans. Wang H. et al., Beijing: The Commercial Press, p.109. cf. Vile, M. (1999) *Politics in the United States,* New York: Routledge of Taylor and Francis Group, p.88.

7.2 The Capitalist Parliamentary System and Interest Groups

As Gong Ruixiang pointed out, in the West, "generally speaking, politics is the struggle launched by various groups with the purpose of taking control of over political organizations such as government organs. In a sense, one could not comprehend the political systems of Western countries or have an intensive understanding of their actual decision-making process without being sufficiently acquainted with interest groups".[24] As democratic politics was first initiated by the bourgeoisie, who pursue the philosophy of individualism on the issues of interest satisfaction and interest structure, the role of interest groups in the democratic politics of capitalist countries has been the most active, typically with the longest history.

7.2.1 Critical Analysis of Interest Groups in Capitalist Countries

In capitalist countries, the concept of the interest group is often used interchangeably with the concept of pressure group, but in fact, they both differ in many aspects, mainly manifested in the fact that the pressure group is solely a political concept, which refers to the interest group that is engaged in politics, while the concept of the interest group can be either political or non-political. According to some Western scholars, interest groups can be transformed into pressure groups only when they take on political roles and attempt to influence the direction of public decision-making and the exercise of public powers for their own benefit. Therefore, pressure groups are tools to safeguard particular interests and achieve special objectives, and their primary feature is to participate in the political process and influence the public policies, but not to seek formal control of the government. Nonetheless, interest groups in capitalist countries are all pressure groups in general. Therefore, I tend to use the concept "interest group" in this book instead. Madison once wrote:

> But the most common and durable source of factions has been the various and unequal distribution of property. Those who hold and those who are without property have ever formed distinct interest in society. Those who are creditors, and those who are debtors, fall under a like discrimination. A landed interest, a manufacturing interest, a mercantile interest, a moneyed interest, with many lesser interests, grow up of necessity in civilized nations, and divide them into different classes, actuated by different sentiments and views. The regulation of these various and interfering interests forms the principal task of modern legislation....[25]

[24] Gong, X. R.(1985). *Bijiao Xianfa yu Xingzhengfa* [Comparative Constitution and Administrative Law], Beijing: Law Press, p.307.

[25] Hamilton, A. et al. (1980) *Lianbangdangren wenji* [The Federalist Papers], trans. Cheng F. R., Zai H. & Shu X., Beijing: The Commercial Press, p.47. cf. Hamilton, A., Madison, J. and Jay, J. (2008) *The Federalist Papers*, New York: Oxford University Press Inc., p.50.

With a view of history, it can be found that interest groups, such as the National Brewers Association and the National Cotton Council of America, appeared in the United States as early as in the late eighteenth century. Later, similar groups successively arose in Britain, France and other Western countries. However, the number of early interest groups was negligible and their influence on society was limited. By the middle of the nineteenth century, various interest groups developed quickly as the wave of industrialization swept across the western countries, where various social contradictions further grew due to the quick differentiation of industries, trades and occupations, and government functions expanded accordingly. The making of various laws and policies by the government involved the interests of different social individuals, which aroused the general concern of the public about government behavior. The British Enterprises Association, the British Shipbuilding Federation, the American Manufacturers Association, the American Chamber of Commerce, the French Shipbuilding Association and some Japanese economic groups were all formed during this period and exerted a pervasive influence on politics at the time. In the twentieth century, especially after the Second World War, with social, economic and cultural development, the expansion of government functions in the management of economy and society, and the progress of science and technology in Western countries, social contradictions were further intensified and complicated causing interest groups to spring up in great numbers. Take the United States as an example. According to the American published *Encyclopedia of Associations,* there were 14,726 non-profit organizations nationwide in 1980, but by 1989, the number increased to more than 40,000. A survey indicated that 60% of Americans attached themselves to one or more groups and 50% of them were activists in those group activities. Thus, it can be seen that there are a huge number of interest groups in contemporary Western capitalist countries. Moreover, the emergence and development of interest groups also shows that the development of interest groups is closely related to government functions. Gong Xiangrui once stated:

> Historically speaking, the domains where government policies first tread are also the areas where pressure groups first appear; practically speaking, where the government intervenes more, pressure groups are more active. The emergence and development of pressure groups are both related to the expansion of government functions, that is to say, where the state power is involved more, there will be more pressure groups.[26]

According to their organizational goals and beneficiaries, interest groups in capitalist countries are classified by scholars into two types: special interest groups and public interest groups,[27] or groups which defend a particular sectional interest and those which seek to promote a cause.[28] As the oldest and broadest kind, special interest groups are generally established on the basis of economic interest relations

---

[26] Gong, X. R. (1985) *Bijiao xianfa yu xingzhengfa* [Comparative Constitution and Administrative Law], Beijing: Law Press, 1985, p.310.

[27] See *Zhongguo da baike quanshu: Zhengzhixue* [Encyclopedia of China: Politics] (1992), Beijing: Encyclopedia of China Publishing House, p.205.

[28] Miller, D. and Bogdanor, V. (eds) (1992). *The Blackwell Encyclopedia of Political Science*, New York: Wiley-Blackwell, p.295.

in pursuit of the special requirements of their members. Special interest groups in capitalist countries generally include: industrial and commercial interest groups, financial interest groups, peasant interest groups and labor organizations. Besides, there are other special groups based on race, ethnicity, gender, age and religion. Whereas, the target areas of public interest groups are very extensive, and any public interest issues with universal significance to the society could fall into the target scope of a public interest group. Generally, the public interest groups in capitalist countries include environmental protection organizations, consumers associations and peace organizations that promote nuclear disarmament, etc.

The existence and progress of the said interest groups and their impacts on the national political life may vary in different historical stages of the development of democratic politics in capitalist countries. If an interest group develops and grows stronger and stronger with the expansion of the government functions, then its political influence is increasingly strengthened through its own growth. To be specific, during the period of the laissez-faire capitalism, interest groups were restrained in both their own development and their political influence, but at the stage of monopoly capitalism, they have gained a rapid growth and a powerful political function and influence. The British scholar M. Vile even considered interest groups one of the three major forces that determined the national policies in the capitalist countries during period of monopoly capitalism. In describing the contemporary American policy making, he continued to claim:

> Arriving at political decisions....Three major sources can be determined from which the eventual solutions to problems are generated: the institutional machinery of government itself, the party system and the interest groups...the role of political parties in terms of policy formation is relatively weak, and a vacuum is created to be filled by the complex structure of interest groups.[29]

Therefore, interest groups play a vital role in the politics of contemporary capitalist countries, and they are ubiquitous and all-pervasive. Also, I believe that the following issues must be clarified in order to gain a correct understanding of interest groups of capitalist countries.

Firstly, individuals who share common interests are seemingly able to form an interest group, but different interest groups could have diverse roles and influences in the politics of capitalist countries and the extents to which various interests are realized could also be unequal. American scholar Keith Graham once noted:

> The issue of equality should be taken into account if we are to research into that of interest. The research would be meaningless without considering equality. There would be one reason to persist in equal distribution of power if it could indeed ensure the uttermost realization of each individual's interest. It is, however, impossible to distribute power equally. In a representative democratic system, interest of only the man who has political power and could order representatives to behave at his will can be satisfied maximally even each individual's interest is given the same consideration.[30]

---

[29] Vile, M. (1999). *Politics in the United States,* New York: Routledge of Taylor and Francis Group, p.87.

[30] Cited in Huang, W. Y. (ed.) (1990) *Guoneiwai Mmnzhu lilun yaolan* [An Overview of Democratic Theories in China and Abroad], Beijing: China Renmin University Press, p.381.

Taking as a criterion, Alan Cawson divided interest groups of capitalist countries based on the relationship between interest groups and the government into two categories: "insider" groups and "outsider" groups.[31] The former can regularly consult with government and play an active role in the making and implementation of policies; the latter is usually regarded unlawful by the government and strives to gain a foothold in political affairs. Therefore, interest groups in capitalist countries today are no longer a part of the mechanism to attract a wide range of different opinions to the democratic process, but rather only attract the privileged ones that exercise the quasi-public powers relatively far from democratic supervision.

Secondly, some bourgeois scholars claim that the participation of various interest groups in state politics marks the full democracy in the governance of capitalist states, but their activities can only be limited to the scope permitted by the bourgeois rule. On the one hand, since the politics in capitalist states is money politics, only those economically strong capitalists can really play an important role in national political life. On the other hand, in certain historical periods, it is true that some labor groups are allowed to exist and even to participate in certain aspects of political life in capitalist countries, but this only serves as a means for the bourgeoisie to alleviate class contradictions and conflicts and defuse tensions between labor and capital. The bourgeois government will take tough repressive measures to consolidate its state power once the activities of these interest groups jeopardize the fundamental interests of the bourgeoisie. Therefore, the so-called pluralistic democracy built upon diverse interest groups in capitalist countries is still a single class democracy of the bourgeoisie in nature, and the existence and activities of interest groups will not change the nature of the bourgeois dictatorship.

Thirdly, as for the working class, it is not without benefit to allow interest groups to engage in state politics.

> In the past, in order to suppress the expression of the will of the proletariat, the bourgeoisie made great efforts to recklessly manipulate the representative constituencies, so that the working class had no chance to speak, but the pressure groups successfully bypassed this obstacle, in this way, the working class could also form and had already formed their own pressure groups.[32]

In political practice, a large number of labor groups are dominated by the upper strata or even the foreman, which makes them unable to adequately express the opinions and demands of the working class, but this situation will definitely change with the improvement of the political awareness of the working class. In this way, the working class can not only fight for democracy and freedom more effectively, but also enhance their solidarity in the process of organizing their interest groups. Moreover, with the development of the interest groups of the working class, capitalist states will have to formulate policies that reflect the interests and demands of the working class. However, there is no doubt that the fundamental requirements of the

---

[31] Miller, D. and Bogdanor, V. (eds) (1992). *The Blackwell Encyclopedia of Political Science*, New York: Wiley-Blackwell, p.295.

[32] Gong, X. R. (1985) *Bijiao xianfa yu xingzhengfa* [Comparative Constitution and Administrative Law], Beijing: Law Press China, p.318.

working class, such as seizing the state power and eliminating the system of man exploiting man can only be realized through proletarian revolution.

7.2.2 Capitalist Parliamentary System as a Basic Way for Interest Groups to Participate in State Politics

Under normal circumstances, when a group has determined its own special interests, the most important issue lies in how to convey them to the decision-making center, so as to exert pressure on the formulation of public policies to promote and realize its own interests. Being both a public opinion organ and a legislative body, the representative institution, i.e. the parliament, has long been a main object upon which capitalist interest groups exert pressure, and the parliamentary system with the parliament as its core has thus become a basic instrument for various interest groups to pursue and achieve their special interests.

In fact, interest groups are allowed to exist and develop not only due to the development of capitalism from the liberal to the monopoly and the increasing expansion of government functions in capitalist countries, but also due to the gradual decline of the capitalist parliamentary system. Although the parliamentary system once served as a channel for communication between the citizens and the government in its early stage and was an effective means for the expression of "public opinion", the parliament could no longer well represent the interests of all aspects of the society, as the modern life became increasingly complex and specialized. The expansion of government functions in the fields of social and economic affairs, especially after the Second World War, provoked the resentment first between the bourgeois class and the working class, and later by other classes. As a result, interest groups emerged as information channels. Since then, this kind of informal political entity has played a significant role in the process of representing public opinion and even has become the basic form of representing public opinions, so to speak. If political parties used to be the main players in a democratic system in the past, interest groups are now playing just as important a role as political parties and will inevitably play an even more important role. When we say that the existence and development of interest groups result, to some extent, from the deficiencies of the capitalist parliamentary system, we do not mean that interest groups will replace it, but only emphasize that interest groups are closely related to the parliamentary system and, under certain circumstances, interest groups can act as a catalyst and remedy for the parliamentary system. Moreover, as the parliamentary system is still the basic form of achieving democracy in modern democratic countries, and the parliament, as the state legislative body, is still the major decision-making center of the country, the political influence of interest groups necessarily depends on the parliamentary system to a great extent. Then, how do interest groups of capitalist countries impose their influence on state politics through the parliamentary system? This question will be discussed specifically below.

(1) Electing Representatives of One's Own Interests to the Parliament

Parliament members make up the main body of the parliament, so to control or influence the parliament is mainly to control or influence its members. Therefore, the election of parliament members is the first step for interest groups to have control over or exert influence on the parliament. Generally, the influence of interest groups upon the parliamentary election mainly includes the following three methods.

First, influencing the election platform of the political party. The election platform is not only the basic policy orientation observed by a political party when it comes to power, but also an important means for the party to gain support from voters and win the election. The usual practice for interest groups to exert their influence on the election platform of a political party is to offer or withdraw their support for the party. For instance, Real estate associations might impose pressure on a political party to include some provisions in its platform that are conducive to the construction of private housing; Peasant associations would demand to be permitted to voice their opinions in the state agricultural plans; some ethnic groups may require a foreign policy to be adopted in the platform that reflects their views on the issue of the Middle East.

Second, directly nominating candidates. In the United States, interest groups mainly impose their influence through lobbying, but in Britain, Germany and Italy, they could directly send their representatives into the parliament. In Britain, for example, of the 269 elected MPs of the Labor Party in 1979, 133 were candidates nominated by the Trade Union.[33] In the German Bundestag, representatives from interest groups accounted for about 1/3, who were either directly dispatched by interest groups or closely tied with them because of their position advantages.[34] In Italy, the Catholic Action Alliance provided the largest number of "Direct Representatives" and held the strongest power in the parliament. Leaders in other social groups also edged themselves into the parliament through election campaigns.[35]

Third, encouraging their group members to vote and provide election funds. During the election campaign, the spokespersons or key figures of the interest group with a large number of members will take an active part in the election campaign to support their candidates through organizing mass rallies, making speeches, promoting their candidates in newspapers, radio and television, and notably collecting donations to provide election funds. Interest groups provide great assistance to intimate campaigning candidates by supporting their nominations, offering political donations, aiding registration of voters and mobilizing them to vote. A well-organized interest group with relatively powerful membership in some districts could provide their candidates a vital base of votes. For example, in the late 1960s and

[33] Cao, P. L. et al. (1993) *Bijiao zhengfu tizhi* [A Comparison of Government System], Shanghai: Fudan University Press, p.97.

[34] Cao, P. L. et al. (1993) *Bijiao zhengfu tizhi* [A Comparison of Government System], Shanghai: Fudan University Press, p.340.

[35] Cao, P. L. et al. (1993) *Bijiao zhengfu tizhi* [A Comparison of Government System], Shanghai: Fudan University Press, p.340.

early 1970s, Political Action Committees (also called Political Committees or Political Education Committees) emerged in the United States. These committees were often organized by business enterprises, industrial associations or individual citizens with similar political views.[36] They offered support to the candidates of their interests financially and morally. In essence, they were tools used by interest groups to affect the election of the Democratic and the Republican. According to the Federal Election Campaign Act of 1974, a Political Action Committee could offer a contribution of no more than 5,000 dollars to a candidate, but the number of Committees that one candidate could receive contributions from were unlimited. Henceforth, Political Action Committees have become legitimate donor organizations with growing influence and increasing numbers in the United States, and in the mid-1980s, there were more than 3000 such committees. In France, major interest groups usually have their own newspapers or propaganda machines, of which they take advantage of printing and distributing various opinions of candidates to their members before each vote, so that they could mobilize voters to support the candidates who promise to represent the interests of their own groups or to boycott those who stand against their own interests. The National Union Committee for the Defense of Independent Workers, an interest group formed in 1970s with about 200,000 members, aimed to defend the interests of small businesses composed mainly of household industries and to side against large enterprises and supermarkets. It had little influence in national parliamentary elections, but in March 1977, during a local election, its members boycotted the then Minister of Commerce and the Minister of Finance, both of whom consequently lost their concurrent posts as city mayor. In the period of monopoly capitalism, especially after the Second World War, the means of election underwent a significant change under the influence of interest groups. Specifically, a new way of campaigning emerged, where candidates could employ campaign managers, public relations firms, political analysts and professional fundraisers, etc. to form a campaign team, which was probably irrelevant to their political party to a large extent. The key to this change was that interest groups provided candidates large sums of money, which enabled them to organize their own campaign team instead of the official campaign organization of his own political party. As a matter of fact, the means by which interest groups imposed their influence on the election was to provide abundant funds as both a precondition and backing of the campaign. As can be seen from the table below, the higher the campaign expenses, the larger the proportion of funds financed by big donors and interest groups.

[36] Li, S. Q. (1988) *Liyi jituan yu Meiguo zhengzhi* [Interest Groups and American Politics], Beijing: China Social Sciences Press, p.98.

Analysis of Source of Campaign Expenses of House of Representatives in 1972[37]

Campaign Expenses	Percentage of Expenses from Small Donors and Party Committees	Percentage of Expenses from big Donors and Powerful Groups
$ 0–30,000	57.9%	27.1%
$ 30,000—70,000	50.6%	34.6%
$70,000—120,000	46.7%	36.5%
> $ 120,000	39.1%	40.4%

(2) Imposing Pressure and Influence Upon Parliamentary Activities

The ultimate goal of interest groups is not just to elect their own representatives or spokesmen, but to manipulate or influence parliamentary activities, such as legislation, appointment and removal, and to spare no efforts to push the parliament to pass the bills that are line with their interests or hinder or oppose those that are not. Therefore, the parliament is not only the conventional venue for political parties, but also a place for interest groups to play an active role. Unlike political parties, which impose their influence on the parliament mostly through organized activities inside the parliament, interest groups exert their influence on the work of the parliament mainly through lobbying groups outside the parliament. The so-called "lobbying groups" mainly include two kinds: one is political brokers specializing in "lobbying members of the parliament", who are employed by various interest groups, bribing and influencing parliament members through various means to result in legislation favorable to their own groups; the other is interest groups themselves or the special offices they set up. In the political practice, Lobbying groups have played a significant role and exerted a great influence on the capitalist parliaments. Karl Schriftgeisser, an American expert on lobbying, once pointed out that "Lobbying is as old as legislation and pressure groups are as old as politics",[38] and the British scholar M. Vile also noted that "Much legislation of importance on the statue books of the United States today originated in the offices of interest groups".[39] In addition, Sir Ivor Jennings provided similar analysis in his book *Parliament*.[40]

In political practices, the major work of interest groups in capitalist parliaments generally includes three aspects: firstly, they manage to win a few or more parliament members to speak and work for themselves; secondly, they actively participate in the formulation of relevant laws and regulations, and coordinate with friendly parliament members to strive for the content of laws and regulations to meet their own demands;

---

[37] Gosnell, H. and R. Smolka (1980). *American Parties and Elections*, trans. Fudan University International Politics Department, Shanghai: Shanghai Translation Publishing House, p.272.

[38] Schriftgeisser, K. (1951) *The Lobbyists: The Art and Business of Influencing Lawmakers*, Boston: Little, Brown and Company, p.3.

[39] Vile, M. (1988) *Meiguo zhengzhi* [American Politics], trans. Wang H. et al., Beijing: The Commercial Press, p.122. cf. Vile, M. (1999) *Politics in the United States,* New York: Routledge of Taylor and Francis Group, p.100.

[40] CF. Jennings, I. (1959) *Yingguo yihui* [British Parliament], trans. Peng B., Beijing: The Commercial Press, pp.205–221.

thirdly, in the process of making laws and regulations in the parliament, they try to do a good job to win over more people, so that they can get majority support in voting to pass laws and regulations they want and opposing the those they do not. The specific practices are as follows:

First, interest groups gain support for their interests by providing parliament members with various materials and information. Legislation regarding tariffs, agricultural prices, finance, social insurance, wages, working hours, and so on all require professional knowledge and background materials that could be provided by lobbyists for reference by parliament members. In the United States, such materials and information must be well-grounded, tenable, rational and convincing, so as to avoid discontent with other members and damage to their prestige. Especially during the deliberation of bills in subcommittees, committees or plenary sessions of the House and the Senate, relevant interest groups and their lobbyists have to, in a timely way, provide the necessary evidence and arguments for debate to the representatives they cooperate with.[41] In Italy, since the parliament lacks a complete and systematic intelligence system and relies heavily on the information offered by external agencies, interest groups often provide one-sided information to the parliament continuously through their representatives to gain advantage in terms of public opinion and legislative basis.[42]

Second, interest groups gain support for their interests by actively playing a role in committees and subcommittees of the parliament. In the United States, interest groups usually strive to testify at relevant hearings held by these committees and they generally prepare their testimony meticulously for such hearings, so as to provide the hearing members with a variety of persuasive materials. In Italy, interest groups could utilize the permanent committee that is entitled to approve and enact laws, to formulate or adopt laws in favor of particular interest groups with the aid of their representatives as much as they could provide. Besides, interest groups also seek to have their own representatives as members of the permanent committee reporting to the whole House. Before reporting the legislative process to the parliament, the reporter may have prepared and collected all kinds of biased arguments to argue hard for his own interest group. He may even alter the facts and single out those materials that benefits his own group most for people's reference, and he can also speed up or delay the discussion of a bill under the pretext of procedural problem or issue of receiving materials. In order to oppose a piece of legislation, the reporter can do anything to delay it at least or to cause it to fail at most.

Third, interest groups gain support for their interests by building legislative alliances. In the United States, some of the most powerful interest groups often tend to work with the legislators who support them to develop shared strategies and tactics for parliamentary struggles and establish a temporary legislative alliance during the deliberation of a bill. Interest groups not only give advice to the legislators,

---

[41] Jiang, J. S. (1992) *Meiguo guohuishi* [The History of American Congress], Haikou: Hainan Publishing House, pp.418–419.

[42] Cao, P. L. et al. (1993) *Bijiao zhengfu tizhi* [A Comparison of Government System], Shanghai: Fudan University Press, p.433.

but also help them draft bills. Consequently, such a legislative alliance, which have no organizational form, but often includes government officials who hold identical stance with their interest groups, becomes a temporary "administrative center".

Fourth, interest groups gain support for their interests by making extensive use of grass-roots lobbying activities. In order to strengthen their influence and pressure on the parliament members, many interest groups mobilize their own members or voters in the electoral districts where parliament members are located to express their demands to them by interviews, letters and telephone. They also promote their campaigns through radio, television and newspaper advertisements to win over public opinion.

Fifth, interest groups gain support for their interests by attending social activities. Social activities are an important means for interest groups to maintain a good relationship with parliament members, and many lobbying activities are carried out in the context of social activities. If an interest group has no friendly relationship with the parliament members, its lobbying cannot go far. Therefore, an interest group and its lobbyists often arrange social activities in different ways according to the preferences of the parliament members.

In political practice, interest groups impose their effect and influence by retaliating against parliament members who repeatedly violate their demands in parliamentary voting and force them to serve their own group, in addition to positively flattering and winning them over as mentioned above. In short, in the parliamentary politics of capitalist countries, interest groups do not only make up for the deficiencies of party politics, but in fact have increasingly played a role as important as that of political parties, which has aroused much concern. For example, the US senator Edward Kennedy once commented on the influence of interest groups on Congress in 1977. He worried that the Congress would not be able to enact legislation in the light of national interests, and noted that during his 16 years' work in the Senate, he witnessed the deterioration of the representative politics on Capitol Hill to its worst state. He argued that the key to this problem was that the Senate and the House of Representatives had drowned in a sea of campaign contributions and lobbying activities for special interests.[43]

7.3 Socialist People's Representative System and Interest Groups

Interest groups are a constituent part of the democratic mechanism, but their specific status and roles manifested in the construction of democratic politics vary from country to country. In capitalist countries, the existence and rise of interest groups

[43] Hrebenar, R. and Scott, R. (1982) *Interest Group Politics in America*, Englewood Cliffs: Prentice-Hall, Inc., p.130.

have facilitated the development of capitalist democracy, while in socialist democratic politics, theoretical and practical understandings of and attention to interest groups must be deepened and improved.

7.3.1 Features of Interest Structure in Socialist Countries

In the previous discussion, we have mentioned more than once the issue of interest in socialist countries, but we have not analyzed it from the perspective of interest structure. Since the interest structure concerns not only the interrelationship between various interest groups and their political status and role, but also the form of political rule of the state, it is necessary to elaborate on the main features of the interest structure of socialist countries. As complicated as it might be, the main features of the interest structure of socialist countries can be summarized by the following three attributes: collectivism, public ownership, and the organic unity of interests in a socialist state.

First, Collectivism is the philosophical foundation for the existence of the interest structure of socialist countries. As mentioned earlier, the interest structure of capitalist countries is based on individualism, an ideological and theoretical viewpoint that treats society and others from a self-centered perspective and sets individual and society in opposition, focusing everything on personal needs and happiness and denying a unified social value standard. Moreover, once individualism develops to the extreme, an individual would harm social interests or the interests of others by any means for the sake of his own personal interests. This inevitably results in insuperable contradictions and severe opposition between diverse interests or interest groups in the interest structure based on individualism. Collectivism, on the other hand, focuses on the fundamental interests of the proletariat in dealing with the relationship between individuals and collectives or individuals and society, emphasizes that the collective interests of the proletariat precede individual interests, and demands that individual interests should be subordinated to collective interests, the immediate to the long-term and the partial to the overall. Obviously, socialist countries focus more on collective interests in terms of the interrelationship between different interests, though they also emphasize protection of legitimate individual interests. This determines that the differences and contradictions between various interests or interest groups in the interest structure of socialist countries are not fundamental and they all can be completely unified under the banner of collectivism.

Second, the public ownership of the means of production is the economic basis for the existence of the interest structure of socialist countries, which is actually the specific manifestation of collectivism in the form of ownership. As previously mentioned, under different forms of ownership of the means of production, individual interests differ in terms of their nature, basis and scope, as do social interests in terms of their features. To be specific, under public ownership, not only the satisfaction of individual production needs often takes the form of common interests, but a large part of individual living needs are also satisfied in the form of common interests. In this way, a truly unified social interest is formed. Therefore, in the interest structure of socialist countries, the common and social interests usually occupy the leading position, and all interest groups can also cooperate with and promote each other in achieving their own interests.

Third, the organic unity of multiple interests is the basic form for the existence of the interest structure of socialist countries. Any society is composed of individuals with certain social interests who are bound to rely on certain social groups, and the realization of individual interests must depend on that of group interests, so it is necessary for individuals to form a certain social interest group according to their common interests. Moreover, any society is comprised of multiple interest groups in different social status, and different interest groups, which are mutually dependent, restricted, influential, penetrating and contradictory, constitutes a multiple social interest system. If the socioeconomic conditions of capitalism determine that the multiple social interest system of a capitalist society is mainly formed on the confrontation of interests between the two major interest groups of the working class and the bourgeois class, then the multiple interest system of a socialist society is a system in which multiple interest groups coexist under the condition of unified fundamental interests. That is to say, despite the existence of multiple interest groups in the socialist interest structure, their fundamental interests coincide, which determines the organic unity of multiple interests between various interest groups.

7.3.2 Socialist People's Representative System as the Core System for Interest Groups to Participate in Deliberation and Administration of State Affairs

In political practice of socialist countries, the participation in deliberation and administration of state affairs is the most fundamental political function for various interest groups. Since interest groups are not constituents of the state organs, their will and interests can be truly reflected and implemented in the process of state and social management only through their participation in the administration and discussion of state affairs. In my view, the essence of political participation by interest groups is to restrict and influence the exercise and execution of state power. As the people's representative organs of socialist countries are institutions that exercise the state power in a unified manner on behalf of the broad masses of the people, the socialist people's representative system, with the people's representative organs as the main body, is the core system through which interest groups can impose their restriction and influence on the state power, which is specifically manifested as follows:

(1) **Selecting Deputies to People's Representative Organs as the First Step for Interest Groups to Participate in Deliberation and Administration of State Affairs**

People's representative organs are composed of people's deputies, and the exercise of state power by the representative organs can only be realized through the activities of people's deputies. Therefore, the selection of deputies is the basic approach for all classes, strata, and groups to exercise their right of being the masters of their countries. According to the constitutions and laws of socialist countries, citizens are entitled to have the right to vote and stand for election as long as they have reached the eligible age and have not been deprived of their political rights by law. Meanwhile, social groups, that is, interest groups, may either independently or jointly recommend candidates for deputies, which provides a constitutional and legal guarantee for various interest groups to elect their deputies to people's representative organs. Moreover, the nature of the socialist state power through which the vast majority of people are their own masters, inevitably requires that the composition of deputies provides broad representation. Therefore, it is of great necessity for various interest groups to select their deputies to the people's representative organs. In this regard, A. A. Bezuglov pointed out in summarizing the situation in the Soviet Union:

> Both the constitution and electoral law guarantee that social groups have the right to propose candidates for deputies, to freely and fully discuss about the candidates, and to designate their own deputies to participate in the affairs of electoral committees at all levels, so as to guarantee the smooth running of elections. And social groups can also play a crucial role in the establishment of the Soviet organs. In addition, they also have the right to be briefed by Soviet deputies and public officials. Finally, the recall law stipulates that social groups have the right to propose to recall the deputies who fail to live up to the trust of voters.[44]

(2) **Direct Participation in or Influence on Activities of People's Representative Organs as the Basic Content for Interest Groups to Participate in Deliberation and Administration of State Affairs**

As we know, the common feature of interest groups in both capitalist and socialist countries is to exert their influence on the activities of representative organs through participation in state politics. The reason is simple: since law-based governance is a basic requirement for a country under rule of law, the law-making body is of paramount importance. If the interest needs of an interest group could be reflected in the contents of the law, the realization and satisfaction of its interests would not be a question. However, different from interest groups in capitalist countries, interest groups in socialist countries can directly participate in the activities of people's representative organs in political practice.

However, the objective effect of such participation and influence is still limited in socialist countries, and for this reason, socialist countries still need to work hard in this regard. To be specific, it must be clear that the "social groups" existing in socialist countries are in fact interest groups, and that these interest groups also have their own special interests, though they share the fundamental interests. In practice, the status and role of interest groups in the people's representative system should be further clarified legally and institutionally. Specifically, interest groups should have the right to propose candidates for deputies, account for a certain proportion in the composition of deputies, collectively supervise the activities of deputies and representative organs,

---

[44] Bezuglov, A. (1983) *Suweiai jianshe xue* [Soviet Construction Theories], trans. Liu, J. H. et al., Beijing: China Renmin University Press, p.185.

and consciously abide by and execute the laws, decrees, resolutions and decisions made by the representative organs.

References

Bezuglov, A. (1983). *Suweiai jianshe xue* [Soviet Construction Theories] (J. H. Liu, et al., Trans.). China Renmin University Press.

Cao, P. L. et al. (1993). *Bijiao zhengfu tizhi* [A Comparison of Government System]. Fudan University Press.

Dahl, R. A. (1981). *Democracy in the United States: Promise and Performance*. Houghton Mifflin Company (4th edn).

de Tocqueville, A. (1988). *De la démocratie en Amérique* [The Democracy of America] (G. L. Dong, Trans.). The Commercial Press (Vol. 1).

Gong, X. R. (1985). *Bijiao xianfa yu xingzhengfa* [Comparative Constitution and Administrative Law]. Law Press China.

Gosnell, H., & Smolka, R. (1980). *American Parties and Elections* (Fudan, Trans.) University International Politics Department, Shanghai Translation Publishing House.

Hamilton, A. et al. (1980). *Lianbangdangren wenji* [The Federalist Papers] (F. R. Cheng, H. Zai, & X. Shu X., Trans.). The Commercial Press.

Hamilton, A., Madison, J., & Jay, J. (2008). *The Federalist Papers*. Oxford University Press Inc.

Hrebenar, R., & Scott, R. (1982). *Interest Group Politics in America*. Prentice-Hall Inc.

Huang, W. Y. (ed.). (1990). *Guoneiwai minzhu lilun yaolan* [An Overview of Democratic Theories in China and Abroad]. China Renmin University Press.

Jennings, I. (1959) *Yingguo yihui* [British Parliament] (B. Peng, Trans.). The Commercial Press.

Jiang, J. S. (1992). *Meiguo guohuishi* [The History of American Congress]. Hainan Publishing House.

Lenin, V. (1907). The Third Duma.

Lenin, V. (1909), 'How the Socialist-Revolutionaries Sum Up the Revolution and How the Revolution has Summed Them Up'.

Lenin, V. (1914). *Conspectus of Hegel's Book The Science of Logic*.

Li, S. Q. (1988). *Liyi jituan yu Meiguo zhengzhi* [Interest Groups and American Politics]. China Social Sciences Press.

Liening quanji [Lenin Collected Works]. (1959).. People's Publishing House (Vol. 13).

Liening Quanji [Lenin Collected Works] (1959). People's Publishing House, (Vol. 38).

Liening quanji [Lenin Collected Works]. (1959). Beijing: People's Publishing House (Vol. 15).

Makesi Engels quanji [Marx and Engels Collected Works]. (1960). Beijing: People's Publishing House (Vol. 3).

Makesi Engesi quanji [Marx and Engels Collected Works] (1958), Beijing: People's Publishing House (Vol. 4).

Makesi Engesi quanji [Marx and Engels Collected Works]. (1965). People's Publishing House (Vol. 1).

Makesi Engesi xuanji [Marx and Engels Selected Works]. (1995). Beijing: People's Publishing House, vol.4.

Marx, K. (1842). *Proceedings of the Sixth Rhine Province Assembly*.

Marx, K. (1847). *The Poverty of Philosophy*.

Marx, K., & Engels, F. (1945). *The German Ideology*.

Miller, D., & Bogdanor, V. (Eds.). (1992). *The Blackwell Encyclopedia of Political Science*. Wiley-Blackwell.

Ornstein, N. J., & Elder, S. (1978). *Interest Groups, Lobbying and Policymaking*. Congressional Quarterly Inc.

Schriftgeisser, K. (1951). *The Lobbyists: The Art and Business of Influencing Lawmakers*. Little, Brown and Company.

Su, H. Z. (1991). *Liyi lun* [On Interests]. Liaoning University Publishing House.

Truman, D. B. (1951/1962). *The Government Process: Political interests and public opinions*. Alfred A. Knopf Inc.

Vile, M. (1988). *Meiguo zhengzhi* [American Politics] (H. Wang et al., Trans.). The Commercial Press.

Vile, M. (1999). *Politics in the United States*. Routledge of Taylor and Francis Group.

Wang, W. G., & Guo, B. P. (1988). *Shehui liyi lun* [On Social Interests]. People's Publishing House.

Wilson, G. K. (1981). *Interest Groups in the United States*. Clarendon Press.

Zhang, X. (1987). *Liyi Lun Jiujiang* [Nine Lectures of Interest], Beijing: China Youth Publishing Group.

Zhongguo da baike quanshu: Zhengzhixue [Encyclopedia of China: Politics] (1992). Encyclopedia of China Publishing House.

Chapter 8
Comparison of Capitalist Parliamentary Systems

The study of the representative system cannot be conducted in isolation from the representative system itself. The survival and development of the representative system is driven both by internal and external causes with internal causes serving the primary role. Although we have discussed the abstract theories and external system of the representative system by illustrating its basic theories and the relevant issues in its establishment and operation, we have not yet made a systematic and comprehensive analysis of the representative system itself. Therefore, beginning with this chapter, we will discuss the structure and functions of the representative system, especially its different manifestations in different countries. Since there are many differences between the capitalist parliamentary system and the socialist people's representative system, we will study them separately and conduct a comparative analysis in order to find out their similarities and differences as well as the reasons behind them.

8.1 Pattern Analysis of Capitalist Parliamentary Systems

Many theoreticians, both in China and abroad, regard the "parliamentary system" as the typical political system of Britain that is different from the presidential system. However, as is repeatedly emphasized in this book, the so called "capitalist parliamentary system" is a capitalist representative system, which is an abstract generalization of various manifestations of the representative system in capitalist state power systems. Therefore, they are different concepts in both connotation and denotation. Meanwhile, as mentioned in Chap. 2, from the development of the capitalist parliamentary system, we can see that the parliamentary system in capitalist countries, though the class nature is identical, will inevitably be manifested in different forms with different characteristics, due to the differences in the balance of class forces, historical and cultural traditions and national psychology, etc. Geir Lundestad, the director of the Norwegian Nobel Institute, stated "in 1945 there were only 51 member

Y. Zhou, *A Comparative Study of Representative Systems*,
https://doi.org/10.1007/978-981-15-4186-5_8

states in the United Nations, but now there are 184[1] and the number is still on the rise." Of the 184 member states, the majority of them have established a capitalist representative system except that some socialist countries have not implemented a democratic system. In this way, the capitalist parliamentary system has taken on an even more diversified manifestation in capitalist countries. Consequently, in the study of the capitalist parliamentary system, it is too trivial to discuss in detail the institutional structure and operating mechanism of the parliamentary systems in each capitalist country. It is easier and more effective to classify them into different types according to their major basic characteristics, and conduct a comparative analysis of the typical types, which require us to conduct a pattern analysis first.

8.1.1 Patterns and Pattern Classification

In scientific research, the establishment of a pattern and the analysis or knowledge of its connotation, denotation and variations are the preconditions for type comparison. But, what is a "pattern"? There is no corresponding entry in authoritative reference books such as *Encyclopaedia Britannica, The Encyclopedia of China* or *Cihai (Encyclopedia of Chinese Words*). Thus, Mr. Zha Youliang gives an encyclopedic qualitative description of what is a pattern from the perspective of pattern theories:

> A pattern, as an important method for scientific operation and thinking, represents certain essential features of the prototypical objects under a certain abstract, simplified, and hypothetical conditions, so as to address some specific problems; acting as a mediator, it is a scientific approach for better understanding and transformation of the prototypes for the construction of a new one. On the one hand, various pattern can be extracted through generalization, induction and synthesis based on practices, and it is possible to formulate theories once these patterns are verified. On the other hand, patterns can also be proposed on the basis of theories through analogy, deduction and analysis, thus promoting the development of practice. A pattern is a similar simulation of objective entities (physical patterns), an abstract description of the real world (mathematical patterns) and visual displays of ideas (image patterns).[2]

This definition seems complicated, but it is a comprehensive and adequate generalization. And in his further elaboration, Mr. Zha also analyzed the meaning of pattern. Generally speaking, there are three main points: first, a pattern is a scientific approach that functions as a mediator in the cognitive process; second, a pattern is a way of thinking to solve problems; third, a pattern is a bridge between theory and practice. However, the reason why a pattern approach is employed in this research is to systematize and regularize the complicated political and legal phenomena by establishing and applying a pattern.

In fact, the classical Marxist writers attached great importance to analogical analysis of various social phenomena by establishing different patterns. In the article

[1] The data was collected in the mid-1990s.

[2] Zha, Y. L. (1994) 'Shenme shi moshilun?' [What is a Pattern Theory?], *Social Science Research*, No.2.

Pre-Capitalist Formations, Marx established all kinds of patterns for pre-capitalist social formations. Engels absorbed Henry Lewis Morgan's patterns and divided the ancient society into three epochs,[3] namely, savagery, barbarism and civilization in *The Origin of the Family, Private Property and the State.* Later on, in his article *Dialectical and Historical Materialism,* Joseph Stalin categorized social formations into five patterns as primitive communal system, slavery system, feudal system, capitalist system and socialist system. In the fields of constitutional law and political science, the so-called monarchy, republic, dual monarchy, parliamentary monarchy, parliamentary republic, presidential system and committee system are all the results of the application of the pattern approach. Hence, as mentioned above, the establishment and application of patterns are preconditions for comparative studies.

How are patterns built and applied? And how are different patterns formed and classified? While addressing these two questions, the following aspects will be discussed. Firstly, the most fundamental problem of establishing a pattern lies in clarifying its connotation and denotation. The connotation of a pattern often reflects its main characteristics and serves as the basis and conditions for establishing and determining the pattern. Take the presidential system as an example. The connotation of the presidential system boils down to three points: first, the executive, headed by the president, is independent of the legislative branch; second, the president, as the head of state, is also the actual head of the executive branch; third, the presidential system is established according to the principle of separation of the legislative, executive and judicial powers, and there is a relationship of mutual checks and balances between the three powers. In this way, the pattern of the presidential system is built with its connotation and characteristics clarified, and the denotation of the presidential system designates all the political systems that conform to the connotation and characteristics of the presidential system. However, it must be clear that the connotation of a pattern is not immutable. Generally speaking, on the premise of keeping the basic meaning unchanged, its connotation can get enriched and developed in accordance with various specific historical conditions.

Secondly, different classifications of patterns hinge on some certain standards, which are derived from the distinctive connotations given to patterns by people. In other words, only under certain standards can different types of patterns be formulated. That is to say, different standards will result in different classifications. Therefore, a given standard must be observed consistently in the same classification. In this regard, Neil J. Smelser's introduction of Arthur L. Kalleberg's criticism on Gabriel A. Almond's classification of political systems is worthy of our reference. Almond divided political systems into the following types: (1) the Anglo-American type, including some Commonwealth countries; (2) the Continental European type, including the Scandinavian and Lowland Countries; (3) the Pre-industrial or partially industrial type; and (4) the Totalitarian type. For Kalleberg, it is impossible to compare the above types for there is no common standard for Almond's classification, in addition, it is also impossible to make the comparison based on the degree of consistency between these systems for Almond did not state the possibility of

[3] See Morgan, H. (1877) *Ancient Society*, London: MacMillan & Company.

finding a common standard among these countries to prescribe their consistency. Kalleberg continued to make a general comment following this criticism:

> The first requirement that must be kept in mind by students of comparative politics is the necessity for carefully distinguishing between classification and comparison.... The second requirement is the need for properly-defined comparative concepts. Truly comparative concept...can only be developed after classification has been completed. Classification is a matter of "either-or"; comparison is a matter of "more or less". Two objects being compared must already have been shown to be of the same class....[4]

Obviously, establishing a consistent standard is the first step for the classification of patterns. In the meantime, it is safe to say, the standard established is not only the basis for the existence of different patterns, but also the mediator or bridge through which the different patterns can be compared with each other in a sense.

Thirdly, in the application of patterns, the following two major issues must also be noted and addressed. For one thing, we cannot take the establishment of a pattern as an end, i.e. pattern for pattern's sake. In other words, the purpose of establishing and applying a pattern is to serve the research of constitutional law and political science, but not the opposite. If the establishment of a pattern was taken as an end, the research work would be mislead. For another, there is distinction between the "standard for classification" and the "standard for comparison". In general, there are similarities and differences between all things in the world, so they all can be compared with each other in principle. Nevertheless, we have to find out a certain angle or connection or a third party as a mediator for a specific comparison between two things or several things. The so called "angle", "connection" or "mediator", also known as the "standard for comparison", is in fact the interface between two or more objects that are compared. If the researcher does not find such an interface, the comparison can hardly proceed. Similarly, if the interface is improperly identified, the research will be seriously affected. The interface can not be speculated subjectively, but must be abstracted out of the objective social and political phenomena. That is to say, the standard for comparison is an objective existence, and the ability of the researcher is to be adept in discovering and grasping it. It is apparent that the "standard for classification" is indeed distinct from the "standard for comparison". If we say that the "standard for classification" is a significant factor for the classification of patterns in the process of pattern building, the "standard for comparison" is the mediator and bridge set for comparative studies after different patterns are established. Therefore, they belong to two different stages in the process of comparative study.

8.1.2 Different Patterns of Capitalist Parliamentary Systems

In past and present political practice, the capitalist parliamentary system has undertaken different manifestations in different countries. Due to the large number of

[4] Smelser, N. (1976/2013) *Comparative Methods in the Social Sciences*, New Orleans: Quid Pro Books, p. 164.

capitalist countries where their specific circumstances and historical conditions are multifarious, the researcher faces difficulty in the study of the capitalist parliamentary system, especially in a comparative study. However, the only effective way to get out of this difficulty is to establish patterns and conduct a comparative analysis through classification of patterns. For this reason, many scholars in Chinese and non-Chinese academic circles have made unremitting efforts in this regard, and they have classified the capitalist parliamentary system into various patterns based on different classification standards. For example, based on the relationship between the legislature and the executive, the capitalist parliamentary system can be classified into dual monarchy, parliamentary monarchy, parliamentary republic, presidential system and committee system[5]; based on the composition of the parliament, it can also be divided into unicameralism, bicameralism and multicameralism[6]; based on the actual role of the parliament, there are "symbolic" parliamentary system and powerful parliamentary system[7]; based on the degree of independence of legislation, a parliamentary system can be categorized into those that reflect social interests and those that legislate independently. Some other scholars even classify the representative government into three types, namely, the republic with "a ceremonial monarch", presidential republic and parliamentary republic.[8]

All classifications listed above are the results of studies conducted by scholars from different angles according to different standards. In this sense, they are all justifiable and irreproachable. However, from the standpoint of this research, none of these classifications are entirely suitable for the research purpose of this book. Therefore, we need to set up another standard and make classifications accordingly before a comparative study. As the organizational system of state political power, the representative system is the basis for the establishment and operation of the structure of the state. Hence, we must set up a standard for classification from this standpoint or angle when classifying patterns of the parliamentary system. Since the parliament is the core and the materialized form of the parliamentary system, the standard established for pattern classification of the parliamentary system in this book lies in the relationship of the parliament with other state organs, especially the executive organs, in the state power system, and the status it occupies in this

---

[5] This classification is advocated by most Chinese scholars. The influence of the capitalist parliamentary system on state organs discussed in Chap. 5 of this book is also grounded on this classification. However, it has a great flaw in that it mixes up the polity, organizational form of political power, executive organ system with the organizational system of political power that belongs to the category of the representative system. This classification has been included into different categories that are intrinsically different as mentioned above, so it is not merely a classification of parliamentary system in fact.

[6] See Li, L. (1991) *Lifa jiguan bijiao yanjiu* [A Comparative Study of Legislative Bodies], Beijing: People's Daily Press, Chapter 3.

[7] Beetham, D. (1989) *Makesi Weibo yu xiandai zhengzhi lilun* [Max Weber and the Theory of Modern Politics], trans. Xu, H. B., Xu K. J. & Kang L. W., Hangzhou: Zhejiang People's Publishing House, pp. 97–106. cf. Beetham, D. (1974) *Max Weber and the Theory of Modern Politics*, London: George Allen & Unwin Ltd., pp. 98–102.

[8] Cao, P. L. et al. (1993) *Bijiao zhengfu tizhi* [A Comparison of Government System], Shanghai: Fudan University Press, p. 3.

relationship. This standard for classification absorbs quite a few aspects involved in the classifications adopted by other scholars. By patterns according to this standard, the capitalist parliamentary system can be divided into four major patterns: the "king in parliamentary system", the pure parliamentary system, the parliament-president parallel system and the semi-parliamentary system.

(1) The King in Parliamentary System

The "king in parliamentary system," in Isao Satou's words, is "the parliament that contains a king," and specifically, "it is a synthesis of the wills of the king, the upper house and the lower house."[9] The United Kingdom is a typical example of the "king in parliamentary system", that is, "the British Parliament is composed of the king, the Upper House and the Lower House."[10] According to Isao Satou, the distinctive feature of British political structure lies in the power of the king and its relationship with parliament.[11] As Mr. Dai Xue pointed out, although the "unwritten" character of the British Constitution makes the contents and provisions extremely complicated, the gist of the Constitution is quite clear: "parliamentary sovereignty" and "rule of law." Generally speaking, "parliamentary sovereignty" means that the parliament is entitled to make laws on any issue it deems appropriate according to its own judgment. Under the Constitution, the Parliament holds an unlimited legislative power, and no other powers can check and balance its power through veto of its legislation. And the "rule of law" indicates that the power of all state organs must derive from the law and be subject to legislative and judicial restrictions. Since "parliamentary sovereignty" and the "rule of law" are the basic contents of modern democracy, they must be coordinated with the monarchy both in theory and in the state power structure to avoid any contradiction with each other. However, this problem has been solved by applying the "fuzzy" concept of sovereignty in the UK.[12] Apart from "parliamentary sovereignty", there are also the concepts of "political sovereignty", "legal sovereignty" and "nominal sovereignty" in British constitutional theories. According to the British Constitution, "the King is the source of all power", which is obviously contradictory to the principle of "popular sovereignty". Consequently, in order to reconcile the relationship between the "sovereignty of the King" and the "sovereignty of the people", Locke proposed the theory of "entrustment". In other words, the status of a monarch comes from entrustment by the people. "Then, where to find the will entrusted by the people? It is in the parliament, so the concept of parliamentary sovereignty emerges."[13] On the other hand, the monarch

---

[9] Satou, I. (1984) *Bijiao zhengzhi zhidu* [Comparative Political System], trans. Liu, Q. L. and Zhang G. B., Beijing: Law Press·China, p. 112.

[10] *Yingguo zhengfu jigou* [The British Government Institutions] (1973), Shanghai: Shanghai People's Publishing House, p. 15.

[11] ibid, p. 115.

[12] ibid, p. 112.

[13] Satou, I. (1984) *Bijiao zhengzhi zhidu* [Comparative Political System], trans. Liu, Q. L. and Zhang G. B., Beijing: Law Press·China, p. 113.

only has "nominal sovereignty", that is, the monarch actually resides in the parliament. In the meantime, in order to reconcile the contradiction between "parliamentary sovereignty" and "popular sovereignty", the distinction is made between "legal sovereignty" and "political sovereignty". "Legal sovereignty" means that the legislation is not restricted by any law, and the "legal sovereignty" in British Constitution refers to "parliamentary sovereignty" with the sovereign, the House of Lords and the House of Commons combined into one. Moreover, since the Parliament is elected by the voters, its members must obey the will of the voters. Therefore, the voters hold the supreme power, which is called "political sovereignty". It follows that Britain has succeeded in "reconciling the relationship between the parliamentary sovereignty and the king"[14] through the theories illustrated above, especially through the establishment of the "king in parliamentary system". Another basic feature of the "king in parliamentary system" in terms of the power structure is that the government and the parliament are required to maintain a mutually coordinated relationship, i.e. the formation of the government must be in line with the will of the majority of the parliament. Once the government loses the confidence of the parliament, there must be a change of government or a re-election of the parliament. In Britain, with the development of the cabinet system and the party system, this coordinated relationship between the government and the parliament is mainly manifested in the fact that the majority party in the House of Commons will organize the cabinet and form the government, and the cabinet is responsible to the House of Commons rather than the monarch. If the cabinet loses the confidence of the House of Commons, it must resign as a body, or the House will be dissolved, but not more than twice. The "king in parliamentary system" was first established in Britain, and gradually spread to the European continent. By the end of the nineteenth century, countries such as Spain, Portugal, Holland, Belgium, Sweden and Norway successively adopted this system. After the Second World War, the "king in parliamentary system" prevailed in many countries in the world, including Canada, Australia, New Zealand, Japan, Thailand and Malaysia, in addition to the European countries, such as Britain, Holland, Belgium, Luxembourg, Norway, Denmark and Spain.[15]

(2) **Pure Parliamentary System**

The "pure parliament system", also referred to as the "parliamentary republic" by some scholars, is actually an application of the British style of the "king in parliamentary system" in a republic. Its basic characteristics are mainly manifested in two aspects. First, the head of state is the president who is elected and has a fixed term of office. Generally, the president has no real power, and his status is similar to that

---

[14] ibid.

[15] Of course, some of the countries mentioned above have not announced explicitly that the monarch is one part of the parliament, like Japan. However, as their power structures and power relations are similar to the "monarchical parliamentary system", the author also classifies them into this category.

of the monarch in the "king in parliamentary system." The basic difference between the "pure parliamentary system" and the "king in parliamentary system" lies in the titles of their heads of state, with the former as the president and the latter as the monarch. Although the president has a similar status with the monarch, the distinctions between them are obvious. For one thing, the monarch takes neither political nor legal responsibilities for his or her behaviors. When the monarch's actions violate the criminal law, neither can the parliament impeach him, nor can the court put him on trial. Whereas, the president shall be charged or impeached and even brought to trial by certain organs (such as the Senate, the Constitutional Court and the Special High Court) when he commits treason or violates the Constitution, though he enjoys the privilege of not being subject to the jurisdiction of the general courts, as stipulated in constitutions of many countries. For example, according to the Basic Law of the Federal Republic of Germany, the Bundestag and the Bundesrat may appeal to the Federal Constitutional Court against any deliberate infringement of the Basic Law and other federal laws by the Federal President. In addition, the Federal Constitutional Court may declare the powers of the Federal President null and void if it determines that the president has deliberately undermined the Basic Law or other federal laws. For another, the monarch generally holds a lifetime and hereditary position, whereas the president is normally elected with a term of office except for a few countries like Tunisia, Equatorial Guinea, Haiti, Malawi and Western Samoa. Although there are various ways to elect a president, in most countries under the "pure parliamentary system", the president is elected by the parliament or members of the parliament. For instance, in the French Third and Fourth Republics, the Republic of Poland and Czech Republic after the First World War, and the Hellenic Republic in modern times, presidents are all elected by their parliaments. According to The 1975 Constitution of Greece, the president must be elected by a 2/3 majority vote of the parliament; in the Republic of Italy, the president is jointly elected by members of both houses of the parliament and three deputies elected by various provincial assemblies; in India, the president is elected by an "electoral college" consisting of members of both houses of the parliament and members elected by the State Legislative Assemblies; in the Federal Republic of Germany, the Basic Law stipulates that the president is elected by the Federal Assembly composed of all members of the Bundestag and an equal number of deputies elected by all the states in proportion to their population.

Second, similar to the "king in parliamentary system", under the "pure parliamentary system", the cabinet must also maintain a coordinated relationship with the parliament. When the parliament has no confidence in the cabinet, either the cabinet must resign or the parliament must be dissolved. Under the "pure parliamentary system", there are various ways to express no confidence in the cabinet and to dissolve the parliament. In some countries, whenever the parliament expresses no confidence in one particular member of the cabinet, the cabinet has to resign en bloc; in other countries, the parliament can only express no confidence in the Prime Minister personally, but not in the other cabinet members. However, when the Prime Minister resigns, the rest of the cabinet members must follow suit. Some countries can dissolve only the lower house but not the upper house; in other countries when the lower house is dismissed the upper house shall be dissolved immediately; in yet other countries, the lower house will be dissolved automatically with the consent of 2/3 majority from its members; and finally in other countries, the president can only dissolve the lower house with approval of 4/5 members of the upper house. Generally, in order to maintain a coordinated relationship with the parliament, the cabinet is usually composed of the members from the political party or the coalition of political parties that holds a majority of seats in the parliament. However, in the political practice, it is difficult to maintain a coordinated relationship between the cabinet and the parliament for a long period of time in countries with a multi-party system.

The "pure parliamentary system" shares similarities with the "king in parliamentary system" in many aspects. Historically, the French Third and Fourth Republics were the most typical examples of a country with a "pure parliamentary system". As Chapsal J. et al. pointed out in evaluating the 1946 Constitution of France, "The guiding ideology of the 1946 Constitution is to give more powers to the National Assembly."[16] Therefore, "the most prominent feature of the government system prescribed in the Constitution of French Fourth Republic is that the National Assembly became the center of state power, and France became a typical multi-party parliamentary country."[17] According to the Constitution, the Parliament is composed of the National Assembly and the Council of the Republic (i.e. the Senate). Elected by universal suffrage, the National Assembly enjoys the right to decide on bills alone, which cannot to be delegated, and it must also elect the Supreme Judicial Council at the beginning of each parliamentary session. The president, head of the state, is elected by the Parliament, and his or her power of appointment must be exercised in accordance with the decision of the National Assembly, his or her pardon power can only be practiced after the resolution of the Supreme Judicial Council, and his or her designation of the Prime Minister has to be voted upon and approved by the National Assembly. In fact, the president is just an ornament of power. What's more, the cabinet is responsible to the National Assembly, instead of the Senate, so the cabinet has to resign en masse once the National Assembly passes the motion of no confidence. In addition, the "pure parliamentary system" was once practiced in countries such as Poland and Czech Republic, and it has been adopted by the Federal Republic of Germany, Italy, Finland, Austria, Greece, Iceland, and some Asian and African countries, such as India and the Republic of Singapore in modern times. In a sense, Switzerland can also be classified into this category.

---

[16] Chapsal, J. et al. (1981) *1940 nian yilai de Faguo zhengzhi shenghuo* [French Political Life Since 1940], trans. Quan, K. K. et al., Shanghai: Shanghai Translation Publishing House, p. 144.

[17] Cao, P. L. et al. (1993) *Bijiao zhengfu tizhi* [A Comparison of Government System], Shanghai: Fudan University Press, p. 179.

(3) **Parliament-President Parallel System**

The so called "parliament-president parallel system" means that the parliament as the legislature and the executive headed by the president are separated from and independent of each other. Not only is the executive not elected by the legislature, but the president and legislature also restrain each other in order to achieve a mutual balance. The United States is the most typical example and was the first country to adopt the "parliament-president parallel system". In addition, the later Weimar Republic of Germany adopted the "parliament-presidential parallel system" as well. The system is characterized by two basic features. First, the parliament and the president are respectively elected by the electorate or the electoral college. In the United States, the Parliament (i.e. Congress) consists of the House of Representatives and the Senate. Initially, only members of the House of Representatives were directly elected by the people. Since the ratification of the Seventeenth Amendment to the Constitution in 1913, voters have also elected members of the Senate. Unlike countries with the "pure parliamentary system", the president of the United States is not elected by the parliament. According to the Constitution, the president is elected indirectly by the electoral college, which is elected by the electorate. And this provision "frees the presidential election from the control of the Congress" and "prevents the political system of the United States from evolving into a parliamentary system."[18] Second, this system is closely related to the way of election in which the parliament and the president are produced. Since both the Congress and the president are elected by the voters, they are formally responsible only to the voters and the Constitution. In this sense, according to Isao Satou, "The relationship between the president (the executive) and the Congress (the legislature) is not interdependent and mutually communicative, but is severed in principle."[19] Nonetheless, since the principle of separation of legislative, executive and judicial powers is strictly applied in countries with the "parliament-president parallel system", legally speaking, the Congress (parliament), the President (government) and the Federal Court are three independent branches with parallel powers and mutual constraints. Specifically, the legislative, executive and judicial powers are not only equal in status, but also mutually restricted, which is adequately reflected in the constitutional system and constitutional practice of the United States. For example, in the United States, the power of appointment and removal of the executive is limited to some extent by the legislature, and the president needs the consent of the Senate to appoint key officials, ministers and ambassadors of the Department of State. Similarly, the legislative power is also restricted by the veto power of the executive as well as the review power of the judiciary. The Constitution of the United State stipulates that every bill passed by the Congress shall be presented to the President for signature before it becomes a law. If the President disagrees, he has the power to veto the bill. However, if the Congress passes the bill again by a two thirds majority, the bill shall become a law without the signature of

---

[18] Li, D. K. (1990) *Meiguo zhengfu he Meiguo zhengzhi* [American Government and American Politics], Beijing: China Social Sciences Press, p. 391.

[19] Satou, I. (1984) *Bijiao zhengzhi zhidu* [Comparative Political System], trans. Liu, Q. L. and Zhang G. B., Beijing: Law Press·China, p. 203.

the President. If the President neither signs nor vetoes the bill passed by the Congress after receiving it within ten days, the bill shall be deemed to have signed into law by the President while the Congress is still in session, otherwise, it shall be invalid when the Congress has adjourned. The Supreme Court also has the authority to review the constitutionality of the federal or state laws, and the laws declared unconstitutional by the Supreme Court cannot be enforced by the lower courts. The organization of the judiciary is prescribed by the legislature according to law. Judges of the Supreme Court are nominated by the president and appointed with the approval of the Senate, and the Senate has the power to hear all kinds of impeachment cases. When the president is on trial, the Chief Justice of the Supreme Court shall act as chairman. In the United States, the functions of the legislative, executive and judicial branch are separated from each other, and there is no such issue of one branch being superior to the others in theory, but in practice, the three branches are often involved in disputes and conflicts due to the ambiguous boundaries of their functions and powers, so they are not entirely parallel in fact. Therefore, the core feature of the "parliament-president parallel system" is that the parliament and the president are not interdependent, but parallel to each other in legal status. This system is mainly practiced'in some countries of Latin America and Africa, such as Mexico, Salvador, Costa Rica, Brazil, Columbia and Venezuela in Latin America, Nigeria, Zaire, Senegal and Gabon in Africa, and in a sense, Indonesia and Sri Lanka in Asia.

(4) **Semi-Parliamentary System**

The "semi-parliamentary system" is also known as the semi-parliamentary and semi-presidential system. According to Miller and Bogdanor, "Such a system would at first sight seem to be a synthesis of the presidential and parliamentary models of government."[20] In other words, this system has the features of both the "pure parliamentary system" and the "parliament-president parallel system", so I would call it "semi-parliamentary system" in comparison with the "pure parliamentary system". The constitutional government system of the French Fifth Republic, i.e. the current system, is typical of this system. There are two basic features in such a system. First, it possesses many features of the "pure parliamentary system". As mentioned above, the French Fourth Republic is typical of the "pure parliamentary system", in which the parliament is the center of state power. However, as Isao Satou pointed out, "If the political structure of the French Fourth Republic centers on the National Assembly, then the new structure is centered on the president."[21] Nevertheless, the French Fifth Republic retains quite a few features of the "pure parliamentary system." For instance, the government is accountable to and supervised by the parliament which has the power to overthrow the government by calling a vote of no confidence. According to the Constitution of the French Fifth Republic, "The Prime Minister, after deliberation with the Council of Ministers, may make the Government's programme or possibly a statement of its general policy an issue of its responsibility before

[20] Miller, D. and Bogdanor, V. (eds) (1992) *The Blackwell Encyclopedia of Political Science*, New York: Wiley-Blackwell, p. 561.

[21] Yang, Z. G. et al. (1992) *Xifang zhengzhi zhidu bijiao* [A Comparison of Western Political Systems], Beijing: World Affairs Press, p. 292.

the National Assembly."[22] The Constitution also stipulates, "Where the National Assembly carries a motion of censure, or where it fails to endorse the programme or a statement of general policy of the Government, the Prime Minister must tender the resignation of the Government to the President of the Republic."[23] In addition, a double-headed executive system may be implemented. There the President takes no political responsibilities, the members of the Government are elected from the parliamentary majority, and the Parliament holds the three traditional powers, i.e. the essential contents of the parliamentary system. Nevertheless, the Constitution "aims at fighting against the abuse of the parliamentary system as it was at the end of the Third Republic as well as during the Fourth Republic, and also against the supremacy of the National Assembly elected by universal suffrage." so "the Parliament has its own powers only in relation to the Government, and it has no power itself."[24] Therefore, the French Fifth Republic is not a "pure parliamentary system", though it has some features of the parliamentary system.

Second, the "semi-parliamentary system" also shares features of the "parliament-president parallel system", so it can also be called the "semi-presidential system" from another angle. For example, In France, the President is elected by universal suffrage, and the highest executive power of the country is in the hands of the President, but not in the hands of the Prime Minister, though there is the central government headed by the Prime Minister. The President is entitled to appoint the Prime Minister and organize the Government. According to the Constitution of the French Fifth Republic, the President shall appoint the Prime Minister and terminate the appointment of the Prime Minister when the latter tenders the resignation of the Government. On the proposal of the Prime Minister, the president shall appoint other members of the Government and terminate their appointments.[25] Although the Prime Minister is nominally the head of government, in fact, he or she acts as the assistant to the President. As the former President Georges Pompidou once said, the Prime Minster is in fact the "Chief Minister" of the government. The President is not only the head of the state, the de facto head of the executive and the commander-in-chief of the armed forces, but also has the power to dissolve the Lower House (the National Assembly), a power which the president does not generally have under the presidential system. Consequently, although the principle of separation of powers is applied in the government system according to the Constitution, that is, the Parliament composed of the National Assembly and the Senate as the legislature, the government led by the Prime Minster as the executive and the Supreme Court as the judiciary, the relationship between the three separated powers in France is neither the American style of checks and balances nor the British style of coordination between the legislature and the executive. In essence, the so-called "separation of powers" is only the division of labor among the three functional branches that centers on the

---

22 Cf. Article 49 of *Constitution of October 4, 1958.*

23 Cf. Article 50 of *Constitution of October 4, 1958.*

24 Chapsal, J. et al. (1981) *1940 nian yilai de Faguo zhengzhi shenghuo* [French Political Life Since 1940], trans. Quan, K. K. et al., Shanghai: Shanghai Translation Publishing House, p. 379.

25 Cf. Article 8 of *Constitution of October 4, 1958.*

power of the President and are subject to his control and domination. According to the Constitution, "The President of the Republic shall see that the Constitution is observed, and shall ensure, by arbitration, the proper functioning of the public authorities and the continuity of the State."[26] Being above the three powers, the President is both the guarantor of national unity and the arbiter of disagreement. In addition, the President, who actually holds the executive power, is not responsible to the Parliament, but the Prime Minster, who has no real executive power, is accountable to the Parliament instead.

In conclusion, the "semi-parliamentary system" is a hybrid system and the product of compromise between the "pure parliamentary system" and the "parliament-president parallel system" for it shares some features of the latter two systems. "Under this hybrid system, the President and the Parliament are the two constituent parts of the pointed arch of the political system in the French Fifth Republic, which support each other, and the keystone is the majority party in the Parliament."[27] To be specific, in the "semi-parliamentary system", although the president is the center of state power, his power, status and role are not fixed, but closely related to changes to the parliamentary majority, unlike in countries with the "king in parliamentary system", "pure parliamentary system" or "parliament-president parallel system", where the power, status and role of the head of state are relatively stable, and are basically not affected by the growth and decline of party forces in the parliament.

This discussion of the basic contents and features of the above four major patterns of systems can only focus on the most important aspects, so it is far from complete. Similarly, the above classification of patterns is only a general and typical division, so it is impossible to exhaust and cover all cases of various countries in the world. Moreover, there are some similarities between various patterns with no distinctive boundaries.

8.1.3 Reasons for Emergence of Different Patterns of Capitalist Parliamentary Systems

If our analysis of different patterns of the capitalist parliamentary system were to stop at the description of their connotations and characteristics, such research would be superficial and inadequate, and its significance and value would be greatly reduced. Only by exploring the reasons why these patterns arise, can we truly justify their existence, comprehensively and systematically assess their impact upon the political practice, and thus predict their vitality and historical trend. Different factors such as the balance of class forces, historical and cultural traditions, and national psychology necessarily result in diverse forms of parliamentary system in different capitalist countries. Yet how do these abstract and generalized factors specifically display and

---

[26] Cf. Article 5 of *Constitution of October 4, 1958.*

[27] Yang, Z. G. et al. (1992) *Xifang zhengzhi zhidu bijiao* [A Comparison of Western Political Systems], Beijing: World Affairs Press, p. 292.

play their roles in the processes? Here, we are going to briefly analyze the reasons why the four different patterns are formed in the four typical countries.

(1) Reasons for Emergence of the "King in Parliamentary System"

As mentioned, the "king in parliamentary system" is the outcome of the attempt to reconcile the relationship of "parliamentary sovereignty" with the monarch, which is only the immediate cause for its emergence. In fact, many factors determined the reconciliation between democracy and monarchy. From the history of British parliamentary politics, these factors are not only economic and political, but also ideological and traditional. From the economic point of view, two points should be highlighted here: for one thing, during the British Bourgeois Revolution when the capitalist economy was not fully developed and still at the stage of workshop handicraft industry, the economic strength of the bourgeoisie, although greatly enhanced, was not powerful enough to eliminate the feudal landlord class, which, as a matter of fact, still exerted considerable economic influence. For another, before the British Bourgeois Revolution, the Kings of England, though in possession of great political power, all shared a common weakness: they spent beyond their means. Since the thirteenth century, Kings had to turn to the representatives from various social groups and shires to obtain their consent for taxation. Therefore, the economic situation was reflected in politics, which determined that the "mutual compromise" was the basic feature of the British Bourgeois Revolution, i.e. both the emerging bourgeoisie and the feudal aristocracy represented by the royal power had to yield to each other to share the power of the state. As a result, democracy and monarchy were made coincide. From the aspect of ideology, during the British Bourgeois Revolution, the political theories and democratic doctrines for the bourgeoisie were not yet fully developed. That is to say, no ready-made systematic constitutional theories could be used to guide the democratic constitutional practices. As Dai Xue pointed out, the British Constitution was not man-made, but grown, so it was the result of intuition rather than abstract theories. Just out of the intuition, it is impossible for the British people to build an architecture of the British Constitution as architects do with a blueprint, but only as bees build their hives.[28] That is to say, the democratic constitutional system is subject to the needs of political struggle. Traditionally, for the British people, the monarch is not only a token of the unity of the United Kingdom, but also the unique symbol of British stability and continuity because of her political neutrality and nonpartisanship. I. Satou pointed out, "This conception can be said to have become a common belief of the British people, which, to be noted, is not only attributed to their irrational emotions, but also rooted in their realistic and empirical minds."[29] Therefore, although the British bourgeoisie demanded the establishment of a democratic constitutional system, it did not compromise with the monarch due to the balance of their various powers, and the "king in parliamentary system" is the

[28] Gong, X. R. (1985) *Bijiao xianfa yu xingzhengfa* [Comparative Constitutions and Administrative Laws], Beijing: Law Press·China, p. 28.

[29] Satou, I. (1984) *Bijiao zhengzhi zhidu* [Comparative Political System], trans. Liu, Q. L. and Zhang G. B., Beijing: Law Press·China, p. 183.

most significant outcome of such a compromise. Even though the bourgeoisie later took full control of the state power, the traditional and national psychological factors provided the strongest support for the continuation of the "king in parliamentary system."

(2) **Reasons for Emergence of the "Pure Parliamentary System"**

The main feature of the "pure parliamentary system" is that the parliament is the center of the state political activities, as exemplified by the French Third and Fourth Republics. From the perspective of historical development, the emergence of the "pure parliamentary system" coincided with the gradual formation of the doctrines of "parliamentary supremacy" and "parliamentary sovereignty" in Europe and the United States in the late 19th and early twentieth centuries. That is to say, the implementation of the "pure parliamentary system" in the French Third Republic was closely related to the concept and trend of "parliamentary supremacy" at that time. Nevertheless, the key question is: As the parliamentary power was gradually weakened and the executive power was continuously strengthened in the capitalist countries of Europe and the United States with the development of the monopoly capitalism, why did France, despite Charles de Gaulle's strong opposition, still "instinctively revive the tradition of the French Third Republic", and bring "a Representative life similar to that of the French Third Republic"[30] to the newly founded French Fourth Republic after 70 years' practice of "parliamentary supremacy" in the French Third Republic? To this question, Mr. Hong Bo has once conducted a systematic analysis. Specifically, he posited the following points: First, France had long been a country dominated by a small-scale peasant economy and small and medium-sized enterprises. After entering the stage of monopoly capitalism, its degree of monopoly and concentration was not as high as that of the United States and Germany, etc. for the trauma of several wars greatly impeded its economic development. In the early years after the wars, France was in a period of economic recovery, and the minority monopoly groups were not strong enough to control the state power for the time being. Second, France was a country that had undergone many political revolutions, which directly resulted in the formation of parliamentary power, so it attached special importance to the parliamentary power. Even the broad masses of the people also regarded the parliament elected by universal suffrage as the embodiment of the power of the people. Third, France was a multi-party country, and no single party was capable of organizing the government alone, so the parliament became a major arena for power struggles, where each party attempted to gain a certain number of seats so as to manipulate policies by dominating the parliament. Fourth, the French parliament has always had much greater power than that of the United Kingdom or the United States, especially in terms of the power to supervise or bring down the government. In this way, the parliament was usually employed as an important means by various political parties or groups to force the government to implement their own policies, so they were all reluctant to weaken the power of the parliament.

[30] Chapsal, J. et al. (1981) *1940 nian yilai de Faguo zhengzhi shenghuo* [French Political Life Since 1940], trans. Quan K. K. et al., Shanghai: Shanghai Translation Publishing House, pp. 4&129.

Fifth, the French people still had fresh memories of the lessons drawn from several historical periods when the reinforcement of the executive power had led to personal dictatorship, so they feared the strengthening of the executive power and expected to limit it through the parliament. Sixth, with the rapid expansion of the armed strength during the anti-fascist war and a great number of seats occupied in the post-war Constituent Assembly, the leaders of the Communist party were superstitious about the parliamentary path and fantasized about a peaceful transition to socialism by holding a parliamentary majority, so they insisted on maintaining the power of the parliament.[31] It should be acknowledged that Mr. Hong Bo's analysis is very comprehensive. In brief, he believes that the "pure parliamentary system" practised in the French Third and Fourth Republic was also a result of economic and political factors. However, one thing I would like to emphasize is that, as we can see from the above discussion, the French attach great importance to theoretical principles in the construction of democratic constitution. In comparing the United Kingdom with France, Isao Satou pointed out, "In France, it was the political theory that preceded the practical political change, whereas in Britain, it was the political philosophy that followed the actual political change."[32] Accordingly, we can conclude that, in a sense, the "pure parliamentary system" is the result of political ideals of the French in terms of the political thought.

(3) Reasons for Emergence of the "Parliament-President Parallel System"

The separation of powers between the legislative, executive and judicial branches and their mutual checks and balances in the United Sates have been widely discussed in Chinese and foreign academia. In order to analyze the reasons for the formation of the "parliament-president parallel system" from multifaceted aspects, we would like to point out first that the establishment of the "parliament-president parallel system" was guided by the doctrine of "checks and balances" determined by the specific historical conditions of the United States. And the specific historical conditions that determined such a doctrine of checks and balances were also reflected in many aspects such as economic and political. In terms of the economic aspect, two main points have to be noted. First, the U. S. Constitution came into force in the late eighteenth century when North America was still largely an agrarian society and the role of the government was relatively simple. The Framers could neither predict nor have confidence in what the central government would be in the future. Given the lessons they had during the colonial period, they thought highly of the future freedom, and only hoped that the government would not infringe on it."[33] Therefore, in order to protect freedom and the so-called civil rights, especially the free development of the capitalist economy, the idea of separation of powers and checks and balances was widely recognized by the Framers. Second, the economic development was bound

---

31 Hong, B. (1993) *Faguo zhengzhi zhidu bianqian* [The Evolution of the Political System in France], Beijing: China Social Sciences Press, p. 198.

32 Satou, I. (1984) *Bijiao zhengzhi zhidu* [Comparative Political System], trans. Liu Q. L. and Zhang G. B., Beijing: Law Press·China, p. 55.

33 Cao, S. L. (1989). *Lun Meiguo de minzhu* [On American Democracy], Wuhan: Wuhan University Press, p. 158.

to intensify the conflict of the property inequality. In order to protect the private property and maintain a stable ruling order, the Framers attempted to write the idea of balanced rule into the Constitution.

> The Framers came up with the idea of a balanced government aiming to reconcile the conflicts between different interest groups and political parties resulting from the property inequality. In other words, it was of great necessity to establish a political institution to guard against the majority rule by one particular interest group. And this balanced government must be a Republic rather than a pure democracy.[34]

In commenting on the Constitutional Convention, Chrisman once noted that, for the sake of property safety, this Convention faced the problem of choosing a better alternative strategies to replace oligarchy (in Britain, the safety of property was ensured by the subordination of the people to oligarchy), so the Framers formulated a complex and impermeable system of checks and balances that could not be penetrated by knife and water to replace the traditional practice of requiring the people to submit to power.[35] From the political point of view, on the one hand, having drawn a lesson from the anarchy during the period of Confederacy, the Framers expected to build a powerful government, but they could never forget the horror of the imperious executive power in the colonial period. Hence, the doctrine of checks and balances was an effective measure to settle this dilemma. On the other hand, the constitutional democracy was a political thought highly advocated in the Declaration of Independence, but the big businessmen and the big bourgeoisie were afraid of the so-called "tyranny of the majority". Elbridge Gerry, a delegate and big businessman of Massachusetts even claimed in the Constitutional Convention that "the evils we have seen around us flow from too much democracy". And so, as Isao Satou pointed out, "The separation of powers can be thought of as a system created for fear of moving towards autocracy. What is feared here is not the former autocratic executive branch, but of the legislature, and especially the lower house, which is most directly connected with the masses of the people. That is why the Framers thought that the theory of separation of powers and checks and balances should target the legislature, particularly the lower house."[36] From the perspective of their ideological concepts, many of the Framers were deeply influenced by the ideas of liberty, equality, human rights and separation of powers proposed by the enlightenment scholars, so they would naturally make an effort to put these ideas into practice in the process of designing the political system. In the meantime, it should also be noted that the delegates to the Constitutional Convention "were all from propertied class who wanted order and security, and the Constitution was a piece of work drafted by these people

[34] Satou, I. (1984) *Bijiao zhengzhi zhidu* [Comparative Political System], trans. Liu, Q. L. and Zhang G. B., Beijing: Law Press·China, p. 205.

[35] Satou, I. (1984) *Bijiao zhengzhi zhidu* [Comparative Political System], trans. Liu Q. L. and Zhang G. B., Beijing: Law Press·China, p. 207.

[36] ibid, p. 205.

entirely from a practical perspective rather than from a general, philosophical and abstract one."[37] This is similar to the United Kingdom to some extent.

(4) Reasons for Emergence of the "Semi-Parliamentary System"

Some scholars asserted that the establishment of the "semi-parliamentary system" in France was highly "accidental", which was in fact the outcome of Charles de Gaulle's return to power through "illegal means" or "coup d'état". However, if we examine the reasons why the reform scheme proposed by Charles de Gaulle was suffocated in the Fourth Republic, but deeply rooted in democratic constitutional system of the Fifth Republic, we can reach a definite conclusion that the final establishment of such a system had a profound historical background and special domestic and foreign conditions. As a matter of fact, it is the inevitable result of historical development and the outcome of various factors functioning together, such as economic and political. The specific manifestations are: First, the concentration and monopolization of production and capital are the most basic reasons for the formation of the "semi-parliamentary system". After the Second World War, the French economy, with its recovery and development, had undergone substantial changes by the end of the 1950s, not only achieving its initial industrialization underpinned by heavy industry, but also starting to move towards the mechanization of its agriculture. And the most striking change was the concentration of production and capital. With the intensification of the private monopoly and the unprecedented development of the state monopoly capitalism and international monopoly capitalism, the concentration and reinforcement of state power were urgently needed. Second, the escalation of the domestic conflicts was the most direct reason for the formation of the "Semi-Parliamentary System". In May of 1958, the French colonial army and the extremist colonialists in Algeria launched a military insurgency, which was echoed by the right-wing extremists in France. Meanwhile, the left-wing parties, labor unions and laboring people attempted to fight back against their conspiracy. And the civil war was on the verge of breaking out. What's worse, the government of the Fourth Republic was paralyzed at the critical moment, which deepened the political and social crisis in France and foreshadowed the urgent need to build a new political system. Third, the "pure parliamentary system" established in the Fourth Republic had adjusted the power relationship between the president, parliament and government on the basis of the lessons drawn from the Third Republic, but failed to solve the problems of frequent government changes and political turbulence. During the Fourth Republic, the French government was reshuffled 20 times, and the average lifespan of each government did not exceed six month, of which the longest was no more than one year, and the shortest was only two days. Therefore, the key issue was to maintain political stability by reforming the political system in France at that time. In this case, General de Gaulle transformed the "pure parliamentary system" centered on the parliament into the "semi-parliamentary system" in response to the requirements

[37] Satou, I. (1984) *Bijiao zhengzhi zhidu* [Comparative Political System], trans. Liu, Q. L. and Zhang G. B., Beijing: Law Press·China, p. 205.

of the objective historical conditions. This system, in his own words, "is partly parliamentary and partly presidential, which not only satisfies our requirement of balance, but also has the characteristics of our country."[38]

From the above analysis of the reasons for the formation of the four different patterns of capitalist parliamentary system, we can conclude that all the patterns, in abstract, are the results of the functioning of multiple factors, such as economic and political, which have various manifestations in different countries or even in different historical periods of a country. Moreover, in dealing with political ideals and political realities, both the United Kingdom and the United States have established a parliamentary system based more on political realities, while France has undergone the transformation from focusing on political ideals to political realities. Anyway, I firmly believe that only when the political system is established in accordance with the specific historical conditions of a country can it solve the political problems in real life and maintain the value of its existence and the vitality for its development. Therefore, we should keep a clear mind about this when learning from and drawing upon the political administration experience of others.

8.2 Comparison of Organizational Structures of Capitalist Parliamentary Systems

In his study of Western political theories, Gabriel A. Almond created the Structural–Functional Theory on the basis of the Political System Theory proposed by David Easton.[39] He argued that all political systems have certain political structures, each of which performs certain functions of its own. Although his theory received much criticism from a few people, I believe that it is of great significance as a research methodology. The Chinese scholar Dong Chongshan has also given an insightful explanation about the structure and function of things in general. According to him, everything is the unity of structure and function. The structure of a thing refers to all the elements within a thing and their interrelations, and the function of a thing is the essential attribute that a thing can interact with its surroundings in a certain form. Hence, there are two major differences between things, namely, the difference in structure and difference in function. To be specific, on the one hand, the structure of a thing determines its function. That is, what kind of structure a thing has, so has what kind of function. On the other hand, the change of function means the change of structure. In this sense, the fundamental difference between things is mainly in their structures, which is also manifested in two aspects. On the one hand, the elements or constituents that make up a thing are different. Elements or constituents of a thing with different natures will definitely result in different structures, regardless of their

[38] de Gaulle, C. (1973) *Xiwang huiyilu* [Memoires d'espoir], Shanghai: Shanghai People's Press, vol.1, p. 289.

[39] Cf. Almond, G. and J. Coleman (eds) (1960) *The Politics of the Developing Areas*, Princeton, New Jersey: Princeton University Press.

interrelationships. On the other hand, the interrelationships between the elements or constituents that make up a thing are different. Different interrelationships between the elements or constituents of a thing will also lead to different structures, whether the elements are the same or not.[40] Admittedly, in the process of conducting a comparative research on different patterns of the representative system and searching for a "standard for comparison" in particular, Almond's structural–functional theory, and especially Mr. Dong Chongshan's general analysis of structures and functions of things have inspired me a lot.

As mentioned earlier, the "standard for comparison" is the interface between two or more objects that are compared. Therefore, in order to make a comparative study of different patterns of capitalist parliamentary systems, we have to identify the interface between them, otherwise, the comparison would be impossible. Since everything is the unity of its structure and function, it is entirely feasible to link all the objects to be compared by taking the structure–function relationship as the "standard for comparison". Hence, in this and next section, we will make a comparative analysis of the parliamentary system in terms of its structure and function respectively.

8.2.1 General Analysis of Organizational Structures of Capitalist Parliamentary Systems

As we have pointed out, the representative system is an organizational system of state power, so is the capitalist parliamentary system. Therefore, if we analyze the organizational structure of the capitalist parliamentary system from the perspective of the organizational system of state power, we are bound to face the extreme complexity of its connotation and denotation. Accordingly, we must first make it clear that the so-called organizational structure of the capitalist parliamentary system actually refers to the composition of the capitalist parliament proper and the interrelationships between its various components, which, to be specific, consists of two main aspects: one is the internal organization structuring of the parliament, and the other is the power relationships formed between various institutions. Since the parliamentary organizations are hierarchically structured and their relationships, i.e., power relationships, are different, we will thus discuss the organizational structure of the capitalist parliamentary system from the macro level of its system and the micro level of its internal organizational structure.

---

[40] Dong, C. S. (1986) *Zhengti Lun* [On Forms of Government], Beijing: China Expectation Press, pp. 123–124.

(1) Macro System of Capitalist Parliaments: Unicameralism, Bicameralism and Multicameralism

Despite the complexity and diversity of the specific formation of various parliaments in capitalist countries, the capitalist parliaments can be divided into three types, i.e. unicameralism, bicameralism and multicameralism from the macro perspective if we take the number of chambers as the standard.

The unicameralism is a parliamentary system under which the parliament consists of only one chamber that exercises the full power. According to the statistics, "Of 150 capitalist countries in the world, 136 countries institutes parliaments, of which 91 countries adopt unicameralism and 45 bicameralism except 14 countries that do not have parliaments or have dissolved them without being restored."[41] From the perspective of historical development, the unicameralism was first initiated during the French Revolution, when King Louis XVI had no choice but to convene the Estates-General in May of 1789 in order to solve his financial difficulties. At first, the Estates-General was proposed to hold separate meetings in two chambers, with one consisting of the nobility and the clergy and the other comprised of the populace, but it was finally terminated due to the strong opposition from the commoners. In June, the deputies of the Third Estate decided to hold a meeting and urged the deputies from the other two Estates to join, proclaiming that those who did not attend were automatically regarded as absentees. As a result, three deputies of the clergy attended the meeting, which passed a motion to change its name and declared the official establishment of the National Assembly. After having failed to sabotage the National Assembly by all means, the Louis government had to yield to it, and the deputies of the aristocracy and the clergy were also obliged to attend the Assembly together with the deputies of the commoners under the King's order, thus making the Assembly a complete unicameral body and a precedent of unicameralism.[42] As for its theoretical origin, the establishment of unicameralism in capitalist countries mainly originates from the doctrine of popular sovereignty proposed by Jean-Jacques Rousseau. As mentioned earlier, sovereignty, in Rousseau's view, is the application of the general will, which, once declared, becomes a sovereign act and constitute a law. Just for this reason, the revolutionaries in the early period of the Great Revolution held that the law was an expression of the general will which should be unique and represented by representative organs, so, in accordance with the principle of popular sovereignty, the parliament should be unicameral. At the same time, they deemed that unicameralism could prevent the restoration of feudalism and help make quick revolutionary decisions.[43]

---

[41] Yang, B. H. and Ming X. (1984) *Zibenzhuyi guojia zhengzhi zhidu* [Political Systems in Capitalist Countries], Beijing: World Affairs Press, p. 128.

[42] Hong, B. (1993) *Faguo zhengzhi zhidu bianqian* [The Evolution of the Political System in France], Beijing: China Social Sciences Press, pp. 117–121.

[43] Hong, B. (1993) *Faguo zhengzhi zhidu bianqian* [The Evolution of the Political System in France], Beijing: China Social Sciences Press, pp. 128–129.

The unicameralism, as a product of the French Revolution during its climax, was later imitated by many capitalist countries, but it has always been accompanied by a debate over its relative superiority or inferiority to the bicamerialism since its birth. Although each side insisted on its own argument, "the rationality and feasibility of a bicameral legislature has been questioned in many countries".[44] Scholars in those countries strongly advocated unicameralism in consideration of both the principle of popular sovereignty and the political practice. They argued that the implementation of the bicameral system in the representative organ with the legislative power could lead to the splitting of the state sovereignty. Moreover, in terms of the relationship between the parliament and the executive, the establishment of two chambers was likely to provoke internal conflicts within the parliament, which would cause the parliament to lose its power to hold the executive in check or even to be manipulated by the executive. In contrast, the unicameralism to be implemented, they believed, was more efficient and could avoid tardiness, easily pass various laws necessary to the state, enhance the sense of responsibility of the parliament members, avoid buck-passing, streamline the institutions, and save manpower and material resources. In this regard, Mr. Li described the development trend of the parliamentary system in terms of the number of chambers:

> In practice, the number of countries with the bicameralism is shrinking, while the number with the unicameralism is on the rise. According to statistics, there were 44 countries adopting bicameralism and 18 unicameralism in 1927, and there were 47 bicameral countries (of which 31 adopted unitary system and 16 federal system) and 16 unicameral ones in 1955. By 1982, of the 152 countries in the world with parliaments, 107 countries were unicameral, 44 bicameral and one tricameral.[45]

The bicameralism is a parliamentary system under which two chambers of the parliament jointly exercise their functions and powers. Historically, the bicameralism was first produced in the United Kingdom. After the mid-thirteenth century, with the development of capitalism in Britain, some small and medium-sized feudal landlords turned to the capitalist exploitation mode by changing their lands into livestock farms and concurrently engaged in commerce, and thus became the new bourgeois nobility. As the economic strength of the new nobility and some free citizens was boosted, they put forward the slogan of "No Taxation without Representation". In 1295, Edward I convened the so-called "Model Parliament", attended by earls, barons, prominent priests as well as the representatives of knights, notable citizens and ordinary civilians. During the reign of Edward III, the parliament had to be held regularly in order to impose extra levies. From 1343 onwards, two forces gradually formed in the parliament, one comprising of big aristocrats and grand clergymen and the other consisting of citizens and bourgeois nobility. The former group developed into the Upper House, i.e. the House of Lords, while the latter became the Lower House, i.e. the House of Commons. Therefore, the bicameral parliament with a strong mark of

---

[44] Li, L. (1991) *Lifa Jiguan Bijiao Yanjiu* [A Comparative Study of Legislature], Beijing: People's Daily Press, p. 121.

[45] Li, L. (1991) *Lifa jiguan bijiao yanjiu* [A Comparative Study of Legislature], Beijing: People's Daily Press, p. 120.

feudalism gradually took shape in the United Kingdom. As mentioned above, from the nineteenth century to the early twentieth century, the bicameralism was adopted by majority countries in the world. Since the mid-twentieth century, the newly independent countries in Asia and other regions mostly adopted unicameralism. Generally speaking, the early developed capitalist countries have mostly adopted bicameralism, including countries that implement federalism, though they differ in the names of the two houses of the parliament. For example, the two Houses in the United Kingdom were initially called the House of Lords and the House of Commons, which were later renamed the Upper House and the Lower House; in the United States and Japan, they are called the Senate and the House of Representatives; In France, the Senate and the National Assembly; in Holland, the First Chamber and the Second Chamber; in Switzerland, the Council of States and the National Council; and in Federal Republic of Germany, the Bundestag and the Bundesrat, etc. Moreover, the composition and functions of the two chambers are quite similar in some respects in some countries, but considerably different in some other countries.

In terms of theoretical origins, the creation of the bicameral system in capitalist countries mainly derived from the doctrine of separation of powers proposed by Montesquieu. He argued that the parliament, as the legislature, was composed of two parts that could restrict each other through the veto power of the opposites, which was also part of the basic British political system and an important factor that made Britain superior over the ancient republics. However, as mentioned earlier, with the emergence of the later unicameral system, the debate over the two systems has never stopped. Scholars who advocate bicameralism often justify the implementation of it based on Montesquieu's theories. First, the practice of bicameralism could prevent the despotism and corruption of the parliament. Comparing the two-chamber system in the United Kingdom with the two-consul system in the ancient Rome, James Bryce held that the two-consul system in the ancient Rome could guard against individual despotism, whereas, the two-chamber system could prevent group despotism. Second, the adoption of bicameralism could prevent imprudent legislation. For example, from the perspective of "restriction", Morris, a delegate to the U.S. Constitutional Convention, maintained that the House of Representatives, which was elected by the people, was prone to act rashly and go to extremes, while the Senate, which was composed of the wealthy upper class, could restrain the "democratic turmoil". Some scholars argued that the law should be cautiously formulated as it is the common code of conduct for the government and the people, and is closely related to the people's interests. And in their opinion, the upper house could play a prudent role to prevent the hasty legislative behaviour of the lower house. Third, the implementation of the bicameralism could ease the conflicts between legislature and the executive. They maintained that, when one house of the parliament clashes with the executive, the other house could mediate between them, so that the two sides would not get into a deadlock to be involved in a fierce struggle. Forth, the practice of bicameralism can coordinate and balance the interests of all parties with adaptation to the realistic demands. Some Western scholars considered that it is impossible for one house to take up all the legislative responsibility, as required by the modern situation in a highly industrialized country, which should be shared by another house.

Moreover, as the conflicts of various interests increasingly intensified, the bicameral system could be used to divide up the legislative power, so as to balance the interests of different classes and strata by the way of achieving the balance of interests among the representatives. The establishment of bicameralism in a federal country can also play a special role in maintaining the balance between the federal country and its states. Although the bicameralism has been highly praised by its supporters, it "has not been only questioned in theory, but also challenged in practice".[46] As for its development in practice, we have already discussed above. In terms of theory, according to some scholars, the idea of using the second chamber to prevent hasty legislation does not hold water; the view that the mutual restriction between two chambers can avoid autocracy and corruption in the parliament is also under doubt. In addition, it is neither advisable nor possible to reconcile class interests in the form of bicameralism.[47]

The "multicameralism" refers to a parliamentary system under which three or four chambers in the parliament jointly exercise their functions and powers. Despite the fact that the overwhelming majority of capitalist countries adopt either the unicameralism or the bicameralism, there are several countries that have once implemented the tricameralism or the quadricameralism, so we should give a brief illustration of them here. In history, the tricameralism was once practiced during the French Second Republic. According to the Constitution enacted by the "Prince President" Louis Napoleon in January of 1852, the legislature was comprised of the Senate, the Legislative Corps and the Conseil d' Etat. Among them, the Senate was responsible for upholding the Constitution and laws and supervising the administration of the colonies; the Legislative Corp was to deliberate over and vote on bills; and the Conseil d'Etat was required to draft laws and administrative regulations under the command of the president, solve administrative problems and speak on behalf of the government when the Senate and the Legislative Corp discussed draft bills. Besides, Bolivia adopted tricameral parliament for a certain period after 1826. Before 1981, the South African parliament was composed of the president, the Senate and the House of Representatives. Since September 3, 1984, a tricameral parliamentary system has been established in South Africa, consisting of the House of Whites, the House of Coloreds and House of Indians, and there were three ways in which members of the parliament could be produced: direct election, indirect election and presidential appointment. The functions of the three houses include enacting laws and decrees on the affairs of their own ethnic groups and deliberating bills on the common affairs concerning all the three races, etc. The tetracameralism was only practiced according to the Constitution promulgated in December, 1799 after Napoleon became first consul in November, 1799. This constitution stipulated that the legislature of the state comprised of the Conseil d'Etat, the Tribunate, Senate and Corps législatif. The form of tetracameralism does not exist anymore.

---

[46] Li, L. (1991) *Lifa jiguan bijiao yanjiu* [A Comparative Study of Legislature], Beijing: People's Daily Press, p. 118.

[47] ibid, pp. 118–120.

(2) Internal Structure of Capitalist Parliaments: Speaker, Committees, Parliamentary Groups and Working Institutions

There is no doubt that parliament members are the most essential element in the internal structure of the capitalist parliament. It can be said that there would be no parliament without parliament members. Therefore, a comprehensive elaboration on the internal structure of the capitalist parliament should begin with its members. Since our focus is on the organizational structure, here we will discuss in brief the Speaker, committees, parliamentary groups and working institutions within the parliament. However, it must be clear that these four structural elements can not be taken as necessary constituents of the parliament, though they are the most basic ones. For instance, in some countries, there are no committees in the parliament, while in some other countries, parliamentary groups are not allowed to exist. Therefore, in political practice, there are bound to be many differences in the internal structures of the capitalist parliaments. Nevertheless, they can still be taken as the most essential elements for analysis.

The Speaker is the presiding officer of the parliament. As the Speaker and the deputy Speaker constitute the main leadership of the parliament together, their positions are of great importance. In a sense, the Speaker is a significant instrument for the ruling party to control the parliament, which ensures that the party's programme can be transformed into the state will. According to the constitutions, laws and political practices of various countries, the ways of producing the Speaker vary from country to country, which can be roughly divided into four types: the elective system, the ex-officio system, the appointment system and the rotation system. Speakers are usually produced by adopting one of the above four ways, of which the elective system is predominant, that is, they are mainly elected from members of the parliament. In some bicameral countries, the Speaker of each house is selected in different ways. For example, in the United State, the speaker of the House of Representatives is elected, and the leader of the Senate is assumed by the vice president naturally. The status of the Speaker also varies greatly in different countries. In some countries, the Speaker of the parliament is one of the chief leaders of the country and can substitute for the president when the president is vacant for any reasons. For example, in the United States, when the president is dismissed, deceased, resigned or unable to perform the presidential duties, the office of the president can be exercised by the president of the Senate. In other countries, the Speaker is merely the leader of the parliament, whose authority is generally confined to the parliament itself and whose role is the presiding officer of parliamentary meetings, etc. In addition, although the constitutions and parliamentary laws of various countries have different provisions on the functions and powers of the Speaker, generally speaking, the Speaker often represents the parliament externally and presides over parliamentary activities internally, including deciding on the agenda, determining which standing committee the bill should be delivered to for deliberation, chairing parliamentary debates, declaring the end of inquiries and the adjournment of parliamentary meetings, convening special parliamentary sessions in accordance with the law, formulating rules of procedure and ensuing their enforcement and so on. Apart from these, the Speaker also carries out activities on behalf of the parliament, such as concurrently assuming state leadership positions, liaising with the current head of the government and working as an acting president under special occasions.

The committees "are considered as the most important structural elements"[48] in the internal structural system of the parliament. As with the speaker, the committee system within the parliament was also originated in the United Kingdom. With the continuous improvement of the parliamentary system and the increasing expansion of the parliamentary scale, the committees were created in response to the political needs of the new situation, the demands of social and economic development and the requirements of the specialized division of labor. In the parliaments of capitalist countries, the committees can be roughly divided into two main categories: standing committees and interim committees. The standing committees are generally also special committees, which are established to conduct preliminary deliberations on certain issues and supervise the activities of the corresponding government institutions. Hence, such committees are usually concerned with activities of a particular government institution, such as finance, administration, judicature, foreign affairs, education, national defense and social affairs, etc., and are authorized to deliberate on bills or other relevant issues in this special field, and the degree of their specialization varies from country to country. In most countries, the mandate of the standing committee is aligned with the duties of individual government departments (e.g. in the United States, Canada, Japan, the Netherlands, Spain, etc.). In some countries, the specialization of the committee is not required to be strictly associated with the government, and the terms of reference of each standing committee can be consistent with two or more government departments or is related to particular topics. For example, in Britain, most of the standing committees are denoted by letters A, B, C, D, etc., except those with special names (such as the Scottish Grand Committee and Private Bill Committees). The standing committees are the most important of all committees in the parliament since their decisions are usually accepted as the parliamentary decisions. Among the standing committees, the Procedure Committee (or the Committee on Rules of Procedure) is particularly important because it wields absolute power over the passage of bills.[49] An American congressman even bluntly referred to the Procedure Committee as the "Office for Unidentified Corpses" where many proposals by congressmen are piled up. The number of parliamentary standing committees in each country varies, ranging from only two in some countries to nearly thirty in some others, which is actually related to the size of the parliament, the time length of legislation and the political traditions of different countries. Moreover, the importance of a standing committee also completely hinges on the political needs of the country. Generally, the candidates to the standing committees are allocated in proportion to the number of seats held by each party in the parliament, and are determined behind the scenes by each party. Normally, the chairmanship of each

[48] Li, L. (1991) *Lifa jiguan bijiao yanjiu* [A Comparative Study of Legislature], Beijing: People's Daily Press, p. 162.

[49] Vile, M. (1988) *Meiguo zhengzhi* [Politics in the USA], trans. Wang, H. et al., Beijing: The Commercial Press, pp. 142–143.

standing committee is held by members from the ruling party, but in some countries, the primary committees are usually chaired by members from the ruling party, while the secondary committees can be chaired by members from opposition parties. The interim committees are set up temporarily to address certain specific issues and will be revoked immediately after the issues are solved. For instances, the committees established to hear or investigate one particular issue or case under a resolution of the parliament; the conference committees formed jointly by members from both Houses when the parliament needs to make resolutions related to the two Houses, or to consider and deal with a bill on which the two Houses disagree, and etc.. In addition, in some countries, there is a Committee of the Whole House consisting of all members of one particular house of the parliament. Different from the plenary session of the parliament, this kind of committee only discusses some specific matters in a particular area, and its rules of procedure are quite flexible. As a matter of fact, its activities are only carried out within one particular house according to specific procedures and its meetings are presided over by the chairman or vice chairman of the committee.

In terms of their functions and powers, the parliamentary committees are normally endowed with the rights to make legislative proposals, review bills and supervise legislation, though there are great differences between countries. As for the power of legislative proposals, for example, in Japan and the Federal Republic of Germany, all parliament members are required to put forward proposals, and the committees also need to propose bills of legislation on matters within their specific areas. With regard to the legislative supervision power, for example, when deliberating bills, the committees in France have the authority to summon relevant government officials to the meeting to provide explanation and information, and to oversee and inspect government activities through the reports of the committees. In the United States, the committees have the powers of pocket veto, amendment and veto on bills, among which the authority to review bills is the most basic power of the committees. As the committees are vested with the power of assisting the parliament in deliberating over bills and play an important part in the process of legislation, they substantially constitute the power network within the parliament. Therefore, the major activities of today's capitalist parliaments have gradually transferred to all kinds of committees, which have become the nucleus of the parliaments. As Thomas Woodrow Wilson pointed out, "Congressional government is committee government."[50] and "What is to be done must be done by or through the Committee. It would seem, therefore, the Congress, or at any rate the House of Representatives, delegates not only its legislative but also its deliberative functions to its Standing Committees"[51]; "The congress does not wield its legislative power any more, which has been transferred to

[50] Wilson, W. (1885/2011) *Congressional Government,* Boston and New York: Houghton Mifflin Company, p. 9.

[51] Wilson, W. (1885/2011) *Congressional Government,* Boston and New York: Houghton Mifflin Company, p. 52.

various committees."[52] Therefore, the establishment of committees, though playing an indispensable role in the actual operation of the parliament, has been strongly criticized by many scholars and politicians.[53]

The parliamentary group is composed of a group of parliament members of the same political party with the same political orientation, which aims to unify the actions of its members in the parliament. It is the product of the development of party politics. In the political practice of modern parliamentary politics, the parliamentary group is a basic unit for political activities in parliament, which plays an important role in electing the Speaker and members of the standing committees, determining parliamentary agendas, and so on. As to the conditions for organizing a parliamentary group, there are often two kinds of situations. One is that its legitimacy is officially recognized and its formation satisfies the conditions of the parliamentary regulations, such as a certain number of seats are required in the parliament. The other is that there is no regulation specified on its formation in countries such as the United States, the United Kingdom and Australia. The parliamentary group in each country usually has its own organizational structure responsible for the leadership and management of its activities and its coordination with the parliament and the government. Generally, the highest decision-making body of the parliamentary group is its plenary session, which elects its chairmen and vice chairmen and the leaders of its working committees. In Austria, for example, the chairmanship and vice chairmanship of the parliamentary group are usually held by important leaders of the party, and under the parliamentary group, some working teams are set up in correspondence to the parliamentary committees, so as to formulate policies of the party when each committee considers a bill. The main tasks of the parliamentary group include: recommending its members to various parliamentary committees according to its strength and proportion of seats in the parliament; proposing legislative motions or bills in line with the interests and decisions of the parliamentary group; making comments on the rules of procedures and urging the leading body of the parliament to convene a meeting; to exercise supervision over the government; to unify thoughts and actions of the parliament members from its party, and to organize and guide activities of the parliamentary group in the parliament, etc. Each parliamentary group usually has its own disciplines. For instance, when voting in the parliament, party members must obey the decisions of the parliamentary group of their own party. In the event that they have different political views, they can be absent from voting, but must not take the opposite stance. Otherwise, they will be subject to the disciplinary punishment of the party.

The working institutions of the parliament, mainly composed of non-parliament members, are responsible for the organization of various parliamentary works, such as policy research, legislative consultation, information collection and analysis, administrative management. Generally speaking, the parliaments in most countries usually

[52] Cited in Zuo, L. S. (1981) *Geguo guohui zhidu* [Parliamentary System in different Countries], Taiwan: Taiwan Cheng Chung Bookstore, p. 28.

[53] Li, L. (1991). *Lifa Jiguan Bijiao Yanjiu* [A Comparative Study of Legislature], Beijing: People's Daily Press, pp. 173–180.

institute some working institutions, such as offices for legislative affairs, administrative bodies and library information systems, though they may differ from country to country in terms of their staff members, duties and functions. For instance, in the Lower House of the United Kingdom, there are Office of Commons Affairs, Speaker's Office, Administration Office, Security Office, Library and other working institutions. In the United States and France, there are even larger working institutions. It is these institutions that guarantee the normal and high-speed operation of the parliamentary machine.

8.2.2 Similarities and Differences in Organizational Structures Between Different Patterns of Capitalist Parliamentary Systems

Since our pattern classification is mainly based on the standard of the status and roles of the parliament, when we compare the different patterns of capitalist parliamentary systems in terms of their organizational structure, we can easily see the following two situations: first, the typical countries of various patterns share striking similarities both in their macro systems and in their internal structures; second, different countries of the same pattern have also many differences in these two aspects. Moreover, in the process of pattern classification, we have already discussed the power structures of different patterns and their basic features, so it is really difficult to compare the similarities and differences in terms of their organizational structures in that differences in specific historical conditions of each country determine that the organization and operation of every political institution will not be exactly the same, and even the same type of institutions may have completely different status and roles in different countries or in different historical periods of the same country. Therefore, we will only attempt to analyze the parliamentary system of different patterns in terms of both their similarities and differences.

(1) **Similarities**

Obviously, different patterns of capitalist parliamentary systems share many similarities in terms of their organizational structures. For instance, they all take the parliament as a reified structure; parliament members are the most basic constituent elements of the parliament; the members are mainly elected and have a certain term of office; various organizations and institutions are set up within the parliament. Here, we would like to point out the following three main aspects.

First, with regard to the macro system, the typical countries that fall into a particular pattern of parliamentary system all adopt a bicameral system, including the United Kingdom with the "king in parliamentary system", the French Third and Fourth Republic with the "pure parliamentary system", the United States with the "parliament-president parallel system" and the French Fifth Republic with the "semi-parliamentary system". Except for the French Fifth Republic that once adopted the pattern of the "semi-parliamentary system" with an exceptionally simple macro system, there are also countries with a unicameral system among the other three patterns. For example, Denmark, Sweden, Luxembourg and New Zealand under the pattern of the "king in the parliamentary system" adopt a unicameral system, so do Finland, Greece and Singapore under the pattern of the "pure parliamentary system" and Costa Rica, Gabon, Senegal, Salvador, Zaire, Sri Lanka, Indonesia under the pattern of "parliament-president parallel system.

Second, most of the parliaments in capitalist countries have set up a speaker, committees, parliamentary groups and working institutions in their internal structures, though there are distinctions between countries of different patterns or different countries of the same pattern in terms of their completeness, status and roles.

Third, countries of different patterns or different countries of the same patterns are all subject to their socio-historical conditions, in particular the influence of class power balance, historical traditions and various political needs in the process of setting up the organizational structures of their parliaments and establishing power relations within them.

(2) **Differences**

Undoubtedly, the differences in the macro system will inevitably lead to the differences in the internal composition and the power relations within a parliament. Therefore, countries with a unicameralism differ from those with a bicameralism in both the organizational structures and the power structures of their parliaments. For example, although Sweden falls into the pattern of the "king in parliamentary system", it does not adopt bicameralism like the United Kingdom, but unicameralism. In this case, not only does the Riksdag exercise the legislative power independently, decide on taxation and the use of public funds, and scrutinize the government and state administration, but also "the partisan rivalry is more intense in a unicameral parliament than in a bicameral one", and at the same time, "the parliament correspondingly becomes more powerful in the relation with the executive."[54] Therefore, countries of different patterns or the same pattern that practise different macro systems are bound to be different in terms of their organizational structures. Such differences are mainly manifested in two aspects: one is whether there are two or more relatively independent divisions that jointly exercise the functions and powers of the parliament and check each other, and the other is whether there are two or more internal systems of organizational institutions in the parliament.

As the four major patterns of typical countries presented in this book all implement the bicameralism in their macro systems, we are next going to analyze the differences in their organizational structures of these bicameral countries. Specifically, their differences are mainly manifested in following aspects.

First, although those countries all adopt the bicameralism, the "king in parliamentary system" emphasizes that the parliament is composed of the king, the upper house and the lower house, with the three in one. However, in the power structures

[54] Cao, P. L. et al. (1993) *Bijiao zhengfu tizhi* [A Comparison of Government System], Shanghai: Fudan University Press, p. 502.

of other patterns, the president, though as head of the state, is not included in the parliament.

Second, in general, members of the lower houses are all elected directly or indirectly by each constituency in proportion to their population, but those of the upper houses are often produced in different ways in countries of different patterns or the same patterns. For instances, in the United Kingdom, members of the Upper House are all the nobility who need not to be elected at all; in Japan, members of the Senate are elected directly by universal suffrage; in France, senators are elected by an electoral college consisting of members of the National Assembly, Regional Councils and General Councils; in Germany, the Bundesrat is composed of members of the state governments, which are also responsible for the election and recall of their members, with at least three seats for each state, four for those with more than two million inhabitants, five for more than six million and six for more than seven million; In Italy, the president has the authority to appoint five senators for life; and in the United States, the senators are directly elected by voters according to the constituencies based on the states, with an average of two senators per state.

Third, the status, the functions and powers as well as the power structures of both the upper house and the lower house are also different between different patterns. Under the pattern of "parliament-president parallel system", the two houses are not only equal in status, but also roughly equal in power. For example, in the United States, both the Senate and the House of Representatives have their own special authority. "As the two Houses enjoy the equal legislative power and status, bills cannot be enacted if one House opposes them; although the Lower House has the power to initiate bills concerning finance, the Senate still holds the amendment rights".[55] However, in other patterns, the functions and powers of the parliament are mainly exercised by the lower houses. For instance, in the United Kingdom, the legislative, supervisory and budgetary powers enjoyed by the parliament are mainly held by the House of Commons. According to the Parliament Acts of 1911 and 1949 in the UK, money bills should only originate in the Lower House, and the Upper House cannot veto any public bills approved by the Commons, but delay them for one year. As for the money bills passed by the Commons, the Lords can only impose a maximum legislative delay of one month. In the French Fourth Republic, the National Assembly was very powerful and almost monopolized the entire legislative power. Even though the Constitution of the French Fifth Republic adjusted the functions and powers between the Senate and the National Assembly and endowed the Senate with more legislative and political authority, in general, the National Assembly still enjoyed relatively more powers and higher status than the Senate. Moreover, under the pattern of the "king in parliamentary system", the transfer of state power has mostly experienced such a developmental trajectory: transferring from the king to the parliament, mainly the upper house, and then to the lower house. After the lower house obtained the supreme power to its peak, it began to lose its power gradually

[55] Li, L. (1991). *Lifa Jiguan Bijiao Yanjiu* [A Comparative Study of Legislature], Beijing: People's Daily Press, p. 98.

and finally descended to "the obedient instrument of whatever political party has a majority of its members".[56]

Fourth, the reasons for the formation of a bicameral system also vary from country to country. For example, the formation of bicameralism in the United States is, on the one hand, based on its colonial traditions and serves as the bond between the states and the Federal government on the other. All in all, it is mainly employed to balance the interests and demands of the people and the states in the legislature, where the will of the people is reflected by the House of Representatives, and the interests of the states are represented by the Senate. Therefore, in a federal country that adopts a bicameralism, the relationship between the two chambers is not primarily one of mutual restriction, but one of reconciliation, so that the conflicts of various interests and classes in the country can be reconciled to the greatest extent in the legislature. The bicameral parliament in the United Kingdom with the Upper House representing privileged classes (the nobility and clergy, etc.) and the Lower House representing the common people results from the polarization of various classes or hierarchies, whose demands can be reflected through the legislature to some extent, and at the same time, the Upper House can prevent the arbitrary use of power by the Lower House. Therefore, the relationship between the two Houses is characterized by mutual restriction.

In addition, in the setting of the internal organizational structure of the parliament, the Swedish Ombudsman System is also very distinctive. In other countries, there are also ombudsmen in the parliaments, who, however, are mainly associated with a particular political parties and the governments, similar to the government whips in Britain, as some scholars pointed out:

> Government whips, with the government's business managers, are responsible for the management of the parliamentary timetable. The whips of the main opposition party (and, less regularly, of smaller parties) are consulted, such contact constituting "the usual channels". The whips act also as channels of communication between front benchers and their supporters and are responsible for persuading hesitant members to support the party line.... The value of whips is such that they are appointed by all parliamentary parties in Britain and are commonly appointed in many other legislatures and public assemblies.[57]

Therefore, voting against the whips is in effect against the party, and in parliaments of those countries, the whips function as a "communication channel" for each political party to oversee and contact its own party members. In sharp contrast, the Swedish Parliamentary Ombudsman System is derived from the principle of "complete openness" in the state organs, especially in the judicial and the administrative systems. Sweden has always maintained the tradition of supervising civil servants in the exercise of their duties, and the Ombudsmen serve as a good "bridge" between public opinion and the supervision of public officials.

The Swedish ombudsmen appeared in the early 19th century. It was originally established for the ombudsmen to make investigations, hear opinions, oversee the

---

[56] Cecil, H. (1986) *Baoshou zhuyi* [Conservatism], trans. Du, N. J., Beijing: The Commercial Press, p. 148. cf. Cecil, H. (1912) *Conservatism*, London: Williams & Norgate, p. 234.

[57] Miller, D. and Bogdanor, V. (eds) (1992) *The Blackwell Encyclopedia of Political Science*, New York: Wiley-Blackwell, p. 640.

work of the civil servants and civil officials and offer assistance to those who felt that they had been unfairly treated by the authorities. Generally, the ombudsmen are elected by the parliament for a four-year term, renewable for two consecutive terms. The elected must be tenured judges with legal higher education and are required to have a good knowledge of law, behave honestly and win the unanimous consent of all parties. They have the right to supervise all activities of judges, prosecutors, police officers, military officers, prison officials, and other state and local institutions (including semi-administrative agencies and state-owned enterprises or companies) and their officials. In accordance with the Constitution, the ombudsmen have the right to attend any meeting of a court or an administrative organ and obtain meeting minutes and other documents of any organ. No document should be confidential to them and any official is obliged to provide them information and reports and answer any question asked by them. Otherwise, the officials concerned will have a fine imposed upon them or they will be punished with other disciplinary measures. If an official is found to have violated the law, neglected his duties, or otherwise misconducted himself, the parliamentary ombudsmen may request the authorities to remove or suspend him from office, or even directly prosecute him. From the perspective of political practice in Sweden, the Parliamentary Ombudsman System not only helps prevent the phenomenon of excessive corruption in the judicial and administrative systems, and alleviate the social conflicts and contradictions, but also helps strengthen people's confidence in the government or even state organs. Consequently, the Swedish Ombudsman System plays an very special role in maintaining social and political stability.

8.2.3 Reasons for Similarities and Differences in Organizational Structures Between Different Patterns of Capitalist Parliamentary Systems

From the view of historical evolution, there are basic intrinsic reasons for the differences and similarities in the organizational structures between different patterns of capitalist parliamentary systems in political practice. The similarities shared by different patterns of capitalist parliamentary systems in the organizational structures are mainly determined by the following two aspects.

First, similarities are determined by the shared nature, tasks and functions of parliaments. The modern democratic ideas sparked by the capitalist commodity economy have not only refreshed people's mindset conceptually, but also brought about a tangible and profound revolution in political practice. If the establishment and operation of state power must be based on the supreme will of an individual or a minority under the natural economy, then under the commodity economy, its establishment and operation must comply, at least formally, with the will of the vast majority of the members of society. Nevertheless, how can the wills of the members of society be measured, and how can these wills be transformed into the will of the state and be put into practice under the protection of the coercive power of the state? The parliament, as a representative body or an organ of public opinions, came into being to address these issues. Specifically, the parliament by its nature is an organ of public opinion, whose task or function is to fully express the public opinions and synthesize them into a "general will" accepted by the vast majority of deputies representing different wills through communication and compromise, i.e. a law must be observed in the governance of the state and the society. Although in some countries, the parliament, as an organ of public opinions and a legislative body, can play a very limited role, and in some other countries, it is only a body that is employed to fulfil a few necessary formalities, no matter which country claims to practice democratic politics and decides to institute a parliament, it will inevitably face the same issues or the same tasks. As a result, it is inevitable for these countries to have the same or similar organizational structures in their parliaments.

Second, similarities between different patterns of capitalist parliamentary democracy are due to the mutual integration and mutual influence between the parliamentary systems of different countries. Historically, the British Parliament was referred to as "the mother of parliaments" as it was both the first bicameral parliament and the first to establish the internal organizations such as Speakers, committees, and parliamentary groups. When other countries are faced with the objective need to establish a parliamentary system and have no tradition or experience in this regard, their only option is to learn from other countries. What's more, most of the old capitalist countries, such as the United Kingdom and France, have had colonial experiences, so their political systems have a stronger influence in their former colonies. For instance, the United States was once a British colony before winning independence, so the British parliamentary system had a great influence on the United States. In comparing the ideological basis of the bicameral system in Britain and the United States, Mr. Man Yunlong once pointed out:

> As a result of the historical movements, the American government system inherited the British model in the forms of both a bicameral parliament and a mixed government consisting of the monarchy (the President), the aristocracy (the Senate) and the democracy (the House of Representatives). However, with regard to its theoretical basis, the American system abandoned the concept of hereditary aristocracy and created the elected Senate under the guidance of the concept of natural aristocracy, parting ways with the British House of Lords.[58]

In analyzing the reasons why bicameralism reappeared in France from 1814 to 1830, Hong Bo concluded that the primary reason was that the French parliament was "influenced by the British parliamentary system, to be exact, it was an imitation of the British parliament, and even their names are the same."[59] Later emerging capitalist countries were even more deeply influenced by the United Kingdom, the United States and France.

[58] Man, Y. L. (1990) 'Hunhe zhengfu xueshuo yu guizu zhengzhi' [The Doctrine of Mixed Government and Aristocracy], *World History*, (6).

[59] Hong, B. (1993) *Faguo zhengzhi zhidu bianqian* [The Evolution of the Political System in France], Beijing: China Social Sciences Press, p. 134.

The fundamental reason for the differences in the organizational structure of different patterns of capitalist parliamentary systems lies in the different national conditions of each country. Although there are certain similarities between different parliamentary systems due to the two aspects mentioned above in various capitalist countries, and the life and vitality of any system are often determined by its ability to adapt to the historical circumstances in which it lives. Therefore, the establishment of a parliamentary system in different countries or during different historical periods of a country is bound to be influenced by the balance of class forces, historical traditions and various political needs. For example, with regard to the choice between unicameralism and bicameralism, some countries, whose territory and population are small in size and whose state affairs are not too burdensome and complicated, should choose the unicameral system according to their actual national conditions because the concentration of power is needed by their leadership due to historical factors. As mentioned, Sweden, for example, adopts a unicameral system, though it belongs to the pattern of the "king in parliamentary system". This is also the case in many newly independent nationalist countries in Africa, as well as Denmark in the Northern Europe. In addition, the fundamental reason why the French Third and Forth Republics and the French Fifth Republic fall into two different patterns, which differ greatly in terms of their organizational structures, especially in terms of their power structures and power relations, is that they existed in varied historical circumstances. Therefore, the specific reasons for their differences could be extremely varied in different countries or during different historical periods of a country.

8.3 Comparison of Functional Effects of Capitalist Parliamentary Systems

The capitalist parliamentary system is no exception to the rule that everything is the unity of structure and function, so it also includes both the organizational structure and the effect produced by the structure, i.e. function. Moreover, if we examine its external features, we will find that the organizational structure of the capitalist parliamentary system is actually a static framework, which is significant in the adoption of constitutions and laws for the establishment of a political system. Furthermore, according to dialectical materialism, the most basic and effective way to evaluate a political system is to investigate its active effect and influence on political practice. Therefore, after discussion of the organizational structure of the capitalist parliamentary system, we must also conduct an analysis of its functional effect in its dynamic operation.

8.3.1 General Functions of Capitalist Parliaments

The general functions of capitalist parliaments actually refer to those that parliaments should have, being generalized in theory and prescribed in the constitutions and laws of capitalist countries. Theoretically, capitalist parliaments arise and exist on the basis and premise that they are needed to wield certain powers and assume certain functions. As the parliament has been an important part of the capitalist state structure since modern times, its functions are closely linked with those of the state, especially with the process of their realization. Specifically, the parliament emerges and exists because certain powers of the state need to be exercised by a certain subject. In the history of Western political thought, various political thinkers proposed a great diversity of complex claims and theories, but the predominant view on the issue of the functions of a parliament is grounded on the need for the division of the state functions with the argument that the state power must be divided in order to realize the state functions. In other words, the functions of the parliament are parts of the state power granted to the parliament according to the principle of separation of powers. Locke, Montesquieu, Kant and so on are representatives of this idea. In terms of political practice, although differences in the national conditions of various countries determine that the functions and powers of the parliaments are not identical, the capitalist parliaments mainly share three general functions and powers according to their constitutions, laws and political practice, namely, the legislative power, the financial power and the power to supervise the government.

(1) **Legislative Power**

In brief, the legislative power is the power to enact, amend and repeal laws, which is a traditional power of modern parliaments. The exercise of the legislative power, or legislative activities, can be traced to ancient times, and came into being with the emergence of private ownership, classes and states. However, who holds power and who is a subject exercising the power differed in different times and in different countries. Before the modern capitalist state took shape, the legislative power was mainly concentrated in the hands of individuals or a minority of people, and typical practice was that the words of monarchs were the laws to be enforced. However, when the forces of the booming commodity economy destroyed the monarchical system based on the old mode of production, which resulted in a brand new system, i.e. the rule of the majority, the subject of legislative power underwent a transfer of profound historical significance in the process of state and social governance. That is to say, the attribution of the legislative power has been transferred from the hands of individuals or a minority to the majority, and "popular sovereignty" is the highest theoretical generalization in this regard. However, in modern democratic practice, legislative power is exercised by the parliament for the following main reasons.

First, modern nation states are not yet equipped with the conditions to implement direct democracy, so the governance of the state and society still has to be realized mainly through the form of representative democracy. Therefore, although in theory, the people are the masters of the country and possessors of all state power, the realization of the state power owned by the people can only be mediated through a certain bridge. This thought has been systematically elaborated by the bourgeois enlightenment thinkers such as Locke and Montesquieu. Both generally hold the view that the state must be established by the consent of the people for the protection of the freedom, equality and property of the people, and any law can only be applied with the consent of the people, so the legislative power should undoubtedly belong to all the people. However, as Montesquieu also stated, "But, since this is impossible in large states, and in small ones is subject to many inconveniences, it is fit the people should transact by their representatives what they cannot transact by themselves."[60] That is to say, the legislative power should be exercised by members of the parliament on behalf of the people.

Second, the nature and role of the parliament make it the most suitable way to exercise legislative power. The representative body is an organ of public opinion, whose members are required to fully express the will of the people and formulate a "general will" acceptable to all through mutual communication and compromise. And the "general will" here is actually the laws that reflect the will and interests of the ruling class. As Zeng Fankang, a Taiwanes scholar of China, pointed out:

> By democratic politics, it is grounded on the fundamental legal principle that the ruling power of state organs comes from the people. The law is the expression of the will of the people, and the parliament is the organ to express the will of the people. Therefore, it is a natural conclusion that the legislative power should belong to the parliament from a logical point of view. What's more, through the exercise of the legislative power by the parliament, various opinions nationwide can be reflected, all kinds of interests can be reconciled, all policies of the state can be formulated, and all activities of the government organs can be guided and supervised. Only in this way, can all rights and obligations of the people be really guaranteed.[61]

Third, the exercise of legislative power by the parliament is also a result of the separation of the state power. If all the powers of the state were centralized and exercised by a single subject, as in slave and feudal societies, where the monarch alone monopolized all powers, it would be neither necessary nor possible to have a relatively independent organ to exercise the legislative power. Nevertheless, with the formation of the doctrine and principle of separation of powers, the state power tends to be divided into three parts, i.e. the legislative power, executive power and judicial power, which has become the basic trajectory of state power operation in modern times. It is quite natural that the parliament, as an organ of public opinion or even as the highest organ of state power in some countries, exercises the legislative power. Just for this reason, the legislative power is the first and foremost among various powers of the parliament.

Western thinkers generally agree that the legislative power should be given to the parliament, but their views differ considerably on the issue of how to wield this

---

60 de Montesquieu (1982) *Lun fa de jingshen* [The Spirit of Laws], trans. Zhang Y. S., Beijing: The Commercial Press, p. 158. cf. de Montesquieu (1777) *The Spirit of Laws*, The Online Library of Liberty © 2004 Liberty Fund, Inc., p. 189.

61 Zeng, F. (1993) *Bijiao Xianfa* [Comparative Constitutions], Taiwan: Sanmin Book Co., Ltd., p. 275.

power. Neither Enlightenment thinkers, Locke or Montesquieu, discussed this issue in detail, but they both advocated that the parliament should enjoy great power to formulate laws. Montesquieu, in discussing the participation of the executive power in legislation, argued particularly that the executive only had the veto power but not the power of legislative initiative. Therefore, he seems to have advocated for the parliament to enjoy full legislative power, including the power of initiative. However, John Stuart Mill argued that it was inappropriate for the parliament to engage in the direct legislative business because "there is hardly any kind of intellectual work which so much needs to be done not only by experienced and exercised minds, but by minds trained to the task through long and laborious study, as the business of making law."[62] And he maintained that legislation should be done mainly by a special committee composed of very few members and that the parliament need only discuss bills and decide whether to pass them or not.

Moreover, from the perspective of constitutional practice, the scope of legislation varies from country to country. The vast majority of countries do not limit the legislative scope of their parliaments, but some do. For example, the parliaments in the United States and Germany can only legislate within the jurisdiction of federal legislation or the common jurisdiction for the federal government and each state, while the legislative power of each state is vested in local parliaments. For another example, the French Constitution of 1958 stipulated that the parliament only has the power to legislate on the following matters: civil rights and obligations, individual nationalities, identities and legal capacity, marriage, inheritance and gifts, crime and punishment, criminal procedure, amnesty, the judicial system and status of judges, the fiscal and monetary systems, electoral systems of the central and local parliaments, establishment of public institutions, protection of civil and military personnel, nationalization of enterprises, and transfer of public property to the private sector. The parliament can also establish legal principles for these matters, such as the state system, the local system, education, property right and real property right, civil and commercial contracts, labor, trade union and social security, and related financial and planning laws, but must not legislate on other matters outside the scope of the items listed above.

According to the constitution and laws of each country, the parliament must comply with certain rules and procedures in the process of exercising its legislative power and carrying out legislative activities. Despite the fact that bills of different types and natures follow a different legislative procedure, generally, the parliamentary legislative procedure mainly includes four stages: the proposal of bills, the deliberation of bills, the passage of bills and the promulgation of bills.

Before a bill is submitted to the parliament for discussion and adoption, the relevant institutions and personnel must first put forward a corresponding motion for the enactment of a law, so the proposal of a bill is the first stage of the legislative procedure in the parliament. However, the specific regulations regarding who proposes a bill differs from country to country. Generally speaking, there are two

[62] Mill, J. (1861/2008). *Considerations on Representative Government*, London: The Electric Book Company, p. 97.

types of sponsors of bills. One type of bill sponsorship is based in institutions and organizations, such as the executives, the heads of state, political parties, and social or economic organizations. In countries under the "parliament-president parallel system", the legislative power rests solely with the parliament. If the government wants to introduce a bill, it has to do so through the members of the parliament on its behalf, so the executive has no right to propose bills. However, in countries under the "pure parliamentary system", the "king in parliamentary system" and the "semi-parliamentary system", the constitutions generally recognize that the executive has the right to propose legislation. In some countries, a head of state also has the right to make a legislative proposal, either in the form of draft laws proposed on his own accord or by other organs or persons in the name of the head of state. For example, Article 35 of the Constitution of Bahrain provides that the Emir has the right of legislative initiative. In other countries, political parties and social or economic organizations also have the right to propose bills. For instance, in Italy, the National Council of Economy and Labor has the right to propose draft laws concerning the economy and labor, and the provincial parliaments also have the right to propose draft laws on regional affairs to both houses of the Italian Parliament; in Finland, the Evangelical Lutheran Church enjoys the right to propose bills to amend the Christian Church Law on church organization and management, and the provincial parliaments can propose draft laws on the affairs of their own provinces. In addition, the standing committees of the parliament in some countries are also granted the right to propose bills. The other of bill sponsorship is based in personnel, mainly members of parliament. The parliament members have the right to propose draft laws, which is clearly stated in the constitutions of many countries, such as Article 39 of the French Constitution, Article 75 of the German Constitution, Article 71 of the Italian Constitution and Article 93 of the Swiss Constitution. In the United States, although most legislative proposals are initiated or drafted by the government departments concerned, they must obtain the consent of at least one parliament member before bringing these proposals to Congress. Still other countries stipulate that a bill can be jointly proposed only with the consent of a sufficient number of parliament members. For example, Germany requires a minimum of 26 members of the Bundestag and Spain 50 members to co-sponsor a bill.

The deliberation of a bill refers to the official examination and debate of a draft bill listed on the agenda in the parliament. In terms of the number of times each bill is debated in the parliament of a capitalist country, there are generally three procedures of deliberation, i.e. first reading, second reading and third reading. The first reading passage generally requires that the bill be referred to the relevant committee for deliberation, which may propose amendments, and then submit a deliberation report to the Assembly of the House, where parliament members may question and debate the report, or propose amendments. Immediately following deliberation, the bill will be put to a vote. The first reading passage is implemented in the parliaments of France, Norway, Spain, Sweden, Japan and Senegal. The second reading procedures are specified as follows: before a bill goes to a committee, the Assembly of the House may first debate on the general principles of a bill, i.e. first reading. After the bill is submitted to the relevant committee, the committee will review and amend it, and then propose a deliberation report to the Assembly of the House, where the parliament members will deliberate carefully on the clauses of the bill and the amendments of the committee for the final vote, i.e. second reading. Countries such as Netherland, Greek, Cameroon, Syria adopt the procedure of second reading. The procedure of third reading generally includes several stages, including a debate on the principles of the bill, discussion in the committee, submission of a report, debate, amendment, and vote on the bill. In the House of Commons of the United Kingdom, first reading means announcing the title of the bill, setting the date for second reading, printing the bill and distributing it to the parliament members. Second reading refers to the debate on the contents and principles of the bill, which, if passed, is submitted to the relevant Standing Committee for deliberation, and then the Committee will report the bill with its amendments to the House of Commons for further debate and amendment, after which, the Commons will return the bill to the Committee for consideration. Third reading refers to the passage of the bill by a vote without a debate unless there are more than six parliament members request it. Countries like the United States, Australia, Canada, India, Ireland, New Zealand, Germany, Austria, Denmark, Malaysia, Thailand and the United Kingdom all adopt the procedure of third reading passage.

The passage of a bill means that the parliament adopts the form of voting to express its official consent to the draft bill and make it law. Therefore, it is the most significant and decisive stage in the entire legislative procedure. Although the parliament always follows the principle of majority decision in the process of voting on bills, the requirements for bills are distinct according to their different nature. Usually, ordinary laws are passed by a simple majority, while the ratification of constitutions or constitutional laws requires more than a 2/3 majority and may be subject to a referendum in some countries. For example, in Germany, a 2/3 majority vote in the Bundesrat is required for amendments and supplements to the Basic Law. Generally, there are nine ways of voting in the parliament, such as shouting, a show of hands, standing up, group queuing, calling the roll, balloting, casting balls or making marks, using a voting machine, and applauding and cheering. Usually, major bills are voted on by secret ballot, often by voting machine. In bicameral legislatures, several other situations should be noted here in the process of passing a bill in the parliament: first, the bill passed by one house must be sent to the other house for consideration, and if it is also passed, it becomes law, such as in the United State and France; second, in countries such as the United Kingdom and Japan, the lower house has the power to pass laws, but the upper house can only veto or delay them; third, the bill must be passed by both houses, and each house can propose amendments to the bill passed by the other house. In case of disputes that cannot be resolved, a consultative meeting between the representatives of the two houses will be held. If no agreement can be reached, the bill will become invalid, as is the case in Canada; fourth, any bill must be passed by both houses. In the event that an agreement cannot be not reached after three months, the two houses must be dissolved, and if the newly elected houses still fail to come to an agreement, the bill will be passed with the absolute majority vote by the parliament members of the joint session of both houses. This procedure has been adopted by parliaments in Australia.

The promulgation of a law refers to formal publication by authorized organs in accordance with the legal procedures and methods after it has been passed in the parliament, so as to bring the law into force officially, which is the final stage of the legislative process. According to the constitutions of capitalist countries, most of them generally provide for the procedure of promulgating laws, though their provisions vary from simplicity to complexity, except for countries such as Indonesia, France, Guinea, Mali, the Philippines and Switzerland. And most countries provide that the power to promulgate laws is exercised by the head of state. However, in some countries, the head of state even has the power to veto or delay the passage of laws, when exercising this power. In addition, the laws in the majority of countries are published in a *Government Gazette* or *Law Gazette*. For instance, in Germany, the laws are normally published in the *Federal Law Gazette*.

(2) **Financial Power**

The financial power, also known as the power of financial supervision, or the power of the budgets and final accounts, is the oldest power of the parliament. It basically means that the financial budgets and final accounts, taxes and public debts, etc. proposed by the government can only be put into practice after they are deliberated and approved by the parliament. Specifically, the financial power of the parliament is achieved through deliberation of finance bills, including various bills concerning the national revenues and expenditures, of which the bills of budgets and final accounts are the most important. The budget bill is normally limited to one fiscal or accounting year, while the bill of final accounts is a summary of the budgetary performance for each fiscal year, which is generally compiled by the financial department and then submitted to the parliament for approval after it is reviewed by the auditing authority. Historically, the financial power of the parliament, like the parliamentary system, originated in the United Kingdom. During the period of English Bourgeois Revolution, the emerging bourgeoisie, through its struggle with the King, established the principle that the King had no right to levy taxes except with the consent of the parliament. In 1627, the *Petition of Right* further specified that no one could henceforth be compelled to provide donations, loans, taxes and other payments of a similar nature without the consent of the parliament. In 1688, the *Bill of Rights* reaffirmed that it was illegal to abuse the royal power to levy taxes for the royal expenses without the approval of the Parliament for a long time, or to levy for the royal expenses beyond the time limit prescribed by the Parliament, or to levy taxes by any other procedure without the approval of the Parliament. In 1706, the British parliament laid down two constitutional principles concerning financial supervision. First, the money should be granted to the King through parliamentary legislation. Second, the parliament would not accept any request for expenditure on public offices or discuss any motion for grants or expenditure from public revenue unless it was proposed by the King. The two principles resulted in a common practice that the appropriation could only be discussed after the King had submitted a written request to House of Commons. Consequently, the Parliament obtained two important powers through the formulation of a series of laws and the formation of the common practices, i.e. the tax commitment power that the King should not impose arbitrary taxes, and the expenditure commitment power that the expenditure of the King should be approved by the Parliament. And these two commitment powers have gradually developed into the power of budgets and final accounts, namely, the financial power.[63]

Parliament has the financial power is closely related to the purpose of government according to the bourgeois thinkers. They argued that people formed a government for the purpose of enjoying their property in peace and security, and in Locke's words, "Men therefore in Society having Property, they have such a right to the goods, which by the Law of the Community are theirs, that no body has a right to take their substance, or any part of it from them, without their own consent."[64] Of course, this does not mean that the government has no right to require people to give up part of their property, just as Hamilton pointed out, "There must be interwoven in the frame of the government, a general power of taxation, in one shape or another."[65] However, the key question is, why the power of taxation, i.e. the financial power of the state, must be kept in the hands of the parliament and exercised by the parliament members on behalf of the people rather than by the executive? To this question, we will discuss it from the following two aspects. First, since people can only enjoy the right that the property which belongs to them by law is not allowed to be taken away without their consent, the best way to collect state funds is to transform a part of the property that originally belongs to them by law into the property that does not belong to them by enacting a bill of taxation. In accordance with the principle that the legislative power belongs to the parliament, this authority can only be owned by the parliament. Second, the government must have the consent of the people if it wants to acquire a part of their property from them. In a representative government, the consent of the people actually means "the Consent of the Majority, giving it either by themselves, or their Representatives chosen by them".[66] Hence, in order to ensure the realization of the purpose of the government, the financial power must be wielded by the parliament on behalf of people.[67]

As the financial power of the parliament has the nature of legislation, finance bills must also go through the legislative procedure similar to that of other bills. Normally, finance bills are proposed by the government to the parliament, but in some countries, the parliament and its members also have the right to propose such bills. In the United Kingdom, finance bills are introduced to the House of Commons

---

[63] Wu, D. Y. et al. (1992) *Bijiao lifa zhidu* [A Comparison of Legislative Systems], Beijing: The Masses Press, p. 289.

[64] Locke, J. (1982) *Zhengfu lun* [On Government], trans. Qu J. N. & Ye Q. F., Beijing: The Commercial Press, p. 86. cf. Locke, J. (1690/1988) *Two Treatises of Government*, London: Cambridge University Press, p. 360.

[65] Hamilton, A. et al. (1980) *Lianbang dangren wenji* [The Federalist Papers], trans. Cheng F. R., Zai H. & Shu X., Beijing: The Commercial Press, p. 145. cf. Hamilton, A., J. Madison and J. Jay (2008) *The Federalist Papers*, New York: Oxford University Press Inc., p. 194.

[66] Locke, J. (1982) *Zhengfu lun* [On Government], trans. Qu J. N. & Ye Q. F., Beijing: The Commercial Press, p. 88. cf. Locke, J. (1690/1988) *Two Treatises of Government*, London: Cambridge University Press, p. 362.

[67] Cf. Zhong, X. (1990) 'Lun zichanjieji de yihui zhiquan lilun' [On the Power of Capitalist Parliaments], *Journal of Capital Norman University*, (4).

by the government and deliberated by the Commons. If the bills are passed in the Lower House, the Upper House has no right to amend or veto them. According to the U. S. Constitution, finance bills should originally be proposed by the Congress, and the budget bills were later changed to be proposed by the government instead for the Congress and its members could not be fully informed of the government's revenue and expenditure, but whatever kinds of finance bills should be introduced to the House of Representatives, which exclusively enjoys the right to accept finance bills and the preemptive right of fiance bill deliberation. However, the U.S. Senate still has authority to deliberate over the bills passed in the House of Representatives in accordance with general legislative procedures, otherwise, the finance bills shall not become laws without the approval of the Senate. In this sense, the two U.S. Houses hold basically equal financial power. In Japan, finance bills should also be proposed to the House of Representatives for deliberation. After the bills have been passed in the House of Representatives, the Senate has the power to consider them. If the resolutions of the House of Representatives and the Senate are different, a consultative meeting between the two Houses shall be held according to law, and if the two Houses still disagree, the resolution of the House of Representatives shall be adopted as that of the parliament. Hence, it is clear that the House of Representatives also has superior power over the Senate in Japan. Different from the United Kingdom, although the Japanese House of Representatives has a superior power over the Senate, it still shows respect for the opinions of the Senate. Besides, there are a small number of countries where the two houses wield completely equal financial power. For example, the Swiss Constitution stipulates that the preparation of the annual national budget, the approval of the national final accounts and the release of public loan decrees are under the jurisdiction of both houses, neither of which enjoys the right of priority or superiority in the legislative process.

(3) **Power to Supervise the Government**

As for the power to supervise the government, John Stuart Mill once stated:

> Instead of the function of governing, for which it is radically unfit, the proper office of a representative assembly is to watch and control the government; to throw the light of publicity on its acts; to compel a full exposition and justification of all of them which anyone considers questionable; to censure them if found condemnable, and, if the men who compose the government abuse their trust, or fulfill it in a manner which conflicts with the deliberate sense of the nation, to expel them from office, and either expressly or virtually appoint their successors .... In addition to this, the Parliament has an office not inferior even to this in importance; to be at once the nation's Committee of Grievances and its Congress of Opinions.[68]

This statement by Mill clearly spells out the supervision function of the parliament over the government. In terms of the theoretical origin, however, the supervision power of the capitalist parliament over the government is derived from the nature of both the parliament and its legislative power. As noted above, the parliament is both

---

[68] Mill, J. (1982) *Daiyizhi zhengfu* [Representative Government], trans. Wang X., Beijing: The Commercial Press, p. 80. cf. Mill, J. (1861/2008) *Considerations on Representative Government,* London: The Electric Book Company, p. 103.

the "organ of public opinion" and the legislative body that exercises the legislative power of the state. Under a democratic political system, only through the supervision of the parliament, as the organ of public opinions, can the actions and activities of the government genuinely reflect the essence of the people being masters of their countries. At the same time, the legislative power, for the Enlightenment thinkers, is the supreme power of a country. Since the legislature has the authority to make laws, it also has the power to supervise their enforcement. As Locke put it:

> When the Legislative hath put the Execution of the Laws, they make, into other hands, they have a power still to resume it out of those hands, when they find cause, and to punish for any mal-administration against the Laws. The same holds also in regard of the Federative Power, that and the Executive being both Ministerial and subordinate to the Legislative, which as has been showed in a Constituted Commonwealth, is the Supreme.[69]

Therefore, as a legislature that exercises the legislative power, the parliament shall naturally have the power to supervise the government. According to the constitutions, laws and constitutional practices of capitalist countries, the power to supervise the government by the capitalist parliament mainly includes interpellation, vote of no confidence, investigation of the state affairs and impeachment.

The power of interpellation, as an important form of parliamentary supervision over the parliament in countries with non-presidential system, is the power of the parliament members to inquire and question the prime minister, cabinet members and ministers on government policy, administrative measures and other matters when the parliament is in session, and request a reply within the statutory time limit. The power of interpellation also originated in Britain and was developed from the right of petition. On the function of the power of interpellation, Ivor Jennings, the British Constitutional scholar, made the typical comments. He argued that "the parliamentary question is the last remedy, not the first" in the mechanism of political operation, and he continued:

> In any event, whether the member wishes to redress a wrong or attack the minister, the power to ask a question is important. It compels the departments to be circumspect in all their actions; it prevents those petty injustices which are so commonly associated with bureaucracies. It compels the administrator to pay attention to the individual grievance.[70]

Both the form and content of interpellation varies depending on the constitutional practices of various countries. Specifically, the forms of interpellation can be divided into oral and written interpellation in terms of the ways of inquiry, and formal and ordinary interpellation according to the consequences of inquiry. Formal interpellation, also known as interrogation,[71] means that the parliament members

---

[69] Locke, J. (1982) *Zhengfu lun* [On Government], trans. Qu J. N. & Ye Q. F., Beijing: The Commercial Press, p. 94. cf. Locke, J. (1690/1988) *Two Treatises of Government*, London: Cambridge University Press, p. 362.

[70] Jennings, I. (1959) *Yingguo yihui* [The British Parliament], trans. Peng B., Beijing: The Commercial Press, p123. cf. Jennings, I. (1957) *Parliament*, Cambridge: Cambridge University Press, pp. 103–104.

[71] Interrogation, also referred to as "great interpellation", is a system of Germany and France, similar to the no confidence vote of the United Kingdom.

address inquiries to the cabinet on its administrative guidelines and important policy measures, which is generally believed to have originated in France. According to the 1791 Constitution of France, the ministers should reply when the parliament asked for explanation. In the 1830s, interrogation was officially adopted in the French Legislature, and it was widely applied in the Third and Forth Republics. Basically, there are two features of interrogation. First, it usually concerns important issues of public interest and thus tends to give rise to general debate. Second, it usually has the nature of a political sanction. At the end of the debate, the legislature will take a vote of confidence or vote of no confidence on all cabinet members or a particular minister. Therefore, interrogation is not merely a means of acquiring information, but an effective form of supervision that holds the cabinet members directly accountable to the parliament. Ordinary interpellation, also known as inquiry, is a form of supervision in which the parliament members ask questions on the matters in the charge of the cabinet members and government ministers, only in a form of question and answer between the questioner and the questioned, and under most circumstances, the questioned only need to reply instead of a debate. Ordinary interpellation is often widely used as a tool to exert pressure on the government and protect the rights and freedom of individuals, with the purpose of obtaining more information from the government about the problems and requiring it to intervene or solve them when necessary. Historically, ordinary interpellation originates in Britain and has later been adopted by the parliaments of many other countries.

There are some restrictions on the exercise of the power of interpellation in different countries, which is particularly true in the use of formal interpellation. For instance, formal interpellation was abrogated in the French Fifth Republic because it was often used as a means to overthrow the cabinet during the Third and Forth Republics, which caused great political instability. Although both formal interpellation and ordinary interpellation are still kept as a tradition in Germany, formal interpellation may only be introduced with a signature of 30 members of the parliament in accordance with parliamentary procedures. The United Kingdom still retains the constitutional tradition with only ordinary interpellation but no formal interpellation. Besides, some countries also have restrictions on the ways of interpellation. For example, according to the Parliamentary Law of Japan, the members of the parliament who propose questions should write a concise keynote report about inquiry items to the Speaker, and oral interpellation can only be utilized in case of emergency. In some countries, there are some restrictions on question time. For example, the French Constitution provides that one meeting per week is reserved for questions from the members of the parliament and answers from the government; according to German parliamentary procedures, the Bundestag should have at least one hour per month for oral questions from members of the parliament, but the subject matter concerned should be provided to the relevant ministers three days in advance.

Pursuant to the relevant provisions, concerned government officials must reply to the questions proposed by the members of the parliament. If the members of the parliament are not satisfied with the answers, they can ask further supplementary questions to be answered by the government officials. In France, this kind of interpellation will be concluded after several rounds of questions and answers. In the United

Kingdom, although only ordinary interpellation is traditionally practiced, under normal circumstances, government ministers can reply in writing after the question time ends. However, in the case of questions on important issues, the members of the parliament can propose to extend the meeting time and change the parliamentary agenda with the consent of more than 40 members. During the extended period, the parliament will hold a debate unless the interpellator is content with the reply from government officials, otherwise, a vote will be needed to determine the result. In this way, an ordinary interpellation is meant to be a formal interpellation.

A vote of no confidence, also known as the power to bring down the cabinet, is the right of the parliament to propose a motion of no confidence in the government and urge it to dismiss the government when the parliament disagrees with the government's policies and guidelines. If the parliament passed a motion of no confidence, the government must resign collectively or ask the head of state to dissolve and reelect the parliament, and the new parliament will decide the fate of the government. The vote of no confidence system originated in the United Kingdom. In 1841, the House of Commons expressed its opposition to and no confidence in the Whig Cabinet, and the Tory Party won the election and made up the Robert Peel Cabinet afterwards, thus establishing the system that the House of Commons could propose a motion of no confidence in the cabinet. This system has three basic features. First, the vote of no confidence is an effective means for the parliament to supervise the government policies, but it is only practiced in countries with the responsibility cabinet system, such as in the United Kingdom, Japan, Italy and Germany, where the cabinet decides the government policies but must be responsible to the parliament. Second, since all polices are decided by the cabinet and the head of state does not take any actual political responsibilities in such countries, the vote of no confidence is only applied to the cabinet, but not to the president or the monarch. Third, in general, the public opinion is directly represented by the Lower House, which usually has the right to take a vote of no confidence. For instance, according to the Constitution of Japan, in case that the House of Representatives passes a motion of no confidence or rejects a motion of confidence, the Cabinet must resign collectively if it fails to dissolve the House within 10 days. However, in a few countries, the government is required to have the confidence of both houses. In Italy, both houses have to express their confidence or no confidence in the government by means of a signed ballot including an explanation of their rationale, and a no-confidence motion must be signed by at least one-tenth of the members of the house and cannot be tabled for discussion until three days after its submission.

In constitutional practice, there are five different ways in which the parliament can express no confidence in the government. First, the parliament can refuse to pass bills on important policies proposed by the government. Second, the parliament can vetoe motions of confidence requested by the government on a policy. Third, the parliament can pass resolutions of censure or motions of impeachment against the government. Fourth, the parliament can pass motions of no confidence in the cabinet or a member of the cabinet, and fifth, the parliament can pass counter proposals against a government proposal. In the meantime, various practices have shown that if there are two or more political parties, most of which hold a certain political strength and influence in a country with the responsibility cabinet system, its cabinet is normally organized by a coalition of various political parties pieced together in the parliament. Although such a coalition with different parties may occupy a majority of seats in the parliament, it often engages in internal strife and falls apart due to each party's own different interests, and the vote of no confidence is often used as a means by the parties to force the cabinet to resign in order to redistribute power, which often results in a political instability. Therefore, some countries have imposed some restrictions on votes of no confidence. One of these restrictions is that a motion of no confidence in the cabinet proposed by the parliament must be signed by a certain number of parliament members. For example, the French Constitution stipulates that a motion of no confidence can be proposed only if it is signed by at least one tenth of the members of the National Assembly. Another restriction is that a motion of no confidence can be put to a vote only after it is proposed for a certain period of time so that the members of the parliament can make full and careful consideration. For example, the German and French constitutions stipulate that the interval between two motions should be two days, while the Italian constitution stipulates an interval of three days.

The power of investigation allows the parliament to investigate the actions of the government, so as to effectively supervise the government. Although this power is not explicitly prescribed in the laws of most countries, and has long been recognized only out of tradition, it has played a very important role in political practice, and in some countries, it is even regarded as an indispensable part of the realization of legislative power.

The power of investigation originated in Britain in the seventeenth century, and is also believed to have originated from the Parliamentary Ombudsman System in Sweden. The parliamentary ombudsmen in Sweden had the right to attend any meeting of the courts or administrative organs and to obtain the minutes and other documents of any institution. No document could be kept secret from them and any official was under an obligation to provide them information and reports. If one refused to do so, he would be subject to fines or other punitive measures. This system in Sweden was later imitated by Finland, Denmark, Norway, New Zealand and other countries. Generally, the power of investigation includes the following aspects: investigation of the exercise of legislative power; investigation of elections; political investigation of illegal acts of the relevant administrative departments and their staff; investigation of issues concerning the violation of civil rights by state organs, etc. The methods of investigation include hearings and investigation meetings held by various parliamentary committees. During an investigation, searches, detentions, and arrests shall not be used, nor shall undue psychological pressure be exerted on witnesses.

However, in some countries, the parliamentary investigation has some of the powers of the judiciary. For instance, the Italian Constitution prescribes that all issues concerning public interests have to be investigated by both houses of the parliament. To this end, each house may appoint committees composed of its members from various parliamentary groups in a proportion to their balance of power. Such investigation committees hold the same authorities as the judiciary in conducting investigations or studies. For another example, the German Bundestag has the power to set up an investigation committee at the request of a quarter of its members, so as to collect necessary evidence either publicly or in secret. In order to provide evidences, the investigation committee can apply certain provisions of criminal proceedings accordingly, and the courts and the administrative agencies are obliged to offer judicial and official assistance to the committee. The resolutions of the committees are exempt from court review.

The power of impeachment refers to the power of the parliament to report, punish and prosecute a violation of laws or crimes by public officials such as the president and senior administration officials. Impeachment can be traced back to the ancient Greek city state of Sparta, where ephors would be elected from the apella to supervise the activities of the King. In 509 B.C., the political reform launched by Cleisthenes in Athens instituted the law of Ostracism, a kind of impeachment. The modern parliamentary power of impeachment originated in the United Kingdom in the fourteenth century, and its creation has its own historical background and theoretical underpinnings. At the time, the responsibility cabinet system had not yet been formed, so the parliament could not dismiss government ministers for their illegal and criminal acts through a motion of no confidence, and it was also difficult to make a fair verdict by resorting to the courts as the system of judicial independence had not been established. Moreover, in accordance with the British laws, the power to prosecute crimes was in the hands of the jury composed of the common people. The Lower House was considered as the representative organ of the people, and the Upper House was the Supreme Court, so impeachment was proposed by the Lower House and tried by the Upper House. Therefore, in 1386, the House of Commons organized a grand jury to prosecute the Earl of Suffolk, Chancellor of the Exchequer, for his abuse of power, and he was removed from his office through the judgement by the petty jury in the House of Lords. Since then, the common practice that the motion of impeachment should be proposed by the House of Commons and tried by the House of Lords has persisted. After the bourgeoisie took power, this practice was confirmed in the Act of Settlement of 1701. Later, as a means of parliamentary supervision of the government, impeachment has been universally adopted by other capitalist countries, but its actual application varies from country to country.

As far as the objects of impeachment are concerned, impeachment only applies to senior officials in monarchical countries, but not to monarchs, while in republics, it is mostly applicable to the president, the prime minister, and the cabinet members, but not to the ordinary officials. In countries such as the United States, Japan and the Philippines, judges can be impeached; in countries such as Norway, the Netherlands, Uruguay and Nicaragua, impeachment can be brought against members of the parliament. However, in most countries, impeachment does not apply to military officers, who will be tried in the military court if they commit crimes. Proposals and trials can generally be categorized as follows. First, a motion to impeach may be proposed by the lower house and tried by the upper house, such as in the United Kingdom and the United States. However, in the United States, when an impeachment is introduced by the House of Representatives, it still needs to be submitted to a special committee or the Standing Committee for investigation, which will then decide whether or not to prosecute. Second, impeachment may be passed and tried by a special institution constituted jointly by both houses. In Japan, for example, the Indictment Committee (the Prosecution Committee) consisting of 20 people elected from among members of both the House of Representatives and the Senate is in charge of the investigation and prosecution of the impeached officials. In the meantime, both houses select seven members respectively to form the Impeachment Tribunal (the Impeachment Court) responsible for the trial of the prosecuted officials. Third, impeachment may be proposed by a resolution of a joint session of both houses of the parliament or one of the two houses with the two thirds majority vote, and is tried by the Constitutional Court. In Germany, for example, only when an impeachment of the president is proposed by 1/4 of the members of the Bundesrat or the Bundestag, and approved by a 2/3 majority of the members can it be submitted to the Federal Constitutional Court for trial, where a verdict is reached by consent of 2/3 majority of judges. In Italy, the impeachment of the president, the prime minister or ministers of departments, who commit crimes in the performance of their duties, is also determined first by the joint session of the two houses of the parliament before being tried by the Constitutional Court. Fourth, the impeachment may be passed by the lower house and tried by the common court. According to the Belgian Constitution, any impeachment case will be passed by a majority vote of the Lower House and referred to the Supreme Court for trial. As for the matters of impeachment, there were no restrictions in the United Kingdom at first, so the impeachment was not differentiated from the vote of no confidence until the nineteenth century in that the impeachment is employed to supervise the violation of laws, which is a legal matter, and the vote of no confidence is used to supervise the dereliction of duties, which is a political issue. However, there are still differences among various countries in the specific matters of impeachment. In Italy, for example, the president is subject to impeachment only for treason or unconstitutional acts, and the prime minister and the ministers of departments for criminal acts committed in the performance of their duties. In the United States, the impeachment matters concerned are rather extensive, including treason, bribery and other high crimes and misdemeanors. However, in accordance with the impeachment cases, the matters to be impeached are only limited to the crimes that are prejudicial enough to the national interests or the officials who are proved to be unsuitable for the performance of their duties. In Germany, the matters subject to impeachment concern the deliberate violation of the Basic Law or the Federal Law. In terms of the consequences of impeachment, there are only two outcomes after an impeachment trial: the impeached person must be punished or should not be punished. And the punishment for the impeached also generally includes two types: removal from office or criminal punishment.

It must be made clear that, in addition to the three major powers of legislation, finance and supervision of government as described above, the capitalist parliament also has the authority to appoint or dismiss senior officials, decide on the declaration of war and ratify international treaties concluded by the government with foreign countries. Moreover, given that the parliament is only a group comprised of parliamentary members, all its activities are specifically manifested as the activities of its members, therefore, the functions and powers of the parliament can only be realized through the activities of its members, and is always reflected specifically in the form of the functions and powers of its members, including the right to propose, discuss, and vote, etc.

8.3.2 *Similarities and Differences in Functions and Powers Between Different Patterns of Capitalist Parliamentary Systems*

Since the capitalist parliamentary system is, on the whole, an organizational system of state power established by capitalist countries for the realization of indirect democracy, and the parliament, as the major materialized form of the parliamentary system, is attributed to the "organ of public opinions" in nature, its powers and functions in different countries are identical in their basic aspects. Therefore, when comparing the different patterns of capitalist parliamentary systems in terms of their functions and powers, the similarities dominate. First, although there may be some differences in the specific provisions and practices of the capitalist parliamentary system in different countries, all parliaments have the basic powers of legislation, finance and supervision of the government. Thus, in theory, the parliaments of the vast majority of countries are at the center of state power. Second, although different patterns of capitalist parliamentary systems have differences in terms of their procedures, approaches and methods in the realization of their various functions and powers, they all share the common ground that they must exercise their functions and powers in accordance with a legal procedures, approaches and methods. In addition, in countries with a bicameral parliament, the lower house is generally superior to the upper house in terms of its functions and powers, so it often plays a central role in the exercise of the parliamentary functions and powers.

However, although similarities predominate, different patterns of capitalist parliamentary systems are, fundamentally speaking, the result of the differences existing. Specifically, there are two major differences. First, of the general functions and powers of capitalist parliamentary systems, i.e. the legislative power and the financial power, are the most traditional powers in the parliaments of various countries. These two powers, whether in their theoretical origins, political needs, or basic contents, are basically the same under different patterns of parliamentary systems. However, in terms of the power to supervise the government, there are greater differences in different patterns of parliamentary systems. In the "king in parliamentary system", the pure parliamentary system and the semi-parliamentary system, the power to supervise the government by the parliament is not only clearly and specifically stipulated in the respective constitutions, but also based on the theory that the legislative power is supreme and the political need that the executive power must be subordinated to the legislative power. However, this is not the case in the parliament-president parallel system. In the parliament-president parallel system, the parliament can also exert pressure and influence on the government through impeachment, but its theoretical origin lies in the separation of powers and checks and balances. That is to say, the power structure of the parliament-president parallel system is different from that of the other three patterns in that the relationship between the legislative power and the executive power is not a integrated one, so the government as an executive does not need to be responsible to the parliament as a legislature. Nevertheless, since the mutual checks between the legislative, executive and judicial powers are stressed to achieve a balance, the parliament is bound to have the power and means to impose restrictions on the government. Despite the fact that the practical effect of such checks is an effective supervision of the government, it is different from the supervision power of the other three patterns in terms of theoretical basis and political needs. In contrast, the parliament in the parliament-president parallel system has no such powers to supervise the government as those of interpellation and votes of no confidence vote. Second, although different patterns of parliamentary systems are all endowed with both the legislative power and the financial power, they differ in terms of the specific procedures, approaches and methods in the process of exercising these powers. For example, in terms of the right to propose bills, in the United States with the parliament-president parallel system, where the typical principle of separation of powers is adopted, the right to propose bills belongs to the members of both houses of the Congress, while the executive organs cannot propose any bills to the Congress. On the other hand, in countries with the "king in the parliamentary system" and the pure parliamentary system, the government should be accountable to the parliament due to the adoption of the principle of separation of powers with the parliament as the focus, but the government is not only an organ for law enforcement, but is also allowed to participate in legislative activities. In this sense, the right to propose a bill is enjoyed by both members of the parliament and the government. In France with the semi-parliamentary system, a compromise has been made in that the power of legislative initiative is vested in both the Prime Minister and the members of the parliament according to its Constitution. In this way, on the one hand, the power to propose bills by the government is confined to the prime minister alone, and on the other, the bills proposed by the parliament members are limited to the extent that they do not reduce the state revenue or increase the burden of the state.

The organizational structure of the capitalist parliament has a very important impact on the exercise of the parliamentary powers and functions. Almond pointed out, "The functional differences among government agencies are related to differences in their structures and procedures."[72] Specifically, for the capitalist parliaments, the differences of their organizational structures will lead to differences in the distribution of their functions and the procedures, approaches and methods by which

[72] Almond, G. et al. (1987) *Bijiao zhengzhixue* [Comparative Politics], trans. Cao P. L. et al., Shanghai: Shanghai Translation Publishing House, p. 303. cf. Almond, G. et al. (1911/1978) *Comparative Politics: System, Process, and Policy*, Boston: Little, Brown, p. 257.

they are performed. The most typical examples are the distinct differences between unicameral and bicameral parliaments in the process of exercising their functions and powers. Generally, in a unicameral parliament, a bill can be enacted once it is passed by the parliament, while in the bicameral parliament, after a bill is enacted by one house, it usually needs to be sent to the other house for deliberation. In addition, such organizations in the parliament as various committees, parliamentary party groups, also affect the exercise of the parliamentary functions and powers to a great extent.

8.3.3 Analysis of Functional Effects of Different Patterns of Capitalist Parliament Systems

The functions of the capitalist parliaments discussed above are mainly generalized from the provisions of the constitutions and laws of various countries. Therefore, we need to further analyze the actual performance of the functions of the capitalist parliaments, i.e. their functional effects. The status and functions of capitalist parliaments are manifested differently in different historical periods. For example, during the period of liberal capitalism, the parliament played a significant role in consolidating political power and building democratic politics for the bourgeoisie, and its status and functions were on the wane when capitalism developed into the stage of monopoly. Although this conclusion, as a general historical trend, resides in the development of various capitalist countries, the actual functional effects of the parliaments, especially the specific circumstances that result in the changes of their functional effects are varied in different patterns of capitalist parliament systems.

Different patterns of capitalist parliamentary systems have certain differences for various reasons in terms of their powers, functions and the procedures for their exercise, but they are basically the same in the main aspects. Therefore, in order to analyze the functional effects of different patterns of capitalist parliamentary systems and see whether their parliamentary functions and powers are effectively exercised, it is necessary to discuss the actual status of different forms of parliaments in their state powers, as well as the factors that restrain and influence the exercise of their parliamentary functions and powers.

(1) **Status of Parliament in Different Patterns of Capitalist Parliamentary Systems**

There is no doubt that the functional effects of the parliamentary system largely hinge on the status of the parliament. The higher status the parliament occupies, the more effective role it plays, otherwise, the examination of the status of the parliament is the primary starting point for the analysis of the functional effects of the parliamentary system. In the four different patterns of capitalist parliamentary systems, the specific status of the parliaments in the state power structure can be roughly divided into three categories. First, the parliament may be at the center of the state power structure, and the whole system of state power observes the principle of "supremacy of the parliament". The "king in the parliamentary system" and the "pure parliamentary system" fall into this category. For example, in the United Kingdom, since the passage of the Bill of Rights in 1689 had ensured the supreme power of the Lower House, and the King withdrew from the struggle for state power, the transfer of state power began to unfold within the parliament, and the parliament completely controlled the entire state power. In this way, the parliament not only had the power to choose the government, but also had firm control of it. This was also the case during the French Third and Fourth Republics: the parliament was the center of political activities of the state; the cabinet was composed of the party or coalition of parties that had the majority of seats in the parliament (the lower house); the government was accountable to the parliament; the president, the head of the state, did not hold real power, but was only a figurehead like the monarch. Under this power structure, the effective exercise of parliamentary functions and powers was guaranteed. It must be noted here that the status of the parliament has changed considerably later on. Second, the parliament may be largely subject to the president, and the president becomes the center of state power instead of the parliament. The parliament under the "semi-parliamentary system" created by Charles De Gaulle is of this category. Under this state power structure, the president not only leads and controls the government, but also enjoys the privilege to decide the major state affairs through a referendum bypassing the parliament in special situations. In the meantime, the parliament is not only deprived of its power to elect the president, but its legislative power is also limited. Both houses of the parliament should give priority to the discussion of the draft laws proposed or approved by the government in the order prescribed by the government. Henceforth, "The parliament is no longer the only source of policies and governments".[73] Third, the status of the parliament in the state power structure may basically be parallel to, but slightly higher than that of the executive and judicial organs. The "parliament-president parallel system" is of this category. In this power structure, although it is emphasized that different powers are separated from and balanced by each other, compared with the other power organs, the parliament has a slight advantage because, in a democratic country under the rule of law, all organs, organizations and individuals should take the law as the fundamental code of conduct. In addition, this power structure emphasizes that different powers should be relatively independent of each other, which also ensures that the parliament can exercise its own power effectively from another aspect.

(2) Factors that Affect and Restrict the Exercise of Parliamentary Functions and Powers

When we examine the status of capitalist parliaments in depth, we find that their status is mainly manifested in three specific aspects: theoretical, legal and practical status. In terms of the functional effects, only the practical status of the parliaments is a reliable barometer of the actual exercise of the parliamentary functions and powers. Then, what are the factors that constrain and affect the practical status of the parliaments, and thus the exercise of the parliamentary functions and powers?

---

[73] de Gaulle, C. (1973) *Xiwang huiyilu* [Memoires d'espoir], Shanghai: Shanghai People's Press, vol.1, p. 289.

Generally speaking, the factors can be divided into two major groups: internal and external. Internal factors refer to the organizational structure, the working system, and especially the parliament's capability to exercise its functions and powers. As the capitalist parliamentary system has operated for hundreds of years, most capitalist countries, particularly some older ones, have already laid a solid foundation and accumulated a rich experience in this regard. Consequently, in the operation of the parliamentary system, the internal factors do not produce significant negative impacts. On the contrary, it is mainly the external factors that restrict and affect the exercise of the parliamentary functions and powers. From the operation of the capitalist parliament, especially the exercise of its functions and powers, external factors such as economics, culture and social stability have great influence on the exercise of the parliamentary functions and powers, among which, the two most direct and important influencing factors are the relationship between the parliament and the government and the relationship between political parties and interest groups. Since we have already discussed the latter earlier, here we will mainly focus on the former.

The analysis of the status of the parliaments in different patterns of capitalist parliamentary systems mainly involves the relationship between the government and the parliament. Despite the fact that capitalist countries follow and implement the principle of separation of the legislative, executive and judicial powers, in the whole power structure of the state and its actual operation, there is always a power at the center, which is either the legislative or the executive. Accordingly, the most important factor that constrains and affects the exercise of parliamentary functions and powers is the power relationship between the parliament, which exercise the legislative power, and the government, which wields the executive power. As discussed above, in the four different patterns of capitalist parliamentary systems, the status of the parliaments roughly fall into three categories, among which the practical status of the parliaments cannot be identical to its theoretical and legal status due to the changes in the power balance between the parliament and the government, as well as the influence of political parties and interest groups. This is most evident in the "pure parliamentary system" and the "king in parliamentary system". From the theoretical aspects and legal provisions, the parliament is at the center of the power structure of the state in these two patterns of parliamentary systems. Accordingly, if such is the actual status of the parliament, then its functions and powers would be fully and effectively exercised. However, this is not the case in the actual operation of these two parliamentary systems due to changes of power balance between the parliament and the government. Addressing this point, American scholar Steven Kelman noted:

> The prime minister is dependent on support from a parliamentary majority to remain in office. But in parliamentary systems with high levels of party discipline, a dynamic occurs to eradicate the apparent supremacy of parliaments. The prime minister and cabinet, selected by parliament, become representatives and leaders of the parliamentary majority. Having been elected by a parliamentary majority, prime ministers are then assured a legislative majority for proposals they present. Prime minister and cabinet take responsibility for developing policy

proposals and use the prodigious resources of government ministries to do so. Parliament becomes a rubber stamp.[74]

In this case, the functional effects of these types of parliamentary systems are imaginable. In discussing the British political system, Hu Kangda specifically analyzed the government control over the parliament, and pointed out that the government gradually diminished the British Parliament so that it no longer played an important part of the decision-making process by controlling the decision-making power, legislation, financial legislation and agenda of the House of Commons.[75] Even in the "parliament-president parallel system", which emphasizes that the parliament and the president should be independent of and parallel to each other, the president has actually become the center of state power. Under the "semi-parliamentary system", in which the parliament is inherently subject to the president, the actual status of the parliament is even less satisfactory.

Therefore, the status and role of the parliament in all types of parliamentary systems have shown a trend of decline. There are mainly three reasons for this phenomenon[76]. First, the economics helps explain the decline of parliamentary power. With the development of capitalism from the liberal stage to the monopoly stage, the capacity of the state to intervene in economic life was increasingly strengthened, while the market economy characterized by free competition was constantly constrained. For such changes in the economic life, the state is urgently demanded to control people's economic behavior as a representative of the interests of the whole society. Since the parliament can no longer meet the needs of economic development due to prolonged legislation and lack of flexibility, the executive is, however, considered superior to the parliament with its advantages of high concentration of power, flexibility and adaptability. Second, politics have influenced parliamentary power. In the early days after the victory of the bourgeois revolution, the capitalist parliament shouldered the heavy responsibility of confirming the achievements of the bourgeois revolution in legal form, and the bourgeoisie also attempted to take advantage of the parliament to fulfill its promise of giving sovereignty to the people, so as to draw over more people, isolate feudal forces to the greatest extent, and consolidate its own rule. Accordingly, the parliament under the control of the bourgeoisie was required to be placed above the monarchical power. Nonetheless, with the consolidation of the political status of the bourgeoisie and the strengthening of its political forces, the capitalist parliament began to go downhill. In this regard, Karl Marx held that the bourgeoisie "first perfected the parliamentary power in order to be able to overthrow it. Now, when it has achieved this, it comes to perfect the executive power, reduces it to its purest form, isolates it, sets it up as the sole target to oppose,

---

[74] Kelman, S. (1990) *Zhiding gonggong zhengce* [Making Public Policy], trans. Shang Z., Beijing: The Commercial Press, p. 38. cf. Kelman, S. (1987) *Making Public Policy: A Hopeful View of American Government*, New York: Basic Books, p. 44.

[75] Hu, K. D. (1993) *Yingguo de zhengzhi zhidu* [The British Political System], Beijing: Social Science Academic Press.

[76] See also Li, L. (1991) *Lifa jiguan bijiao yanjiu* [A Comparative Study of Legislature], Beijing: People's Daily Press, pp. 81–82.

in order to concentrate all its forces of destruction against the executive power."[77] Third, the ideology influenced the role of parliament. During the bourgeois revolution, bourgeois concepts such as democracy, freedom, equality and human rights were reflected in political systems in the form of people's participation in politics. The creation of the parliamentary system made the ideal a reality. However, after the mid-nineteenth century, with the emergence of the sociological jurisprudence and the doctrine of state sovereignty, political participation of individuals was integrated with the society and the state, so the significance of the parliament as a representative organ of public opinions has sharply declined for individual citizens, but people have increasingly recognized the executive as a symbol and representative of the state and society. For these reasons, the status of the parliament has been on the decline and that of the executive has been on the rise since the mid-to-late nineteenth century. Under such circumstances, the situation has become increasingly unfavorable for the exercise of parliamentary functions and powers.

Nevertheless, in the four different patterns of parliamentary systems, the extent to which the status of the parliament declines and the exercise of its functions and powers weakens are not exactly the same. This phenomenon is extremely serious in the "pure parliamentary system", the "king in parliamentary system" and the "semi-parliamentary system", but in the "parliament-president parallel system", it is not so prominent, for the balance of powers between the parliament and the government are always changing. As Steve Kelman pointed out, "There have been surges and declines in the relative strength of the president and Congress during American history. The power of the presidency grew from the 1930s through the 1960s. Congress reasserted itself during the 1970s." He continued:

> Congress does not gain the apparent ascendency over the executive that comes from selecting its head. But it keeps the real power that comes from uncertainty about whether it will pass legislation. When the president belongs to one party and the congressional majority to the other, the automatic approval common in parliamentary countries would be impossible even if there were high party discipline in Congress. Even when the president and the congressional majority are of the same party, the imperfection of party discipline in Congress still rules out automatic majorities. ...if the president proposes, Congress, to cite an oft-repeated adage, still disposes.[78]

Therefore, under the "parliament-president parallel system", the status and role of the government headed by the president are increasingly strengthened, which differs from the other three patterns in such aspects as the parliamentary processes and procedures.

---

[77] *Makesi Engesi xuanji* [Marx and Engels Selected Works] (1995), Beijing: People's Publishing House, vol. 1, p. 675. cf. Marx, K. (1852) *The Eighteenth Brumaire of Louis Bonaparte.*

[78] Kelman, S. (1990) *Zhiding gonggong zhengce* [Making Public Policy], trans. Shang Z., Beijing: The Commercial Press, p. 39. cf. Kelman, S. (1987) *Making Public Policy: A hopeful View of American Government*, New York: Basic Books, p. 45.

References

Almond, G., & Coleman, J. (Eds.). (1960). *The politics of the developing areas.* Princeton University Press.

Almond, G. et al. (1911/1978). *Comparative politics: System, process, and policy.* Little, Brown.

Almond, G. et al. (1987). *Bijiao zhengzhixue* [Comparative politics] (Cao P. L. et al., Trans.). Shanghai Translation Publishing House.

Beetham, D. (1974). *Max weber and the theory of modern politics.* George Allen & Unwin Ltd.

Beetham, D. (1989) *Makesi Weibo yu xiandai zhengzhi lilun* [Max weber and the theory of modern politics] (Xu, H. B., Xu, K. J. & Kang L. W., Trans.). Zhejiang People's Publishing House.

Cao, S. L. (1989). *Lun Meiguo de minzhu* [On American democracy]. Wuhan University Press.

Cao, P. L., et al. (1993). *Bijiao zhengfu tizhi* [A Comparison of Government System]. Fudan University Press.

Cecil, H. (1912). *Conservatism.* Williams & Norgate.

Cecil, H. (1986) *Baoshou zhuyi* [Conservatism] (Du, N. J., Trans). The Commercial Press.

Chapsal, J. et al. (1981). *1940 nian yilai de Faguo zhengzhi shenghuo* [French political life since 1940] (Quan, K. K. et al., Trans). Shanghai Translation Publishing House.

de Montesquieu. (1777). *The spirit of laws.* The Online Library of Liberty © 2004 Liberty Fund, Inc.

de Montesquieu. (1982). *Lun fa de jingshen* [The spirit of laws] (Zhang, Y. S., Trans.). The Commercial Press.

Dong, C. S. (1986). *Zhengti Lun* [On forms of government] (pp. 123–124). China Expectation Press.

de Gaulle, C. (1973) *Xiwang huiyilu* [Memoires d'espoir] (vol. 1). Shanghai People's Press.

Gong, X. R. (1985) *Bijiao xianfa yu xingzhengfa* [Comparative constitutions and administrative laws]. Law Press·China.

Hamilton, A., Madison, J., & Jay, J. (2008). *The federalist papers.* Oxford University Press Inc.

Hamilton, A. et al. (1980) *Lianbang dangren wenji* [The federalist papers] (Cheng, F. R., Zai, H., & Shu, X., Trans.). The Commercial Press.

Hong, B. (1993). *Faguo zhengzhi zhidu bianqian* [The evolution of the political system in France]. China Social Sciences Press.

Hu, K. D. (1993). *Yingguo de zhengzhi zhidu* [The British political system]. Social Science Academic Press.

Jennings, I. (1957). *Parliament.* Cambridge University Press.

Jennings, I. (1959). *Yingguo yihui* [The british parliament] (Peng, B., Trans.) The Commercial Press.

Kelman, S. (1987). *Making public policy: A hopeful view of american government.* Basic Books.

Kelman, S. (1990). *Zhiding gonggong zhengce* [Making public policy] (Shang, Z., Trans.). The Commercial Press.

Li, D. K. (1990). *Meiguo zhengfu he Meiguo zhengzhi* [American government and American politics]. China Social Sciences Press.

Li, L. (1991). *Lifa jiguan bijiao yanjiu* [A comparative study of legislative bodies]. People's Daily Press.

Locke, J. (1690/1988). *Two treatises of government.* Cambridge University Press.

Locke, J. (1982). *Zhengfu lun* [On government] (Qu, J. N., & Ye, Q. F., Trans.). The Commercial Press.

Makesi Engesi xuanji [Marx and Engels Selected Works] (1995). vol. 1. People's Publishing House.

Man, Y. L. (1990). 'Hunhe zhengfu xueshuo yu guizu zhengzhi' [The doctrine of mixed government and aristocracy]. *World History, 6.*

Marx, K. (1852). *The eighteenth brumaire of louis bonaparte.*

Mill, J. (1861/2008). *Considerations on representative government.* The Electric Book Company.

Mill, J. (1982). *Daiyizhi zhengfu* [Representative government] (Wang X., Trans.). The Commercial Press.

Miller, D., & Bogdanor, V. (Eds.). (1992). *The blackwell encyclopedia of political science.* Wiley-Blackwell.

Morgan, H. (1877). *Ancient society*. MacMillan & Company.
Satou, I. (1984). *Bijiao zhengzhi zhidu* [Comparative political system] (Liu, Q. L., & Zhang, G. B., Trans.). Law Press·China.
Smelser, N. (1976/2013). *Comparative methods in the social sciences*. Quid Pro Books.
Vile, M. (1988). *Meiguo zhengzhi* [Politics in the USA] (Wang, H. et al., Trans.). The Commercial Press.
Wilson, W. (1885/2011). *Congressional government*. Houghton Mifflin Company.
Wu, D. Y., et al. (1992). *Bijiao lifa zhidu* [A comparison of legislative systems]. The Masses Press.
Yang, B. H., & Ming, X. (1984). *Zibenzhuyi guojia zhengzhi zhidu* [Political systems in capitalist countries]. World Affairs Press.
Yang, Z. G., et al. (1992). *Xifang zhengzhi zhidu bijiao* [A comparison of western political systems]. World Affairs Press.
Yingguo zhengfu jigou [The British Government Institutions] (1973). Shanghai People's Publishing House.
Zeng, F. (1993). *Bijiao Xianfa* [Comparative constitutions]. Sanmin Book Co., Ltd.
Zha, Y. L. (1994). Shenme shi moshilun? [What is a pattern theory?]. *Social Science Research, 2*.
Zhong, X. (1990). Lun zichanjieji de yihui zhiquan lilun [On the power of capitalist parliaments]. *Journal of Capital Norman University, 4*.
Zuo, L. S. (1981). *Geguo guohui zhidu* [Parliamentary system in different countries]. Taiwan Cheng Chung Bookstore.

Chapter 9
Comparison of Socialist People's Representative Systems

As previously mentioned, the emergence of the socialist people's representative system is a step of great historical significance in the development of the representative system. Compared with the capitalist parliamentary system, the socialist people's representative system is different both in terms of the basis for its existence and its internal structure and operation, especially its different manifestations in different socialist countries, though it has a relatively short history and is only practiced in a few countries in the world today. Nevertheless, in order to study the representative system comprehensively and systematically, a comparative analysis of the socialist people's representative system is necessary.

9.1 Pattern Analysis of Socialist People's Representative Systems

The proletariat, like other classes, is faced with the arduous task of organizing and realizing state power after seizing it. However, in terms of the form of government, socialist countries can only take the form of a republic while countries governed by exploiting classes can take the form of either republic or monarchy. As Engels put it, "A republic, in relation to the proletariat, differs from a monarchy only in that it is the ready-made political form for the future rule of the proletariat."[1] He further explained, "Our party and the working class can only rule under the political form of a democratic republic, which is even a special form of the dictatorship of the proletariat."[2] In the process of socialist state power construction, this republican form of government is

[1] *Makesi Engesi xuanji* [Marx and Engels Selected Works] (1995), Beijing, People's Publishing House, vol.4, p.734. cf. Engels, F. (1894) Letter to Paul Lafargue at Le Perreux.

[2] *Makesi Engesi quanji* [Marx and Engels Collected Works] (1965), Beijing, People's Publishing House, vol.22, p. 274. cf. Engels, F. (1891) A Critique of the Draft Social-Democratic Programme of 1891.

Y. Zhou, *A Comparative Study of Representative Systems*,
https://doi.org/10.1007/978-981-15-4186-5_9

manifested as the organizational form of state power in the people's representative system, but the practical operation of the people's representative system in each socialist country is bound to have its own characteristics due to the different specific historical conditions of various countries. As Lenin pointed out, "All nations will arrive at socialism – this is inevitable, but all will do so in not exactly the same way, each will contribute something of its own to some form of democracy, to some variety of the dictatorship of the proletariat, to the varying rate of socialist transformations in the different aspects of social life."[3] Therefore, classification of the socialist people's representative system is the first step in the comparative analysis of it.

Classification should be made on the premise of a clear standard, as is discussed previously in Chap. 8. Only under certain standards can different types of patterns be formulated, however, different standards may result in different classifications. Since socialist countries are few and far less complex than capitalist countries, in theory, they all adhere to the guidance of Marxist-Leninist theory of state, and in practice, most of them learn from and draw on the experience of the Paris Commune, the first dictatorship of the proletariat, and Soviet Russia, the first socialist state power. And especially in the theory and practice of socialist people's representative system, some basic categories have already been formulated, which provided sufficient standards for classification. Next, we are going to discuss the three major conventional patterns of the socialist people's representative systems: the Soviet System, the System of People's Congresses and the System of People's Assemblies.

9.1.1 The Soviet System

The "Soviet System",[4] founded on the basis of the Russian workers' movements and the October Revolution, was the first form of socialist people's representative system in history. It is the product of the combination of the Marxist theory of the state and the specific historical conditions of Russia. According to the 1918 Soviet Russian Constitution, the highest organ of state power is the All-Russian Congress of Soviets, composed of deputies from workers, peasants, Red Army and Cossacks. When the All-Russian Congress of Soviets is not in session, the highest power organ of the state in the Russian Federation is the All-Russian Central Executive Committee, which is elected by and responsible to the All-Russian Congress of Soviets, and is the supreme legislative, executive and supervisory body of the Federation. And the highest organ of state administration is the Council of People's Commissars of Soviet Russia, composed of the All-Russian Central Executive Committee, under which there are several commissariats, responsible to the All-Russian Congress of Soviets and the All-Russian Central Executive Committee. The local organs of state power in provinces, states, counties, and townships are the respective Congresses of

[3] *Liening quanji* [Lenin Collected Works] (1958), Beijing: People's Publishing House, vol. 23, pp. 63–65. cf. Lenin, V. (1916) *A Caricature of Marxism and Imperialist Economism.*

[4] It has been discussed briefly in 2.3 of this book.

Soviets, where the executive committees at different levels of government are elected. When the Congresses are not in session, the executive committees at all levels are the supreme organs of local power. The Soviets and their executive committees in villages and towns are the most basic organs of state power, which are directly elected by voters. With the founding of the Soviet Union, the system of Soviet Congresses was adjusted accordingly, and the organs of state power were renamed as the Congress of Soviets of the Soviet Union, Congresses of Soviets of the Union Republics and Autonomous Republics, Congresses of Soviets of provinces, counties and townships and Soviets of cities, villages and towns.

The 1924 Constitution of the Soviet Union not only confirmed these changes, but also explicitly stipulated that the Congress of Soviets of the Soviet Union was the supreme organ of state power in the whole the Soviet Union, with the Central Executive Committee as the highest organ of state power when the Congress was not in session. Different from the 1918 Constitution, the Central Executive Committee of the Soviet Union at this time was composed of two parts: the Soviet of the Union and the Soviet of Nationalities. Between sessions of the Central Executive Committee, its presidium exercised the supreme power of legislation and executed and released decrees, in turn the Council of People's Commissars was an organ that executed and released decrees of the Central Executive Committee of the Soviet Union. The 1936 Constitution of the Soviet Union, based on the realities, changed the name of the Soviet of Workers', Peasants' and Soldiers' Deputies into the Soviet of Laborers' Deputies, and established the soviet system of laborers' deputies, including the Supreme Soviet of the Soviet Union, the Supreme Soviets of the Union Republics, the Supreme Soviets of the Autonomous Republics, and the Soviets of Laborers' Deputies in the border regions, states, autonomous states, ethnic states, districts, counties, cities, towns, and villages. According to the Soviet Constitution, the Supreme Soviet was the highest organ of state power in the Soviet Union with two equal chambers: the Soviet of the Union and the Soviet of Nationalities. When the Supreme Soviet of the Soviet Union was not in session, its elected presidium would exercise its powers, with the Council of People's Commissars as the executive organ. The Supreme Soviet also elected the Supreme Court and appointed the Procurator General of the Soviet Union. Compared with the 1924 Constitution, the 1936 Constitution not only improved the organizational structure of the state power organs and enhanced their powers, but also established and further developed the soviet representative and other systems. The 1977 Constitution of the Soviet Union changed the name of the Soviet of Laborers' Deputies to the Soviet of People's Deputies. Although the two names did not make any difference in essence, the transformation process did witness the improvement of the Soviet System in two main distinct aspects: first, the authority of the soviets was expanded, and especially the supervisory power of the Supreme Soviet was significantly strengthened; second, the status of the soviet deputies was raised. However, From March of 1985 onward, the Soviet System gradually underwent great changes. In particular, the establishment of the People's Congress System and the Presidential System in 1989 marked the transition of the Soviet Union embarking on the road of western parliamentary democracy, and "turning the former Soviet Union from the traditional soviet system into the parliamentary democracy with separation of powers".[5]

9.1.2 System of People's Congresses

Under the leadership of the Communist Party of China, Chinese people of all nationalities have founded and developed a System of People's Congresses, which inherited and developed the experience of the political power construction in the people's revolutionary base areas by referring to the practices of the Soviet Union and other people's democratic countries. Early in China's First Revolutionary Civil War, the working class and peasant class established political organizations with the characteristics of the people's revolutionary democratic regime in its early form, such as the Congress of Canton-Hong Kong Striking Workers and the Strike Committee in 1925, the Citizens' Assembly and its elected Civil Government in 1927 after the triumph of Shanghai Workers' Armed Uprisings, and Peasant Associations established after the victory of peasant insurrections in various areas. During China's Second Revolutionary Civil War, the congress system of workers', peasants' and soldiers' deputies was established in all revolutionary base areas. In November 1931, the First National Congress of Chinese Soviet was held in Ruijin, Jiangxi province, where the Temporary Central Government of Chinese Soviet was founded with the National Soviet Temporary Central Executive Committee elected as the supreme organ of state power. During the War of Resistance Against Japan, the revolutionary democratic regimes in the anti-Japanese base areas adopted the form of a Consultative Council, which organized the government and led local government affairs when the council was not in session. During China's War of Liberation, poor peasant leagues and peasant associations were established to exercise the functions and powers of local governments in all rural areas where land reform was carried out. The peasant leagues and associations formed the basis on which the people's representative assemblies at district and village (township) levels were established to elect the people's governments. Comrade Mao Zedong pointed out that this "is an extremely valuable experience" and that "once such a people's representative assembly has been established, it should become the power organ for the local people."[6]

In the days following the founding of the People's Republic of China, the Chinese People's Political Consultative Conference (CPPCC) was convened, which assumed the functions and powers on behalf of the National People's Congress (NPC) and formulated the Common Program as the interim constitution. On the basis of summarizing the experiences of the political power construction in China's democratic revolutions, the Common Program for the first time defined the system of the People's

[5] Wang, Z. T. and Gao, J. H. (1993) *Lishi jubian: Shehui zhuyi de cuozhe jiqi jiaoxun* [Historical Upheaval: Setbacks and Lessons of Socialism], Jinan: Shandong People's Press, pp. 164–166.

[6] Cf. *Mao Zedong Xuanji* [Selected Works of Mao Tsetung] (1991), Beijing: People's Publishing House, vol.4, p. 1308.

Congresses as China's organizational system of political power. The 1954 Constitution marked the formal establishment of the People's Democratic Dictatorship and the System of the People's Congresses in China. However, after 1958, local authorities began to ignore the system of the People's Congresses the system gradually lost power in the central authority. During the decade of turmoil in the Cultural Revolution, this System was even more severely undermined. The 1978 and 1982 Constitutions, along with the Electoral Law and the Organic Law re-enacted, further improved and developed the System of the People's Congresses in China. According to the Constitution of People's Republic of China, under the System of the People's Congresses, the National People's Congress is the highest organ of state power, while the local people's congresses at all levels are local organs of state power at local levels. Both the National People's Congress and local people's congresses at and above the county level have permanent bodies that exercise their corresponding functions and powers in accordance with the law when the people's congresses at the same level are not in session. The National People's Congress and local people's congresses at all levels also elect their respective administrative, judicial and procuratorial organs at the same level. These state organs, elected by the people's congresses, must be responsible to and supervised by the people's congresses, and all state organs, including people's congresses at different levels, are responsible to the people and subject to their supervision. In addition, as organs of state power, the people's congresses at all levels actually have a wide range of functions and powers. Since the ratification of the 1978 Constitution, the System of the People's Congresses in China has been on a track of healthy development.

9.1.3 System of People's Assemblies

The System of People's Assemblies is the specific form of the socialist people's representative system in the Democratic People's Republic of Korea (D.P.R.K), which is similar to the System of the People's Congresses in China in terms of its basic contents and characteristics. In June of 1948, a leaders consultative council of various political parties and social organizations from both North Korea and South Korea was held in Pyongyang, which declared the unilateral election held by South Korea in May of 1948 as null and decided on a general election by the whole Korean people from both the North and the South. In late August, elections were held separately in different forms in the northern and southern halves of the country, and 572 members were elected. On September 2, 1948, the first session of the Supreme People's Assembly was held in Pyongyang. The Constitution adopted at this assembly officially confirmed the System of People's Assemblies as the basic form for the Korean people to realize their rights as masters of the country. According to the Constitution, the highest organ of state power in the D.P.R.K is called the Supreme People's Assembly, which is the only legislature of the country. It has the right to approve and amend the Constitution, enact laws, produce and supervise the state leaders, such as electing the president of the state, organizing the highest administrative organ, appointing the leaders of the supreme judicial and procuratorial organs. In addition, the Supreme People's Assembly has the power to determine the economic development plans, approve the state budget, declare war and peace and decide other major issues. Meanwhile, the highest power organ of the D.P.R.K also has its permanent body called the Standing Conference of the Supreme People's Assembly. In addition, it has established the Central People's Committee as the highest leading body of state power. Like the System of the People's Congresses in China, the D.P.R.K instituted the Government Administration Council as the executive organ of the supreme organ of state power, which is responsible to and reports its work to the highest organ of state power.

From the above introduction to the formation processes and general situations of the three patterns of the socialist people's representative system, i.e. the Soviet System, the System of People's Congresses and the System of People's Assemblies, there emerge three commonalities: first, they were all created during their respective revolutionary wars and continued to develop and improve with their respective political and economic development, but they also experienced twists and turns in the process of their development; second, they all resulted from thoroughly smashing the old state apparatus of their own countries and constantly summarizing and learning from the experiences and lessons of their own and others in the construction of political power; third, they all inherited and reflected the principles of the Paris Commune and adopted the people's representative system, which was a political form to consolidate the proletarian dictatorship and to ensure the right of the people to be their own masters.

The differences in the actual balance of class forces and historical traditions in various countries determine that the three major patterns mentioned above also differ in the process of their emergence and development. First, in terms of origins, the Soviet System originated from the Soviet of Workers' Deputies, while the System of People's Congresses in China originated in the Citizens' Assembly during the Shanghai Workers' Armed Uprisings and Peasant Associations in the rural areas, and so on. Therefore, they are marked with the imprint of the economic and political struggles of the time, though each of them has its own characteristics in origin. Second, there are distinctions in their class relations when the people's representative system has been instituted in the form of a basic law in various countries. Before the socialist transformation of the ownership of means of production was basically completed in China, there existed alliances and cooperative organizations between the working people and the non-working people, such as the Chinese People's Political Consultative Conference, which was the organizational form of the people's democratic united front based on the alliance of workers and peasants under the leadership of the working class (through the Communist Party), but this sort of alliance did not exist in Soviet Russia. Third, there were also differences in the right to vote at the initial stage of the people's representative system. According to the 1918 Constitution of Soviet Russia, exploiters and others who harmed the interests of the working people did not have the right to vote, while in China, according to the 1954 Constitution, only bureaucratic comprador capitalists, landlords and counter-revolutionaries were deprived of their political rights, excluding the national bourgeoisie.

9.2 Comparison of Organizational Structures of Socialist People's Representative Systems

As an organizational system of state power, the socialist people's representative system is also the unity of structure and function. Specifically, only when the socialist people's representative system is materialized into certain organs and organizations, can it function effectively in political practice through the activities of these organs and organizations. Therefore, a comparative study of the socialist people's representative system must first begin with a comparative analysis of its different patterns from the perspective of the organizational structure.

9.2.1 General Analysis of Organizational Structures of Socialist People's Representative Systems

Although the socialist people's representative system is rich in content and covers a wide range of areas, as discussed in Chap. 8 on organizational structures of capitalist parliamentary systems, the organizational structures of socialist people's representative systems mainly refer to the internal composition of the people's representative organs and the interrelations of its various constituent parts. Here, we will discuss it from both the macro and micro levels.

(1) **Macro System of Socialist People's Representative Organs: Unicameralism & Bicameralism**

In terms of the number of houses, socialist people's representative systems can be also divided into unicameralism and bicameralism. For instance, the System of People's Congresses in China and the System of People's Assemblies in the D.P.R.K are unicameral systems, while the Soviet System is a bicameral system. Despite the fact that there are both unicameralism and bicameralism in the practical operation of the socialist people's representative system, many people, since the classical Marxist writers, have advocated unicameralism and opposed bicameralism in their critique of the capitalist representative system. Lenin declared during April and May of 1917, "The Constitution of the Democratic Republic of Russia shall guarantee that: the first article is to establish the dictatorship of the people; the supreme power of the state must be vested entirely in people's representatives, who shall be elected by the people and be subject to recall by the people at any time, and who shall constitute a single popular assembly, a single chamber."[7] And he also stated, "Is the two-chamber system a sound condition for political life? We do not think so. The Progressists and the Cadets think it is. For holding such views, we accuse the liberals of being anti-democratic, of being counter-revolutionary. And by formulating this

[7] *Liening quanji* [Lenin Collected Works] (1957), Beijing: People's Publishing House, vol. 24, p. 428. cf. Lenin, V. (1917) 'Preliminary Draft Alterations in the R.S.D.L.P. Party Programme'.

accusation against the liberals, we level an even greater accusation at all the Rights."[8] In response to the liberal's argument that the implementation of bicameralism, though a violation of democracy, could be agreed upon by more people, Lenin pointed out that "the liberal goes on to explain his idea as follows: the more modest the demand, the wider is the circle of those who agree with it", "But we reason differently. Our main premise is that unless the masses are politically conscious there can be no change for the better." And "If we refrain from explaining the harm of the two-chamber system, … we alienate the masses – in the sense that the masses, to whom democracy is not just a diplomatic signboard, not a showy phrase, but their own, vital cause, a question of life and death, would lose their confidence in the partisans of the two-chamber system; and also in the sense that relaxing the attacks on the two-chamber system implies inadequate political education of the masses, and unless the masses are politically conscious, wide-awake and full of determination, no changes for the better can be brought about."[9]

When talking about the organization of the Republic of the Russian Federation in April of 1918, Stalin criticized bicameralism and said to a journalist from *Pravda*, "The United States and the Swiss Confederation actually take the form of bicameralism, with a house elected according to the principle of universal suffrage on the one hand, and a federal house composed of various states on the other. It is the bicameralism that has in fact slowed down the bourgeois legislation. Needless to say, the working people of Russia will not accept such a bicameral system, not to mention that this system is completely incompatible with the basic requirements of socialism."[10] He also noted, "There will not and should not be a so-called second house between the Central Executive Committee and the People's Committee... [and]....Whatever forms practice creates, it will never revive the bicameralism that has already been eradicated and buried by our revolution".[11] In May 1918, in his speech at the preparatory conference on the founding of the Tatar-Bashkir Republic, Stalin criticized the bicameralism of the bourgeois state as "a system that stagnates the legislation and strangles any revolutionary cause", and pointed out, "We are opposed to the introduction of this political system building to the country, not only because socialism fundamentally denies bicameralism but also because of the practical considerations of the current situation."[12] To be specific, because the bourgeoisie has not been suppressed yet, the economic destruction and food panic have not been eliminated,

[8] *Liening quanji* [Lenin Collected Works] (1959), Beijing: People's Publishing House, vol. 18, p. 113. cf. Lenin, V. (1912) 'The Nature and Significance of Our Polemics Against the Liberals'.

[9] *Liening quanji* [Lenin Collected Works] (1959), Beijing: People's Publishing House, vol. 18, pp. 114–115. cf. Lenin, V. (1912) The Nature and Significance of Our Polemics Against the Liberals.

[10] *Sidalin quanji* [Stalin Collected Works] (1956), Beijing: People's Publishing House, vol. 4, p. 66. cf. A talk with the *Pravda* journalist in April of 1918, published in No. 62–63 of *Pravda*.

[11] *Sidalin quanji* [Stalin Collected Works] (1956), Beijing: People's Publishing House, vol. 4, p. 67. cf. The opening speech delivered by Stalin at the preparatory conference on the founding of the Tatar-Bashkir Republic in May of 1918, published in No. 96–101 of *Pravda*.

[12] *Sidalin quanji* [Stalin Collected Works] (1956), Beijing: People's Publishing House, vol. 4, p. 67. cf. The opening speech delivered by Stalin at the preparatory conference on the founding of the Tatar-Bashkir Republic in May of 1918, published in No. 96–101 of *Pravda*.

and the new socialist world has not been established, "at this time, the country must have a strong all-Russian state power capable of completely suppressing the enemies of socialism and organizing a new communist economy, [and]…. If the local and regional autonomous power organs are established in parallel to the central state power, any political power will, in fact, be collapsed and fall back to capitalism."[13] Mikhail Kalinin stated that "in the capitalist state, the second house (the upper house) is the one for the survival of the class that is stepping off the stage of history… it is the safety door used for the ruling classes to protect themselves and prevent the lower house from taking certain 'rebellious' measures against them."[14]

Indeed, now that all the power of the socialist state belongs to the people, the unity principle of state power shall be the basis of the people's representative system, and even of the entire state power. Therefore, considering the unity principle of state power, the unicameral organizational structure shall be established in all socialist people's representative organs, not to mention the fact that in the practical operation of the capitalist parliamentary system, one of the two houses always tends to be conservative, thus fully revealing the deficiencies of the bicameral system. However, regardless of its drawbacks, the practice of bicameralism does happen in the organizational structure of the socialist people's representative system. So, why have some countries also adopted the form of a bicameral system in the process of establishing the organizational structure of the socialist people's representative system?

There is no doubt that the adoption of a bicameral system in socialist countries is not intended to use the upper house to restrain the lower house. At the early stage of development of the Soviet System, the bicameral system was adopted mainly to deal with the issue of nationalities. In this regard, Stalin once made a systematic discussion, and in February of 1923, he proposed to the Political Bureau of the Communist Party of Russia building a second House in the Central Executive Committee of the Soviet Union. In the outline of his report, which was submitted to the 12th National Congress of the Communist Party of Russia and approved by the Central Party Committee, he explained his rationale for the establishment of the Soviet of Nationalities:

> The supreme organ of the Union should fully reflect not only the common needs and demands of all nationalities in the Union, but also the special needs and requirements of individual nationalities. Therefore, apart from the present Central Organ that represents the working people of the whole Union irrespective of nationalities, special organs representing various nationalities should be established in accordance with the principle of equality. And the Central Organ of the Union organized in such a way will make it possible for us to listen to the needs and demands of all nationalities, give them timely help, and create an environment of complete mutual trust, so as to wipe out the above-mentioned heritage with the least harm.[15]

---

[13] *Sidalin quanji* [Stalin Collected Works] (1956), Beijing: People's Publishing House, vol. 4, p. 182. cf. The opening speech delivered by Stalin at the preparatory conference on the founding of the Tatar-Bashkir Republic in May of 1918, published in No. 96–101 of *Pravda.*

[14] Cited in Kirichenko, M. (1956) Qian *Sulian zuigao guojia quanli jiguan* [The Highest Organ of State Power in the Former Soviet Union], trans. Sen, Y., Beijing: Law Press·China, p. 34.

[15] *Sidalin quanji* [Stalin Collected Works] (1956), Beijing: People's Publishing House, vol. 5, p. 156. cf. Stalin, J. (1923) National Factors in Party and State Affairs. The so called "heritage" here refers

In 1936, in his report *On the Draft of the Former Constitution of the Soviet Union*, Stalin explained why the second chamber was established in the U.S.S.R.:

> A single-chamber system would be better than a dual-chamber system if the U.S.S.R. were a single nation state. But the U.S.S.R. is not a single-nation state. The U.S.S.R., as we know, is a multi-national state. We have a supreme body in which are represented the common interests of all the working people of the U.S.S.R. irrespective of nationality. This is the Soviet of the Union. But in addition to common interests, the nationalities of the U.S.S.R. have their particular, specific interests, connected with their specific national characteristics. Can these specific interests be ignored? No, they cannot. Do we need a special supreme body to reflect precisely these specific interests? Unquestionably, we do. There can be no doubt that without such a body it would be impossible to administer a multi-national state like the U.S.S.R. Such a body is the second chamber, the Soviet of Nationalities of the U.S.S.R.[16]
>
> He continued:
>
> Reference is made to the parliamentary history of European and American states; it is pointed out that the dual-chamber system in these countries has produced only negative results -- that the second chamber usually degenerates into a centre of reaction and a brake on progress. All that is true. But this is due to the fact that in those countries there is no equality between the two chambers. As we know, the second chamber is not infrequently granted more rights than the first chamber, and, moreover, as a rule the second chamber is constituted undemocratically, its members not infrequently being appointed from above. Undoubtedly, these defects will be obviated if equality is established between the chambers and if the second chamber is constituted as democratically as the first.[17]

Obviously, although the Supreme Soviet of the Soviet Union, as designed by Lenin and Stalin, also consisted of two chambers, the implementation of a dual-chamber system was not to prevent the passion and impulsion of the deputies as in a single chamber, nor to cheat the masses, but to satisfy the requirements for properly solving the domestic national problems, so as to take care of both the common interests of the whole country and the special interests of individual nationalities. Of course, in the practical operation of the socialist people's representative system, other countries with multi-nationalities adopted unicameralism. This is not only connected with the traditions of various countries, but it is also closely related to theoretical principles, such as the unity of state power and the consistency of people's interests. However, whether a socialist country should adopt a unicameralism or a bicameralism, "it all depends on the practical needs instead of the abstract judgment of which one is better or worse."[18]

---

to the remnants of Russian chauvinism and nationalism, and the inequality of all nationalities in economy and culture (noted by the author).

[16] *Sidalin xuanji* [Stalin Selected Works (II)] (1979), Beijing: People's Publishing House, p. 415. cf. Stalin, J. (1936) 'On the Draft Constitution of the U. S. S. R.'.

[17] *Sidalin xuanji* [Stalin Selected Works (II)] (1979), Beijing: People's Publishing House, p. 415. cf. Stalin, J. (1936) On the Draft Constitution of the U. S. S. R.

[18] He, H. H. (1988) *Bijiao xianfaxue* [Comparative Constitutional Law], Wuhan: Wuhan University Press, p. 269.

(2) Internal Composition of Socialist People's Representative Organs: Permanent Organs, Committees and Working Institutions

Deputies elected by voters are the most central and basic constituent elements of the socialist people's representative organs. However, only when individual deputies are organized into a certain power-wielding body can they practically exercise the functions and powers of the people's representative organs. The unicameralism and bicameralism mentioned above in the so-called macro system are the typical manifestations in this regard. However, whether in unicameralism or bicameralism, the people's representative organs can only truly exercise its functions and powers fully and effectively through its internal organizations. To be specific, the internal organizations mainly include the permanent organs, committees and working institutions.

The Permanent Organs are those that are often established when the socialist people's representative organs are out of session, through which the broad masses of working people in a socialist country regularly exercise the highest power of the state. Under the capitalist parliamentary system, since parliamentary activities are frequent and there are often long terms of session, there is no need for a permanent organ. For instance, regular sessions of the U.S. Congress usually last for nine months, starting on January 3 every year, with no definite ending time specified by the Constitution, but no later than the starting time of the next session; the Diet of Japan sits for 150 days, and the House of Commons in Britain has an average session time of 165 days, etc. However, in socialist countries, the duration of a regular session of the people's representative organ is very tight. Many countries stipulate in the Constitution that the supreme organ of the state shall hold a session once or twice a year. For example, according to Article 112 of the 1977 Constitution of the U.S.S.R, the Supreme Soviet of the former Soviet Union shall convene twice a year, and Article 77 in the Constitution of North Korea stipulates that regular sessions shall be convened once or twice a year and so on. However, in political practice, the real time spent in session every year is approximately 20 days. Thus, the establishment of a permanent organ is crucial to maintain the regularity and continuity of the work and activities of the people's representative organ, so as to keep the channel open at all times for people to be masters of their own country. For this reason, the Soviet Russia Constitution of 1918 clearly states that the All-Russian Congress of Soviets is the supreme power organ of the state, and the All-Russian Central Executive Committee, elected by and responsible to the All-Russian Congress of Soviets, act as the supreme organ of state power when the Congress is not in session, which is also stipulated in its subsequent constitutions and in all constitutions of other socialist countries. For instance, according to the 1977 Constitution of the U.S.S.R, the Presidium of the Supreme Soviet is the permanent organ of the Supreme Soviet of the U.S.S.R, elected by the joint session of the two chambers of the Supreme Soviet from among deputies, which reports all its work to the Supreme Soviet, and exercises the functions and powers of the supreme power organ of the state within the limits of the Constitution between the sessions of the Supreme Soviet of the U.S.S.R; the Constitution of the D.P.R.K stipulates the Standing Committee of the Supreme People's Assembly as its permanent organ; according to the 1982 Constitution of China, the National People's Congress of the People's Republic of China is the highest organ of state power, and its permanent organ is the Standing Committee of the National People's Congress, etc.

Both in the theory and practice of the socialist people's representative system, it is of positive significance to set up a permanent organ of the people's representative organ. First, the establishment of a permanent organ is more conducive to attracting the broad masses to participate in the management of the state affairs. Compared with capitalist countries, socialist countries have far more deputies to the people's representative organs than the number of parliament members in the capitalist countries. The reason is that the parliament in capitalist countries have no permanent organ, so that all work must be fulfilled by the parliament itself. Therefore, it is difficult for too many parliament members to manage a large volume of work during the session of the parliament, otherwise, the work efficiency will be greatly reduced. In socialist countries, since the daily work of the people's representative organs is handled by the permanent bodies, though there are also a large number of deputies, the functioning and effectiveness of the people's representative organs will not be affected. On the contrary, the large number of deputies not only means that the people's representative organ has a broad mass base, but also indicates that it can attract more people to participate in the management of the state, so that the democratic nature of the socialist state power can be fully reflected. Second, the establishment of a permanent organ can greatly improve the work efficiency of the people's representative organs. Despite the fact that the large number of deputies demonstrates a high level of democracy, too many of them will result in deficiencies of inadequate discussion of issues and activity inconveniences, but such defects can be remedied by permanent organs. Third, the establishment of a permanent organ also gives full and continuous play to the functions of various special committees. In capitalist countries, the special committees are just subsidiary institutions of the parliament and their functions are bound to be affected once the parliament is in recess. Whereas, in socialist countries, the special committees serve not only the people's representative organs, but also the permanent organs when the people's representative organs are out of session. In this way, the work of the permanent organ can be improved in quality and efficiency with the assistance of the special committees, and the work of the special committees can continue as well. Fourth, although the permanent organ is vested with the right to regularly exercise the state power when the people's representative organ is out of session, the most fundamental and significant issues shall still be handled and decided by the people's representative organ. Moreover, the permanent organ shall be responsible to and supervised by the people's representative organ, so the establishment of a permanent organ will not undermine the authority of the people's representative organ, but will further strengthen its role and authority on the contrary.

The Committees are important organizations within the people's representative organ and the subsidiary working institutions of the people's representative organ and its permanent organ. Generally, there are two types of major committees: the standing committees or special committees and interim committees. The people's representative organ is the organ of state power, which not only has the power of legislation, appointment and removal, and supervision, but also the power of decision-making on major affairs. With the increasing complexity of modern legislation and the growing volume of government work, it is difficult for the deputies to gain complete knowledge of work in all areas. In addition, it is impossible for the people's representative organ to meet in session all the year round, which calls for the establishment of various committees to undertake the preparatory work such as considering bills and assisting the people's representative organ to strengthen the supervision of the government, etc. There are various committees within the people's representative organs in socialist countries. For instance, the 1936 Constitution of the Soviet Union expressly provided that the Supreme Soviet of the Soviet Union could organize an investigation committee or a review committee on any issue when necessary. Before 1957, the two chambers of the Supreme Soviet had 4 respective committees, and the number was increased to 16 after 1966 in order to strengthen the role of the committees. According to the Communiqué of 1980, 17 committees were established in each chamber of the Supreme Soviet respectively, including credentials committee, bills committee, planning and budget committee, foreign affairs committee, industry committee, agriculture committee, youth affairs committee, etc., 34 in all. According to the 1954 Constitution of P.R.C, the National People's Congress shall establish a nationalities committee, law committee, budget committee, deputies credentials committee and other committees as are necessary. At present, the National People's Congress of China maintains 9 special committees, including the Ethnic Affairs Committee, the Constitution and Law Committee, the Financial and Economic Committee, the Education, Science, Culture and Public Health Committee, the Foreign Affairs Committee, the Overseas Chinese Affairs Committee, the Internal and Judicial Affairs Committee, the Environmental Protection Committee, and the Agriculture and Rural Affairs Committee.

Generally, committee members are elected by the people's representative organ. For example, the members and chairman of the committees in the Soviet Union were selected from among the deputies to the Soviet of the Union and the Soviet of Nationalities. According to the statistics, in 1979, the number of deputies of the two chambers of the Soviet Union elected to various committees accounted for 76 percent of the total. In China, the candidates for various committees of the National People's Congress shall be nominated by the presidium of the Congress from among the deputies and shall be decided by a vote of the Congress. Generally, the functions and powers of the committees mainly include: the powers to make legislative proposals, to examine records, to supervise and inspect, and to make work suggestions. First, committees have the power to make legislative proposals. For instance, all the committees of both chambers of the Supreme Soviet of the U.S.S.R had proposal rights. And the committees of the National People's Congress in China continue to have the right to submit proposals relevant to their own committees to the Presidium of the National People's Congress and the Standing Committee of the National People's Congress within the scope of the respective functions and powers of the Congress and the Standing Committee. Second, committees have the power to examine proposals. The Soviet Union did not submit all the proposals to the committees for review. For instance, of the 27 bills passed by the Supreme Soviet from 1958 to 1962, only 14 were examined by the relevant committees; of the 241 proposals received between 1962 to 1966, only 53 proposals were submitted to the committees concerned. At the present stage in China, the deliberation work for the special committees of the National People's Congress are enormous and heavy, such as reviewing the bills and inquiries entrusted by the Presidium of the National People's Congress or the Standing Committee of the National People's Congress, to which a report on their work shall be submitted when necessary; reviewing the administrative regulations, decisions and orders formulated by the State Council that are in conflict with the Constitution or laws on behalf of the National People's Congress; reviewing the orders, instructions and regulations formulated by the ministries and commissions under the State Council; reviewing the local regulations and decisions formulated by the people's congresses and their standing committees at the levels of province, autonomous region and city directly under central government jurisdiction; and reviewing the decisions, orders and regulations formulated by the people's governments at the levels of province, autonomous region and city directly under central government jurisdiction. Third, committees have the power of supervision and inspection. For instance, in the Soviet Union, the committees had the power to hear and question reports on issues under their jurisdiction submitted by the responsible officials of the government organs and other all-Soviet organizations, to obtain relevant information and data, and to oversee the activities of government organs and organizations, as well as their enforcement of the laws. Finally, committees have the power to make work suggestions. For instance, the committees of both chambers in the Soviet Union had two kinds of powers to make a suggestion: first, to make work suggestions to both chambers and the Presidium, including a suggestion of submitting a certain proposal or issue to the whole people for discussion; second, to make work suggestions to the central and local administrative organs. In addition, the committees also had the power to make suggestions to the Council of Ministers of the Soviet Union, and so on.

Under the socialist people's representative system, the working institutions mainly refer to the agencies established under the permanent organs of the people's representative organs, which are the basic conditions for ensuring the proper and efficient operation of the people's representative organs and their permanent organs. In the Standing Committee of the National People's Congress in China, there is the Council of Chairmen composed of a chairperson, vice chairpersons and a secretary general, responsible for handling the important daily work of the NPC Standing Committee. In addition, the Legislative Affairs Commission and the General Office of the NPC Standing Committee under the Council of Chairmen are established to provide services for the conferences of the NPC and its standing committee, to assist the work of the special committees, and to serve the NPC deputies and the members of the Standing Committee to exercise their powers according to law. For example, the major duty of the Legislative Affairs Commission is to assist the NPC Standing Committee and NPC Law Committee to draw up, research and amend draft laws; the General Office of the NPC Standing Committee is responsible for studying and handling the specific daily affairs through its respective subordinate organs under the leadership of the Secretary General. In addition, the Standing Committee may also establish other working committees as needed.

9.2.2 Similarities and Differences of Organizational Structures of Socialist People's Representative Systems and Their Reasons

There are clear similarities between the Soviet System, the System of People's Congresses and the System of People's Assemblies in terms of organizational structure. Firstly, they are all political forms universally adopted from the central to the local levels in their own countries. For instance, under the Soviet System, there are the Supreme Soviet of the Soviet Union, the Supreme Soviets of the Union Republics and the Autonomous Republics, and local Soviets of People's Deputies at all levels; in China, there are both the National People's Congress and the local people's congresses at all levels, etc. Secondly, they have all replaced the bourgeois principle of separation of powers with the organization and activity principle of democratic centralism, and the power structure of the state has thus been formed with a extremely distinct features. Specifically, though all state organs have a division of functions and powers, there is no check and balance relationship between the two. The legislature is not an organ that simply exercises the legislative and supervisory power, but an organ of state power with all power of the state, and the administrative, judicial and procuratorial organs of the state are produced by the organs of state power at all levels. Thirdly, since the people's representative organ is of a conference nature, a permanent organ is usually established to exercise the state power when the representative organ is not in session, and the committees and working institutions assist the people's representative organ and its standing committee to exercise the relevant functions and powers, and so on. There are two main reasons for these similarities. First, these countries have the same nature of state power and follow the same guiding ideology and theoretical principles for the construction of political power. Fundamentally opposed to the capitalist state power, the socialist state power is the one in which the broad masses of the working people are the masters of the country, which is the central focus that must be centered on in the practical operation of the organizational system of state power. Furthermore, the Marxist-Leninist theory of state is the fundamental guiding ideology for the political power construction in all socialist countries, and it is the identical guiding ideology that inevitably leads to such similarities in terms of the organizational structure, though the implementation of this ideology is usually combined with the practical reality of each socialist state. Second, all these countries once took the Paris Commune and the Soviet System as models to learn from. As the first proletarian dictatorship in world history, the Paris Commune created a series of democratic principles and accumulated rich experience and lessons, which had far-reaching influence on later socialist countries. The Soviet Russia was the first socialist state power in the world established after the triumph of the October Revolution. Whereas, some socialist countries, such as the People's Republic of China and North Korea were founded after the victory in the Second World War. Therefore, all the objective circumstances have determined that the emerging socialist countries must draw on the experience of the Soviet Union, which already had a history of nearly 30 years, in the process of building a socialist people's representative system and a brand new socialist political power. Consequently, different patterns of socialist people's representative systems are bound to have some similarities in their organizational structures.

Likewise, different patterns of socialist people's representative systems also have differences in terms of organizational structure. When comparing things and phenomena of the same nature, one must analyze both similarities and differences. However, the analysis of differences is the main focus, especially the historical background that caused the differences and their dynamic effect on things and phenomena, so as to offer valuable insights for reference. The main differences between the socialist representative systems are found in the macro system and in the selection of deputies. First, there are differences in the macro system of the people's representative organs. For example, both the System of People's Congresses and the System of People's Assemblies adopt unicameralism, while the Soviet System applies a bicameralism in the central government. Second, there are also differences in the way deputies are selected. For instance, deputies to the National People's Congress of China are indirectly elected, while the deputies to the two chambers of the Soviet System are directly elected by voters.

In a nutshell, the fundamental reason why different patterns of socialist people's representative systems utilize different organizational structures lies in the different national conditions and new developments made by each country on the premise of adhering to the basic principles of Marxism-Leninism. As mentioned previously, the Soviet System adopted bicameralism mainly because the Soviet Union was confronted with the ethnic problems that needed to be solved, while the adoption of a unicameralism in China was determined by its own national conditions, such as historical tradition, mutual relations among various ethnic groups and the features of the ethnic distribution, though China is also faced with the ethnic issues.

9.3 Comparison of Functional Effects of Socialist People's Representative Systems

The socialist people's representative system is the basic form for the broad masses of the working people in socialist countries to achieve the status of being masters of the country. In this regard, we have already analyzed various perspectives, mostly limited to the organizational forms and basic theories. Now, it is necessary to examine the impact of the socialist people's representative system on political practice in terms of its functional effects.

9.3.1 General Functions and Powers of Socialist People's Representative Organs

As discussed before, according to the theories of the parliamentary power in capitalist countries, the power of the parliament refers to that part of state power invested in the parliament in line with the principle of separation of powers. However, according to socialist theories of state and constitutional theories, the people's representative organ is the organ of state power through which the broad masses of working people realize their right to be masters of their own country. And since all power of the state belongs to the people in socialist countries, in theory, the people's representative organ is a plenipotentiary authority of the socialist state that exercises the power of the state on behalf of the whole people. However, as the people's representative organ is an institution of a conference nature, and its meeting times are limited, so it is difficult for it to exercise all power of the state. Therefore, in accordance with the principle of democratic centralism, a division of labour among state organs is necessary under the premise of insisting on the unified exercise of state power by the people's representative organ. In this way, in the political practice of a socialist country, the actual power of the people's representative organ is limited by the explicit provisions of the Constitution and laws. In other words, the people's representative organ is plenipotentiary in theory, but in practice, its power is also restricted to a certain scope. Based on the provisions of the constitutions and laws in socialist countries as well as the practical operation of the socialist people's representative system in each country, the general functions and powers of the socialist people's representative organ can be summarized into four categories: the functions and powers in the legal system, the power of appointment and removal, the power of supervision, and the power of decision.

(1) **Functions and Powers in Legal System**

The functions and powers of the people's representative organ in the legal systems of socialist countries mainly include two parts: the legislative power and the supervisory power to oversee the enforcement of the Constitution and laws. Generally, the local people's representative organs at all levels have no legislative power of in socialist countries, so here we will focus on the relevant functions and powers of the highest people's representative organ. Since a Constitution is also a kind of law, the legislative power should include the power to make and amend the Constitution. However, whether the representative organ in various countries is entitled to make and amend the constitution of the country is an extremely complex and requires urgent research due to the peculiarities of a given constitution. In capitalist countries, the parliament has no constituent power, and even the power of constitutional amendment can only be partially enjoyed. For instance, the U.S. Congress was constituted under the Federal Constitution, and there was no Congress at all before the Constitution was created, so there is no way to talk about the constituent power of the Congress. Moreover, a constitutional amendment can become part of the Constitution only when it is proposed by 2/3 of members from both houses of the Congress or 2/3 of state legislatures, and ratified by 3/4 of the state legislatures or 3/4 of the constitutional conventions of each state. Comparatively, the power of the U.S Congress to amend the Constitution is also extremely limited. However, the constitutional history of socialist countries shows that the supreme people's representative organ has both the constituent power and the constitutional amendment power, though in some socialist countries, only the constitutional amendment power is vested in the supreme organ according to their constitutions. For example, the 1918 Constitution of Soviet Russia was drafted by the Constitutional Committee of the All-Russian Central Executive Committee and passed at the Fifth All-Russian Congress of Soviets; the 1954 Constitution of the People's Republic of China was also drafted by the Constitution Drafting Council and passed at the first plenary session of the First National People's Congress. The constitutions of some socialist countries, on the other hand, explicitly provide that the supreme people's representative organ has the constituent power. For instance, the Constitution of the D.P.R.K stipulates that the supreme people's representative organ has the power to adopt and amend the Constitution. With regard to the amendment of constitutions, According to the Soviet Constitution, the Constitution can only be amended with the approval of at least a 2/3 majority of all deputies in each chamber of the Supreme Soviet; the Chinese Constitution provides that the Constitution can only be amended if proposed by the NPC Standing Committee or by more than 1/5 of the NPC deputies, and adopted by a 2/3 majority of all NPC deputies. It can be seen that the constitutions of socialist countries have all vested the power of adopting and amending the constitutions in the supreme people's representative organ of the state. At the same time, the constitutions of socialist countries also provide that the supreme people's representative organs enjoy the power to enact and amend ordinary laws. For instance, the Constitution of the Soviet Union stipulates that the Supreme Soviet is the highest legislative organ and enjoys the supreme legislative power of the country. As for the supervision of the enforcement of the Constitution and laws, the constitutions of socialist countries generally vest this power in the supreme people's representative organs.

Although local people's representative organs at all levels generally do not have the legislative power of the state, they still make significant contributions to the legal system. In fact, the legislative power is vested in the people's representative organs in countries with a federal form of state structure, such as the Union Republics and the Autonomous Republics of the Soviet Union. Even in countries with a unitary state structure, the local people's representative organs have the power to enact local laws and regulations. For example, in China, the people's congresses and their standing committees in provinces, autonomous regions, and cities directly under central government jurisdiction, and those of the capital cities and of relatively larger cities approved by the State Council have the power to enact local laws and regulations. Moreover, in order to ensure the enforcement of the Constitution and laws of the state, the constitutions of various countries generally prescribe that the local people's representative organs at all levels have the responsibility to ensure the enforcement of the Constitution and laws of the state within their administrative regions.

(2) **Power of Appointment and Removal**

As organs of state power, the people's representative organs in socialist countries also have the power to organize other state organs at the same level by means of election or appointment. As stipulated in the Constitution of the Soviet Union, the Supreme Soviet is the only organ that has the power to set up the Soviet Union organs that report work to it. It has the power to select the Presidium of the Supreme Soviet, organize the Council of Ministers, elect the Supreme Court, and appoint the Supreme Procurator-General and the chairman of the Committee of People's Control, and also has the power to remove the chairman of the Presidium of the Supreme Soviet or the senior leaders of other state organs at any time by means of secret ballot; the Supreme Soviets of Union Republics and Autonomous Republics shall have the power to elect the Presidium of the Supreme Soviet and organize the Council of Ministers of the republic; and the local soviets of people's deputies can elect the local soviet executive committees as their executive organs and organs for issuing orders.

According to the Chinese Constitution, the National People's Congress has the power to elect the Chairman, the Vice-Chairmen, the Secretary-General and the members of the NPC standing committee, and the President of the state, the Chairman of the Central Military Commission, the President of the Supreme People's Court, the Procurator-General of the Supreme People's Procuratorate. In addition, the National People's Congress has the power to decide on the successful candidate for the premier of the State Council based on nomination by the president of the state, and on the successful candidates for vice-premiers, state councilors, ministers of ministries or commissions, the auditor-general and the secretary-general of the State Council upon nominations by the premier; it also has the power to decide on the successful candidates for vice-Chairmen and other members of the Central Military Commission upon nomination by the Chairman of the Central Military Commission. The National People's Congress has the power to remove individuals from the positions above according to legal procedures. However, Local people's congresses at all levels shall elect separately, and have the power to remove from office the heads of the people's governments at their corresponding levels, and local people's congresses at and above the county level shall elect, and have the power to remove from office presidents of the people's courts and chief procurators of the people's procuratorates at their respective levels. The election or removal of Chief Procurator of the People's Procuratorate at a lower level must be reported to the Chief Procurator of the People's Procuratorate at the next level up for submission to the standing committee of the people's congress at that level for approval, etc.

(3) **Power of Supervision**

Since the other state organs are elected or organized by the people's representative organs at their respective levels, they are necessarily responsible to them and subject to their oversight. On the other hand, it is only through the oversight of the other state organs that the people's representative organs at various levels can ensure that the state power is to be collectively exercised by them, so as to genuinely secure the status of the working people being the masters of the country. Therefore, the supervisory power is one of the most important functions of the people's representative organs.

For instance, according to the Constitution of the U.S.S.R, the Supreme Soviet of the Soviet Union shall supervise the enforcement of the Constitution and ensure that the constitutions and laws of the Union Republics are in conformity with the Constitution and laws of the Soviet Union; the Supreme Soviet shall supervise all state organs that report their work to it; the Supreme Soviet of the Soviet Union shall direct the activities of the Committee of People's Control, and the leading of the people's control system; the Supreme Soviet of a Union Republic shall supervise its Presidium and Council of Ministers; local Soviets of People's Deputies shall exercise control over the observance of laws by enterprises, institutions and organizations subordinate to higher authorities located in their area, coordinate and supervise their activities regarding land use, nature conservation, building, employment of manpower, production of consumer goods, and provide social, cultural, communal and other services and amenities for the public.

According to the Constitution of the People's Republic of China, the National People's Congress (NPC) is empowered to supervise the work of other state organs created by it, and the NPC standing committee shall be responsible to and report its work to the NPC; the National People's Congress can change or revoke inappropriate decisions of the NPC Standing Committee; the State Council, the Central Military Commission, the Supreme People's Court and the Supreme People's Procuratorate shall all be responsible to the NPC; local people's congresses at all levels have the power to oversee the work of their standing committees, people's governments, people's courts and people's procuratorates at their corresponding levels. In terms of the content of supervision by the people's representative organs in socialist countries, it mainly includes legal supervision and work supervision; in terms of the specific supervisory system, there are reporting systems, inquiry systems, and law and regulation review and approval systems, etc.

(4) **Power of Decision on Major Issues**

All the people's representative organs in socialist countries have the power to decide policy on major issues. For the supreme people's representative organ, its power of decision mainly includes: reviewing and approving the national economic and social development plan and the report on its implementation; reviewing and approving the state budget and the report on its implementation; formulating the general guideline of foreign policies and ratifying treaties and agreements concluded with foreign countries; deciding on issues concerning war and peace and issuing mobilization orders; establishing regional administrative organizations, etc. For instance, the following decision powers were vested in the Supreme Soviet as defined by the Constitution of the U.S.S.R: admitting new republics to the U.S.S.R and approving the establishment of new autonomous republics and autonomous regions; reviewing and approving the government work report submitted by the Council of Ministers, and ratifying the national plan for economic and social development, the state budget and the reports on the execution of the budget and plan; deciding on the specific domestic and foreign policies during the period and ensuring their enforcement. As for local people's representative organs at various levels, they mainly have the power to decide on important matters in their respective administrative areas. For instance, according to the Constitution of the U.S.S.R, local Soviets of People's Deputies at all levels had the right to adopt decisions on major issues in their administrative areas within the power accorded them by the laws of the Union of Soviet Socialist Republics, the Union Republics and the Autonomous Republics, and all enterprises, institutions, and organizations, as well as public officials and citizens, within the jurisdiction of the particular Soviet, are obliged to implement the decisions of the corresponding local Soviet.

According to the Constitution of P.R.C., local people's congresses at and above the county level have the power to review and approve the economic and social development plans and budgets of their respective administrative areas as well as report on their implementation, and discuss and decide on the major issues concerning politics, economy, education, science, culture, public health, and civil and ethnic affairs; the people's congresses of townships, ethnic townships and towns have the power to decide, in accordance with state plans, economic, cultural, and public service construction plans, review and approve the reports on their finance and budget implementation, and decide on the implementation plan of civil affairs within their administrative areas, etc.

9.3.2 Structures and Functions of Socialist People's Representative Systems

It should be clear that, although different patterns of socialist people's representative systems may differ in one way or another in terms of functions due to the differences in the national conditions of each country, there is not much difference between them in their most basic and important aspects. Therefore, if they are compared from a functional point of view, we will find that they are quite similar. However, the differences in the organizational structure between different patterns of socialist representative systems determine that the ways in which they exercise their powers and realize their functions and the procedures they use to do so are different. Typically, the adoption of a unicameralism or bicameralism in the macro system will have different effects upon the exercise of functions and powers of the people's representative organs. If a unicameral system is adopted, such as the System of People's Congresses and the System of People's Assemblies, all functions and powers will be exercised by a single chamber. However, if a bicameral system is applied, such as the Soviet System, there will be different ways of exercising its functions and powers. Under the Soviet System, the two chambers, the Soviet of the Union and the Soviet of Nationalities, were equal in their exercise of powers. Each enjoyed the same right to propose bills, and all bills had to be adopted by a majority of deputies present in both chambers before they become laws.

In addition, the internal organizational structure of the people's representative organ also has a great effect on the exercise of the functions and powers of the representative organ. To be specific, whether its permanent organ is well-organized, whether its committees and working institutions are well-equipped, and whether all its relevant systems can operate effectively, are directly related to the way the people's representative organ exercises its powers and the realization of its functional effects.

9.3.3 Analysis of Functional Effects of Socialist People's Representative Systems

As mentioned previously, in theory, the socialist people's representative organ is a plenipotentiary body, whose functions and powers are limited to the scope prescribed by the Constitution and laws due to the division of labour among state organs, its functions and powers is still very extensive as seen from the above overview. However, in political practice, the people's representative organ was once called "rubber stamp" by some politicians and scholars in the West, and even the broad masses of working people in socialist countries were not quite satisfied with the functional effects it created in political practice. So, what are the practical functional effects of the socialist people's representative system? What are the main factors that constrain and influence its functional effects?

From the perspective of historical development, with the construction of democracy and the strengthening of legal system in socialist countries, the functional effects of the socialist people's system have been improved day by day. The specific manifestations are as follows: first, the status and authority of the people's representative organs in various countries have been enhanced. In summarizing the history of the development of the Soviets of People's Deputies, Nie Yunlin pointed out that from 1917 to 1985, "the Soviet System was greatly developed and strengthened: the social foundation of the soviet regime was continuously expanded; the status and role of the soviets at all levels, especially the local soviets, were significantly improved."[19] Although the people's congresses at all levels in China once suffered a calamity during the Cultural Revolution, they have quickly recovered and strengthened, and their status and authority have been rapidly improved since the Third Plenary Session of the 11th CPC Central Committee. Second, the capacity of exercising the functions and powers by the people's representative organs in all countries has been enhanced. One of the most important prerequisites for giving a full play to the functional effects of the socialist people's representative system is that the people's representative organs are capable of exercising the functions and powers conferred on them by the Constitution and laws in the political practice. The people's representative organs of socialist countries have greatly enhanced their ability to exercise their functions and powers through various measures, such as intensifying the building of their organizational structures and working systems and improving the quality of their relevant members and staff. Third, the role of the people's representative

[19] Nie, Y. L. (1992) *Qian Sulian Shehui zhuyi minzhu zhidu yanjiu* [A Study of the Socialist Democratic System of the Former Soviet Union], Wuhan: Wuhan Press, p. 87.

organs in various countries has been increasingly strengthened in the political practice. With the enhancement of the status of the people's representative organs and the improvement of their ability to exercise their functions and powers, the people's representative organs have played an increasingly important role in political practice.

At present, the functional effects of socialist people's representative system is far from perfect despite vast improvement. In fact, its functional effects have not been brought into full play for various reasons. From the perspective of the practical operation of the socialist people's representative system, although the factors that constrain and influence its functional effects are many, they can be categorized into two main groups: internal and external. In terms of internal factors, the internal organizational structures and the working systems of the people's representative organs are far from perfect and still have room to be improved. Therefore, the system's ability to exercise its functions and powers, though improved, has not reached the level it should. To be specific, some countries have not yet established a permanent organ in the local people's representative organs, or the ability and quality of its members are not very satisfactory. In addition, the number of committees is insufficient, the tasks and duties of each committee are not clearly defined, and the quality and knowledge of the members need to be improved. Further, the working methods and procedures need to be institutionalized and systematized, and such systems as the proposal system, inquiry system, recall system, liaison system, etc. have not been fully built and enhanced. Due to the above mentioned problems within the socialist people's representative system, the performance of its functional effects is hindered.

While internal factors may be better handled by strengthening socialist democracy and its legal system, external factors are comparatively more difficult to deal with. From the political practice of socialist countries, the external factors that directly and significantly influence the exercise of the functions and powers by people's representative organs involve the relationships between the people's representative organs and the following institutions: the administrative organs, the people's courts and the people's procuratorate, and the organizations of the ruling party at their respective levels. Of these relationships, the most important is the relationship between the people's representative organs and the organizations of the ruling party at their respective levels, that is, the relationship between the governing power of the ruling party and the state power of people as the masters of country.[20] Undoubtedly, mismanagement of this relationship will restrict and affect the exercise of the functions and powers of the people's representative organs and prevent the full play of the functional effects of the socialist people's representative system. However, for quite a long time, in the political practice of socialist countries, the problem of no clear distinction between the functions of the party and those of the government and substitution of the party for the government is exceptionally serious, which has even resulted in the practice that the state power is replaced by the governing power. Therefore, it is necessary to clarify their interrelationship conceptually and handle it well in practice. As a matter of fact, when the broad masses of working people become the

[20] Qiu, D. H. (1993) *Zhongxi minzhu zhengzhi lun* [On Chinese and Western Democratic Politics], Beijing: Chinese Workers Publishing House, p. 118.

masters of the country, two kinds of powers are bound to emerge in the country: one is the leadership power (i.e. governing power) of the ruling party, and the other is the ruling power (i.e. state power) of people as the masters of the country. Although it seems that there is no significant difference between the governing power and the state power in the process where the ruling party fulfills its political platform through the state organs of power and the broad masses of working people realize their will and manifest the status of the ruling class through the power organs of their own, in reality, they are two power systems with different functions that are irreplaceable for each other. For this reason, in socialist political practice, on the one hand, the socialist state must adhere to the leadership of the ruling party over the organs of state power, i.e. the people's representative organs, and on the other hand, this leadership should mainly focuses on the guidelines, principles and policies, and can only be realized when it is transformed into binding laws through the organs of state power. Therefore, the leadership of the ruling party over the state is mainly political leadership, indirect and in principle, and the governing power cannot directly intervene in the state power, let alone replace it.

References

Engels, F. (1891). *A critique of the draft social-democratic programme of 1891.*

Engels, F. (1894). *Letter to Paul Lafargue at Le Perreux.*

He, H. H. (1988). *Bijiao xianfaxue [Comparative constitutional law].* Wuhan University Press.

Kirichenko, M. (1956). Qian *Sulian zuigao guojia quanli jiguan* [The highest organ of state power in the former soviet union] (Sen, Y., Trans.). Law Press·China.

Lenin, V. (1912). The nature and significance of our polemics against the liberals.

Lenin, V. (1912). *The nature and significance of our polemics against the liberals.*

Lenin, V. (1916). *A caricature of marxism and imperialist economism.*

Lenin, V. (1917). *Preliminary draft alterations in the R.S.D.L.P. party programme.*

Liening quanji [Lenin Collected Works] (1957). vol. 24. People's Publishing House.

Liening quanji [Lenin Collected Works] (1958). vol. 23. People's Publishing House.

Liening quanji [Lenin Collected Works] (1959). vol. 18. People's Publishing House.

Makesi Engesi quanji [Marx and Engels Collected Works] (1965). vol. 22. People's Publishing House.

Makesi Engesi xuanji [Marx and Engels Selected Works] (1995). vol. 4. People's Publishing House.

Mao Zedong Xuanji [Selected Works of Mao Tsetung] (1991). vol. 4. People's Publishing House.

Nie, Y. L. (1992). *Qian Sulian Shehui zhuyi minzhu zhidu yanjiu* [A study of the socialist democratic system of the former soviet union]. Wuhan Press.

Qiu, D. H. (1993). *Zhongxi minzhu zhengzhi lun* [On Chinese and western democratic politics]. Chinese Workers Publishing House.

Sidalin quanji [Stalin Collected Works] (1956). vol. 4. People's Publishing House.

Sidalin quanji [Stalin Collected Works] (1956). vol. 5. People's Publishing House.

Sidalin xuanji [Stalin Selected Works (II)] (1979). People's Publishing House.

Stalin, J. (1923). *National factors in party and state affairs.*

Stalin, J. (1936). On the draft constitution of the U. S. S. R. The opening speech delivered by Stalin at the preparatory conference on the founding of the Tatar-Bashkir Republic in May of 1918, published in No. 96-101 of *Pravda.*

Wang, Z. T., & Gao, J. H. (1993). *Lishi jubian: Shehui zhuyi de cuozhe jiqi jiaoxun* [Historical upheaval: Setbacks and lessons of socialism]. Shandong People's Press.

Chapter 10
Comparison Between Capitalist Parliamentary Systems and Socialist People's Representative Systems

The most basic stance and starting point of this book is premised on the assumption that both the capitalist parliamentary system and the socialist people's representative system are the specific manifestations of the same category of representative system. For this reason, this book takes the capitalist parliamentary system and the socialist people's representative system as the corresponding reference systems for each other in order to draw some basic conclusions through analysis and comparison. However, in comparing the capitalist parliamentary system with the socialist people's representative system, we find some issues concerning the organizational structures and functional effects, in particular, the interrelationship between the two systems remain unsolved. This chapter is an attempt to address these problems.

10.1 Comparison of Organizational Structures

As mentioned before, the organizational structure is the most basic materialized form and the main carrier of the basic functions of the representative system. Whether the capitalist parliamentary system or the socialist people's representative system, they are both confronted with the basic problem concerning organizational structure. Moreover, as the basic forms of indirect democracy, both the parliaments and the people's representative organs are the organs of public opinions, which determines that the two systems have both similarities and differences in their organizational structures.

Y. Zhou, *A Comparative Study of Representative Systems*,
https://doi.org/10.1007/978-981-15-4186-5_10

10.1.1 Similarities

The concepts of "same" or "identical" in dialectical logic cannot be understood as absolutely equivalent, but as "the sameness in differences" or "the sameness with differences and opposites". Therefore, summary of the similarities in organizational structures between the capitalist parliamentary system and the socialist people's representative system here can only be relative. Meanwhile, due to differences in specific historical conditions such as national conditions in various countries, the similarities are not necessarily found in all countries. In addition, this research focuses mainly on the macro aspects, so our generalizations are necessarily imperfect. Specifically, the two systems have four points in common in the organizational structure.

(1) **Both Direct and Indirect Election Adopted in Selection of Members and Deputies**

In theory, direct elections ensure that voters can directly exercise their right to vote, and thus fully reflect public opinion, in form, however, both direct election and indirect election are adopted in both the selection of members to the capitalist parliaments and deputies to the socialist representative organs. Under the capitalist parliamentary system, members of the lower house are directly elected in countries such as the United Kingdom, the United States, France, Germany, Italy, Switzerland, Brazil and Japan, while some of the members of the upper house are still elected indirectly, such as in the French Senate and the Belgium upper house, though fewer and fewer countries have adopted indirect election since the nineteenth century. The same is true under the socialist people's representative system. For example, the deputies to the Soviets at all levels in the Soviet Union and the people's deputies below the county level in China are directly elected, whereas, the deputies to the people's congresses at and above the county level in China are elected indirectly. However, in terms of the practice of electoral system, the capitalist parliamentary system and the socialist people's representative system have their own foci on the use of the two methods of election of members and deputies: the former mostly adopts direct election, and the latter mainly adopts indirect election.

(2) **Candidates Nominated by Both Parties and Electors**

The Japanese scholar Isao Satou compared provisions of the 1936 Constitution of the Soviet Union with the systems of capitalist countries. According to the 1936 Constitution, the right to nominate candidates should be exercised by labor unions, mass groups, and Communist Party organizations. Although such provisions were criticized by some western scholars, Isao Satou argued that this practice laid a solid foundation for the election of the deputies truly representing the people because a repeated evaluation of the candidates was required during the nomination process. According to Isao Satou, "In the system of free nomination of candidates in capitalist countries, there is no such public discussion and evaluation of the nominees by voters, so the system of free nomination of candidates is nothing but a window dressing."[1] Moreover, since the Soviet deputies at all levels had the obligation to report their work to the electorate and could be replaced at any time according to the decisions of the voters. Yang Bohua and Ming Xuan also noted, "in a sense, it is the reproduction of the mandat imperatif system that once existed, but here we can see the difference between the soviet deputies and the parliament members of capitalist countries in that the former takes the people as its true foundation."[2]

Isao Satou mainly focused on the differences between the two systems in his comparative study, but according to the current laws and electoral practices, whether in the capitalist parliamentary system or in the socialist people's representative system, there are occasions where both political parties and voters can propose candidates for deputies in the process of candidate nomination. As stipulated in the Chinese Electoral Law, any ten or more voters or deputies can jointly nominate a candidate, and political parties and people's organizations can nominate candidates alone or jointly. However, the number of voters needed to nominate a candidate varies according to the laws of different countries. For instance, in countries such as France, Japan, Sweden, Finland, Brazil and Argentina, the nomination of candidates requires no support from any voter; in India, only one voter is required to support the nomination, 2 voters in New Zealand, 4 in Sierra Leone, 6 in Australia, 10 in UK, 15 in Switzerland, 25 in Netherlands, 200 to 500 in Austria (National Council) and Belgium (Chamber of Representatives) and 100 in Belgium (Senate).[3] At present, the nomination of candidates by political parties has become a common practice in various countries around the world, which has been widely adopted, whether in legal provisions or in traditions, by countries such as the UK, the US, France, Germany, Italy, Japan and the Soviet Union.

In electoral practice, there are also differences in determining candidates between the capitalist parliamentary system and the socialist people's representative system. Under the capitalist parliamentary system, candidates recommended by political parties are more advantaged. In general, it is extremely difficult for citizens to be nominated as candidates or elected without the backing of a powerful political party. Under the socialist people's representative system, however, it is often emphasized that candidates recommended by political parties should stand in equal position with those recommended by voters or other people's organizations, so even those nominated by voters or other people's organizations are also likely to become formal candidates.

(3) **Both Unicameralism and Bicameralism Adopted**

In the previous two chapters, we have discussed the macro systems used in the capitalist parliamentary system and the socialist people's representative system. Under

---

[1] Satou, I. (1984) *Bijiao zhengzhi zhidu* [Comparative Political System], trans. Liu Q. L. and Zhang G. B., Beijing: Law Press·China, p.252.

[2] Ibid.

[3] Yang, B. H. and Ming, X. (1984) *Ziben zhuyi guojia zhengzhi zhidu* [The Political System of Capitalist Countries], Beijing: World Affairs Press, p.102.

the capitalist parliamentary system, unicameralism is adopted in countries such as Sweden, Finland, Luxembourg, Greece, Denmark and Portugal, while bicameralism is implemented in countries such as the United States, the United Kingdom, France, Germany, Japan and Canada. Whereas, under the socialist people's representative system, unicameralism is adopted in China and North Korea, while bicameralism was once practiced in the Soviet Union. Therefore, it is obvious that, in terms of the number of chambers, both unicameralism and bicameralism are the forms that can be adopted by the two representative systems of different natures. However, in the political practice, differences arise in the actual application of the macro systems in different countries. For example, although both the capitalist parliamentary system and the socialist people's representative system may take the form of bicameralism, there are differences when it is practiced in different countries. First, the two chambers are formed for different reasons. In theory, bicameralism in capitalist countries is mainly established on the basis of the doctrine of separation of powers for the purpose of keeping one chamber in check by the other, while bicameralism in socialist countries is aimed to address the issues of nationalities, so as to reflect both the special interests and the general interests of all ethnic groups. Therefore, in terms of the interrelationship between the macro system and the form of state structure, bicameralism in a socialist country is related to the structural form of federal states in that they are both designed for the resolution of ethnic issues. However, the bicameralism of capitalist countries is not necessarily related to the form of state structure. Although such a connection exists in the United States, it does not in France and Japan. Second, there are differences in the way both chambers are produced. Under the capitalist parliamentary system, the lower house is generally elected, but the upper house is mostly created by means of appointment, election plus appointment, selection, designation and ex officio appointment, etc. For example, the House of Lords in UK and the Senates of Canada, Jamaica and Bahamas, etc. are not elected. Whereas, under socialist people's representative system, both chambers are elected. Third, there are also differences in the scope of the two chambers' functions and powers. Generally, the lower house has more powers than the upper house in capitalist countries, but this is not the case in socialist countries. In the Soviet Union, the two chambers had completely equal power.

(4) **Committees and Working Institutions Within Organizational Structures**

Committees were created to meet the needs of political and economic development and specialized division of labor, which are the important conditions for the proper and effective operation of the representative organs, and the working institutions are the organizations that offer various services to parliament members or deputies and representative organs. Both the committees and the working institutions play important roles in the exercise the powers and work of the representative organs. For this reason, both the capitalist parliamentary system and the socialist people's representative system have set up various committees and working institutions in their internal organizational structures, but they differ in many aspects in political practice. First, generally, there are relatively more committees under the capitalist parliamentary system than those under the socialist people's representative system. For example, the 99th United States Congress (1985–1987) had a total of 294 committees and sub-committees, among which the Senate had 16 standing committees and 90 sub-committees and 4 special committees, and the House of Representatives had 22 standing committees, 153 sub-committees (14 of them were called "task forces") and 5 special committees. In addition, there were 4 joint committees of the two houses. Whereas, the National People's Congress of the People's Republic of China only has 9 committees. Second, the functions and powers of the committees under the capitalist parliamentary system are generally greater than those of the committees under the socialist people's representative system. For instance, the committees of the US Congress have not only the power to propose legislation, but also the powers to shelve, amend and veto bills, etc. For example, the proposed bills that were shelved during the Eisenhower Administration accounted for 23% of the total number of the government proposals in 1960, and 10% of the proposals were shelved during the Johnson Administration from 1965 to 1967. In the United States, the review reports of the committees play a decisive role in determining whether a proposal will become a bill. The committees in countries such as Germany, Italy and Sweden are similar to those in the United States. In Italy, for example, 20% of the government proposals and 80% of individual proposals of parliament members are usually shelved by the committees. However, the functions and powers of the committees of the socialist representative organs are much more limited. Of the 27 bills adopted by the Supreme Soviet of the Soviet Union between 1958 and 1962, only 14 bills were reviewed by the committees, and of 241 bills received from 1962 to 1966, only 53 bills were referred to the committees. Third, the committees under the capitalist parliamentary system play a much bigger role in political practice than those under the socialist people's representative system. The wider range of functions and powers will naturally result in greater political effect in actual political practice. For this reason, in capitalist countries, the committees have become the core of the parliaments, and the main activities of the parliaments have gradually been shifted to various committees. As Woodrow Wilson pointed out, "The congressional government is a government controlled by various committees of Congress."[4] Whereas, in socialist countries, although the status of the committees in the people's representative organs has been improved, it still needs to be further strengthened compared with the committees of the capitalist parliaments.

The four points above are just some of the similarities in the organizational structure between the capitalist parliamentary system and the socialist people's representative system. But why do they share these similarities? This can be explained from the following two facets. First, both of them belong to the category of the representative system and are both manifestations of indirect democracy as opposed to direct democracy. Therefore, "representation" and "deliberation" are their most basic common features. Although the capitalist parliamentary system and the socialist

[4] Cited in Zuo, L. S. (1981) *Geguo guohui zhidu* [Parliamentary Systems in Various Countries], Taipei: Taipei Central Publishing House, p.28. cf. Wilson, W. (1885/2011) *Congressional Government,* Boston and New York: Houghton Mifflin Company, p.9.

representative system may be fundamentally different in terms of the objects of representation and contents of deliberation, they are consistent in the form of representation. This determines that they are bound to share commonalities in terms of their organizational structures. Second, both systems draw lessons from and influence each other. Given that the representative system was first developed by the bourgeoisie, and the socialist people's representative system share some similarities with the capitalist parliamentary system in certain forms and conditions, it is no surprise that in the process of establishing the socialist people's representative system, the socialist countries draw on the relevant experience of the capitalist parliamentary system, which result in some similarities in terms of their organizational structures.

10.1.2 *Differences*

In addition to the above-mentioned similarities, there are also differences between the organizational structures of the capitalist parliamentary system and the socialist people's representative system. According to dialectical logic, differences or dissimilarities can be understood as those between the specific and related things rather than those between the abstract and irrelevant things and aspects, that is, differences in similarities. Specifically, in terms of organizational structure, differences between the capitalist parliamentary system and the socialist people's representative system are mainly manifested in the following aspects:

(1) **Differences in Class Bases of Members of Representative Organs**

Parliament members or deputies are the core and most basic components of both the capitalist parliaments and the socialist people's representative organs. However, there are great differences between the two systems in the source of their members or deputies. Under the capitalist parliamentary system, the vast majority or even all of the members of the parliament are men of property or agents of the propertied class. As mentioned earlier, in order to prevent the working people from participating in elections, the electoral laws of the early capitalist countries mostly set restrictions on the right to vote in terms of property status, educational level, length of residence and other conditions. In addition, the working people were deprived of the opportunity to be elected to the parliaments by stipulating a deposit payment system. In the twentieth century, such restrictions have been gradually reduced and even eliminated in some major capitalist countries, but it is still difficult for the working people to obtain the opportunity to be elected to the parliaments. The reason is that the bourgeoisie has shifted its focus from the electoral principles and forms to the electoral procedures in terms of controlling the parliament through elections. In this way, the bourgeoisie still control the election of the parliament members by controlling electoral procedures, so as to enable its representatives to enter the parliament to serve its political and economic interests. Moreover, since the election of members of the parliament in capitalist countries is based on economic strength, whoever has more money is more likely to be a member of the parliament, which is difficult to truly reflect the democratic intention of the representative system, and can hardly guarantee the quality of the social management personnel as well. Under the socialist people's representative system, members of the representative organs are all deputies of the broad working masses. According to the constitutions and electoral laws in socialist countries, all citizens of legal age, except those deprived of political rights by law, are eligible to vote and stand for election, regardless of ethnicity, race, gender, occupation, family origin, religious belief, educational background, property status and length of residence. Moreover, the electoral procedures in socialist countries have truly unified the principles of socialist electoral system with the reality. Therefore, the people's deputies of socialist countries are those who are elected in accordance with the will of the people, delegated by the people to the representative organs and trusted by the people.

(2) **Differences in Internal Organizational Structures**

The Speaker and parliamentary groups are unique to the parliaments of capitalist countries. As mentioned earlier, under the capitalist parliamentary system, the Speaker is the presiding officer of the parliament, who usually acts as an instrument for political parties to control the parliament and to ensure their party programs are transformed into the will of the state. As a basic unit of political activities within the parliament, parliamentary groups play an important role in electing the Speaker and standing committees of the parliament as well as determining the parliamentary agenda, etc. However, such important capitalist parliamentary organizations have no counterparts in the socialist people's representative organs. Rather, there is a president of the Supreme People's Assembly in North Korea and a chairman of the National People's Congress in China, but they are the heads of the standing committees of the people's representative organs rather than the presiding officer or heads of the people's representative organs proper. For example, the Organic Law of the National People's Congress in China stipulates that "The Presidium shall preside over the sessions of the National People's Congress" and "The Chairman of the Standing Committee shall preside over the meetings and work of the NPC Standing Committee" etc., so the permanent organs are unique to the socialist people's representative organs. However, there is no need to set up a permanent organ for the capitalist parliament because the capitalist parliament often has long regular sessions and its work and activities can maintain a certain degree of continuity, while the working features of the socialist people's representative organs determine that the establishment of a permanent organ is not only necessary, but also of positive significance.

(3) **Differences in Organizational and Operational Principles**

Since the organization and operation of the whole state structure in a capitalist country are based on the principle of separation of powers with checks and balances, the capitalist parliament is bound to strictly follow this principle in its organization and operation. Moreover, the bourgeois democracy is essentially the democracy of the bourgeoisie and its bureaucrats, that is to say, the capitalist parliament implements, in its actual organization and operation, the bourgeois and bureaucratic centralism.

And such bureaucratic centralism practiced in the organization and operation of the capitalist parliament guarantees the realization of the will and interests of the whole bourgeoisie, and the monopoly bourgeoisie in particular. Whereas, the socialist people's representative system is organized and operates according to the principle of democratic centralism. Under the socialist people's representative system, the broad masses of the people can, through the representative organs elected democratically, exercise the state power, administer the country and supervise and recall incompetent deputies of the representative organs at all levels. Therefore, democratic centralism has laid an organizational foundation for the socialist people's representative organ to become a unified and highly authoritative organ of state power that can fully express the common will of the people and safeguard their fundamental interests.

(4) **Differences in Power Structures**

The principle of separation of powers with checks and balances determines that the capitalist parliament is, in general, only a legislative body for exercising the legislative power of the state. Therefore, although the parliament plays an important role in the overall structure of state power, generally, it does not occupy an absolute dominant position. In addition, the purpose of setting up the two houses is mainly to keep each other in check. Therefore, separation and balance are the basic characteristics in the power structure of capitalist parliamentary system. Whereas, the principle of democratic centralism determines that the socialist people's representative organ is not only the legislative body for exercising the legislative power of the state,[5] but also the plenipotentiary organ that exercise the power of the state in a unified manner. Specifically, the people's representative organ occupies an absolute and dominant position in the whole structure of state power. Even in countries with a bicameral system, the goal is not that the two house keep each other in check, but to better exercise the state power in a unified way. Therefore, centralization and unification are the basic features in the power structure of the socialist people's representative system.

Ultimately, there are more differences than similarities in the organizational structures between the capitalist parliamentary system and the socialist people's representative system. Actually, even in discussing their similarities, we have also mentioned some of their differences. Therefore, it is quite natural to reach such a conclusion that the systems are quite different. So, why are there so many differences between them? In my view, these differences result from the different natures of the two systems. The capitalist parliamentary system is the organizational system of political power in capitalist countries, through which it generally aims to mobilize and organize the forces of the entire bourgeoisie, safeguard and realize the interests and will of the bourgeois class and consolidate the state power of the bourgeoisie. Whereas, the socialist people's representative system is the organizational system of political power in socialist countries, through which it aims to safeguard and realize the interests and will of the working people and consolidate the state power of the working

[5] In some countries, the supreme people's representative organ has the power to exercise the legislative power of the state, but local representative organs do not have.

class. These fundamentally different natures determine that they are bound to be different in their organization of the representative organs and the establishment of relevant institutions. These two systems' differences are due to the different historical conditions of various countries. The political setup of any country cannot be divorced from its objective historical conditions. Therefore, countries with different historical conditions will have different manifestations in terms of their organizational structures in the process of establishing their representative systems.

10.2 The Comparison of Functional Effects Between Capitalist Parliamentary Systems and Socialist People's Representative Systems

Since the organizational structure is manifested in concrete political institutions, it is practical and tangible, though it often appears in a static form. Therefore, it is more convenient to compare the similarities and differences between the capitalist parliamentary system and the socialist people's representative system in terms of the organizational structure. Although it is much more difficult to compare the capitalist parliamentary system and the socialist people's representative system in terms of the functional effects not only because the functional effects are more flexible and dynamic, but also because the standard for comparison and evaluation are not easy to establish, a comparative study of the functional effects of the two systems is necessary. Therefore, this section will also focus on the discussion of both similarities and differences in terms of their functional effects.

In terms of similarities, they can be mainly summarized into two aspects. First, they both exercise the legislative and supervisory powers of the state, and play an important role in national political life. Under the capitalist parliamentary system, the parliament is not only the organ of public opinion, but also the legislative body that exercises the legislative power of the state. As we all know, the core of modern democratic politics lies in that the people are the masters of the country, so every law should be implemented only with the consent of the people, and the legislative power should be vested in all the people. However, due to various subjective and objective reasons, only the parliament can exercise the legislative power on behalf of the people. In addition, the nature and role of the parliament as well as the principle of separation of powers with checks and balances also determine that it is most appropriate for the parliament to exercise the legislative power. Although the parliaments of various capitalist countries differ in their legislative scope, procedures and principles, they are all legislatures of the state. Under the socialist people's representative system, although the nature of the people's representative organs (usually the supreme people's representative organs) differs from that of the capitalist parliaments, and there are also fundamental differences in the purpose and content of legislation, especially, in terms of the will and interests to be reflected and protected by legislation, similarly, they also exercise the legislative power of the state. The same is true of the supervisory power. Although the supervisory function of the capitalist parliament is inferior to that of the socialist people's representative organ due to the principle of separation of powers with checks and balances, the capitalist parliament still plays an important role in supervising the government in that it is equipped with a mature system and a perfected form and vested with such an authority by law. Whereas, the absolute and dominant position of the socialist people's representative organ determines that its supervisory function is more powerful. Second, their actual functional effects are subject to their internal and external factors. As mentioned earlier, both the capitalist parliaments and the socialist people's representative organs have their respective theoretical, legal and practical status, and the "actual functional effects" of the representative organs mainly refer to their practical status. Taking a historical overview of both the capitalist parliamentary system and the socialist people's representative system, the status quo of their functional effects totally depends on the setup of the internal organizational structures and construction of the working systems of the representative organs, as well as coordination with relevant external institutions and organizations. To put it simply, if the internal organizations and working systems of the representative organs are not well developed, their work efficiency is bound to be low in exercising their functions and powers. And their functional effects achieved will definitely be unsatisfactory as a result. On the other hand, if they only have a strong capacity for exercising their functions and powers, but fail to coordinate the external relations well, the external factors will undoubtedly limit their capacity to play a role in their functioning. In this case, their functional effects will not be desirable either.

In terms of differences, they can also be summarized into two main aspects. First, the scope of functions and powers of the socialist people's representative organs are much broader than that of the capitalist parliaments. Theoretically, as repeatedly mentioned, the socialist people's representative organs are the plenipotentiary organs that exercise state power collectively. Although, for subjective and objective reasons, the actual functions and powers of the people's representative organs prescribed by the constitutions and laws are also limited within a certain scope, the socialist people's representative organs are much superior to the capitalist parliaments in terms of the content of their functions and powers and their status occupied in the overall structure of state power. For example, the capitalist parliaments can not rival the socialist people's representative organs in its power of appointment and removal, its power of supervision and its power to decide on important matters. In addition, the socialist people's representative organs also have the executive function. While comparing the 1936 Constitution of the Soviet Union with the capitalist parliamentary system, Mr. Isao Satou pointed out that "the Supreme Soviet of the former Soviet Union, different from the parliaments of capitalist countries, also had the nature of the executive organ".[6] He also argued that, if the Council of Ministers of the Soviet Union was regarded as an executive organ, it would, in this sense, be more subordinate than a cabinet in the parliamentary cabinet system. Indeed, under the people's representative

[6] Satou, I. (1984). *Bijiao zhengzhi zhidu* [Comparative Political System], trans. Liu Q. L. and Zhang G. B., Beijing: Law Press·China, p.245.

system, the administrative organs, as the executive organs, are elected by the people's representative organs, to which they are responsible and report their work. Therefore, although execution is the business of the administrative organs, it is self-evident that the people's representative organs also have an executive function if we look at the connection between the administrative organs and the people's representative organs. Further, there are differences in the direction of development. As stated in Chap. 8, due to economic, political and ideological reasons, the status and role of the parliament tend to be declining in various patterns of the capitalist parliamentary systems, instead, the status and role of the administrative organs are increasingly rising. Whereas, under the socialist people's representative system, although the status and role of the people's representative organs are on the rise, their functional effects are not yet satisfactory for various reasons. If we examine the socialist people's representative system from a longitudinal survey of its historical development, we can easily find that the status and role of the people's representative organs have been significantly improved to a great extent.

10.3 Some Reflections

In comparing the capitalist parliamentary system and the socialist people's representative system, one of the most prominent distinctions lies in their different nature. To be more specific, they belong to the different organizational systems of state power in two different types of countries. However, further discussion is necessary.

10.3.1 Historical Connections Between Representative Systems with Different Natures

As different organizational systems of state power, although the capitalist parliamentary system and the socialist people's representative system are fundamentally opposed to each other, there are historical connections between them. That's to say, the socialist people's representative system is a successor to the capitalist parliamentary system in a sense, and there is a "influence-acceptance" relationship between them, which is determined mainly by the following three macro reasons:

First, according to the Marxist view of historical development, Marx and Engels once pointed out, "Men make their own history, but they do not make it as they please; they do not make it under self-selected circumstances, but under circumstances existing already, given and transmitted from the past."[7] In other words, they also noted "… at each stage [of history] … a mass of productive forces, capital funds and conditions, which, on the one hand, are indeed modified by the new generation,

---

[7] *Makesi Engesi xuanji* [Marx and Engels Selected Works] (1995), Beijing: People's Publishing House, vol.4, p.732. cf. Marx, K. (1852) *The Eighteenth Brumaire of Louis Bonaparte.*

but also on the other prescribes for it its conditions of life and gives it a definite development, a special character."[8] Therefore, such a succession of conditions of social life, especially material conditions of life, determines that the former and latter social systems "are manifested as various development stages in their interrelationship", and there is a certain "connection" or "coherence"[9] between various stages. Therefore, a certain "coherence" exists between the socialist people's representative system and the capitalist parliamentary system, both of which are only different stages in the development of the representative system.

Second, according to the dialectical negation, a new thing is the negation of an old thing, which means the fundamental negation of the nature of the old thing rather than the total abandonment of all elements in the old. As Engels put it, "Negation in dialectics does not mean simply saying no, or declaring that something does not exist, or destroying it in any way one likes."[10] Thus, the negation in dialectics includes the affirmation of the old thing. The superiority of the new over the old is not only manifested in its new essence, but also in its courage to critically inherit all the reasonable parts of the old that can serve the survival and the development of the new. There is no exception for the relationship between the socialist people's representative system and the capitalist parliamentary system.

Third, according to the dialectical relationship between content and form, content determines form, but form has its own relative independence. The development of new content requires a new form to serve it, and it can also make use of certain elements of the old form. In his book *"Left-Wing" Communism: An Infantile Disorder*, Lenin criticized the "Left-Wing" doctrinairism for not understanding that "an old form" can be filled with "new content", and he argued that a new content can open up the way through various forms, including the old ones. The Soviet and the proletarian regimes can and should utilize, transform, and subjugate all old forms.[11] As a matter of fact, the Soviet power "has developed incomparably farther and deeper that feature of bourgeois democracy which marks historically its great progressive nature as compared with medieval times...at the same time, swept away those negative aspects of bourgeois democracy".[12] Therefore, it is absolutely necessary for the socialist people's representative system to learn from the capitalist parliamentary system in terms of form and procedure.

If we analyze the specific reasons why the socialist people's representative system has inherited something from the capitalist parliamentary system only from the perspective of the representative system, we can conclude three points: First, as

---

[8] *Makesi Engesi quanji* [Marx and Engels Collected Works] (1960), Beijing: People's Publishing House, vol.3, p.43. cf. Marx, K. (1846) *The German Ideology*.

[9] Cf. *Liening xuanji* [Lenin Selected Works] (1995), Beijing: People's Publishing House, vol.1, pp.33-34.

[10] *Makesi Engesi xuanji* [Marx and Engels Selected Works] (1995), Beijing: People's Publishing House, vol.3, p.484. cf. Engels, F. (1878) *Anti-Dühring*.

[11] *Liening xuanji* [Lenin Selected Works (1995), Beijing: People's Publishing House, vol.4, pp.197-198. cf. Lenin, V. (1920) *"Left-Wing" Communism: An Infantile Disorder*.

[12] *Liening xuanji* [Lenin Selected Works] (1995), Beijing: People's Publishing House, vol.3, p.723. cf. Lenin, V. (1931) *Draft Programme of the R. C. P.* (B.).

far as the polity is concerned, both the socialist people's representative system and the capitalist parliamentary system belong to a republic. Liu Zhenduo also noted, "However, the republican forms of government in any country, as long as they are "republican", will share a common feature, that is, the legislative power, which is crucial to state power, is held by the representative organs elected by the citizens. And there are also some similarities in the methods, rules and procedures by which the representational and representative organs are produced and operate."[13] Second, they both are manifestations of indirect democracy corresponding to direct democracy. Under direct democracy, citizens participate in the decision-making of major state affairs in person, so its corresponding systems, procedures and methods are bound to be closely related to the characteristic of "directness"; under indirect democracy, citizens participate in, decide on and manage the major state affairs through their representatives, so its corresponding systems, procedures and methods are bound to be closely related to the characteristic of "indirectness". Therefore, both the socialist people's representative system and the capitalist parliamentary system, as specific forms of realizing indirect democracy, naturally share some similarities in their relevant systems, procedures and methods. Third, although the natures of the capitalist parliamentary system and the socialist people's representative system are different, modern democratic regimes are all faced with the same issues of efficiency and ultimate goal: Whether or not and how do they reflect the popular will, realize the popular sovereignty, and promote social progress? Although there may be great differences between them in term of the scope of the "people" and the content of the "popular will", the same issues they face determine that they are bound to learn and draw on each of their respective methods in the process of solving these problems.

Therefore, although the capitalist parliamentary system is the key content of the political system of the capitalist countries, the socialist countries can also learn and draw on some of its relevant systems and forms. As Lenin pointed out, "The way out of getting rid of the parliamentary system is, of course, not to abolish the representative organ and electoral system, but to change a representative organ from a talking shop into a working institution."[14] Under the condition that the proletariat takes power, the parliamentary system, as a special capitalist system, no longer exists, but "the representative bodies are still there", for "we cannot imagine democracy, even proletarian democracy, without representative institutions".[15] Therefore, it is not only possible but also necessary that there is a historical connection between the socialist people's representative system and the capitalist parliamentary system.

---

[13] Liu, Z. D. (ed.) (1991) *Xinxing guojia lun* [On New Forms of States], Beijing: SDX Joint Publishing Company, p.46.

[14] *Liening xuanji* [Lenin Selected Works] (1995), Beijing: People's Publishing House, vol.3, p.151. cf. Lenin, V. (1917) *The State and Revolution.*

[15] *Liening xuanji* [Lenin Selected Works] (1995), Beijing: People's Publishing House, vol.3, p.152. cf. Lenin, V. (1917) *The State and Revolution.*

10.3.2 Representative Systems of Different Countries Cannot Be Simply Imitated

When discussing rights, equality and fraternity in a civilized society, Engels once quoted the words of Lewis Henry Morgan, "It [civilization] will be a revival, in a higher form, of the liberty, equality and fraternity of the ancient gentes."[16] When we say that the socialist people's representative system has a certain historical connection with, and an inheritance from the capitalist parliamentary system, we do not mean that the former is a simple reversion to the latter. On the contrary, it must be and can only be "a revival in a higher form" under new historical conditions. What is meant here, however, is that the representative system, after its development to the socialist stage, must change and develop with the changing conditions of socialism. If this view is associated with the conditions of various countries, any representative system adopted by different countries cannot be simply copied.

As a matter of fact, in the history of political thought, scholars at all times and in all parts of the world have argued that it is not possible to simply imitate a political system of another country. Aristotle once pointed out in *Politics*: "The reason why there are many forms of government is that every state contains many elements."[17] Rousseau also stated from the perspective of natural conditions, especially the climatic conditions that "For ages there has been much debate about the best form of government, without considering the fact that each of them is the best in certain cases, and the worst in others."[18] The author of *Nordic Democracy* specifically emphasized that the modern Nordic democracy was formed under its historical tradition and special social background that could not be copied by other countries.[19] Sun Yat-sen, the forerunner of the Chinese bourgeois revolution, noted:

> ... for thousands of years, the social conditions and customs in China have been greatly different from those in Europe and the United States. Since the Chinese society is different from that of Europe and the United States, its politics of social management is naturally different from that of Europe and the United States. For this reason, we cannot completely imitate them... it would be a huge mistake if we blindly import the foreign politics of social management to China regardless of its own national conditions.[20]

And Ma Qihua even put it more clearly:

---

[16] *Makesi Engesi xuanji* [Marx &Engels Selected Works] (1995), Beijing: People's Publishing House, vol. 4, p.179. cf. Engels, F. (1884) *The Origin of the Family, Private Property and the State.*

[17] Lipset, S. (1993) *Zhengzhi ren* [Plitical Man], trans. Liu G. M. and Nie R., Beijing: The Commercial Press, p.2. cf. Lipset, S. (1960) *Political Man: The Social Bases of Politics,* New York: Doubleday & Company, Inc., p.8.

[18] Dunn, S. (ed.) (2002) *The Social Contract and First and Second Discourses* by Jean-Jacques Rousseau, New Haven and London: Yale University Press, p.200.

[19] Wisti, F. (ed.) (1990) *Beiou shi minzhu* [Nordic democracy], trans. Zhao Z. Q., Beijing: China Social Sciences Press, The Preface, p.2.

[20] Cited in Gu, B. X. (1988) *Minquan zhuyi minzhu zhengzhi lun* [On Civil Rights and Democratic Politics], Taipei: San Min Book Co., Ltd., p.561.

> Any system must be suitable for the conditions of the country, so it is quite normal that different countries have different systems, and even the same system will not always suitable for different national conditions, just as the shoes of the same size do not fit the feet of different sizes. Generally speaking, the system created must match its national conditions, just like shoes customized by measuring the feet must fit one's feet, and the naturally formed system, which is like a pair of shoes growing on the feet, is the most suitable. As for the transplanted system, its effectiveness depends on whether it can match the conditions of the country to which it is transplanted. Otherwise, we have to cut the feet to fit the shoes.[21]

Similarly, the classical Marxist writers have also explicitly discussed this issue. When the Soviet Union made its civil code in 1922, Lenin pointed out that, on the one hand, everything that the literature and experience of the West-European countries contained on the protection of the working people had to be used, and on the other hand, he also emphasized that "We must not play up to Europe and copy the old bourgeois concepts of civil law, but create new ones".[22] Comrade Mao Tse-tung also pointed out that our policy was to learn the strong points of all nations and all countries including the political, economic, scientific and technological fields, literature and art, "But we must learn with an analytical and critical eye, not blindly, and we mustn't copy everything indiscriminately and transplant mechanically."[23]

Ultimately, the representative systems of different countries cannot be simply imitated for various reasons. To be more exact, one of the most fundamental reason lies in the different national conditions of various countries. In his comparative analysis of the political forms in different countries, Wang Huning argued that the political form adopted by a country would be affected by such variables as the political form, political development path, social and cultural structure and economic development level, and he concluded that "the diversity of multiple factors such as historical, social and cultural determine the diversified political forms".[24] Indeed, the vitality of any political system, including the representative system, depends, to a large extent, on how well the system fits the national conditions of the country concerned. Therefore, although the capitalist parliamentary system and the socialist people's representative system have many unique features of their own, as we have mentioned repeatedly, what can be absorbed by the system of people's congresses of China is definitely determined by the specific historical conditions in China. Based on the above discussion and analysis, I believe that there are two erroneous tendencies we must resolutely oppose concerning the issue of the representative system: one is to erase the distinctive nature between the socialist people's representative system and the capitalist parliamentary system and blindly worship the capitalist parliamentary system; the

---

[21] Ma, Q. H. (1975) *Zhengzhixue jingyi* [Essentials of Politics], Taipei: Pamir Book, p.705.

[22] *Liening quanji* [Lenin Collected Works] (1957), Beijing: People's Publishing House, vol.33, p.173; *Liening wengao* [The Manuscripts of Lenin] (1978), Beijing: People's Publishing House, vol.4, p.222. cf. Lenin, V. (1922) Letter to D. I. Kursky with Notes *On the Draft Civil Code.*

[23] *Ma Zedong xuandu* [Selected Readings of Mao Tsetung's Works] (II) (1986), Beijing: People's Publishing House, p.740.

[24] Wang, H. N. (1987) *Bijiao zhengzhi fenxi* [Analysis of Comparative Politics], Shanghai: Shanghai People's Publishing House, p.90.

other is to deny the historical connections between them, or even totally reject the absorption of the reasonable elements of the capitalist parliamentary system.

10.3.3 Functional Effects of Representative Systems Depend on Multiple Factors

We have previously analyzed the factors that restrict the functional effects of the capitalist parliamentary system and the socialist people's representative system from both internal and external aspects. Although the internal organizational structure and working systems as well as the relevant external relationships are important factors that restrict the functioning of the representative system, they are just the direct and conspicuous constraints. In introducing Lipset's views, Lin Ying noticed that "how to adapt the reform of the political system to the economic development and the change of social and economic structure is a key issue in realizing political modernization and democratization".[25] The same is true for the realization of functional effects of the representative system. During the rising period of capitalism, the fundamental reason that the capitalist parliaments occupied a relatively high status and played a greater role, from the economic point of view, lies in that the capitalist economy provides them a solid foundation of free and equal competition. However, with the concentration and monopoly of capital, the executive power of the state has become increasingly powerful, and the state power has been gradually concentrated in the hands of the executive organs, thus forming a kind of extra-parliamentary power with the executive power as the core. And the "growth of the extra-parliamentary power has led to the decline of the status of the parliament".[26] In socialist countries, from the economic point of view, the fundamental reason why the status and role of the people's representative organs have been far less than satisfactory for quite a long time and the functional effects of the socialist people's representative system have not been fully brought into play lies in the fact that their weak economic base has failed to provide material guarantees for the functioning of the people's representative system. Moreover, the planned economic system has changed the executive organs into the center of state power, which undermines the authority of the people's representative organs. Therefore, in order to give a full play to the functional effects of the representative system in the political practice, we must also provide a sound economic base for it.

Meanwhile, there are also some underlying factors that determine and restrict the functional effects of the representative system, such as public awareness of participation, cultural traditions and national psychology. The representative system can be

[25] Lipset, S. (1993) *Zhengzhi ren* [Political Man], trans. Liu G. M. and Nie R., Beijing: The Commercial Press, The Preface to the Chinese edition.

[26] Kardelj, E. (1981) *Minzhu yu shehui zhuyi* [Democracy and Socialism], trans. Qiu Y. J. and Zhou X. B., Beijing: People's Publishing House, p.48.

called the representative democracy only if it is based on the public opinions, otherwise, the functions of the representative system will be completely lost in the process of realizing indirect democracy. As G. Almond once pointed out, "For if democracy means anything, it means that in some way governmental elites must respond to the desires and demands of citizens."[27] But on the other hand, "Insofar as people do not live up to the ideal of the active citizen, democracy is a failure."[28] However, he also noted:

> ... recent studies of political behavior call the rationality-activist model into question, for it is becoming clear that citizens in democracies rarely live up to this model. They are not well informed, not deeply involved, not particularly active; and the process by which they come to their voting decision is anything but a process of rational calculation... that the informed, involved, rational, and active citizen is more frequently found in the successful democracies than in the unsuccessful democracies.[29]

This conclusion, reached by Almond on the basis of a comparative study of the civic cultures in Britain, the United States, Germany, Italy and Mexico, fully displays the significance that public participation matters to the success or failure of democratic politics. As an important part of democratic politics, the representative system relies heavily on public participation. If citizens do not have a strong sense of participation and fail to actively participate in political practice, the functional effects of the representative system will never be satisfactory. However, in countries with backward economy and culture with deep-rooted feudal customs, it is much more difficult to develop an awareness of political participation and democratic habits than to establish the representative system itself. Therefore, developing the awareness of public participation and building an effective participation mechanism are important issues in the process of giving play to the functional effects of the representative system.

Cultural traditions and national psychology are part of the concrete manifestations of the aforementioned "national conditions". The most prominent constraint they exert on the functional effects of the representative system is manifested in their ability to use the territory they have already occupied and the power they have developed to facilitate or resist the functioning of the representative system. The best explanation for this conclusion comes from the political practices of various countries. For example, although the representative systems were also established in many newly independent countries in Asia, Africa and Latin America, they were inevitably resisted by their original cultural traditions and national psychology in their political practices for lack of the corresponding cultural and ethnic bases. In this way, it is difficult to give a full play to the functional effects of the representative system. After the triumph of the October Revolution, Lenin once pointed out that the Soviet power "in principle has provided an immensely higher proletarian democracy, which has created a model of such democracy for the whole world–how this lack

[27] Almond, G. (1963) The Civic Culture: Political Attitudes and Democracy in Five Nations, New Jersey: Princeton University Press, p.476.

[28] Ibid, p.475.

[29] Ibid, p.474.

of culture is reducing the significance of Soviet power and reviving bureaucracy".[30] History has repeatedly proven that in order to make the representative system truly a basic form for the realization of the people as the masters of the country, not only must a nation continuously enhance the system construction, but also greatly promote the economic and cultural construction, so as to improve the political and cultural quality of the people and develop their democratic and legal conception such as the awareness of political participation.

10.3.4 Concluding Remarks: Development Trends of Representative Systems

In the 1920s, Austrian-American legal philosopher Hans Kelsen asserted that "modern democracy can survive only when the parliamentary system identifies itself to be an instrument capable of solving the contemporary social problems". And he further pointed out that "the destiny of the parliamentary system determines that of the democracy".[31] Alvin Toffler also suggested that the "Representative government was a stunning advance over earlier power systems", and he continued, "Representative government made possible orderly succession without hereditary dynasty. It opened feedback channels between top and bottom in society. It provided an arena in which the differences among various groups could be reconciled peacefully."[32] American political scientist, Giovanni Sartori, summarized two contributions of the representative system in 1987: "First, it reduces power to less power; in a system of representative government nobody is in a position to exercise an absolute (i.e., limitless) power. Second, and concurrently, in a system of representative government the people actually exercise power (political power) by being able to control and change the people in power."[33] In short, the representative system provides prerequisites for the people to exercise their power and achieve democracy. However, for some futurologists, such as J. Naisbitt, although the representative democracy was "a practical way to organize a democracy", but "now we have outlived the historical usefulness

---

[30] *Liening quanji* [Lenin Collected Works] (1956), Beijing: People's Publishing House, vol.29, p.152. cf. Lenin, V. (1919) 'Report on the Party Programme at the Eighth Congress of the Russian Communist Party'.

[31] Mastellone, S. (1992) *Ouzhou zhengzhi sixiang shi:Cong 15 shiji dao 20 shiji* [History of European Political Thoughts: From 15th Century to 20th Century], trans. Huang H. G., Beijing: Social Sciences Academic Press, p.400.

[32] Toffler, A. (1984) *Di sanci langchao* [The Third Wave], trans. Zhu Z. Y, Pan Q. and Zhang Y., Beijing: SDX Joint Publishing Company, p.133. cf. Toffler, A. (1981) *The Third Wave,* New York: Bantam Doubleday Dell Publishing Group, Inc., p.75.

[33] Sartori, G. (1993) *Minzhu xinlun* [New Theory of Democracy], trans, Feng K. L. and Yan K. W., Beijing: Orient Press, p.76. cf. Sartori, G. (1978) *The Theory of Democracy Revisited (Part One: The Contemporary Debate),* New Jersey: Chatham House Publishers, Inc., p.71.

of representative democracy and we all sense intuitively that it is obsolete".[34] So, what is the fate of the representative system? How will it develop in the future? I would like to address the questions from the following two aspects.

10.3.5 Are Representative Systems Declining?

In discussing how the principles of the representative system are changing with the development of history, Isao Satou pointed out:

> The concept of representation is based on the premise of agreement with the represented. At the beginning, the so-called agreement of the modern representative system was in fact the agreement with the interests of citizens. However, with the development of capitalism, the unity of the civil society has gone, and the modern parliament has no longer been able to perform its function of correctly reflecting the interests of citizens, where the people outside the parliament have gained more right to say, and there comes the phenomenon that the pressure group directly resorts to the government, political parties and citizens outside the parliament and tries to influence them.[35]

This is the change in the status and role of the capitalist parliament that we discussed in Chap. 8. Professor Cao Peilin called this change "the evolution from the representative democracy to the executive centralized democracy" and he believed that it is "the trend of historical development".[36] To be specific, with the development of capitalism, the contradictions inherent in capitalist countries are intensifying, and the government can no longer guarantee the normal operation of the capitalist social movements if only responsible for "law and order". Therefore, the government, as the general capitalist, has to "undertake the direction of production",[37] and while ensuring the external conditions of the capitalist reproduction, it is also required to play a role in all the internal areas and processes of social reproduction. Therefore, the representative government with the parliament as the center has to change its internal power structure by gradually transferring the power from the parliament to the executive organs. Cao Peilin summarized three basic features of the executive centralized democracy:

> First, the executive centralized democracy in various countries still retains the democratic forms and infrastructures, such as universal suffrage, parliamentary system, cabinet responsibility system. Second, the power of the parliament has been significantly reduced, and the

---

[34] Naisbitt, J. (1984) *Da qushi: Gaibian women shenghuo de shige xin fangxiang* [Ten New Directions Transforming Our Lives], trans. Sun D. Z., Beijing: China Social Sciences Press, p.162. cf. Naisbitt, J. (1982/1986) *Megatrends: Ten New Directions Transforming Our Lives*, New York: Warner Books, Inc., p.177.

[35] Satou, I. (1984) *Bijiao zhengzhi zhidu* [Comparative Political System], trans. Liu Q. L. and Zhang, G. B., Beijing: Law Press·China, p.338.

[36] Cao, P. L. (1993). *Bijiao Zhengfu Tizhi* [Comparative Government System], Shanghai: Fudan University Press, p.20.

[37] *Makesi Engels xuanji* [Marx and Engels Selected Works] (1995), Beijing: People's Publishing House, vol.4, p.752. cf. Engels, F. (1880) *Socialism: Utopian and Scientific*.

> parliamentary system in the traditional sense no longer exists. Under the executive centralized democracy, it is not the case that the parliament is responsible for legislation and the executive is responsible for the implementation of it, but that the executive implements laws formulated by itself. And the parliament merely performs the procedures of authorization and approval; it is not the parliament that supervises the executive, but the executive supervises the parliament. And the executive can direct the activities of the parliament and in some countries even set procedures for the parliament. Third, the executive power has been greatly strengthened, and the head of the executive becomes the center of power.[38]

Both Isao Satou's and Cao Peilin's views are consistent with our analysis above in terms of the functional effects of the capitalist parliamentary system: The power structure of the modern capitalist countries has changed in that the executive rather than the parliament has become the center of state power. Therefore, considering the status and role of the parliament, the capitalist parliamentary system is actually declining. However, it is hard to jump to this conclusion if examined from a static point of view, especially in terms of the constitutional and legal provisions, as well as the organizational structure and working mechanism of the capitalist parliamentary system. From the perspective of political history of the capitalist parliaments, with the continuous accumulation of experience in the governance and management of the bourgeoisie, the capitalist countries have made certain improvements both to the provisions of their constitutions and laws governing the parliamentary system and to its organizational structure and working mechanisms. Therefore, if we simply examine these aspects, we can say that the capitalist parliamentary system is constantly developing. But the life and significance of any political infrastructure lies fundamentally in its functional effects. Since the status of the capitalist parliament has declined in the power structure of the capitalist state and its role and influence in the political practice has also been reduced, the capitalist parliamentary system is indeed going from boom to bust in terms of the overall political infrastructure of the capitalist state, especially the political practice of the whole capitalist countries in spite of the development of capitalist parliamentary system.

Although the capitalist parliamentary system is in decline, this does not signify the decay of the representative system generally because the development trend of the capitalist parliamentary system is not universal. There are two major types of representative systems in modern countries: the capitalist parliamentary system and the socialist people's representative system. Contrary to the development direction of the capitalist parliamentary system, the status and role of the socialist people's representative system are on the rise, which is not only reflected both in its own self-construction and in its functional effects. The development trend of the socialist people's representative system can be explained in three main points. First, the status of the people's representative system is increasing due to the nature of state power in socialist countries where the people are the masters of the country. In socialist countries, all power belongs to the people, but people often exercise the state power through the people's representative organs at various levels of the country. Therefore, the nature of the socialist state requires the improvement the status of the people's

[38] Cao, P. L. et al. (1993) *Bijiao zhengfu tizhi* [Comparative Government System], Shanghai: Fudan University Press, p.20.

representative organs and enhancement of the role of the people's representative system.

Second, the status of the people's representative system is increasing due to the construction of socialist democracy and enhancement of the legal systems. Most socialist states suffered a bitter experience whereby the construction of democracy and legal system were overlooked. Nevertheless, they proceeded to embark on the road to vigorously develop democracy and their legal systems after learning from their own mistakes. For example, as noted in Resolution of the Central Committee of the Communist Party of China on Certain Questions in History of Our Party Since the Founding of the P.R.C:

> A fundamental task of the socialist revolution is to gradually establish a highly democratic socialist political system. Inadequate attention was paid to this matter after the founding of the People's Republic, and this was one of the major factors contributing to the initiation of the "Cultural Revolution". Here is a grievous lesson for us to learn. It is necessary to strengthen the building of state organs at all levels in accordance with the principle of democratic centralism, and make the people's congresses at all levels and their permanent organs authoritative organs of the people's political power.[39]

With the building of the socialist democracy and the strengthening of the legal system, the status and role of the socialist people's representative system are bound to be promoted. Third, the status of the people's representative system is increasing due to the transformation of the economic management system. Various economic management systems can be built on the basis of public ownership of the means of production. Although the planned economic system can play a positive role under certain historical conditions, the excessive intervention of the government in the economy and the practical role of the government in political practice have made the government dominant in the entire power structure of the state. In this way, the status and role of the people's representative organ will be restrained accordingly. However, with the shift from the planned economy to the market economy, "the visible hand" has been replaced by "the invisible hand" in process of economic management. As a result, the functions of the government shall be transformed, and its status and role in the power structure of the state shall also be adjusted. In addition, the market economy is essentially a rule of law economy in which laws play an extremely important role not only in the governance of state and society, but also in the management of the economy. Therefore, the status of the people's representative organ as the legislative body is bound to increase and become the center of the power structure of the socialist state, and the functional effects of the socialist people's representative system is sure to develop in an upward trend. Moreover, the three factors will exist in socialist countries for a long time and determine that the socialist people's representative system will thrive in the long run.

In short, it is too hasty and one-sided to conclude that the representative system is on the wane. If the centralization and monopoly of capital leads to the administrative centralization and decline of the capitalist parliamentary system in capitalist

[39] Annotated version of Resolutions on Several Historical Issues of the Party since the Founding of the PRC (1983), Beijing: People's Publishing House.

countries, the socialist people's representative system in the socialist countries is increasingly prospering as the intervention of the government in the economy turns to be more indirect with the transformation of government functions.

10.3.6 Will Representative Democracy Be Replaced by Direct Democracy?

Ideally, direct democracy is the best form of realizing democracy, and the representative system is but a compromised democracy. However, as mentioned earlier, the situation of modern nation-states determines that the representative system is both a great progress from ancient democracy to modern democracy and a necessity for the development of democracy itself. In other words, democracy cannot be realized without the implementation of the representative system. In this sense, the representative system constitutes the basic form of democracy in modern countries. However, in the actual practice of the representative system in various countries, its deficiencies have also been revealed. Gu Buxian, the Taiwanese scholar of China, categorized the drawbacks of the representative system into three aspects. First, the essence of popular sovereignty has been changed. Specifically, Gu Buxian explained that under the representative system, "The people only have the right to vote. And the representatives will run all government affairs on behalf of the people once they are elected. In this way, the people are only the masters of the country in name, but not in reality..., [and] the elected representatives become the real masters instead."[40] Second, the parliament has too much power. Gu also noted, "...the sovereignty of the state has been transferred from the hands of the people to the hands of the parliament, or the center of politics has shifted from the people to the parliament, it is quite natural that the priority, supremacy and excessive power of the parliament give rise to its despotism."[41] Third, the government is relatively weak. Gu continued to explain, "A too powerful parliament will directly result in a weak government."[42]

Although Gu's conclusion is generalized from the perspective of ideal democracy based on capitalist countries, there are undoubtedly some defects in the representative system. To be specific, the representative system is feasible but not democratic enough. For this reason, many political scientists and thinkers have explored ways to solve such a perplexity and attempted to reconcile its feasibility with democracy. The Direct Civil Rights proposed by Sun Yat-sen was designed to reconcile the merits and demerits between direct democracy and indirect democracy.[43] And some scholars refer to direct democracy as Referendum system. As Sa Mengwu noted:

---

[40] Gu, B. X. (1988) *Minquan zhuyi minzhu zhengzhi lun* [On Civil Rights and Democratic Politics], Taipei: San Min Book Co., Ltd., pp.398-399.

[41] Ibid, p.400.

[42] Ibid, p.404.

[43] Ibid, p.394–395.

> Since direct democracy is not available and indirect democracy fails to achieve the ideal democratic politics, some countries have to make a compromise between indirect democracy and direct democracy and thus adopt the referendum system, where citizens are entitled with the right to express their opinions by voting when it comes to some important issues of the country, though the parliament is the legislative body.[44]

With regard to global political practices, Miller and Bogdanor noted, "...some countries combine the representative democracy with a moderate direct democracy in that they refer certain issues to all citizens for decision by means of referendum. These countries include Switzerland, Italy, France and some states of the United States. In addition, Switzerland, Italy, and some states of the United States also adopt a motion procedure, and the recall procedure is still practiced in some states of the US."[45] In his study of the Swiss political system, the Japanese scholar Yamaguchi Yasushi, especially noticed that "the direct democratic forms of political participation such as Referendum are still full of life in Switzerland".[46]

The Social Autonomy once practiced in some socialist countries is also a specific manifestation of direct democracy. For example, in the process of promoting the People Autonomy, the Soviet Union attached great importance to direct democracy, and regarded it as an important form for the people to participate in and manage the social affairs of the state.

Ultimately, the deficiencies of the representative democracy directly result in the revival of direct democracy. Specifically, since the representative system is not democratic enough, the direct democratic system can be adopted to make up for its deficiencies rather than replace it. As Vernon Bogdanor pointed out:

> The referendum and initiative are used not to replace representative institutions but to supplement them when it is felt that they are not working effectively; they are also advocated so as to secure greater popular legitimacy and support for government policies.... However, these instruments of direct democracy tend to arouse controversy only when their frequent use is advocated. Where, as in most democracies, they are employed only very infrequently, they tend to be taken for granted as a useful if limited adjunct to the normal machinery of the democratic state."[47]

In discussing British politics, Ralph Miliband noted, "It is certainly true that representative government has never run the slightest risk of being superseded by direct government."[48] When talking about the extension of the suffrage in Britain, C. S. Emden also suggested, "This kind of development need not raise the apprehension

---

[44] Sa, M. W. (1986) *Zhengzhixue* [The Politics], Taipei: San Min Book Co., Ltd., p.205.

[45] Miller, D. and Bogdanor, V. (eds) (1992) *The Blackwell Encyclopedia of Political Science*, New York: Wiley-Blackwell, p.177.

[46] Yamaguchi, Y. (1991) *Zhengzhi tizhi* [Political System], trans. Han T. Y., Beijing: The Economic Daily Press, p.46.

[47] Miller, D. and Bogdanor, V. (eds) (1992) *The Blackwell Encyclopedia of Political Science*, New York: Wiley-Blackwell, p.525.

[48] Miliband, R. (1982) *Capitalist Democracy in Britain,* New York: Oxford University Press, p.39.

that representative government is in the process of being superseded by direct government."[49] Therefore, political practice indicates that the revival of direct democracy is not intended to supersede the representative system.

However, in light of democratic ideals and social development, the trend is to maximize people's political participation and develop direct democracy. Since the representative system is only a compromise to democracy, then striving to fulfil the ideal of democracy shall be the development direction of the democratic system. Furthermore, the development of productive forces, the advancement of science and technology and the improvement of citizens' quality create conditions for the expansion of political participation. Therefore, direct democracy undoubtedly constitutes an important part of democracy if we examine the development history of modern democratic politics from a diachronic perspective. Japanese scholar Tomoaki Iwai explained the relationship between direct democracy and representative democracy thusly:

With the rapid development of technology, especially the development of computer science and new media, the representative system that was originally formed for technical reasons may lose its function of representation. Undoubtedly, it is definitely feasible that the functions of the representative system will soon be replaced with the development of technology. And the will of the people, which could only be expressed indirectly through intermediaries in the past, can now be transmitted directly in an instant.[50]

John Naisbitt argued that, thanks to the telecommunication revolution and the well-educated electorate, "...today, with instantaneously shared information, we know as much about what's going on as our representatives and we know it just as quickly... [Therefore]...now we have outlived the historical usefulness of representative democracy... [and]... politically, we are currently in the process of a massive shift from representative to participatory democracy".[51] Yamaguchi Yasushi called this transformation as shift from "multipolar democracy" to "consensus democracy".[52] In these scholars' view, representative democracy will be superseded by direct democracy, and the future democracy will be a "participatory democracy" with direct democracy as its "heart and soul".

However, others have different opinions about "participatory democracy". According to Daniel Bell, participatory democracy is largely a form of opposition to social specialization and technocracy in post-industrial society, but not the panacea as advertised by its advocates. He also predicts that participatory democracy will continue to grow but will not have a promising future because the extension of

---

49 Ibid.

50 Iwai, T. (1990) *Lifa guocheng* [Legal Process], trans. Li W., Beijing: The Economic Daily Press, p.171.

51 Naisbitt, J. (1984) *Da qushi: Gaibian women shenghuo de shige xin fangxiang* [Ten New Directions Transforming Our Lives], trans. Sun D. Z., Beijing: China Social Sciences Press, p.162. cf. Naisbitt, J. (1982/1986) *Megatrends: Ten New Directions Transforming Our Lives*, New York: Warner Books, Inc., pp.176-177.

52 Yamaguchi, Y. (1991) *Zhengzhi tizhi* [Political System], trans. Han T. Y., Beijing: The Economic Daily Press, pp.181–189.

the political arena and the participation of much more people means that it will take more time and cost more to reach agreement and get things done. Based on this, he concludes that more participation will lead to more frustration. Giovanni Sartori has challenged participatory democracy from various aspects, and pointed out that the referendum democracy as "a macro democracy that replaces representative democracy" is "by now, technologically feasible. Each voter would dispose of a video terminal in which the issues and their proposed solutions are displayed… and [people] would simply have to press yes–no–abstain buttons."[53] He also commented on participatory democracy as follows:

> It sets an outright zero-sum mechanism of decision making, that is, a literal majority rule system that rules out minority rights. On each issue, the winning majority takes all, the minority loses all. Not only majority rule would become absolute or unlimited, but no tradeoffs, no compensations, could occur among issues either. Since every referendum-type decision is a discrete and self-contained decision, it cannot be tempered by "exchanges", by cross-issue adjustments or corrections (not even if required on the grounds of consistency). In short, the objection is that referendum democracy is a conflict maximizing structure that represents not only the perfect but also the most unintelligent (since it would be purely mechanical) incarnation of a systematic "majority tyranny".[54]

In terms of feasibility, Giovanni Sartori argued:

> There remains the question of feasibility…direct, real self-government cannot be presumed; it requires the actual presence and participation of the people concerned. It is impossible to have direct democracy at a distance and meaningful self-government among absentees. The gist is that the greater the number of people involved, the less effective is their participation– and this to a vanishing point. Thus, when vast territories and entire nations are involved, direct democracy becomes an unusable formula. I have also and concurrently held that an electronic, "referendum democracy", while technically feasible, would be disastrous and, in all likelihood, suicidal…. In conclusion, I would say that democracy based on personal participation is possible only under certain conditions; and correspondingly, that when these conditions do not exist, representative democracy is the only type possible.[55]

I present the views of these scholars in detail here because they are in line with my argument proposed in Chap. 3. Both direct democracy and representative democracy are merely means, approaches and methods. In case that the conditions are not equipped for full implementation of direct democracy, the optimal approach to democracy is to combine representative democracy with direct democracy. Whether representative democracy or direct democracy is given priority in a specific period is mainly determined by its objective needs and historical conditions. According to the situation both at present and into the foreseeable future, although direct democracy will develop with the improvement of such conditions as science and technology

[53] Sartori, G. (1993) *Minzhu xinlun* [New Theory of Democracy], trans, Feng K. L. and Yan K. W., Beijing: Orient Press, p.123. cf. Sartori, G. (1978). *The Theory of Democracy Revisited (Part One: The Contemporary Debate)*, New Jersey: Chatham House Publishers, Inc., p.115.

[54] Ibid, p.124.

[55] Sartori, G. (1993) *Minzhu xinlun* [New Theory of Democracy], trans, Feng K. L. and Yan K. W., Beijing: Orient Press, p.286. cf. Sartori, G. (1978) *The Theory of Democracy Revisited (Part Two: The Classical Issues)*, New Jersey: Chatham House Publishers, Inc., p.283.

and the quality of citizens, and the status and role of the representative democracy will be more likely to be restricted in the process of achieving democracy, representative democracy will coexist with direct democracy, and will not be replaced by direct democracy soon. As Jose Ortega pointed out, "People are now speaking ill of the parliament everywhere, but no attempt has ever been made to replace the parliament in any major countries, and there is even no alternative utopian scheme of political forms proposed that are at least ideally more desirable."[56] The criticisms of the parliament, though valid, but cannot lead to the conclusion that the parliament should be abolished. On the contrary, people have fully realized the necessity of parliamentary reform. For example, the socialist people's representative system is facing the challenge of further enhancement and improvement in many aspects, such as the strengthening of the organizational and institutional construction of the socialist people's representative organs, and properly handling and coordinating the relationship between the socialist people's representative system and other related systems, so as to enhance the capacities of the people's representative organs to exercise their functions and powers, to improve their status and authority, and to give a full play to the socialist people's representative system.

References

Almond, G. (1963). *The civic culture: Political attitudes and democracy in five bations.* Princeton University Press.

Cao, P. L., et al. (1993). *Bijiao zhengfu tizhi* [Comparative Government System]. Fudan University Press.

Dunn, S. (Ed.). (2002). *The social contract and first and second discourses by Jean-Jacques Rousseau.* Yale University Press.

Engels, F. (1878). *Anti-Dühring.*

Engels, F. (1880). *Socialism: Utopian and scientific.*

Engels, F. (1884). *The origin of the family, private property and the state.*

Gu, B. X. (1988). *Minquan zhuyi minzhu zhengzhi lun* [On Civil Rights and Democratic Politics]. San Min Book Co., Ltd.

Iwai, T. (1990). *Lifa guocheng* [Legal Process] (W. Li, Trans.). The Economic Daily Press.

Kardelj, E. (1981). *Minzhu yu shehui zhuyi* [Democracy and Socialism] (Y. J. Qiu & X. B. Zhou, Trans.). People's Publishing House.

Lenin, V. (1917). *The state and revolution.*

Lenin, V. (1919). 'Report on the party programme at the eighth congress of the Russian communist party.

Lenin, V. (1920). *"Left-Wing" communism: An infantile disorder.*

Lenin, V. (1922). Letter to D. I. Kursky with Notes *On the Draft Civil Code.*

Lenin, V. (1931). *Draft Programme of the R. C. P.* (B.).

Liening quanji [Lenin Collected Works]. (1956). People's Publishing House (Vol. 29).

Liening quanji [Lenin Collected Works]. (1957). People's Publishing House (Vol. 33).

Liening wengao [The Manuscripts of Lenin]. (1978). People's Publishing House (Vol. 4).

[56] Mastellone, S. (1992) *Ouzhou zhengzhi sixiang shi: Cong 15 shiji dao 20 shiji* [History of European Political Thoughts: From 15th Century to 20th Century], trans. Huang H. G., Beijing: Social Sciences Academic Press, p.504.

Liening xuanji [Lenin Selected Works. (1995). People's Publishing House (Vol. 4).
Liening xuanji [Lenin Selected Works]. (1995). People's Publishing House (Vol. 1).
Liening xuanji [Lenin Selected Works]. (1995). People's Publishing House (Vol. 3).
Lipset, S. (1960). *Political man: The social bases of politics*. Doubleday & Company Inc.
Lipset, S. (1993). *Zhengzhi ren* [Plitical Man] (G. M. Liu & R. Nie, Trans.). The Commercial Press.
Liu, Z. D. (Ed.). (1991). *Xinxing guojia lun* [On New Forms of States]. SDX Joint Publishing Company.
Ma, Q. H. (1975). *Zhengzhixue jingyi* [Essentials of Politics]. Pamir Book.
Makesi Engels xuanji [Marx and Engels Selected Works]. (1995). People's Publishing House (Vol. 4).
Makesi Engesi quanji [Marx and Engels Collected Works]. (1960). People's Publishing House (Vol. 3).
Makesi Engesi xuanji [Marx and Engels Selected Works]. (1995). People's Publishing House (Vol. 3).
Marx, K. (1846). *The German ideology*.
Marx, K. (1852). *The eighteenth Brumaire of Louis Bonaparte*.
Mastellone, S. (1992). *Ouzhou zhengzhi sixiang shi: Cong 15 shiji dao 20 shiji* [History of European Political Thoughts: From 15th Century to 20th Century] (H. G. Huang, Trans.). Social Sciences Academic Press.
Ma Zedong xuandu [Selected Readings of Mao Tsetung's Works] (II). (1986). People's Publishing House.
Miliband, R. (1982). *Capitalist democracy in Britain*. Oxford University Press.
Miller, D., & Bogdanor, V. (Eds.). (1992). *The blackwell encyclopedia of political science*. Wiley-Blackwell.
Naisbitt, J. (1982/1986). *Megatrends: Ten new directions transforming our lives*. Warner Books, Inc.
Naisbitt, J. (1984). *Da qushi: Gaibian women shenghuo de shige xin fangxiang* [Ten New Directions Transforming Our Lives] (D. Z. Sun, Trans.). China Social Sciences Press.
Sa, M. W. (1986). *Zhengzhixue* [The Politics]. San Min Book Co., Ltd.
Sartori, G. (1978). *The theory of democracy revisited (Part one: The contemporary debate)*. Chatham House Publishers Inc.
Sartori, G. (1993). *Minzhu xinlun* [New Theory of Democracy] (K. L. Feng & K. W. Yan, Trans.). Orient Press.
Satou, I. (1984). *Bijiao zhengzhi zhidu* [Comparative Political System] (Q. L. Liu & G. B. Zhang, Trans.). Law Press·China.
Toffler, A. (1981). *The third wave*. Bantam Doubleday Dell Publishing Group Inc.
Toffler, A. (1984). *Di sanci langchao* [The Third Wave] (Z. Y. Zhu, Q. Pan & Y. Zhang, Trans.). SDX Joint Publishing Company.
Wang, H. N. (1987). *Bijiao zhengzhi fenxi* [Analysis of Comparative Politics]. Shanghai People's Publishing House.
Wilson, W. (1885/2011). *Congressional government*. Houghton Mifflin Company.
Wisti, F. (ed.). (1990). Beiou shi minzhu [Nordic Democracy] (Z. Q. Zhao, Trans.). China Social Sciences Press
Yamaguchi, Y. (1991). *Zhengzhi tizhi* [Political System] (T. Y. Han, Trans.). The Economic Daily Press.
Yang, B. H., & Ming, X. (1984). *Ziben zhuyi guojia zhengzhi zhidu* [The Political System of Capitalist Countries]. World Affairs Press.
Zuo, L. S. (1981). *Geguo guohui zhidu* [Parliamentary Systems in Various Countries]. Taipei Central Publishing House.

Postscript to the First Edition

This book is completed with supplementation and revision on the basis of my doctoral dissertation *Research on Some Problems of Representative System*. As the issue of "representative system" is an old topic, when I chose it as the research object of my doctoral dissertation, many teachers and friends were worried that it would be difficult to come up with new ideas of the old issue. But the following reasons drove me to stick to it: First, with further study and research of constitutional law, I have come to realize the importance of democracy to the study of constitutions, and even that the core of a constitution lies in democracy. Therefore, one cannot study constitutions without studying democracy. However, the history of human democratic development has constantly shown that the form of democracy is of great importance to the Constitution. Thus, the representative system, as the basic form of democracy, has naturally become the center for the study of democratic forms. Second, in the West, many scholars have long held a misconception that socialism means dictatorship and autocracy, but not democracy at all. In some socialist countries, there are also quite a few people complaining about the low level of democracy. Then, can democracy be compatible with socialism? In my view, the answer is affirmative. But what are the main obstacles to the development of socialist democracy? Looking at democratic practices in socialist countries, although there are many obstacles, I am afraid that imperfect forms may be a very important aspect of them. Third, although the representative system is an old issue, there are still many questions that need to be clarified, such as, whether the representative system is the capitalist parliamentary system? Whether the socialist people's representative system is a kind of representative system? And whether the capitalist parliamentary system and the socialist people's representative system are similar or even identical in some aspects? And so on. Although Chinese and foreign scholars have made great achievements in their research, there are still some gaps and limitations. For example, the lack of studies in theoretical generalizations and summaries, especially the basic principles; more studies are limited to case studies, or even just an introduction to static institutions and systems. From the scientific point of view, such studies will inevitably be subject to many restrictions. It is the above considerations that pushed me to further research

Y. Zhou, *A Comparative Study of Representative Systems*,
https://doi.org/10.1007/978-981-15-4186-5

on this issue. As for the research results, we would be very happy to accept valuable suggestions and criticisms from all readers.

It has been 10 years since I was admitted to the graduate program of Wuhan University to study for a Master of Constitutional Law under the supervision of my respectable professor Mr. He Huahui in the winter of 1984. In the past 10 years, my role has changed from a student to a teacher, and then to both a student and a teacher, and such an experience is really a bitter taste. Even now, I am still terrified at the memory of those days when I had to teach more than 400 h of classes a semester in addition to other daily tasks while writing my doctoral dissertation. Fortunately, I met numerous kind people who gave me selfless guidance and help in all aspects, and finally got me through the difficult time. First of all, I would like to express my heartfelt gratitude to my supervisor, Professor He Huahui and his wife, Ms. Zhao Zongquan. In the past 10 years, none of my academic progress can be separated from their earnest and patient instructions. Without their guidance and help, I would not be where I am today.

My sincere gratitude also goes to Prof. Xu Chongde from Renmin University of China, Prof. Jiang Bikun from Zhongnan University of Political Science and Law, Prof. Diao Tianding from Zhongnan University of Finance and Economics, Prof. Chen Jialing from Hubei Academy of Social Sciences, Prof. Liu Dehou and Prof. Li Long from Wuhan University, for reviewing my dissertation and attending my oral defense in the extreme heat of that summer. They not only gave a detailed, thorough and thoughtful evaluation to my dissertation, but also offered me a lot of constructive suggestions for my subsequent revisions.

I would like to extend my grateful thanks to Prof. Wu Jialing from Ningxia University, Prof. Xiao Weiyun and Prof. Wei Dingren from Peking University, Prof. Chen Yanqing from Legislative Affairs Commission of the NPC Standing Committee, Prof. Lian Xisheng and Prof. Sun Bingzhu from China University of Political Science and Law, Prof. Wu Jie from People's Public Security University of China, Prof. Zhang Guangbo from Jilin University, Prof. Pu Zengyuan and Prof. Cheng Jiyong from Shanghai Academy of Social Sciences, Prof. Zheng Jiuhao from Hangzhou University, for their valuable views and suggestions on the issue of representative system.

I would also like to express my thanks to my friends including He Yejian, Wang Bo, Zhao Guoxiang, Liu Jitao, Luo Yi, Liu Gang, Yin Xinli and Hu Wei, and my schoolmates such as Tong Zhiwei, Zhou Min, Zou Pingxue and Zhu Fuhui, for their generous and selfless help both in academic discussion and in daily life, which still remain fresh in my mind.

Last but not least, I would like to thank the leaders and my colleagues of Wuhan University Law School for helping me through some practical difficulties in the process of my dissertation writing, revision and publication, my parents and my parents-in-law for providing me favourable conditions for my study, and my wife, Chen Danpin, not only for almost undertaking all the housework, but also for helping me to collect and transcribe most of the manuscript, so that I could successfully complete my dissertation.

Finally, it is worth mentioning that the successful publication of this book has received great support and help from the leadership of Wuhan University Press and the editor-in-charge, Guo Yuanyuan. I would like to express my sincere thanks to them.

Due to my limited knowledge and time restriction, there are a lot of shortcomings and mistakes in this book. I am pleased to accept any criticism and correction.

Zhou Yezhong
Luojia Hill
November, 1994

Postscript to the Revised Edition

This book was first published by Wuhan University Press in 1995 and reprinted in 2005 by the same Press. Although it has been in publication for nearly 20 years, the topic covered in this book is still of great theoretical value and practical significance to China at a new historical era. This is both the most prominent consensus that Dr. Guo Yishi and I have made in recent years in the process of writing our book, *A Study of Chinese Style Representative Democracy*, and much of the core content of my thinking on the issues of China's future political development and political reform over the years.

First of all, the subject matter discussed in this book is of great significance both to the development of socialist democracy and to the adherence to the development of the socialism with Chinese characteristics. After the end of the ten-year turmoil of the Cultural Revolution, the CPC and the Chinese people have drawn two important conclusions: one is that our task must focus on economic construction, and the other is that our socialist democracy must be developed and our socialist legal system must be improved. Comrade Deng Xiaoping also profoundly pointed out that there would be neither socialism and nor socialist modernization without democracy. The reports to The 17th and the 18th National Congress of the CPC clearly stated that people's democracy is the life of socialism and the development of socialist democratic politics is the unswerving goal of our Party.

However, as has been analyzed in this book, direct democracy is the most ideal form to achieve democracy for the actualization of "people being masters of the country", but the complexities of various factors such as vast territory, large population, and the conditions of social development determine that the representative democracy is a great progress from ancient democracy to modern democracy in the history of world civilization. Therefore, representative democracy is the basic form of modern democracy in modern countries. In this case, if Chinese people want to develop a socialist democracy, they must try to explore and develop the representative democracy with Chinese characteristics.

Second, the main issue of concern in this book are also of vital importance for exploring and following the laws governing the construction and operation of representative democracy. There is no doubt that democracy is a universal value commonly

Y. Zhou, *A Comparative Study of Representative Systems*,
https://doi.org/10.1007/978-981-15-4186-5

pursued by human beings. On the issue of universal values, I have always held a basic view: while affirming the existence of universal values in many areas of human society, we should not one-sidedly equate Western values with universal values, nor should we confuse values with their forms of realization. Since democracy and human rights are the achievements of human civilization jointly created in the long process of historical development and the common values pursued by mankind, now the key problem lies in what forms, approaches or methods should be adopted for countries to realize democracy and human rights. The author believes that they should choose the ones that are most conducive to the realization of democracy and human rights based on their own national situations and their objective historical conditions. In other words, the forms of value realization are diverse rather than unique. If people criticize a country for its political practice by taking one or two forms of realization as the sole criterion, it is not only unscientific in theory but also harmful in practice. It is such an understanding that tells us at least two things: First, it is justifiable and legitimate for different countries to have diverse forms manifested in the development of representative democracy; Second, a comparative study of different representative systems and their manifestations will not only help us explore and summarize the basic laws of the construction and operation of representative democracy, but also help us reflect on and improve the representative democracy in China through learning and reference.

Thirdly, the topic of this book is crucial to China's political development and reform in the new era. As for the basic trajectory of China's modernization, I believe that it must go through three stages of development with different foci, i.e. from the stage of economic construction with economic reform as the focus, to the stage of social construction with social reform as the focus, and then to the stage of political construction with political reform as the focus. Although at each stage, the economic, political and social work are in progress at the same time, the focus of each of the three stages is different. Specifically, between the Reform and Opening Up and the 16th CPC National Congress, our focus was on the economic reform, and the focus had been shifted to social reform since the 16th CPC National Congress, especially the 6th Plenary Session of the 16th CPC Central Committee with adoption of *the Decision of the Central Committee of the Communist Party of China on Several Major Issues Concerning the Construction of a Socialist Harmonious Society*. When we have made great breakthroughs in the economic and social reforms, which have laid a solid foundation for political reform, we will enter the stage of political construction with political reform as the focus.

So, what is the focus or fundamental work for China's political development and reform in the new era? China should earnestly uphold and improve the System of People's Congresses. To this end, people should first of all have a new understanding of the status and role of the System of People's Congresses, i.e. the System of People's Congresses in the new era is not only the fundamental political system of China, but also the fundamental institutional vehicle of China's socialist democratic politics, as well as the fundamental approach for the governance of the country by the Communist Party of China. This new understanding not only shows the importance of Chinese style representative democracy based on the System of People's Congresses in the process of China's political development, but also shows that the focus and breakthrough of China's political reform lies in practically improving the status of the people's congresses and their standing committees at all levels and giving full play to the role of the System of People's Congress.

Based on the above understanding, a comparative study of the basic theories, system construction and actual operation of the representative system is of great theoretical significance and practical value. Therefore, when the Commercial Press intended to include this book in its republication plan, I readily agreed and made some revisions to the original manuscript. Specifically, there are three major revisions made: first, several inappropriate expressions that are not scientific; Second, some notes and references that are not accurate or unconventional; Third, several ghost words and printing errors in the text. It must be noted that, although it is a revised edition, the overall framework, basic contents and main ideas of the book have not been greatly adjusted. Even some of the expressions seem a bit outdated now, in order to keep the original work as a product of the conditions at that time, I do not deliberately make any modification. I earnestly request my readers to understand and forgive me for this treatment.

Zhou Yezhong
Luojia Hill, Wuchang
June, 2013

MIX
Papier aus verantwortungsvollen Quellen
Paper from responsible sources
FSC® C105338

If you have any concerns about our products,
you can contact us on
ProductSafety@springernature.com

In case Publisher is established outside the EU,
the EU authorized representative is:
Springer Nature Customer Service Center GmbH
Europaplatz 3, 69115 Heidelberg, Germany

Printed by Libri Plureos GmbH
in Hamburg, Germany